McCall's
NEEDLEWORK
TREASURY

A Learn & Make Book

By The Editors of
McCall's Needlework
& Crafts Magazine

Random House · McCall's

Foreword

McCall's Needlework Treasury is a carefully planned handbook to provide reference and inspiration for all who are interested in needlecraft. Some will find the book invaluable as a source for identifying and learning handcraft techniques. Others wishing to identify heirloom pieces made in America will find valuable information and helpful illustrations to aid them in their search. McCall's Needlework Treasury, while covering the needlework field, gives special attention to the types of needlework of greatest interest to the needlewoman of today.

Our book is a "learn-and-make" book. There are instructions for each type of stitchery illustrated. Some of the projects are easy enough for a child, while others are for the experienced and gifted needlewoman. Since this is a book for all who wish to learn, from children to senior citizens, the items to make are chosen for their practical use as well as design. By following the step-by-step illustrated details with their written instructions, the student of needlework can proceed from the simplest embroidery stitches to the beautiful combinations of these stitches which are used to create the rich effects of crewel embroidery; or one can advance from casting on knitting stitches to learning intricate knitted patterns such as are used in Aran Isles and Scandinavian designs.

By presenting outstanding museum examples of both traditional and modern needlework, with the basic how-to for creating them, we hope to enable present day needlewomen to acquire the inspiration and knowledge she needs to create the museum pieces of the future!

During my twelve years as editor of the Mc-Call's Needlework and Crafts publications, I have seen interest in all types of handwork increase: knitted and crocheted garments have become high fashion; well-known artists have switched from paint to yarn to create wall hangings of the highest artistic quality; expert craftsmen have developed new design trends in handmade rugs. As a result, needlework has sparked the imagination of decorators who often plan entire rooms around beautiful needlework pieces.

The material in this book has been compiled by the editors of the McCall's Needlework & Crafts publications. The following associate editors have assisted me and given their expert knowledge to the writing of sections in this book: Embroidery—Eleanor Spencer; Knitting, Crochet, and Tatting—Gena Rhoades; Quilts, Rugs and Hand Loom Weaving—Ellene Saunders.

NANINA COMSTOCK

Color Illustrations

Acknowledgments

The items chosen to feature in this book have been made from basic yarns, threads, and other materials readily available; therefore, we have omitted brand names when listing the required materials. We wish to express our gratitude to the following companies who have developed designs especially for our use, or have supplied us with materials: American Thread Co., The Artcraft Press, Emile Bernat and Sons Co., Bernhard Ulmann Co., Columbia-Minerva Corp., D.M.C. Corp., John Dritz and Sons, Heirloom Needlework Guild, Inc., Hero Mfg. Co., Lily Mills Co., Paragon Needlecraft, A. & H. Shillman Co., Inc., Ralph C. Springer Co., Tuxedo Yarn Co., Walbead, Inc., Wm. E. Wright & Sons Co., and Yankee Homecraft Corp.

We are also indebted to The Metropolitan Museum of Art, The Newark Museum, The Cooper Union Museum, The Smithsonian Institution, and Museum of Fine Arts, Boston, for the photographs and information we obtained through their study departments and collections.

Contents

Our Needlework Heritage

Since needlework has been from the earliest civilizations an important part of every culture, we in the United States have inherited a wealth of material from many sources, including the American Indians. Our museums contain beautiful examples from this country and others in which the native needlework originated and developed. While the designs are strikingly individual and typical of both the area and the era of their origin, there is a worldwide similarity of the stitches and the basic techniques throughout history. Following are brief historical notes on typical ancient embroideries, the great interest in needlework which started in England as early as the 13th century, and the development of needlework in this country which was strongly influenced by many European styles. More detailed information about the origin of each kind of needlework is given at the beginning of the chapter or section where it is featured.

ANCIENT EMBROIDERY

The origins of embroidery are lost in obscurity. The few examples of early Egyptian, Greek, and Roman embroideries often show fine strips of pure gold or other metals wound around a foundation thread of linen. These gold-covered threads were couched to the surface of the fabric to cover areas in a solid gold effect, or were used to outline colored silk, wool, or linen embroidery. Also, there are rare examples of fabric appliqués which were used for wall hangings or to decorate garments.

Silk embroidery was developed in the Orient along with silk fabrics. The earliest Oriental garments of richly hued silks were embroidered with silk, metallic thread, or jewels. Seed stitch, chain stitch, outline stitch, featherstitch, and satin stitch were used, and tiny bits of metal similar to modern sequins were often added to the design. Mirror fragments were used in some of the embroideries of India, held in place by close chain stitching. Also in India, the Punjabs used a darning stitch to create fine allover ornamentation. Although European styles have changed through the centuries, Oriental designs and workmanship still follow the old traditions, colors, and designs.

When silkworms were first smuggled out of the Orient, they were cultivated in Italy and southern France. Fine silk fabrics, brocade, and velvet were made up into wall hangings or garments, all richly embroidered with silk floss and metal threads.

Embroidery and appliqué formed a part of the early wall decorations in European homes. Castles during the Middle Ages and up to the 17th century were built of stone, sometimes without mortar. Drafts blew through the walls unless hangings were used. One of the most famous early pictorial hangings is the Bayeux Tapestry, which is not a tapestry but an embroidery in wool on linen worked in outline, rope stitches, and laid work. It tells the story of the Norman conquest of England in the 11th century.

THE ENGLISH TRADITION

During the 16th century, Catherine of Aragon, the first wife of Henry VIII, introduced Spanish "black work" in England. Turkey tufting, which is believed to have been an imitation of Turkish carpets, was also popular in the Tudor Period. Elizabeth I and her cousin, Mary Queen of Scots, were both skilled needlewomen. Many embroideries of their time were done in wool or silk on a coarse linen similar to a very fine canvas with threads of an even count; this was called "canvas work." It was popular to make samplers or "exemplars" of the variety of stitches one could work on canvas. While many stitches were made, the most important one was tent stitch, the forerunner of needlepoint.

Another early form of embroidery in England was "needle worke cruell," which derived its name from the type of wool used, "a thin worsted yarn of two threads." This embroidery was worked on a linen background in various stitches. It reached its height of popularity during the early 17th century at the time of James I and is often called Jacobean work. Today the name "crewelwork" refers to embroidery of the same type as the early work. A very good example is shown on page 18.

Bed hangings of the 17th and 18th centuries, often worked in crewel, provided the sleeper with privacy and kept out cold night breezes. When heavy fabric was not available, several thicknesses of material were layered together and held with stab stitching, thus popularizing the quilting technique.

EARLY EMBROIDERY IN AMERICA

American embroideries are descended from so many others that it is very difficult to know just where our individuality begins. For example, during the early 1700's our ancestors were making samplers similar to those being made throughout Europe at the time; crewel-embroidered bedspreads were closely related to the Jacobean designs being embroidered in England; needlepoint (then called "tent stitch") chair seats and pictures were as popular here as abroad. Most of the New England designs either came from or were strongly influenced by England.

Needlework teachers in the colonies not only sold imported designs but created their own in related subjects, coloring, and technique. An interesting example is the famous "Fishing Lady" of Boston worked in tent stitch (page 11). The exact origin of this design is not known; however, about eight different embroideries have been discovered which are very similar, using the same motifs arranged in different ways. It is believed that a key to the source of the designs is given by the following information which appeared in the Boston News-Letter for April 27/May 4, 1738, stating that there was "To be had at Mrs. Condy's near the Old North Meeting House; all sorts of beautiful Figures on Canvas, for Tent Stick; the Patterns from London, but drawn by her much cheaper than English drawing; All sorts of Canvas, without drawing; also Silk Shades, Slacks, Floss, Cruells of all Sorts, the best White Chapple Needles, and every thing for all Sorts of Work."

Early American crewel embroideries showed slight changes from those in England both in design and

Pastoral Landscape with Fishing Lady, sometimes called "Boston Common," is an example of the embroidery which flourished in Boston during the 18th century. It is one of eight embroideries with a similar subject from the vicinity of Boston. The pieces are dated from 1743 to 1748. Detail at right, approximately actual size, illustrates size of stitch used in canvas work of this period.

Birds, Beasts and Flowers is a detail from a colorful crewel-embroidered petticoat border made in New England, 1725 to 1750.

Sampler shows a combination of simple cross-stitch letters with a rich floral border of flowers, foliage, and a pineapple in satin stitch, stem stitch, and French knots. It was embroidered by Eliza J. Benneson, 1835.

Innocence and Friendship is a typical "mourning piece," embroidered with silk floss and chenille on silk. Background is painted, cottage roof is actual straw. A broad margin of black glass surrounds the elaborate picture, worked by Mary P. Paul, of Philadelphia, in the late 18th century.

The Caswell Carpet, made by Zeruah Higley Guernsey Caswell, is one of the best-known large-scale embroideries. Squares worked in tambour stitch were joined to make the 12' x 13½' carpet. It is recorded that two young Patawatomi Indians who lived with Zeruah's family while attending Castleton Medical College worked on the carpet, designing the two squares marked with their initials. This impressive embroidery was completed in 1835, after two years' work.

THE METROPOLITAN MUSEUM OF ART, GIFT OF KATHERINE KEYES, 1938,
IN MEMORY OF HER FATHER, HOMER EATON KEYES.

13

stitches, the most notable difference being the use of a modified Oriental or Roumanian stitch to replace the long-and-short stitch. The New England needle-woman found that she could conserve her crewel and still obtain a charming effect by executing this stitch so that she picked up with her needle only a few threads of linen ground, allowing most of the woolen threads to lie on the surface. Among interesting examples of early crewel embroidery in this country are the narrow embroidered bands running around the hemlines of petticoats. These designs are less formal than the English, and sometimes the borders showed landscapes with beasts and buildings, as well as floral ornaments. (See page 11.)

Many of the crewel designs were worked in native dyed wools. The early settlers who found it expensive to import yarns from England had to depend on their own inventive ability, and a number of colors used by them were discovered by accident or through experiment. Many a New England colonist raised her own indigo plants and boasted the possession of an indigo tub in the rear kitchen. Here lambs' wool was tinted various shades of blue. Attempts were made to match the Canton blues of the chinaware from the Orient, and crewel embroideries worked in these shades were called "Blue and White Work."

Instruction in embroidery was part of the education of every well brought up young girl in America. Their samplers varied according to the part of the country where they were made.

The young girls of New England were apt to combine only a few simple stitches, using them for a small picture, a flower border, and an alphabet. There might also be a rather lugubrious verse along with the embroiderer's name and date of working.

Many of the samplers made by the early Pennsylvania Dutch settlers are long narrow strips of linen in a fairly open mesh. These show drawnwork and a variety of quite complicated stitches.

Samplers from various parts of the country were genealogical charts, with sturdy trees, each branch labeled with the names and dates of each ancestor.

An interesting type of embroidery sprang up from the teaching of the Moravian sect. These people migrated from Moravia in central Europe and settled in Bethlehem, Pennsylvania, in 1740. The art of embroidering memorial samplers (see page 12) was taught in their schools. Later, this kind of embroidery became a fad in other areas, with less morbid subjects, such as ships and pastoral scenes. These pictures were a combination of a tinted satin background and silk embroidery in a variety of stitches.

In the early 1800's the alphabet samplers became more elaborate and often had rich floral borders requiring skillful workmanship. (See page 12.)

While young girls were making their samplers, there was a great deal of embroidery being done for practical use in the home. Cross-stitch was worked on canvas to produce large carpets. Chairs and benches were upholstered with canvas worked in Bargello or flame stitch (see page 51). Turkey work was used as an upholstery fabric, for bed covers and rugs.

Popular in Europe at this time, and widely used here, was a kind of embroidery called "tambour." This is an embroidered chain stitch worked with a fine needle resembling a crochet hook. The Caswell carpet (page 13) is a unique example.

Floor coverings were a necessity and many rag rugs were hooked and braided from leftovers. The hooked rugs more than any others reflected the personality of the maker. Sometimes they were painstakingly made with great care for detail, or at other times were only a bold splash of color. The antique rooster rug (page 16) shows the latter approach, while the rug on page 138 was more carefully made. Edwin D. Frost is responsible for our heritage of many floral rugs from the Victorian era. He collected over 700 hooked rug designs and made copper stencils of the patterns; however, no two hand-hooked rag rugs are ever just alike.

A practical use of needlework by the settlers of New England, New Amsterdam, Virginia, and the Carolinas was quilt making. Among early quilts we find beautiful all-white examples—some puffed with padding (see page 128), some embroidered with heavy white cotton cord, and others worked with wicking, thus giving us the name "candlewicking" (see page 133).

The art of quilt making has continued through many stages. During the Revolutionary era, flower sprays were cut from French toile and appliquéd on the backgrounds; combinations of appliqué, patchwork, and quilting depicted patriotic emblems or the other interests of the maker. The uncounted number of patchwork designs which appeared in the 19th century were inspired by almost anything from a "duck's foot" to a "log cabin." Some of the more intricately designed quilts were often highly personalized, as is shown by a representation of the family homestead in the center of the quilt detail on page 16.

Just as white quilts were popular in the 18th century, so were other types of "white work." This term applies to white embroidery in general, which was greatly influenced by the French; some of the best examples come from Louisiana. It is interesting to note that the tambour stitch used to embroider the Caswell carpet was equally popular in white work for embroidering dainty veils, shawls, and collars of fine net. Interest in white work continued until about the middle of the 19th century.

While original native quilt designs and the French-inspired white work were a part of every trousseau,

FEATURED IN McCALL'S NEEDLEWORK & CRAFTS MAGAZINE, SPRING-SUMMER 1953

Lovely afghan or carriage robe from the Victorian era has designs cross-stitched on an afghan-stitch crochet background, rich fringe. The insignia in the lower left corner indicates it may have been made for a clergyman. Red rose detail has been adapted for working in other sizes and stitches on canvas. See illustrations, pages 52 and 53.

15

Detail of appliquéd and embroidered quilt made by Emiline Dean Jones, about 1835.

Antique hooked rug made with uncut loops of fabric strips on a burlap background.

Unusually well-designed example of Berlin work, with sculptured and beaded accents.

it was Berlin work which dominated the 19th century. This kind of embroidery had been called "canvas work" during the 15th and 16th centuries, but in the early 1800's it received the name "Berlin work" because the patterns originated in Berlin. These patterns, drawn on "paint paper" or painted on canvas, often copied celebrated pictures to be worked in needlepoint, using silk, then beads, and finally the brightly-colored Berlin wool. Other characteristic subjects were birds, flowers, and arabesque motifs in bold color. The Berlin type of design was prevalent during the Victorian era, and was adapted to a variety of embroidery techniques. See afghan, page 15.

EMBROIDERY IN THE 20th CENTURY

During the last quarter of the 19th and first quarter of the 20th century needlewomen did a great deal of knitting, crocheting, and tatting. They also made embroidered antimacassars, bureau runners, doilies, and other household linens, known as "fancy work." Designs were available stamped on material, as perforated patterns, or as hot iron transfers. They were used for both white work and embroidery in silk on linen using Kensington stitch in the realistic colors of flowers and fruits.

Starting in the 1920's there was a revival of interest in crewel embroidery and needlepoint. Most of the designs were copies of old pieces and were used to upholster both antique furniture and reproductions. At the same time many needlewomen embroidered unique designs which were created to their specifications by artists who either painted the needlepoint designs on canvas or made perforated patterns to stamp the designs on linen. In the 1930's there was a nationwide revival of rug hooking. Many of the designs were adaptations of the old Frost patterns, but a few were original.

During World War II merchandise was scarce and kits containing both patterns and materials were produced, thus making certain that the customer had the yarns in the right colors. This service may have been responsible for a steady increase in handcrafts since the beginning of the 1950's.

Today there is an ever-increasing demand for unusual and well designed needlework patterns. Top artists not only design for other needlewomen; they themselves are literally painting with yarns, creating contemporary rugs and wall hangings which are museum pieces. Right now we are in the most exciting period of all needlework history. We have a vast heritage of handwork techniques, a limitless variety of yarns and other materials with which to work, and the needle arts are recognized by museum authorities as fine arts media of the 20th century.

Embroidery

From time immemorial women have embroidered on clothing, accessories and linens to accent their intrinsic qualities or add new interest. One of the great advantages of the art is that it can be as simple or as complex as the needleworker cares to make it. Many of the basic stitches are the heritage of assorted cultures and are centuries old. To these have been added variations and new techniques eminently suited to today's functional and exciting use of color and design.

Whether you choose to make a line-for-line copy of a design, adapt it with modifications, or create an entirely new piece of work, you will find that embroidery offers something for everyone with an eye for beauty.

17

Crewel Embroidery

Crewelwork, or Jacobean embroidery, became fashionable first in the 17th century, and expressed the extravagant taste of the time for richly-embroidered decorations. Early designs, which customarily featured exotic flowering trees combined with birds and animals, resulted from an exchange of ideas between Asia and Europe. Although the first crewel embroidery was worked in shades of one color, generally blue or green, later designs sometimes used varied and brighter coloring; greens and blues still predominated.

The exotic Tree of Life was, and is, the most popular basic design. An elaborate example is the hanging shown below from the Metropolitan Museum of Art. The odd thing about these trees is that a single trunk with its many branches will carry a wide variety of flowers and fruits. Even the leaves vary in shape. Thus crewel embroidery gives you a chance to express your own individual design ideas since the kind of forms you use is limited only by your own imagination.

Swirl the trunk gracefully up the center of the area, decreasing its diameter as you get to the top of the tree. At the base of the trunk embroider satin stitch scallops of brown and green to represent earth and grass; spot with flora and fauna.

TREE OF LIFE DESIGN
COURTESY METROPOLITAN MUSEUM OF ART.

Contemporary version of crewel work,
is a Paragon Needlecraft Crewel Kit.

Embroidery Stitches

All basic embroidery stitches are easy. What may appear to be a difficult, complicated work is often the result of a well thought-out combining of several basic stitches to produce a richly-embroidered piece.

This is especially true in crewel embroidery which can be as varied as you choose—from confining it almost exclusively to long and short stitch, to using all the stitches presented here.

The more familiar you are with these basic stitches, the greater the excitement you can derive from developing your own combinations.

For practicing the stitches you will need embroidery wools or thread, a linen or linen-like textured fabric, and embroidery needles which are available in sizes 1 to 6. An embroidery frame is optional, but it is often preferred to enable you to keep your stitches even and smooth.

RUNNING STITCH

WHIPPED RUNNING STITCH

THREADED RUNNING STITCH

RUNNING STITCH   Worked along a line that is either straight or curved. It consists of evenly spaced stitches even in size. It may have variations with one stitch longer than the others placed at even intervals. It may be used for a flower stem, or to form veins in leaves. It may fill in an open area with an allover design of many rows.

WHIPPED RUNNING STITCH   A combination of two stitches. First the running stitch is completed with evenly spaced stitches. Then the blunt pointed needle is threaded with contrasting color and worked through the stitches without going through the fabric. This gives the effect of a twisted cord.

THREADED RUNNING STITCH   Another variation. The running stitch has a second thread worked through in a wave by passing the blunt pointed needle first through the right of one stitch then through from the left of the next stitch. This differs from the twisted stitch in which the second thread is always passed through from the right to the left.

STRAIGHT STITCH   May be made as single stitches here and there in a design, or separated straight stitches in a ring or semicircle to form a flower. It may be made in various lengths and in clusters, but each stitch is always separated from the others.

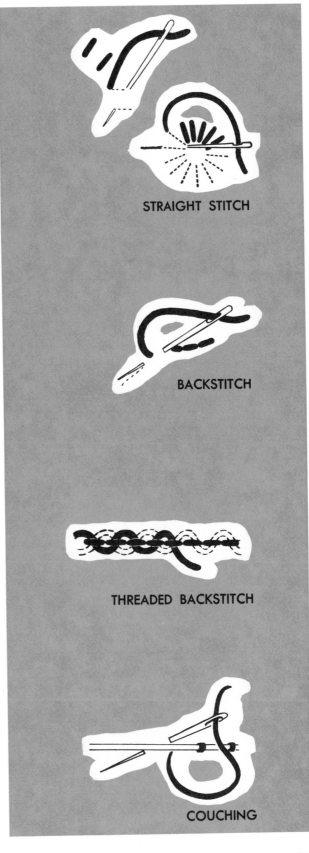

STRAIGHT STITCH

BACKSTITCH   Short stitches are placed end to end for a slim outline. This may be used alone for stems or borders, or to outline solid areas. The stitches just meet in the row, but the thread is carried under the fabric for twice the distance. Work from right to left, and carry the thread along the outline.

BACKSTITCH

THREADED BACKSTITCH   Made in the same way as the threaded running stitch. A second color is worked in and out of the stitches of the backstitch without piercing the fabric. A third color may thread through to make loops on the opposite side as well. See dotted lines in illustration.

THREADED BACKSTITCH

COUCHING   Lay thread to be couched across fabric. Use an embroidery frame. With the same color or a contrasting color of thread, take small stitches at even intervals over the laid thread. Couching can be used solidly for special effects on small areas.

COUCHING

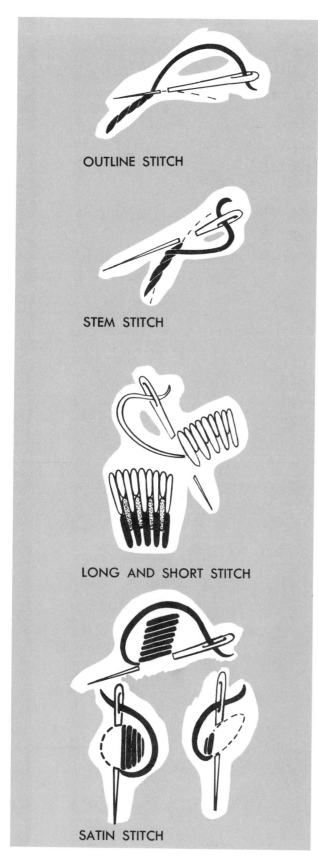

OUTLINE STITCH

STEM STITCH

LONG AND SHORT STITCH

SATIN STITCH

OUTLINE STITCH Bring needle up through fabric. With thread to left of needle, insert needle a short distance away and on the line and bring needle out again on the line. This stitch makes a fine line and is used around edge, for veining and detail lines.

STEM OR CREWEL STITCH This differs from outline stitch in that the thread is held on the opposite side of the line; the needle is inserted to the right of the line and brought up to the left of the line, making a thick outline. This stitch may be used as a filling by working rows along side of each other.

LONG AND SHORT (KENSINGTON) STITCH Used to fill areas solidly, and shade colors. The first row is alternating long and short stitches, as shown. Following rows are stitches of equal length, worked at ends of short and long stitches. Regularity of the following rows depends on shape to be filled. Start at outer edge and work toward center or downward, keeping stitches generally in the same direction. Plan the stitches in an area so they fill it naturally and gracefully; it is helpful to mark with pencil the direction of some of the stitches. Shade colors into each other in rows.

SATIN STITCH Straight stitches worked side by side, usually slantwise, to fill small areas. For straight areas, work slantwise from top to bottom; for small circles, work center long stitch vertically first, then fill each side; for leaf shapes, work diagonally, starting at left edge.

SATIN STITCH LEAF   When area is large, divide into sections; work separately, changing direction of stitches for each section. Keep neat, firm outline and smooth, parallel stitches.

OPEN LEAF STITCH   Start at base, left of center. Insert needle on opposite margin part way up, bring out at base, right of center. Continue as shown, alternating from side to side.

FISHBONE STITCH   Starting at point, work as shown, slanting each succeeding stitch more until correct angle is obtained. Try with two needles and two shades of the same color.

FLAT STITCH   Work in similar manner as shown for small leaves and petals. For larger areas, work bands of stitch side by side, interlocking bands at sides to resemble braid effect at center.

LAZY DAISY STITCH   A popular stitch for making flower petals. Bring thread up at base of petal, hold loop with thumb and anchor it with a small stitch. Work lazy daisy petals in a ring with base of each close, for a round flower. May also be used as a filling stitch by scattering lazy daisies at random.

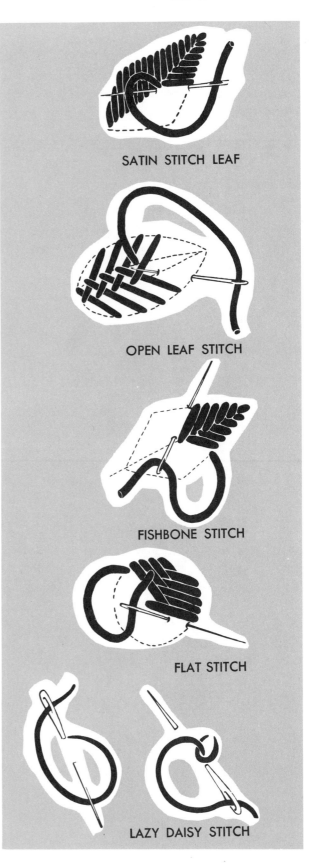

SATIN STITCH LEAF

OPEN LEAF STITCH

FISHBONE STITCH

FLAT STITCH

LAZY DAISY STITCH

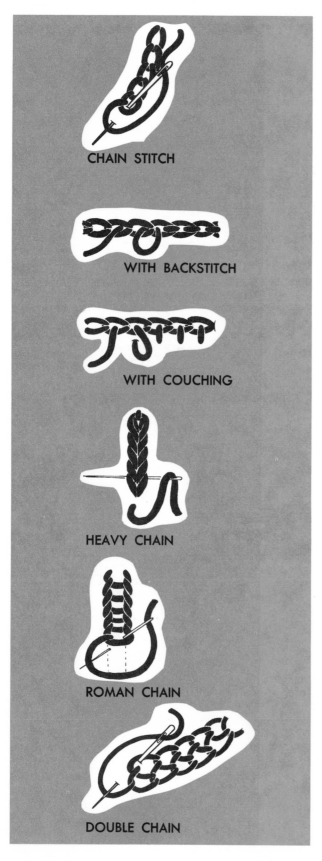

CHAIN STITCH

WITH BACKSTITCH

WITH COUCHING

HEAVY CHAIN

ROMAN CHAIN

DOUBLE CHAIN

CHAIN STITCH Worked from top down. Bring needle up through fabric; hold loop with thumb and insert needle again at same place. Bring needle up a short distance away with thread looped under needle; repeat. Use for heavy outlines or as a filling, making rows of chains follow the outline of shape being filled.

CHAIN WITH BACKSTITCH, WITH COUCHING Make backstitch down center of chain; or couch down on one side of chain as shown, using another color of yarn.

HEAVY CHAIN Start with a small vertical stitch; then make a small loop through stitch, without picking up the fabric. Continue making loops under the second one above.

ROMAN CHAIN Made in a similar manner to regular chain, except that the loop ends are wide apart. Keep the width of the loops even and make them close together.

DOUBLE CHAIN Use when a broader border decoration is desired. This is done in same way as regular chain stitch except that the needle is angled from right to left, then from left to right as shown.

BUTTONHOLE STITCH   Worked from left to right. Bring needle up through fabric. Holding thread under left thumb, form a loop; then pass needle through fabric and over the looped thread; repeat.

CLOSED BUTTONHOLE STITCH   Made in same manner as above, but with stitches close together. May be used to make scalloped edges as shown, or to fill an area by working several touching rows.

HERRINGBONE STITCH   Worked between two lines. Bring thread up through lower line, insert needle in upper line a little to the right and take a short stitch to the left. Insert needle on lower line a little to the right and take a short stitch to the left. May be used for thick stems, or to connect two solid areas for softening effect.

COUCHED HERRINGBONE   First make herringbone stitch. Then couch down with separate thread in contrasting color, if desired, where stitches cross.

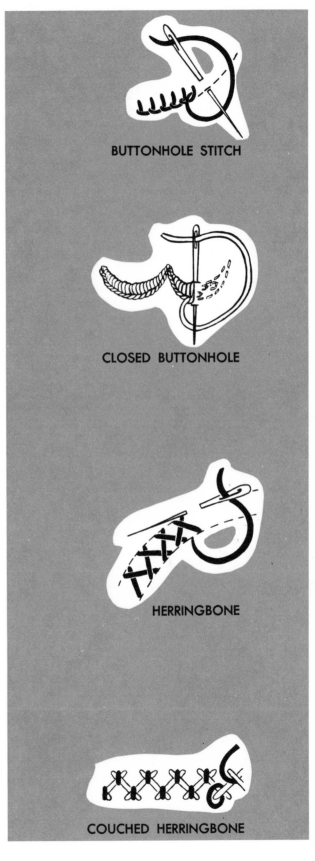

BUTTONHOLE STITCH

CLOSED BUTTONHOLE

HERRINGBONE

COUCHED HERRINGBONE

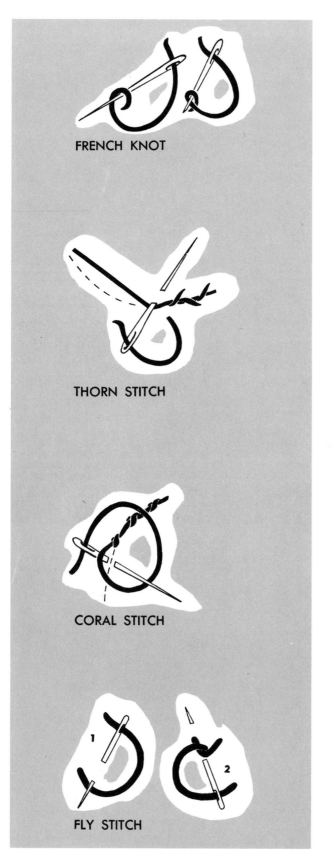

FRENCH KNOT

THORN STITCH

CORAL STITCH

FLY STITCH

FRENCH KNOT Bring thread up through fabric. Wrap thread over and under needle, crossing beginning thread; insert needle in fabric close to where it came up. Thread may be used double to produce larger knots if desired.

THORN STITCH Work in an embroidery frame. First lay a long thread across area. Take diagonal stitches from side to side to hold long thread in position as shown. Used for some stems to produce a special effect.

CORAL STITCH Work from right to left. Bring thread up through fabric and hold with thumb. Take a small stitch across line, under and over thread. Pull up thread to form a small knot; repeat. May be used for fine stems.

FLY STITCH Similar to lazy daisy stitch, but the ends of the loop stitch are widely separated. Make a small backstitch to anchor the center in place, bringing needle up in position for next stitch. Can be used as a scattered space filler where a simple, textured background is desired.

FEATHERSTITCH   Worked along a single line outline with the needle slanted to touch the line. Placed first to the right, then to the left and so on alternately each time, the thread is passed under the needle for a buttonhole loop. This is similar to the chain stitch, but the loop is open, not closed. The branches may be kept all even with each stitch the same length, or they may be varied in length.

CLOSED FEATHERSTITCH Worked along a double outline, with the needle kept erect along that line instead of being pointed toward the center. The same method of alternating the stitches from right to left is used as in plain featherstitching, but each stitch is taken at bottom of the stitch above.

STRAIGHT FEATHERSTITCH   Formed in the same way with a double guideline and perpendicular stitches, but the ends of the thread do not meet the stitch above.

There are many fancy variations of featherstitching. Two stitches may be taken at each side before alternating the side. This forms Double Featherstitch. Or three stitches may be taken to form Treble or Triple Featherstitching. A definite scallop or zigzag may be used as a guide in featherstitching.

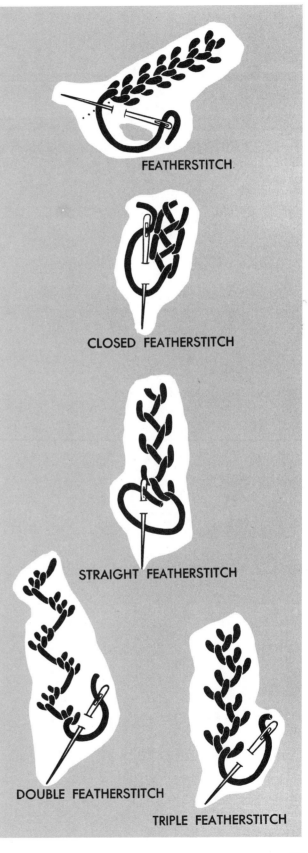

FEATHERSTITCH

CLOSED FEATHERSTITCH

STRAIGHT FEATHERSTITCH

DOUBLE FEATHERSTITCH

TRIPLE FEATHERSTITCH

Embroidery: filling stitches

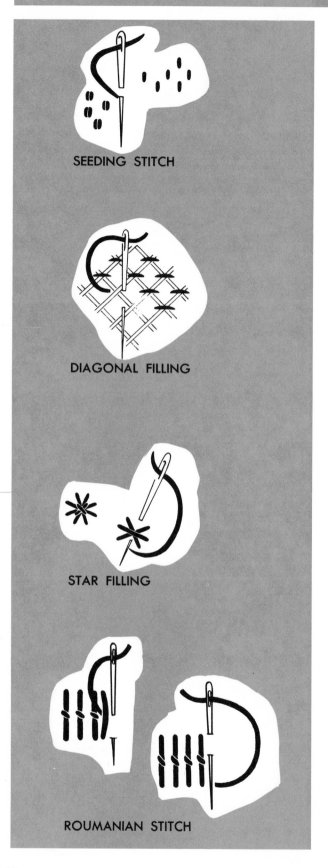

SEEDING STITCH   Take two small stitches side by side, or one small single stitch. Scatter over area to be filled, alone or combined with other stitches.

DIAGONAL FILLING   Take stitches diagonally across area to be filled, in opposite directions. With contrasting color of thread, take short stitches across diagonal stitches where they cross, proceeding diagonally from top left to bottom right as shown.

STAR FILLING   Work an upright cross, then a diagonal cross. They all are held together with a small cross worked over center of large crosses. May be used in combination with other stitches as filling.

ROUMANIAN STITCH   May be used as a solid filling by making rows of stitches close together; or for borders or spot decorations. It is made in two steps. One long stitch is fastened in the center with a short couching stitch as shown in the diagrams.

ORIENTAL STITCH   Since satin stitch is very popular in Oriental embroideries it is natural that one variation should be so named. This stitch is used to cover a fairly large area. Long floating threads of satin stitch are first placed vertically over the area. Another thread is then laid across them and held in place with short anchoring stitches spaced equally, as in couching. These anchoring stitches may match or contrast in color. The couched threads may also be laid across the background threads diagonally.

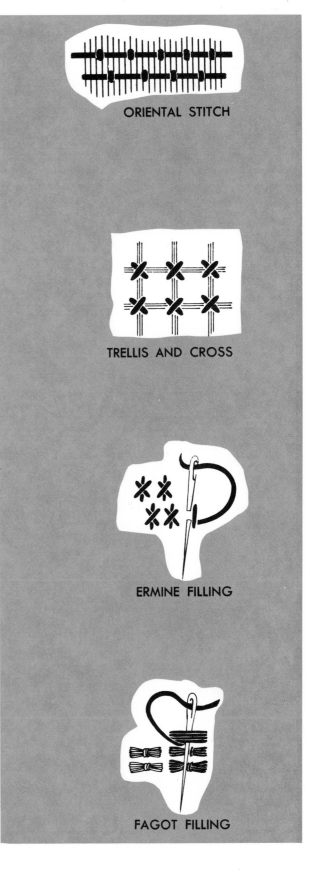

ORIENTAL STITCH

TRELLIS AND CROSS   Take long stitches across area to be filled in, horizontally and vertically. Where stitches cross, work a small cross in same or contrasting color of thread. French knots are sometimes worked in center of squares.

TRELLIS AND CROSS

ERMINE FILLING   Take an upright stitch. Bring up needle to right of upright, nearly at bottom; insert needle near top at left of upright. Bring needle out at left near bottom and insert at dot on right, near top. Use in rows, alternating spacing to fill area.

ERMINE FILLING

FAGOT FILLING   Take four or five stitches close together across fabric. Tie the stitches together at middle with two small stitches through fabric and around stitches to make a bundle.

FAGOT FILLING

Embroidered Ornaments

These gay tree ornaments may also double as useful pincushions. They are embroidered with a variety of stitches detailed elsewhere in this section. Use crewel wool and six-strand cotton to embroider the bird for which we give the actual-size pattern and the directions.

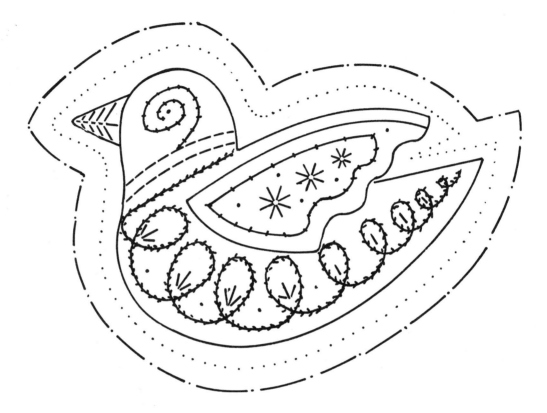

STITCH KEY

• SEQUIN	_ _ _ _ BACKSTITCH
———— OUTLINE STITCH	+++++ COUCHING
⌄⌃ ⸜⸝ STRAIGHT STITCH	⤜⤜⤜⤜ THORN STITCH

EQUIPMENT: Embroidery needles. Pencil. Tracing paper. Carbon paper. Scissors.

MATERIALS: Cotton broadcloth: green, blue, red. Matching sewing thread. Cotton for stuffing. Fine wool yarn and six-strand embroidery cotton: white, yellow, dark green, orange, black, red, bright blue, light yellow, yellow-green. All-purpose glue. Sequins, assorted colors.

DIRECTIONS: Trace pattern, including all embroidery details. Using carbon paper, mark pattern on double broadcloth; mark embroidery details. Cut out double fabric for design on dot-dash line. Dotted line is seam line.

Embroider design on one fabric piece, following embroidery stitch key which indicates the stitch to use for each part of design. Plain solid line is outline stitch. Use wool yarn and embroidery cotton in colors shown, or use your own color combinations. Leave second fabric piece plain.

When embroidery is complete, stitch the two fabric pieces together on seam line with right sides facing and leave an opening for turning. Turn right side out and press. Stuff firmly with cotton. Turn in edges of opening and sew closed inconspicuously. Glue on sequins at single dots on pattern. Sequins may be sewn on, topping each with a seed bead.

30

COURTESY VIETNAM HANDICRAFT DEVELOPMENT CENTE
DESIGNER, KEN J. UYEMURA OF RUSSEL WRIGHT ASSOCI

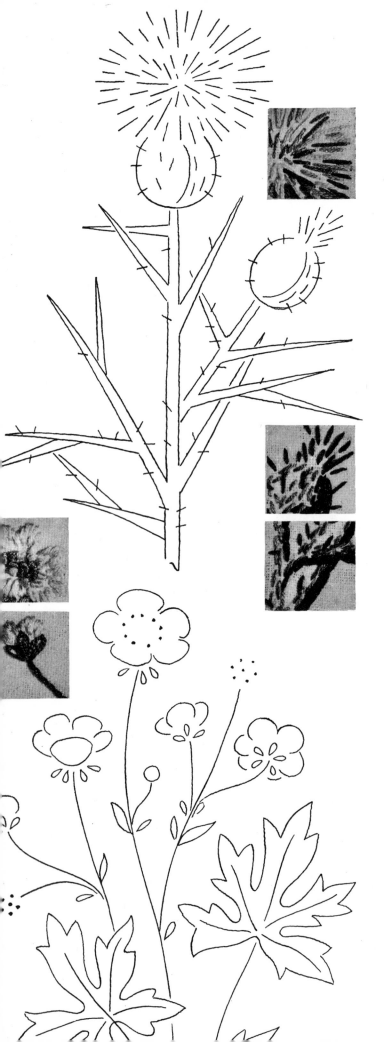

Embroidered Flower Prints

The three flower pictures shown on the opposite page were embroidered in so few simple stitches that even a beginner can enjoy making them. Cut linen 8″ by 11″ for each picture. Choose one of these flower designs or pick your own from china, a chintz design or a flower print.

If the design is the right size trace it as it is. We chose flower sprays 6½″ to 8″ long. See actual-size details at left. Draw your outline in this simple way on a piece of tracing paper or drawing paper. Use Scotch tape to fasten linen and drawing on a windowpane; with drawing underneath trace outline with medium soft pencil. Or place carbon between linen and paper, with paper uppermost and draw over design with a hard pencil.

Choose simple stitches as here. We used outline stitch and slanted satin stitch for stems. Kensington stitch shades the petals of the Wild Rose.

The enlarged details at the left show the stitch treatments for the Thistle and for the Buttercup. Embroider flowers in natural colors using 4 strands of six-strand cotton.

Make your flower prints a sampler of all the stitches you know. Have fun experimenting with different stitches to see how lifelike you can make the flowers appear by relating the stitches to the form and texture of the flower.

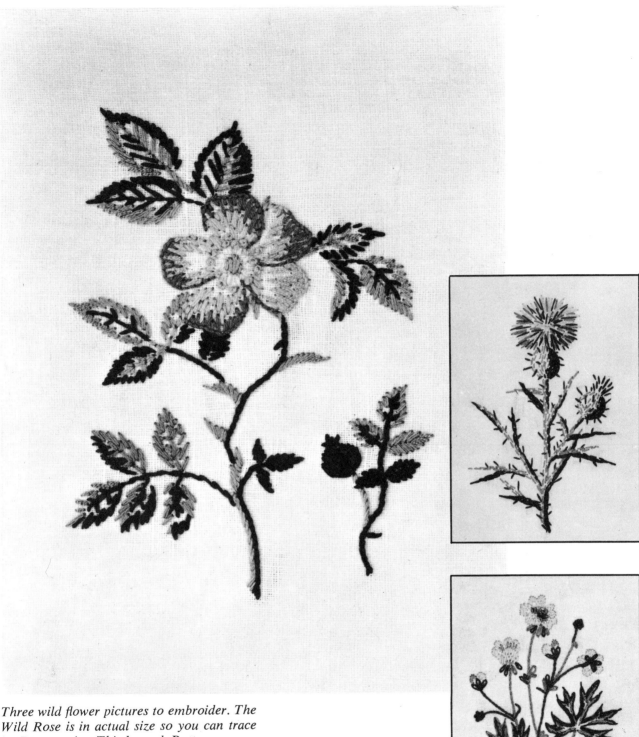

Three wild flower pictures to embroider. The Wild Rose is in actual size so you can trace it. Patterns for Thistle and Buttercups are on opposite page.

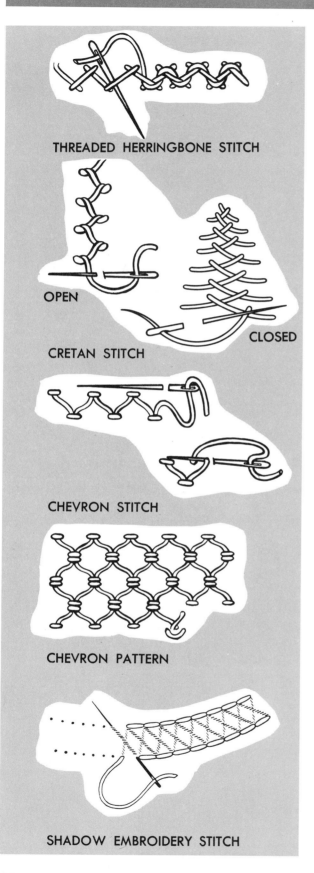

THREADED HERRINGBONE STITCH

OPEN

CRETAN STITCH

CLOSED

CHEVRON STITCH

CHEVRON PATTERN

SHADOW EMBROIDERY STITCH

THREADED HERRINGBONE STITCH Created by running contrasting thread through the zigzags of the herringbone stitch without going through the fabric beneath. Diagram shows method of looping the thread around the crossed ends of the stitch.

CRETAN STITCH Made with the needle turned toward the center of the row, and the zigzags worked back and forth from right to left alternately as in catch stitch. *Closed Cretan Stitch* simply involves setting the stitches closer together. They may be closed up tight if desired in the same way as in closed chain stitch.

CHEVRON STITCH Involves herringbone stitch with a second step at each diagonal end. This consists of a perpendicular stitch marking each end.

CHEVRON PATTERN Is an allover area of chevron stitch simply consisting of repeated rows of the stitch. Each end stitch can be elaborated with repetition, or it may be worked out with a contrasting color stitch to resemble smocking.

SHADOW EMBROIDERY STITCH or CROSSED BACK-STITCH On the right side of the work this stitch resembles two rows of backstitch and on the wrong side it looks like a closed herringbone stitch. Slant the needle and take a backstitch, bring it out above and to the left; then work the line above in same manner. Work on sheer materials for shadow effect.

Embroidery On Ticking

This attractive and amusing embroidery technique was worked out using stripes of ticking as guidelines. The border stitches, opposite, and edge stitches on next page, as well as chain stitch, threaded running stitch, and herringbone stitch, are especially suitable. Use bold, bright colors to embroider household articles, or personal items like the eyeglass case. Embroider all articles which will require frequent washing with six-strand cotton; for others, wool yarn may be used. Do not embroider over seam allowances.

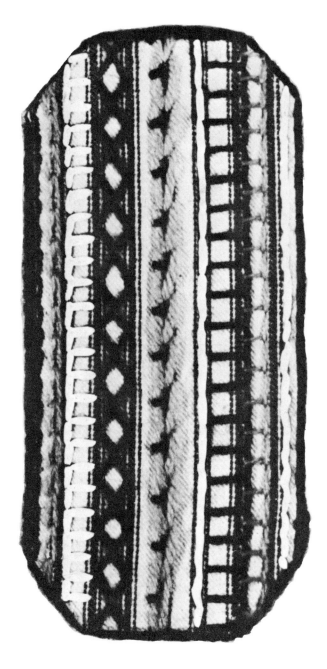

EYEGLASS CASE: Cut two pieces of ticking and two pieces of bright cotton (for lining), 7″ x 4″. Cut off corners diagonally about ¾″ in from tip. Embroider both pieces of ticking. Turn under seam allowances on all pieces (turning under seam allowances on lining slightly more than ½″). Hem linings to inside of ticking pieces. Whipstitch ticking pieces together along sides and across one end. Finish with braided, twisted or crocheted cord; whipstitch cording to all edges.

Embroidery: edge stitches

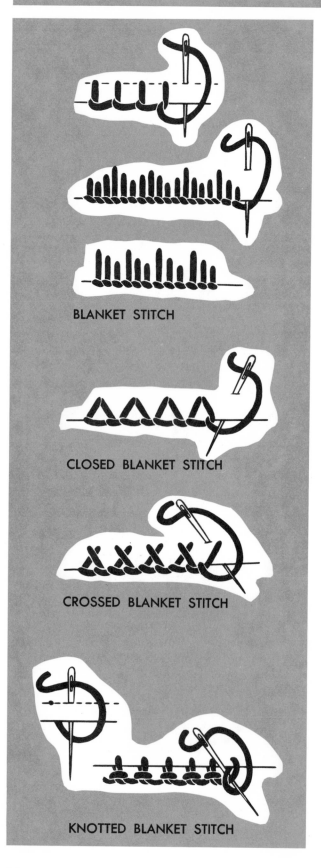

BLANKET STITCH

CLOSED BLANKET STITCH

CROSSED BLANKET STITCH

KNOTTED BLANKET STITCH

BLANKET STITCH   A quicker stitch made in the same way as buttonhole stitch, but more widely spaced. This may be used on a raw edge of material that will not ravel, or on a turned edge of other fabric. The hem turn should be basted in place first, then the stitches placed over the width of the hem, and close enough together to hold it firmly in place. These two stitches are often used in applique work. For a most decorative effect vary the depth of the stitches of either buttonhole stitch or blanket stitch. These edgings may be done in varied colors, or a single color. See diagram of two variations, one a pyramid border, and one a sawtooth border.

CLOSED BLANKET STITCH   Forms tiny inverted V's all along the edge. The needle is slanted to the left as shown in the diagram for the first stitch. The next stitch starts at the top of the same stitch and slants toward the right, taking up a bit of the lower edge to hold it firmly in place. Alternate stitches 1 and 2 all across the edge.

CROSSED BLANKET STITCH   Worked on the same premise of alternating angled stitches but the tops of the stitches cross instead of joining at the top.

KNOTTED BLANKET STITCH   Worked in two steps. First a loosely worked blanket stitch is formed. Then with the stitch still free from the fabric the needle is passed through the loop again to form a knot.
This stitch or any of the above edge stitches may be used on knitted garments to form an edge finish, and may be substituted for a crocheted edge finish. In delicate yarns or embroidery thread it is very useful for baby garments.

Embroidery: raised wool

You can create a lovely flower picture of your own like the museum piece right which is an example of shaded wool embroidery in a raised effect. If you hesitate to use your own design, choose a flower picture and sketch it on a dark colored fabric with chalk or dressmaker crayon. Place the fabric in an embroidery frame and work in crewel yarns or leftover wools. In this embroidered piece, the multicolored flowers and leaves are worked mostly in satin stitch, with some petals and leaves stitched on top of others. Other stitches used are stem stitch, French knots and lazy daisy stitch. See detail, below, of satin stitch petals and French knot center. Add seed beads and details in embroidery floss.

FLORAL SPRAY MADE BEFORE CIVIL WAR.
COURTESY SMITHSONIAN INSTITUTION

SATIN STITCH PETALS
FRENCH KNOT CENTER

Embroidery: tufted wool

This is also from an original museum design. The detail at the right is part of a black broadcloth table cover.

To embroider a similar tufted design, outline the flower pattern on dark fabric with chalk or crayon. Embroider the stems first in outline or stem stitch. Then start with the larger flower at the center. Tuft the area by sewing with turkey work loops as shown in detail.

Start with unknotted yarn end on front of work and make a small anchoring stitch. Loop yarn above needle and take another small stitch as shown, holding the loop; then with yarn below needle take another small stitch to anchor the loop. Continue placing each stitch close to preceding stitch. Shade the colorings as you work. Complete the tufting of a petal or the whole flower, then shear off the loops, cutting parts shorter than others to give a rounded, realistic form to the pile.

DETAIL, DECORATED TABLE COVER.
COURTESY SMITHSONIAN INSTITUTION

TURKEY WORK LOOPS

Canvas Work: Needlepoint

There are conflicting opinions as to the terms describing needlepoint. The differences may result from the fact that needlepoint has come down to us from various countries and in various stitches. Briefly, needlepoint is embroidery on canvas; the most common stitch is half of a cross-stitch which is also called "tent stitch."

Needlepoint-tapestry is an often used expression which shows the relation of needlepoint to the tapestry designs of the middle ages. This is especially true when the needlepoint is worked in an upright Gobelin stitch which gives the effect of a woven tapestry.

This early work was done on a loosely-woven material like coarse linen. Later, canvases were made especially for the purpose—both in single thread canvas, or with threads arranged in pairs to make "double thread canvas." The double thread canvas was often worked in needlepoint combining the fine petit point stitch, used for detailed shading, with gros point used for large flat design areas. To make this combination, the double thread canvas was "split"; that is, the meshes opened with a needle or pin to form a single thread canvas for working in petit point.

As with all other forms of embroidery it is very difficult to give exact dates, and even places where the technique originated. Canvas work dates back to the sixteenth century, but reached its peak during the late seventeenth and early eighteenth centuries. Needlepoint was extremely popular in Colonial America where it was used for pictures, as an upholstery fabric, and for fashion accessories.

During the Victorian era, Berlin work came into popularity. It is often characterized by brilliant worsteds and combinations of geometric and floral designs. The majority of the designs were developed as hand-painted patterns on squared paper, especially made for copying in needlepoint or cross-stitch on canvas. The best of these designs came from Berlin, thus naming it.

The current revived interest in needlepoint started to gain momentum during the late twenties and continues to increase in popularity with the ever-growing interest in handcrafts. Designs are available in department stores and shops all over the country, although there is a growing number of needlepoint enthusiasts designing original pieces in a large variety of stitches.

HOW NEEDLEPOINT DESIGNS ARE SOLD

Embroidered Centers The majority of imported needlepoint pieces have the center already worked, with only the background left to be filled in. Needlepoint pieces with the designs already worked were formerly planned primarily for dark backgrounds, such as maroon and black. Today, the lighter, modern furniture requires lighter backgrounds and many new designs are being planned for these colors.

Tramé Pieces The design has yarn laid in long stitches across the canvas in the exact pattern. The colors used in tramé patterns are approximately the colors to be used in working the piece in needlepoint. The needlepoint is worked over the long laid stitches following the correct color arrangement. This helps to pad the piece, and is easy to follow.

Painted or Tinted Pieces These are becoming more available in department stores as well as in specialty shops. The design is painted directly on the canvas in colors approximating the colors to be used in working the needlepoint. You can paint your own designs on needlepoint canvas, using oil paints mixed with benzine.

Charted Designs Many designs for pictures and other needlepoint pieces are available in chart form. Following a chart, a design may be worked on any size canvas mesh desired to produce a large or small piece. Each square on the chart represents a stitch in the canvas.

On the opposite page is shown a contemporary needlepoint picture worked in modern decorator colors. This is a tinted canvas by Heirloom Needlework Guild.

Needlepoint

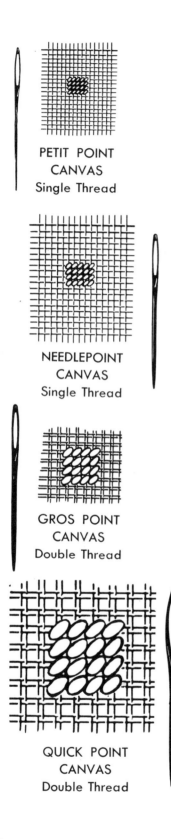

PETIT POINT
CANVAS
Single Thread

NEEDLEPOINT
CANVAS
Single Thread

GROS POINT
CANVAS
Double Thread

QUICK POINT
CANVAS
Double Thread

Needlepoint is the general term for an embroidery stitch used to cover canvas, as well as for the embroidered piece. When this stitch is worked on canvas 20 meshes to the inch or smaller, it is called petit point. When worked on 14 to 18 to the inch mesh, it is called simply needlepoint. On 8 to 12 to the inch mesh, it is called gros point. Larger meshes, 5 and 7 to the inch, have been used in the past for making rugs and are sometimes referred to as large gros point. However, we have coined a name for this larger stitch. We call it quick point.

YARNS TO USE WITH DIFFERENT CANVASES

In general you can use one strand of crewel wool or split tapestry wool on canvas 18 to 22 meshes to the inch. Use two strands of crewel wool on 14 to 16 mesh canvas. Use one strand of tapestry wool on 8 to 12 mesh canvas. For rug canvas, use rug wool or two strands of tapestry wool. It is important to use together wool and canvas by one manufacturer because they are coordinated.

It is possible to combine in one needlepoint piece crewel wool, tapestry wool and rug wool, provided sufficient strands of the finer yarns are used to balance the weight. This is done only when special colors are unobtainable in the correct yarn. Other yarns may be used if they have a tight, firm twist. However, care must be taken in the choice. For example, knitting worsted is not suitable for needlepoint, because the twist is not firm enough, and it wears thin from constant pulling through the canvas.

NEEDLES A blunt tapestry needle is always used. Needles range in size from fairly fine to the large rug needles. Sketches on this page show sizes.

STITCHES What stitch should be used? First, there is the half cross-stitch. This just covers the canvas with practically no yarn at the back. (See details on p. 41.) This stitch does not cover the canvas as well as the continental stitch or the diagonal stitch. The half cross-stitch is practical when working a picture or areas which will not receive hard wear; it is a yarn-saver since almost all the yarn appears on front of canvas.

Three methods for working basic needlepoint stitch

HALF CROSS-STITCH Start at upper left corner of canvas. Bring needle to front of canvas at point that will be the bottom of first stitch. The needle is in a vertical position when making stitch (see detail). Always work from left to right; turn work around for return row. Catch yarn ends in finished work on back.

CONTINENTAL STITCH Start design at upper right corner. To begin, hold an inch of yarn in back and work over this end. All other strands may be started and finished by running them through wrong side of finished work. Details 1 and 2 show placement and direction of needle; turn work around for return row. Always work from right to left. Finish design, then fill in background.

DIAGONAL STITCH Begin by tying a knot at end of yarn and putting needle through canvas to back, diagonally down from upper right hand corner of work. Never turn work; hold it in the same position. *Step 1:* The knot is on top. Bring needle up at A, down through B and out through C. *Step 2:* Needle in D, out through E. *Step 3:* Needle in F, out through G. *Step 4:* Start next row in at H and out through I.

You are now ready to work from the Big Diagram. Each stitch is drawn on Big Diagram with a blunt and a pointed end. Put needle in at pointed end, out at blunt end.

Stitch No. 5 is your next stitch. It extends from space 1 to A. Complete stitches to 10 on diagram in numerical order to finish diagonal row. Stitch No. 11 starts next row diagonally upward.

After starting row going up, needle is horizontal. Needle slants diagonally to begin new row down, as in Step 1. Going down, needle is always vertical, as in Step 2; and again, when the last stitch is made, the needle slants diagonally to begin next row up, Step 3.

Work as far as knot; cut knot off. All other strands of yarn may be started and ended by running them through finished work on back. Work background to design; then work design. Fill in remaining background.

HALF CROSS-STITCH

The needle is always in a vertical position when making the stitch.

CONTINENTAL STITCH

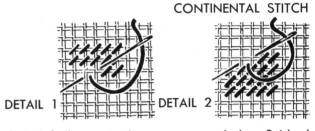

DETAIL 1   DETAIL 2

Detail 1 shows starting a new row below finished portion. Detail 2 shows starting a new row above finished portion.

DIAGONAL STITCH

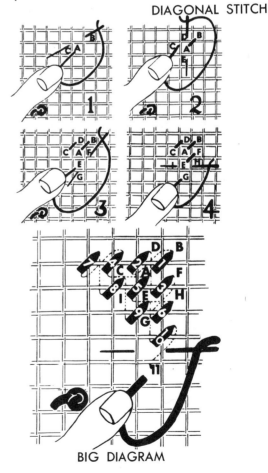

BIG DIAGRAM

CONTINENTAL STITCH

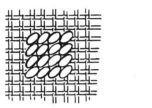

FRONT   BACK

HALF CROSS-STITCH

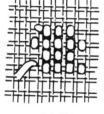

BACK

DIAGONAL STITCH

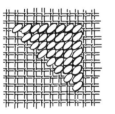

FRONT   BACK

Advantages of the two preferred stitches

The continental stitch is the one most promoted. It uses more wool than the half cross-stitch; however, it covers the canvas on both front and back (see detail). As a result, the finished piece is more attractive and the wearing quality is increased. The slight padding on the back makes it durable and practical for upholstery pieces and rugs.

The diagonal stitch, contrary to popular belief, does not use more wool than the continental stitch. It uses the same amount. This stitch covers the canvas and reinforces it, as it is actually woven into the canvas, and works up into a strong embroidered piece (see detail).

Blocking

Cover a wooden surface with brown paper and mark on this the size of canvas, being sure corners are square. Place needlepoint, right side down, over guide and fasten with thumbtacks placed ¾" apart near edge of canvas. Wet thoroughly with cold water; let dry. If work is badly warped, restretch, wet and dry again. If yarn is not colorfast, apply salt generously to back of needlepoint before wetting.

Quick point picture to work from a chart

Quick point is the needlepoint stitch worked over large-mesh canvas with thick wool—usually rug yarn, sometimes doubled tapestry wool. Its newness lies in its name and in its application. In the past the technique has been confined principally to making rugs; we have applied it to smaller-scale designs like that shown here. Quick point has all the fascination of fill-in painting, with a needle replacing the brush. Experienced needleworkers will enjoy doing it while watching television. Quick point is as quick as its name. It affords needlepoint lovers the pleasure of seeing smooth results spring into being in an incredibly short time with a minimum of concentration.

A fascinating study of Siamese cats sketched from life. Worked up in quick point on 5 mesh-to-the-inch canvas with rug yarn, the picture is 13″ x 19″. The chart for copying this picture and list of materials needed is given on pages 44 and 45.

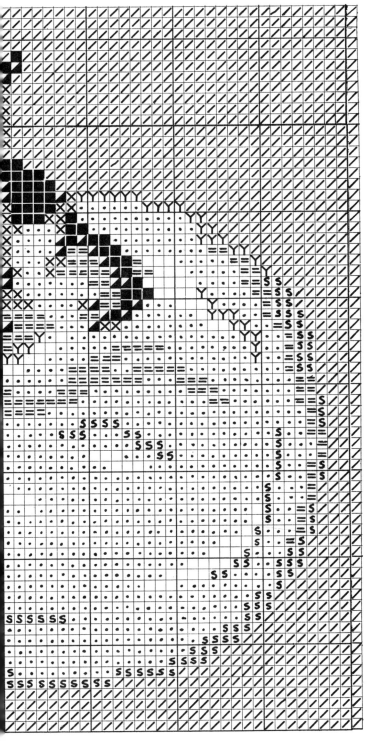

COLOR KEY

- ☑ LIGHT BLUE
- ◩ DARK IVORY
- ☒ LIGHT BROWN
- ■ BLACK
- ☐ WHITE ⊡ ANTIQUE WHITE
- ▣ OLD IVORY
- ⑤ MEDIUM TAUPE
- ◢ MEDIUM BROWN

SIZE: 13½″ x 19¼″.

MATERIALS: Wool rug yarn (40 yard skeins): 1 skein each Medium Taupe, Light Brown, Medium Brown, Black, Old Ivory, Dark Ivory, White; 3 skeins Antique White; 4 skeins Light Blue.

Rug canvas, 5 meshes to the inch, 20″ x 25″. Large-eyed rug needle.

More stitches on canvas

Needlepoint offers a variety of other interesting stitches, ranging in texture from the ribbed effect of upright Gobelin to the elegant Florentine stitches. For footstools and chair seats these can be used instead of tent stitch for backgrounds and borders to make handsome tone-on-tone fabrics or to form a brilliant pattern in two or more colors. Details on this page show finished work actual size, as well as the method of working upright, wide, and encroaching Gobelin stitches.

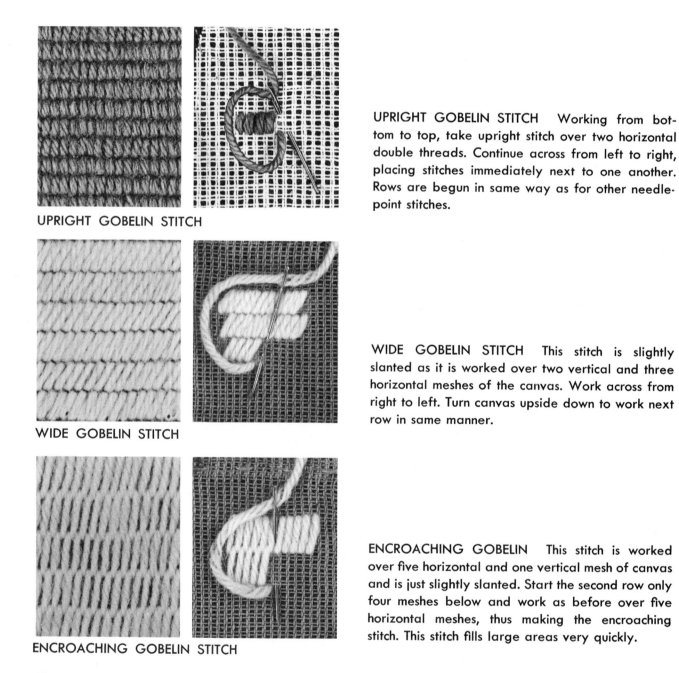

UPRIGHT GOBELIN STITCH

WIDE GOBELIN STITCH

ENCROACHING GOBELIN STITCH

UPRIGHT GOBELIN STITCH Working from bottom to top, take upright stitch over two horizontal double threads. Continue across from left to right, placing stitches immediately next to one another. Rows are begun in same way as for other needlepoint stitches.

WIDE GOBELIN STITCH This stitch is slightly slanted as it is worked over two vertical and three horizontal meshes of the canvas. Work across from right to left. Turn canvas upside down to work next row in same manner.

ENCROACHING GOBELIN This stitch is worked over five horizontal and one vertical mesh of canvas and is just slightly slanted. Start the second row only four meshes below and work as before over five horizontal meshes, thus making the encroaching stitch. This stitch fills large areas very quickly.

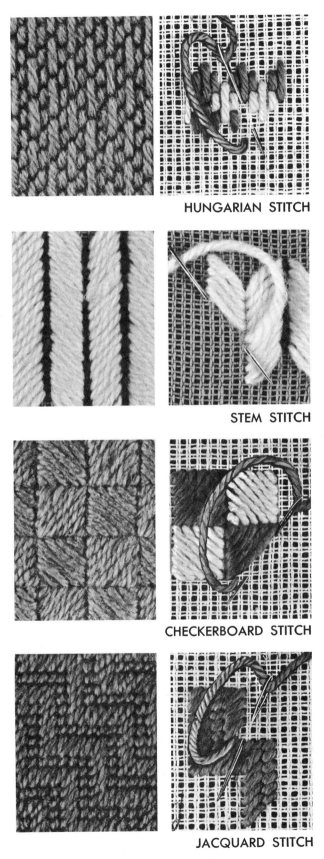

HUNGARIAN STITCH Work upright stitches over two, four and two double threads, making a diamond shape. Skip one vertical mesh, continue across from left to right. Dovetail succeeding rows, alternating contrasting colors or using one shade.

HUNGARIAN STITCH

STEM STITCH Work diagonal stitches from top to bottom, over four meshes of canvas each way, making each stitch one mesh below. Work the second row in diagonal stitches in opposite direction. When diagonal stitches are completed, work backstitch in another color of yarn between the diagonal rows.

STEM STITCH

CHECKERBOARD STITCH Work diagonal stitches left to right over one, two, three, four, five, four, three, two, one double threads, forming a square. Make other squares in same way, alternating direction of stitches and changing color, if desired.

CHECKERBOARD STITCH

JACQUARD STITCH From left to right, work diagonal stitches over two double threads, taking six stitches down and six across; continue row for desired length. Next row, work over one double thread, make same number of stitches, arranged in the same way.

JACQUARD STITCH

47

RICE STITCH

FERN STITCH

STAR STITCH

MOSAIC STITCH

RICE STITCH or **CROSSED CORNERS CROSS-STITCH** Work cross-stitch over two double threads. Using crewel wool in contrasting color, take diagonal stitches over each arm of crosses, having the stitches meet in space between crosses.

FERN STITCH Work rows from top to bottom. The first half of stitch is worked over two meshes of canvas each way; the second half is also worked over two meshes of canvas each way, to the opposite side of center stitch with needle coming out again one mesh below the beginning stitch.

STAR STITCH Each star consists of eight stitches all meeting in the center. Each star should be worked the same way. Work over two meshes of canvas for each stitch of star, bringing needle down through center mesh each time and working around to complete star. Backstitch may be worked around the completed star.

MOSAIC STITCH Consists of long and short stitches taken alternately in diagonal rows. Work over one and two meshes of canvas. In each succeeding diagonal row a short stitch is worked into a long stitch and a long stitch into a short one.

Checkerboard pillow

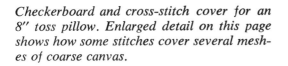

Checkerboard and cross-stitch cover for an 8″ toss pillow. Enlarged detail on this page shows how some stitches cover several meshes of coarse canvas.

MATERIALS: Rug canvas, 5 meshes to the inch, ½ yard, 40″ wide. Foam rubber 8″ square and 2″ thick, or two 1″ thick pieces. Needlepoint wool, nine 40-yard skeins. Large-eyed, blunt needle. Carpet thread.

Cut two pieces of canvas for top and bottom of pillow, each 12″ square. Cut four pieces for sides, each 6″ x 12″.

To Embroider: Pillow is done in cross-stitch and checkerboard stitch, using single strand of yarn for crosses, double strand for checkerboard stitch. Starting 2″ in from both sides at top right corner, work a row of 41 cross-stitches across, and from same corner 41 stitches down. Complete other two sides to form square.

Divide inside of large square into 64 smaller squares 5 meshes wide and 5 meshes deep (8 squares to each side). Work horizontal and vertical rows of crosses on these dividing lines. Fill in squares with checkerboard stitch (see detail). Make back of pillow in same way.

Work side pieces in cross-stitch, making 11 rows 41 stitches long; leave 2″ of canvas all around.

Block each piece.

To Assemble: Fold excess canvas to wrong side all around each piece and baste. With carpet thread whip sides to edges of top, taking close stitches.

Whip ends of sides together. Pin bottom to edges of three sides and whip together. Insert foam rubber, whip last side to bottom. Finish joined corners of sides with a row of crosses.

Make a twisted cord (see Index) and sew around edges on top and bottom of pillow.

STITCH DETAIL OF CHECKERBOARD
AND CROSS-STITCH PATTERN

49

Canvas Work: Colors and textures

The two examples below were worked on canvas with 10 meshes to the inch in crewel wools. Made into pillows, they are a stunning counterpoint to the checkerboard pillow pictured on p. 49.

The first sample is oblong cross-stitch with backstitch. Cross-stitch loops are worked between some rows of cross-stitch.

The second example is a checkerboard design of cross-stitch loops and couched needlepoint squares. Using double crewel wool, lay yarn in rows, diagonally across the canvas to form a square; couch yarn using double wool in another color and working in the diagonal needlepoint stitch. Work alternate squares in cross-stitch loops.

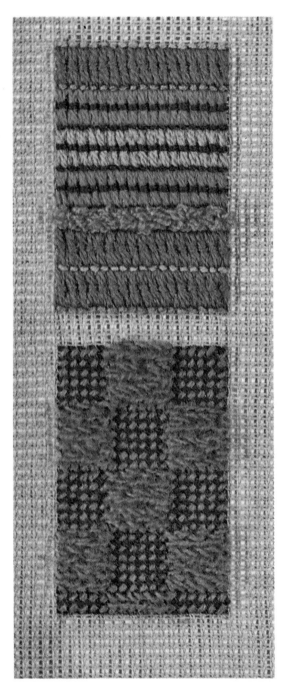

OBLONG CROSS-STITCH   BACKSTITCH

| Fig. 1 | Fig. 2 | Fig. 3 |

Work from left to right over four horizontal meshes of canvas and one vertical mesh, Fig. 1. Work back crossing stitches, Fig. 2. Make a backstitch, Fig. 3, over center of each cross-stitch and between rows of cross-stitch.

CROSS-STITCH LOOPS

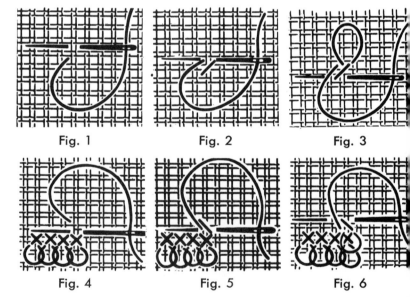

| Fig. 1 | Fig. 2 | Fig. 3 |
| Fig. 4 | Fig. 5 | Fig. 6 |

Starting at upper right, make first half of cross and pull yarn tight, Fig. 1. Take next stitch above cross, Fig. 2, and form loop ¼″ long while completing cross, Fig. 3. Work across in this manner from right to left. For next row, turn work and work as shown in Figs. 4, 5 and 6, holding loops below work.

Florentine work

Florentine, Bargello, or Hungarian work is of ancient origin and was generally used for covering cushions. Later it came into use for upholstery fabric and such personal items as handbags. It is also known as Flame Embroidery, because of the distinctive zigzag patterns which characterize this work. Traditionally, several shades of one color are used to give a soft and gradual ombre effect, but for a more striking effect, several different colors may be combined in one design. The work consists of perpendicular stitches which can be made all the same length, or in a combination of long and short perpendicular stitches, covering from two to six meshes of the canvas. The canvas used is usually single thread, 10 meshes to the inch. Depending on the color combinations and stitch arrangements, various effects are obtained which give names to the patterns, such as diamond, skyscraper and sawtooth.

Bargello stitch is easily worked from a graph pattern. Work the first row in peaks, following chart below; starting at the center, work to right and then left to finish row and establish the pattern. For succeeding rows, follow first row, in long or short stitches as indicated on chart, until all the surface is covered. Fill in the corners of the design to completely cover the area.

A Bargello design may be carried out for chair upholstery to cover both seat and back as shown. It is advisable to plan the color scheme and work a small section of one seat to determine how much yarn will be required. Suppose you are working the chair seat and back shown here. Outline areas on your canvas to correspond with seat and back of chair. Work one-quarter of the back and determine how much yarn you used. Then purchase enough to cover that area, multiplied by the number of times necessary to cover all of back and seat, before continuing with the work.

Chair covered with Bargello work

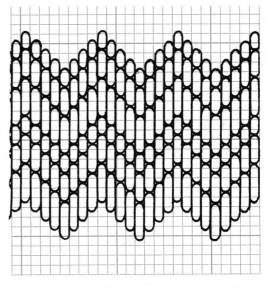

CHART FOR BARGELLO DESIGN

51

Adapting a design to a different size or use

Almost everyone has a favorite cross-stitch or needlepoint design which she has worked and would like to use again for something else. Often, too, when looking for a design for a particular article, you will find the right thing, but in the wrong size. Any needlepoint or cross-stitch de-sign can be enlarged or reduced by using a material or canvas with a larger or smaller thread or mesh count than that of the original design. See (on the opposite page) how the Victorian Rose design pictured below can be varied in size depending on background count. See in color, p. 15.

The Victorian Rose motif, chart opposite page, enlarged to scatter-rug size, makes a huge and beautiful bloom. It is cross-stitched with two strands of wool rug yarn over 3½ mesh-to-the-inch rug canvas. Four meshes equal one stitch of the original design. One large cross covers the four meshes to equal one square on chart. Actual size 23" x 25".

To vary size of rose motif, follow the original design or the color chart on this page, letting each stitch of the original represent one mesh, or block of meshes, on the new background. To illustrate what we mean, actual-size details of variations are shown here. They do not include all the canvases and materials on which the design could be worked, but they do represent a number of the possibilities.

To figure the overall size of your design on the new background, count the number of stitches lengthwise and crosswise on the original. Then count off an equal number of meshes on the new background (or, if several meshes are to represent one stitch of the original, as in the rose detail at the bottom of page 52, count off the corresponding meshes).

Select the type of yarn or the number of strands of embroidery cotton best suited to the mesh. Estimate the amount of yarn needed by working a 1″ square. Figure the number of square inches to be covered by each color and multiply by the amount used to work the 1″ square. This gives you the approximate yardage for each color. To compute this in skeins, divide it by number of yards in skein.

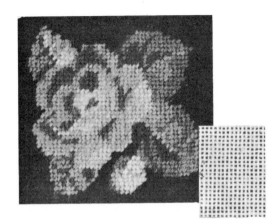

Petit point with crewel wool on 22-to-the-inch single thread canvas.

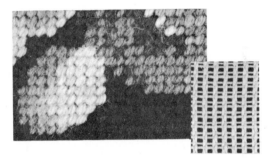

Needlepoint with tapestry yarn on 10-to-the-inch double thread canvas.

Needlepoint with wool rug yarn on 5-to-the-inch double thread rug canvas.

Cross-stitched with rug yarn on 3½-to-the-inch double thread rug canvas.

CHART FOR VICTORIAN ROSE

COLOR CHART

ROSE:
⬒ DEEP PINK
⬓ LIGHT RED
⧯ SCARLET
◪ DARK RED
CENTER:
☐ YELLOW
◩ BURNT ORANGE
◈ TERRA COTTA

GOLD LEAVES:
◉ RICH GOLD
⊡ GOLDEN BROWN
⊙ BROWN
⊞ DARK BROWN
GREEN LEAVES:
◿ PALE GREEN
◩ JADE GREEN
⊠ DEEP GREEN
◼ DARK GREEN

Cross-stitch

Cross-stitch is easy to do and attractive whether used for ornamenting clothes, for monogramming, or for home decoration. Cross-stitch pieces are often worked on linen in six-strand embroidery floss. Several different ways to do the stitch are described and illustrated on the opposite page. All yield equally good results if care is taken to make sure that the strands of thread or yarn lie smooth and flat. Secure the end of your thread on the wrong side by running it under the work.

A McCALL'S TRANSFER PATTERN

How to cross-stitch

In working cross-stitch over a stamped transfer (Method A), work across all stitches in each row from left to right before crossing back in the other direction. Be sure crosses touch. Details 1 and 2.

Method B shows the design following the mesh of coarse fabric such as monk's cloth. Here the design may be worked from a chart without a transfer pattern simply counting each square of equal size for one cross-stitch.

Method C shows a checked material used as a guide for the cross-stitch design. Here the corners of the blocks are guidelines.

Method D illustrates the use of round thread linen or sampler linen. The threads may be counted, and each cross-stitch made the same size. For instance in the illustration a 3 thread square is counted for each stitch. This same method was used for many of the Victorian pictures, with the design stitched on coarse canvas or stiff scrim mounted on a needlepoint frame. The design may be painted on the canvas or outlined with crayon.

Method E is illustrated in the larger picture at the right. Here Penelope canvas, or cross-stitch canvas, is basted to the fabric on which the finished design is to be shown. The design is then worked counting the threads as shown, and making the crosses over the threads. When design is completed the bastings are removed and the threads of the canvas drawn out, leaving the finished design on the fabric. This canvas is available in several size meshes. Choose the finer sizes for smaller designs, larger sizes for coarser work in yarn.

1 2

METHOD A

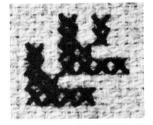

METHOD B

METHOD C

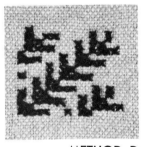

METHOD D

Typical cross-stitch borders from an old sampler.

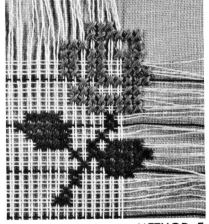

METHOD E

Making a cross-stitch sampler

Few gifts as happily combine challenge and fun for the giver with an assured welcome from the receiver as individual samplers do. Design your sampler either around the particular hobby or interest of the recipient, or plan a special-occasion sampler for a bridal couple, or a friend's baby. These samplers are easily worked on even mesh linen, or by using Penelope canvas as a guide. Some suggestions for details suitable for such samplers are shown in chart form on page 57. Some of the designs may be worked in a single color, while others combine two or three colors. The alphabet of cross-stitch block letters on page 66 may be used in combination with the motifs given here.

Other samplers similar to the old one shown here are to be found in museums in various parts of the country. Your public library may have books illustrating old samplers, parts of which you can copy or trace to work out your design.

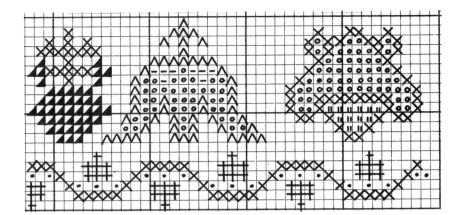

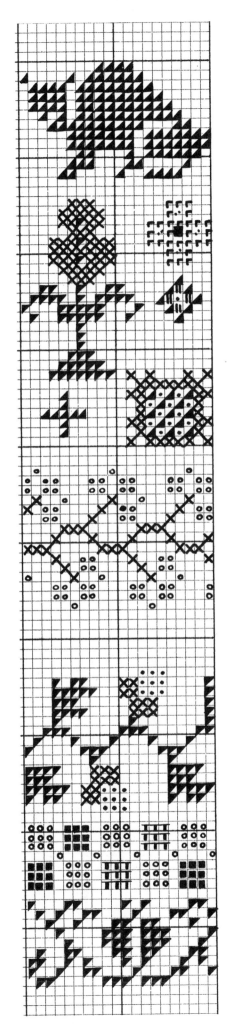

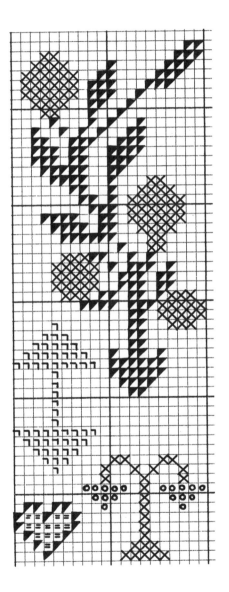

Here are a few motifs which may be used in cross-stitch samplers. Each symbol represents a different color. Other designs may be found in cross-stitch booklets, or evolve your own on graph paper.

Cross-stitch on gingham

Checked gingham fabric offers an easy guide for working cross-stitch designs. Each cross is worked within a check of the gingham with the ends of crosses at corners of the check. Gingham comes in many sizes of checks, from four to the inch to 10 to the inch or more. For big bold designs, use four to the inch. For most designs, however, you will find that gingham with 8 checks to the inch is easiest to work on. Many designs are worked out especially for gingham and in some of these the embroidery is to be done in the white checks of the fabric only. However, almost any cross-stitch design can be followed, utilizing all of the checks of the gingham. The apron below has a daffodil design in yellow and green floss on green-and-white checked gingham.

GENERAL DIRECTIONS: Gingham with checks 8, 9 or 10 to the inch is most suitable for working these cross-stitch designs. When working on 10 checks to the inch, use three strands of six-strand embroidery floss in the needle. On 8 checks to the inch, use full six strands in the needle.

Cross-stitching is usually done on the white checks of gingham only. But for a more solid look, or special design, the dark checks are utilized also. Place gingham in an embroidery hoop to obtain even stitches and prevent pulling of thread. Work bottom stitch of crosses all in one direction, then complete crosses with top stitches all in opposite direction (see stitch detail on this page).

Follow charts in working cross-stitch designs. When the design is all one color, an X symbol is used on the chart. If more than one color is used, X is used for one color and various symbols used for the other colors.

You may find embroidering easier if you first mark the designs in hard pencil on the gingham, following charts.

APRON: MATERIALS: Gingham with 9 or 10 checks to the inch, ¾ yard, 36″ wide. Matching sewing thread. Six-strand embroidery floss in yellow, green, and white. White rickrack.

DIRECTIONS: Cut gingham for skirt, 29″ wide and 22½″ long. Cut two ties, 3½″ x 28″. Cut waistband, 3½″ x 16½″. Cut pocket, 5¼″ x 6″. Embroider designs across bottom of skirt, leaving 2½″ for hem and a margin below design as desired. Embroider daffodil design in yellow and green; wide border in white with white rickrack sewn between rows of crosses. Sew on other rickrack as shown. Fold waistband in half lengthwise as guide for placing border. Embroider border across waistband near fold; sew on rickrack underneath border. For pocket, embroider border along one shorter edge for top, about 2″ from edge.

Make ¼″ hems at sides of apron skirt and 2″ hem at bottom. Gather top edge in to 16″. Stitch one long edge of waistband to skirt top, with embroidered side of band and right side of skirt facing. Fold waistband in half to back, turn in edge and sew to skirt. Turn in raw ends of waistband. Hem both long edges and one end of ties. Stitch raw ends of ties in waistband.

For pocket, make a 1¼″ hem at top. Turn in ¼″ all around remainder of pocket. Stitch to apron, 3½″ down from waistband and 6″ in from side.

CROSS-STITCH DETAIL

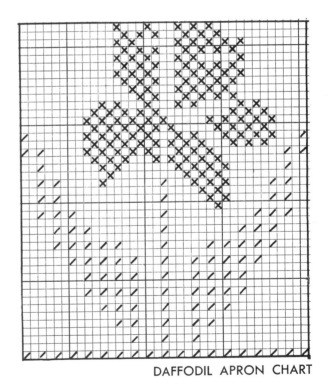

DAFFODIL APRON CHART

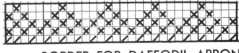

BORDER FOR DAFFODIL APRON

Cross-stitch variation on gingham

A combination of cross-stitch and straight stitches produces medallion-like designs to work on checked gingham. Medallions in other shapes and other arrangements can be used to make an endless variety of designs. A chart is given below, showing the cross-stitches and straight stitches. This was used to make one of the pot holders shown on the opposite page. Make your own designs on graph paper to embroider on such household items as tablecloths, place mats, curtains.

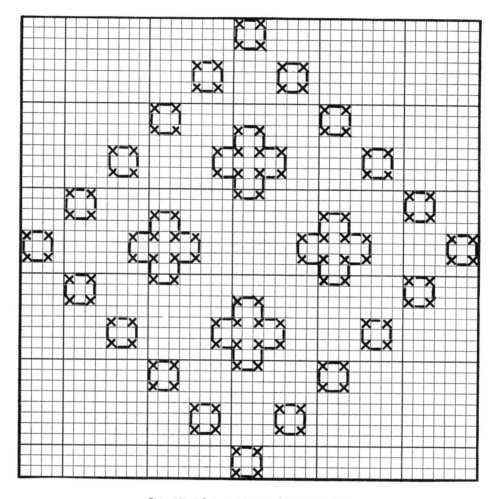

CHART FOR MEDALLION DESIGN

MEDALLION POT HOLDER: MATERIALS: For each pot holder, checked gingham with 8 checks to the inch, 14″ square. Cotton batting, or other padding, 7″ square. Black six-strand embroidery floss. White sewing thread. 1″ plastic ring.

DIRECTIONS: Cut two pieces of gingham 7″ square. From remainder of gingham, cut 1″ wide strips diagonally across fabric; place one strip across another at right angles and stitch together diagonally from the end of top strip to end of bottom strip to make a continuous piece. Sew bias strips together until piece is long enough to fit around gingham.

On one gingham square embroider medallion design following chart, left. Work straight stitches connecting crosses as indicated on chart. With right side of bias strip facing right side of embroidered square and raw edges matching, stitch bias strip all around square with ¼″ seam; ease strip around corners and join ends by turning in edge of one end and sewing to square under opposite end. Place padding between gingham squares with right sides out and baste together. Quilt through all three thicknesses with tiny running stitches in a diamond shape, outlining embroidered motifs. Turn bias strip to back of pot holder; turn in raw edge and slip-stitch in place. Sew ring at corner.

Gingham with eight checks to the inch was used to make this simply designed apron and the pot holders. Directions are given on opposite page for making a pot holder with self-bound edges and embroidering it.

Assisi Embroidery

Assisi work, named for the Italian village of its origin, is a very distinctive type of needlework. Traditionally it is done on pale ivory linen and embroidered in red, blue, and black, or a combination of two colors. Simplicity of design is important to show the true characteristic of this technique. At its inception, as now, the designs were worked from charts and embroidered by counting the threads of the linen. This is a simple embroidery technique and its charm lies in the artistry, neatness and skill of the embroiderer.

The design is first outlined with a running stitch or straight stitches and worked back again in the same way to fill in between the first line of stitches. This step when finished resembles backstitch. See stitch detail below. The background is then filled in solidly with cross-stitch, leaving just the design area open. The cross-stitch must be done very carefully, counting an equal number of threads vertically and horizontally for each stitch, and making all stitches even. Work first half of all crosses in one direction and the second half all in opposite direction. After the Assisi work is completed, narrow borders can be added in cross-stitch and straight stitch in simple repeat patterns.

This makes a very attractive pillow, with the cross-stitching covering the entire pillow top.

STEP 1

STEP 2

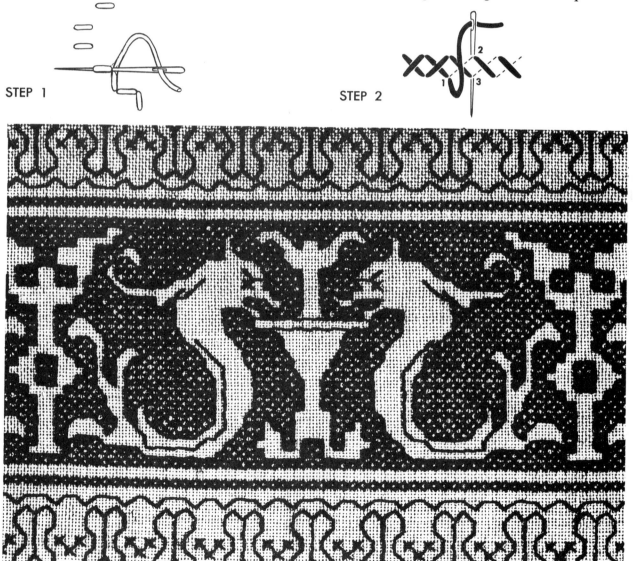

COURTESY D.M.C. EMBROIDERIES

Monogramming

Your monogram should be very personal. Whether you wish to monogram apparel or household linens, choose a style of letter which you think best expresses your own tastes and the sort of social life you lead. A few alphabets are given on the following pages. When you have chosen one, trace the letters, enlarging or reducing them, by following the square method. (See Index.)

TABLE LINEN. A dinner cloth should be monogrammed at opposite ends or opposite right hand corners above the area that hangs down 12″ to 15″ over the side of the table. If centered it should be above the table setting. Use only one monogram for a lunch cloth, or tea cloth, and place that similarly. Monograms on place mats may be arranged perpendicularly or horizontally at the left hand side. Or they may be centered above the plate position. For napkins the marking should correspond to the treatment of the cloth or mat, but be smaller in size. Some prefer a single initial on the napkin. Always place the initials on the dinner napkins so the base of the initial faces the corner. Then when each adjoining side is folded under for correct service the monogram will be upright parallel with the fork.

LINENS for the hope chest are monogrammed with the maiden name, with the surname initial centered. For a married woman the three initials used are her first name, maiden surname and married name with the marriage surname larger and in the center. If the three initials are the same size, and placed either perpendicularly or horizontally, then the married surname comes last.

SHEETS are monogrammed in the center of the turnover just above the hem. Pillowcases may be monogrammed in the center of the area just above the hem or toward the top of the case to one side.

TOWELS are usually monogrammed at the center just above the hem, so that when folded the monogram will appear a few inches above the hemstitched hem, or the decorative border of terry cloth towels.

HANDKERCHIEF monograms, or monograms for lingerie or men's shirts are usually quite small in size, and should be embroidered with finer thread, or a single strand of six-strand cotton.

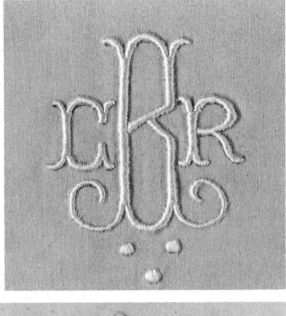

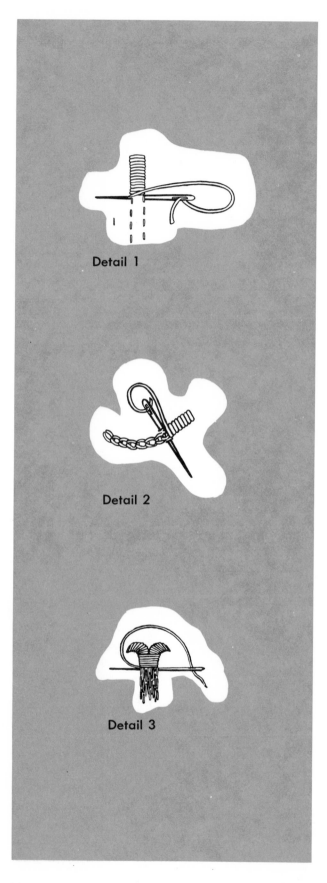

Detail 1

Detail 2

Detail 3

SATIN STITCH may be done by hand, or by machine. In either case you will find it essential to use an embroidery hoop to hold the work firm while working. After the design for the letters has been transferred or drawn in outline with dressmaker crayon, set the frame in place. For hand embroidery use two strands of six-strand cotton or No. 25 or 30 embroidery cotton. The latter comes in white only and is used as a single strand.

The first step in hand embroidering a monogram is the underlying padding. This is used to give the work the richly rounded effect so desirable. Use slightly heavier embroidery thread than the covering thread. Outline each letter with running stitch, carrying this thread just inside the stamped outline, having a short stitch on the wrong side with a longer stitch on the right side, Detail 1. Then fill in the area inside this outline with the same stitch. Or use chain stitch, Details 2 and 3.

You are now ready to add the surface covering. Thread needle with the other thread, and work over the padding placing the needle exactly through the fabric right on the stamped outline. Each stitch should be even in length, and placed just a thread apart each time. The closer the spacing of the stitches the smoother the finished effect will be. If your letter has a formal swirled end or a shaped curve such as in a C or S turn the stitches gradually to fit the curve. In a corner such as in an E or an M the turn may be more abrupt. The stitches may either swing gently out in a fan or may be tapered into each other in a miter.

CHAIN STITCHING (See Index) may be used for informal linens used daily. These may be script instead of block letters and may be a first name in lieu of a monogram.

OUTLINE STITCH may also be used for such individual markings. It may be used alone, or in combination with the chain stitch, or to outline a monogram of French knots. It is often of another color forming a shadow outline along one side of the lettering, or carried all around.

FRENCH KNOTS (See Index) are particularly suitable for working a monogram on bath towels. The raised quality looks well with the tufts and makes an effective monogram. These should be worked quite large for the utmost effectiveness.

CROSS-STITCH MONOGRAMS may be used on linen towels, and are particularly suitable for small guest towels or fingertip towels. The monogram is usually simple block letters set in line. Follow the usual directions for working cross-stitch, making all the slanting stitches in one direction first, then adding the cross top stitch in the other direction. You may work these over Penelope cloth mesh, then pull out the threads.

These letters and those on the following page can be traced and used in the size drawn or they can be enlarged or decreased in size by copying on graph paper with larger or smaller squares.

Several ways of arranging monograms from these script letters are shown here, incorporating decorative motifs as well. These monograms are planned for satin stitch. However, if a very large monogram is desired, the letters may be filled in with rows of chain stitch.

Embroidery: Openwork

Openwork, also called punch stitch, is sometimes mistakenly called drawn work, although no threads are drawn from the fabric. The reason for the name punch stitch is that a large three-sided punch needle is sometimes used when working on coarse fabric. This needle separates the threads of the fabric, making an open space. A punch needle is not necessary, however. A regular needle may be used, but a much thicker one than for ordinary embroidery.

Loosely woven linen is best to use, as the threads must be counted and each stitch taken over the same number of threads, usually four. However, fine linen or lawn, or even satin may be used. Thread should be strong, a little finer than the material, and usually the same color.

The four-sided square is made in four steps and worked horizontally. On the back of the work cross-stitches are formed in the process of making the blocks. For a diagonal row, work the top and one side stitch for length desired; then work back with the bottom and other side stitch to complete the squares. As each stitch is taken, the thread is pulled tightly, thus accenting the holes.

Because the needles used are large and have big eyes, you may find it easier to tie the end of the thread to the needle eye when working. Pull thread tight after each stitch. Bring thread to front of fabric, count up four threads, insert needle at this point and bring out again at beginning point. Insert needle again at top of stitch and bring out four threads to left and four threads down, Step 1. Insert needle in beginning hole and bring out in hole four threads to left. Insert again at beginning stitch and bring out four threads up and four threads to left, Step 2. Insert needle four threads to right in hole of first stitch, bring out in hole to left. Insert again in hole to right and bring out four threads to left and four threads below, Step 3. Complete square with two stitches in same manner as before, as shown in Step 4. Continue making squares for length desired. Turn work to make next row, and work in holes of previous row.

Openwork is used mainly for backgrounds and filling spaces. It can be done as shown in the samples below in oblong or square spaces, or used as borders. Designs can be worked out in bold geometric fashion, working diagonally and straight. Since the threads are not drawn, it can also be worked in circles and curved lines, as in intricate fruit, flower and leaf shapes. This work often is used in combination with other embroidery to fill open areas of a design.

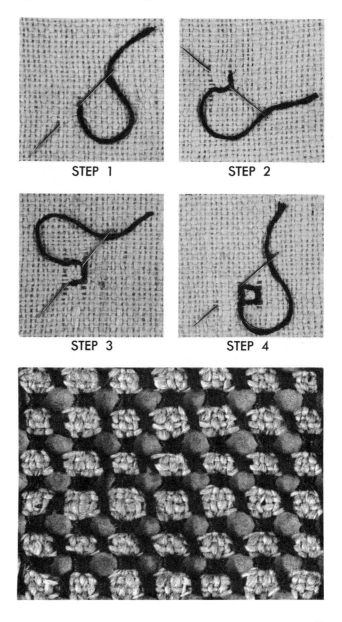

STEP 1 STEP 2

STEP 3 STEP 4

Cutwork or Richelieu Embroidery

The illustration above is an example of a design executed in round and oval eyelets, and is sometimes called Madeira work. The eyelets are all beautifully worked in overcast stitch, with satin stitch leaves and dots. The photograph is actual size and can be traced and worked on squares of fine linen, or used as corner motifs.

An actual-size detail at left shows typical contemporary cutwork in a rose pattern, as used on a tablecloth. Here the embroidery is almost completely buttonhole stitch, with details of satin stitch and outline stitch. Courtesy of Paragon Needlecraft.

PUNCHED EYELETS may be made up to ¼" in diameter. Use an embroidery stiletto or a knitting needle to pierce the hole in the fabric after marking the placing of each. Outline with running stitch to support the buttonhole stitches before punching the holes. Then whip edges with close overcasting, or buttonhole. If desired, shaded eyelets may be made with one side more narrowly edged than the other. The buttonhole loop may be at the outside of the petal if desired. See small oval shape thus formed.

CUTWORK EYELETS are made as diagramed with the center slashed and snipped to fit after the outline has been reinforced with tiny running stiches. As the edge is buttonholed or whipped the fabric is held back to the running stitch outline.

CUTWORK in other shapes or larger areas is made in the same way. The design is outlined in running stitch for reinforcement. Use small pointed embroidery scissors to cut the necessary slashes as you sew the outline areas with buttonhole stitch or overcast whipping. Trim off extra fabric after the edges are sewn. If the area to be cut out is rather large, make ladders of several strands of embroidery thread crossing from side to side before cutting away the fabric underneath. These ladders are covered with buttonholing.

PICOTS may be used to decorate these ladders or the edge detail. To form such picots loop several strands of thread and buttonhole them, or make a French knot part way along the bar.

HEDEBO This form of cutwork embroidery has many variations. The open areas may be round, oval, or of various shapes. The edges are first finished with buttonhole stitch, then ladders of thread worked across the opening in various angles. These are then worked over and over with the twist, sometimes interlaced with a modified spiderweb design. This Danish work is interesting for the advanced needleworker.

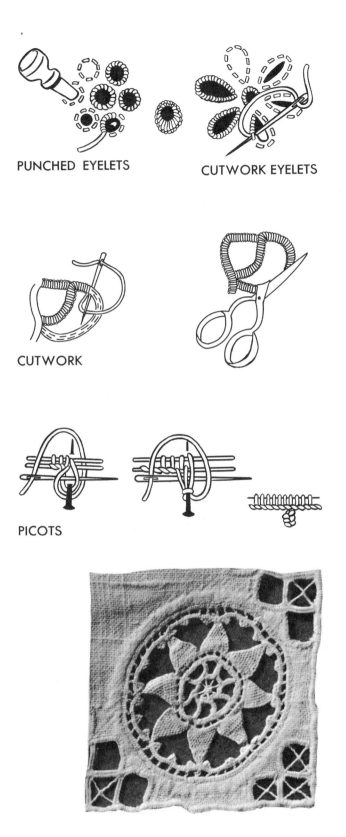

PUNCHED EYELETS   CUTWORK EYELETS

CUTWORK

PICOTS

THE METROPOLITAN MUSEUM OF ART.
PURCHASE, ROGERS FUND, 1908.

69

Drawn Work: Hemstitching

Drawn work describes those kinds of embroidery in which some of the warp or weft threads are drawn from the fabric; the remaining threads are pulled together with a fine needle threaded with a matching or contrasting color. Illustrations are examples of drawn work used to finish hems and make borders. Directions are given on these pages for plain hemstitching with zigzag and twisted thread variations, and for Italian hemstitching which makes a more elaborate border. Suitable fabrics for hemstitching vary from the finest linen to burlap. Threads, too, can be widely varied.

GENERAL DIRECTIONS: Any linen or cotton fabric with a plain weave may be used for hemstitching. To draw out threads, insert a pin under one thread near edge of fabric and pull it up; then carefully draw the thread from fabric all the way across. Try to ease it out without breaking it. Hemstitching is done on wrong side of fabric, from left to right.

Plain Hemstitching: Draw out two or three threads across fabric, depending on its coarseness. Secure thread at left edge of drawn section without making a knot by taking a few stitches over end of thread. Put needle under next three or four upright threads of drawn section from right to left (Fig. 1). Pull thread taut, insert needle in second row of threads above drawn section (Fig. 2) and pull thread tight. Continue across, as in Figs. 1 and 2, always picking up same number of threads. Secure thread at end. Bottom edge of drawn section may be hemstitched also as shown in Fig. 4.

A hem may be made at same time hemstitching is done. Turn fabric over twice to make hem desired width, and baste. Draw out threads just below edge of hem. Starting at left, hemstitch as in Figs. 1 and 2, inserting needle in 2nd row of threads above and through bottom edge of hem (Fig. 3). Repeat these two steps across, catching hem edge and picking up same number of threads each time.

For a more decorative border (Fig. 4), pull out about eight threads and work across in same manner as Figs. 1 and 2, picking up six threads at a time. To hemstitch lower edge of drawn section and make zigzag design, pick up first three threads only, then continue across, picking up six threads at a time (Fig. 4).

To make twisted groups of hemstitched threads (Fig. 5), pull out 10 or more threads and work plain hemstitching evenly at top and bottom of drawn section, picking up four threads at a time. Turn work over to right side, secure thread at right-hand edge in middle of drawn section. Pick up second group of threads at left with needle pointing from left to right. Bring this group of threads over and to the right of first group by inserting needle under first group and turning it to the left, keeping second group on needle. Continue across in same manner, always picking up second group of threads first.

PLAIN HEMSTITCHING

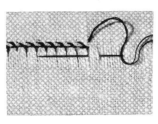

FIG. 1

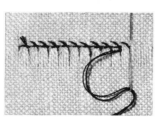

FIG. 2

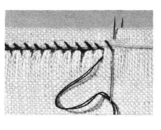

FIG. 3

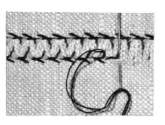

FIG. 4

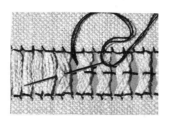

FIG. 5

Italian Hemstitching: This is based on the same two steps as plain hemstitching, except in the second step, the needle points downward instead of upward, unless otherwise stated.

To make border shown in Fig 6, baste hem. Draw out two threads just below hem, skip three threads, draw out next two threads, skip three, etc., for desired width. Make first row of hemstitching, picking up four threads at a time. With needle pointing downward for second step, insert needle in hem first, two threads up from fold, then through all thicknesses and out at drawn section. Continue across in same manner. To make succeeding rows, insert needle in space between groups of threads of preceding row (Fig. 6).

A wide decorative border, the right side of which is shown in Fig. 7, is worked as follows: Baste hem. Draw out two threads just below hem, skip three threads, draw out ten threads, skip three threads, draw out two threads. Work first two rows of hemstitching as shown in Fig. 6, picking up four threads at a time. On next row, fasten thread at base of wide drawn section and work a row of plain hemstitching as in Fig. 4, picking up eight threads at a time. On last row, fasten thread in last drawn section and work a row of hemstitching like second row, inserting needle in space between groups of threads and at base of groups.

To make border in Fig. 8, baste hem. Draw out ten threads just below hem, skip four threads, draw out two threads, skip four threads, draw out ten threads. Work first row as for Fig. 6, picking up nine threads at a time. Turn work around. Work second row along other edge of same drawn section, picking up three threads at a time and inserting needle in second row of threads above. Turn work around. Work third row in narrow drawn section, picking up three threads at a time and inserting needle in second row above. Turn work. Make fourth row in same drawn section along other edge in same manner. Turn work. Make fifth row in next wide drawn section, picking up three threads at a time and inserting needle in second row of threads above. Turn work. Make last row along other edge of wide drawn section, picking up nine threads at a time and inserting needle in second row of threads above. Be sure that nine-thread groups are in line with groups in first drawn section.

Many other decorative borders may be made by combining examples above and drawing out different numbers of threads.

The border of a white linen towel is worked in green. Spaces between thread clusters give the design lightness.

ITALIAN HEMSTITCHING

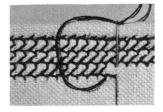

FIG. 6

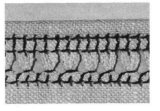

FIG. 7

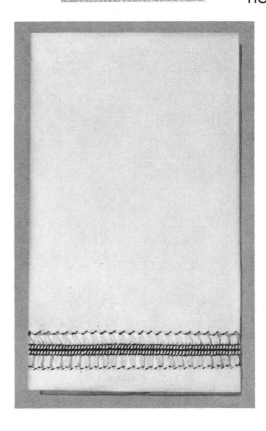

FIG. 8

Drawn Work: Needleweaving

Needleweaving has been a favorite in many countries for centuries. This technique of drawing threads from a fabric and then replacing them by weaving a design over the remaining threads is ideal for working colorful borders on linens. Here we give designs done in a thread heavier than the threads removed, thus producing an enriched, contrasting texture. These heavier threads of pearl or six-strand cotton are woven with a blunt needle, following simple repeat patterns on charts. The designs are striking when worked in strong colors, more subtle when done in white.

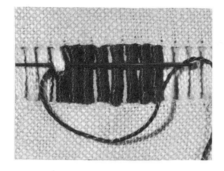

FIG. 1

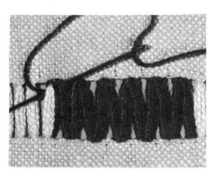

FIG. 2

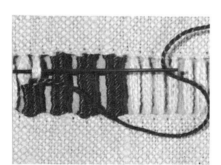

FIG. 3A

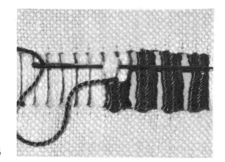

FIG. 3B

GENERAL DIRECTIONS: Choose coarse or fine linen or other fabrics from which threads can be drawn easily. Use pearl cotton or all strands of six-strand cotton and a blunt needle for weaving.

Draw out enough threads to make desired border. Both edges of the drawn section should be hemstitched first (see Index). Use thread to match fabric for hemstitching. Take an equal number of vertical threads in each stitch (usually 3, 4 or 5) according to weight of fabric being used. Then do needleweaving on right side of fabric over and under each group of threads divided by hemstitching—never split these groups. Always be sure that weaving threads are close together so they cover vertical threads of drawn section.

To begin work, fasten end of thread by placing it along first group of threads and working over it. To end off, run needle back into weaving for about four rows and cut thread close to work.

Practice the following six basic formations before starting to work borders on opposite page.

Vertical Bars (Fig. 1): Fasten thread at lower right and work closely around first group from bottom to top. End off thread. Make each bar separately in same way.

Zigzag Bars (Fig. 2): Fasten thread at bottom right and work one vertical bar, but do not end off. Work two stitches around first bar and next group of threads at same time, then work down 2nd group of threads. Work around bar just completed and next group of threads at same time. Continue in same way.

Double Bars (Figs. 3A and 3B): Fasten thread at lower right, weave under first group of threads and over 2nd group (Fig. 3A). Then weave under 2nd group and over first group (Fig. 3B). Continue weaving closely under and over first and 2nd groups from bottom to top. End off thread. Make each double bar separately.

Broken Double Bars (Fig. 4): Fasten thread at lower right and weave double bar same as above, halfway up drawn section; then weave under first group, over 2nd and under 3rd. For 2nd half of bar, weave over 3rd group of threads and under 2nd, then back over 2nd group and under 3rd. Continue weaving over and under 3rd and 2nd groups to top. End off thread. Start next broken bar at bottom, weaving 3rd and 4th groups of threads halfway up and continuing to top on 4th and 5th groups. Work across in same manner. First bar is finished by working to top.

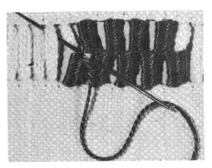

FIG. 4

Alternating Blocks (Fig. 5): Fasten thread at lower right, weave under first group of threads, over 2nd group, under 3rd, over 4th. Then weave back under 4th, over 3rd, under 2nd, over first. Continue weaving in this manner halfway up drawn section. Then weave under first group, over 2nd, under 3rd, over 4th, under 5th, over 6th. Weave back under 6th, over 5th under 4th and over 3rd. Continue weaving to top on 3rd, 4th, 5th and 6th groups of threads. Fasten off threads. Start next block at bottom on 5th, 6th, 7th and 8th groups of threads and weave halfway up. Then weave on 7th, 8th, 9th and 10th groups of threads to top. Continue across in this manner. Finish first 2 groups of threads as a double bar.

FIG. 5

Pyramids (Fig. 6): Fasten thread at lower right, weave under and over first 8 groups of threads and back under and over to first group. Weave back and forth for one-quarter depth of drawn section. Then weave over and under one group less of threads on each side (6 groups) for 2nd quarter of depth. Weave under and over one less group on each side (4 groups) for 3rd quarter of depth. Weave over and under 2 center groups for last quarter, to top of drawn section. End off thread. Start next pyramid upside down at bottom of drawn section. Weave under and over 2 groups of threads for first quarter; over and under 4 groups for 2nd quarter; under and over 6 groups for 3rd quarter; over and under 8 groups for last quarter. End off thread. Continue across in same way.

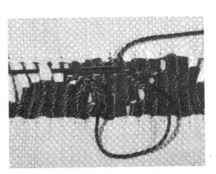

FIG. 6

Many interesting designs can be made with these basic formations.

Shown from top to bottom: Narrow Border of Triangles is worked in navy, light blue and contrasting gold; Medium Border of Vertical Diamonds in salmon and navy, and Wide Border of Reverse V's in light and dark green.

Teneriffe Embroidery

This type of embroidery involves the same technique as for needleweaving. However, no threads are drawn from the fabric for Teneriffe. Long straight stitches make the web or spoke and then you work over and under these long stitches to weave the design. It is a simple matter to use checked gingham as the background to form an even outline for your design. Form designs of squares, triangles, diamonds and circles, using the checks of the gingham as a guide for placing the long straight stitches. The apron and pot holder below show Teneriffe used as a border.

74

Teneriffe apron and pot holder

MATERIALS: Gold-and-white checked gingham with 4 checks to the inch, 1⅛ yards, 36″ wide. White sewing thread. Pearl Cotton No. 5: two balls each hunter green and steel blue. Tapestry needle No. 20. Bone ring, 1″. Terry cloth, 6¾″ square.

DIRECTIONS: Apron: Keeping selvages at sides, make skirt 36″ wide and 22½″ long. Turn up a 4″ hem; press, but do not sew. Make Teneriffe border following directions below. Gather top edge of skirt to measure 16¾″. Cut waistband 17¼″ long and 5″ wide. Fold in half lengthwise. Turn in long edges and ends. Insert gathered top edge of skirt between halves of waistband and stitch across. Cut two ties each 27″ long and 5″ wide. Stitch ¼″ hems on both long edges and one end of ties; fold end over to adjacent side and stitch together forming triangle. Repeat for other tie end. Make a tuck in raw end of each tie and insert in ends of waistband; stitch across.

Cut pocket 8″ wide and 9″ deep. Make design across top following directions below. Press sides under ½″ and bottom edge ¼″. Make 2″ hem along top. Stitch pocket to skirt 5″ below bottom edge of waistband and 3¾″ in from right side.

Pot Holder: Cut two pieces of gingham each 9″ square. Follow weaving directions below for border. With right sides together and squares matching, stitch along three sides making 1″ seams. Turn to right side and insert terry cloth padding. Fold in remaining edges and stitch together. Make a few small stitches through all thicknesses to secure.

With blue, single crochet (see Index) closely around bone ring and sew to one corner of pot holder.

To Weave Teneriffe Design: For apron, start design at right corner of third square in from right edge and 4½″ up from pressed hem. With green, make three straight stitches for bottom triangle web as shown at point A on chart. Each square on chart represents a check on gingham. Bring thread to front of gingham at bottom of triangle and weave design as shown in Fig. 1; run needle over and under spokes of web, working back and forth to fill spokes. Do not pull thread too tightly: push rows of threads down toward point to fill closely. At top, bring needle to back of work and fasten. Work top triangle in same way. With blue, make center web on four squares of gingham, starting each of eight stitches from center, between the two triangles as illustrated in chart. Starting at center of web, loop around each spoke of web as shown in Fig. 2; work around web twice. Work next triangles and center wheel reversing colors. Repeat straight across apron to complete border, ending with green triangles and blue web.

For pocket, begin design 4½″ up from 9″ edge and ½″ from 8″ edge. Work design across as for apron until it measures about 7″ across, beginning and ending with blue triangles.

For pot holder, make design on one piece only. Begin in right corner of 13th square in from left edge and 6th square up from lower edge. Starting at point A on chart, work with green as for apron. Then reverse colors moving to the left. For corners, follow chart and work the two outside corner points with green and the center web with blue; work the two inside corner points with blue. Repeat design, alternating colors, except for corners, around entire pot holder; make corners all the same.

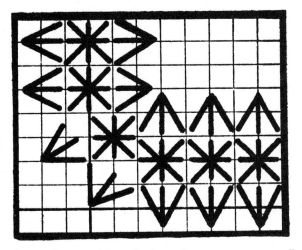

Chart for working design shown on apron. Each square represents one check of gingham fabric.

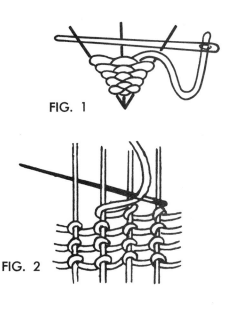

FIG. 1

FIG. 2

Hardanger Work

Hardanger work is based on the square blocks of cutwork. This is done on coarse even mesh linen with the threads drawn and cut away in blocks as each motif is worked. The cross threads are used as a basis for stitches woven through to form sturdy ladders. The adjoining areas are decorated with satin stitch blocks or open blocks after the edges of the openings have been whipped with straight even stitches. Designs for this work should be kept to the block forms typical of Norwegian embroidery. This embroidery is most effective for luncheon sets.

1. Kloster block of five stitches worked over four threads of linen.

2. Designs are made up of combinations of these blocks turned in different directions.

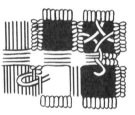

3. Kloster blocks in place, center ready to be cut.

4. Typical block of open Hardanger showing drawn threads with blocks cut away. Weaving or darning stitches worked through the ladders and over and over edge stitching. Spider stitch worked in open block.

5. Open block worked in outline running stitch similar to Holbein stitch.

Fagoting

The technique of joining fabric pieces with a decorative stitch to produce an open, lacy effect is called fagoting. Almost any material can be used, but silk, satin, linen and cotton are best. Seams can be joined by fagoting them together, or a much more ambitious project—a blouse, for example—can be produced by fagoting strips of material to each other. To do the decorative stitch, use embroidery silk, pearl cotton, or six-strand cotton.

The edges of the fabric to be joined are first hemmed by slip-stitching neatly. The two pieces of fabric are then basted to a piece of stiff paper, leaving the desired amount of space between. The space may vary for different pieces, but must be kept constant on one article. The tension of the embroidery should be kept even throughout. When the fagoting is completed, clip the basting and remove it from the paper. The sample on this page shows the two most familiar stitches—Trellis and Twisted Bars—plus Sheaf Stitch, Grouped Buttonhole and Knotted Insertion Stitch. Vary them as you wish after you have done a little experimenting with the ones shown here.

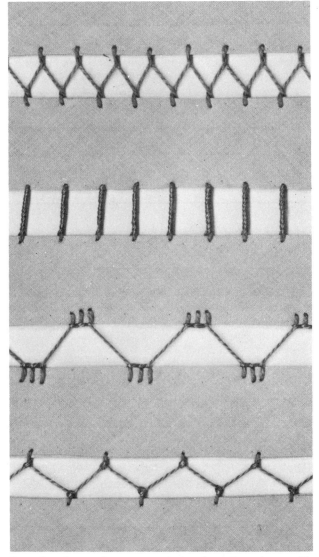

Sample above shows actual-size fagoting done with double thickness of bias tape between embroidery.

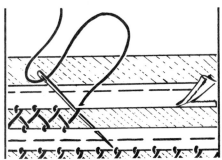

TRELLIS STITCH Similar to Open Cretan Stitch worked on the edge of two pieces of fabric.

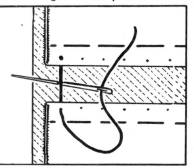

TWISTED BARS First make a straight stitch from bottom to top between the two fabrics.

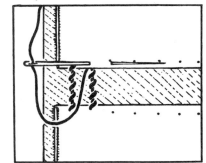

Next, overcast the bar from top to bottom to fill the space neatly and evenly. Start next bar to left.

77

Embroidery on Net

Net or tulle with hexagonal meshes is used for the background of this embroidery and is worked in a manner so it resembles the fine old pillow laces. The embroidery may be done in a simple darning stitch, or more elaborately by using a variety of stitches. Some stitch details are shown on these pages. Combine them to make your own designs on net. The embroidery can be done with a fine thread to make a dainty lace, or you may use heavier threads or yarn. The net should be of a good quality so that the meshes will not break while being embroidered. Use a needle with a blunt tip and darn in ends of threads to start and finish. Never make knots because they show. You may draw your design on stiff paper and tack the net to this as a guide for embroidering. Or you may want to follow a pattern by counting the mesh of the net. You may find it easiest to outline your design first with a simple running stitch, then embroider in any stitches desired.

DARNING This is worked in rows back and forth, going over and under one mesh for each stitch, or more, depending on embroidery thread being used. The top detail shows a fine yarn being darned. In this detail three rows of darning are put alternately over and under each mesh. The second detail shows a heavy yarn being used with just one row through each mesh of the net.

OUTLINING This is merely a running stitch worked over and under each mesh to outline a design. To fasten the embroidery thread, fold it over on back of work and embroider over it. Run the end back into the embroidery to finish off a thread.

OVERCASTING To overcast, the embroidery thread is worked over two or more meshes of net solidly. When using a fine thread at least two stitches should be made over each mesh to fill; for a heavier yarn, make just one stitch over each mesh.

The sampler at left is a simple geometrical design, using many of the stitches shown.

OPEN BUTTONHOLE STITCH   This is worked just the same as buttonhole stitch on any fabric. Make one buttonhole stitch in each mesh of the net. Can be worked horizontally, vertically or diagonally and in fine or coarse thread.

CLOSED BUTTONHOLE STITCH   This is the same as open buttonhole stitch except that a number of stitches are worked over each mesh to fill solidly. This stitch is normally used when working with a fine thread.

COUCHED BUTTONHOLE   If a design is first outlined, this is the way buttonholing would be done. When working by the counting method, first run a single thread in and out of the meshes to the desired outline. Then work buttonholing over the outline.

EYELET ROW   This is worked in two rows back and forth. Work in and out of each mesh of net, going below and around one side of first mesh, then above and around one side of next mesh. Continue across row in this manner, then work back around the same meshes to complete the eyelets.

STEM AND EYELET   First darn a single line for the stem, then work completely around one mesh for eyelet. Alternating the darning, work around eyelet again and down stem.

STAR   When using a fine embroidery thread, two stitches should be taken for each arm of star; with a heavier yarn, make one stitch for each. Take stitches over two meshes or more, down through center mesh and out at next diagonal, horizontal, or vertical row of meshes. Continue around in this manner to make a star with six evenly spaced arms.

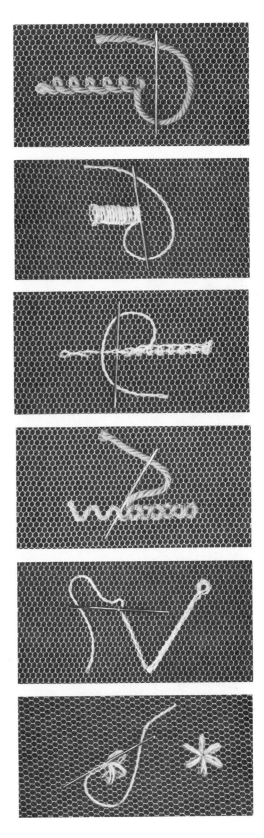

Smocking: English

Smocking is easy to do when you have mastered the simple stitches which are based on the familiar embroidery stitches, such as outline stitch and backstitch, together with a kind of whipped stitch. These are combined with fullness introduced either by gathers set before the smocking is begun, or by following pattern dots. You may smock with a transfer pattern as your guide, or create your own design.

There are two methods of smocking—English smocking for which the material is gathered in pleats first and regular smocking in which the gathers are made as the pattern is followed.

The best fabric to use for smocking is one with a firm weave and even grain. Cotton poplin, chambray, piqué and gingham are popular. Patterned fabrics such as squared and striped materials provide their own guide lines, as do also such materials as dotted Swiss and dimity. Use six-strand cotton to embroider, carrying out the design in a single color, in two, three or four colors, as you wish, and as the pattern recommends. If the garment is washable, make sure that you use washable, colorfast thread. If the fabric is silk or wool, or other material that is to be dry cleaned, then you can use silk floss.

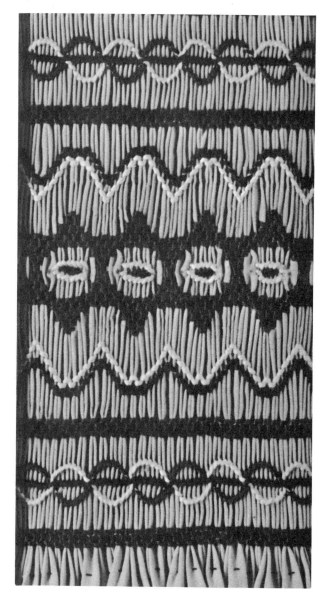 

Above are two fine examples of English smocking. You will note the even, deep-pleated appearance of the gathers which is the characteristic of this type of smocking —noted for its elasticity.

For every inch of finished smocking, about 2½ inches of fabric is required.

Rows of dots are marked on the back of the fabric, ¼″ apart. There are transfer patterns of rows of dots which can be stamped onto the fabric with a hot iron. There are also machines that will gather the fabric evenly for English smocking. After the marking is done each row of dots is gathered on the wrong side forming uniform pleated folds. The smocking is then worked on the right side of the material by using stitches described and shown here.

First mark center of smocking area with a vertical contrasting basting thread. Pull up gathering rows (about 3 at a time) so material to be smocked is slightly smaller than the desired finished size. Fasten threads.

Smocking is now worked on the right side of material, using four strands of six-strand cotton. Starting at left-hand edge and working from left to right, pick up the top of each pleat of material, following instructions for desired smocking design. Gathering threads are removed after smocking.

TO SMOCK: Gather stamped dots with contrasting sewing thread as in Fig. 1. To start, bring needle up between first and second pleats, then insert needle again, picking up first pleat (Fig. 2).

Cable Stitch: With thread below needle, pick up next pleat and pull up. (Fig. 3). With thread above needle, pick up next pleat and pull down (Fig. 4).

Outline Stitch: With thread above needle, pick up each pleat across (Fig. 5).

Two-Step Wave: With thread below needle, pick up first pleat as in Fig. 3. With thread below needle, pick up next pleat (½ step up) and pull up (Fig. 6). With thread below needle, pick up top pleat and pull up (Fig. 7). With thread above needle, pick up next pleat and pull down. With thread above needle, pick up next pleat (½ step down) and pull down (Fig. 8). With thread above needle, pick up bottom pleat and pull down (Fig. 9). With thread below needle, pick up next pleat, pull up.

Three-Step Wave: Begin same as two-step wave (Figs. 6 and 7). Then continue in same manner up one more step. With thread above needle, pick up next pleat and pull down. With thread above needle, work down three steps in same manner as two-step wave.

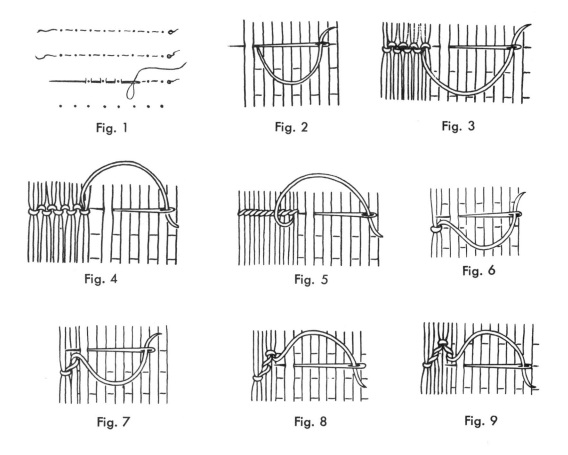

Fig. 1   Fig. 2   Fig. 3

Fig. 4   Fig. 5   Fig. 6

Fig. 7   Fig. 8   Fig. 9

Smocking: Regular

The regular method of smocking is based on picking up dots arranged in a pattern as they are given in McCall's Transfer Patterns. Following these dots, which are stamped on right side of material, forms the smocking pattern, and pulls the material up into tiny pleats or folds. In regular smocking, the needle picks up the dots and the stitch covers them. In English smocking, the needle picks up the top of the gathered pleats.

The cable stitch, outline stitch and wave stitch are done in the same manner as for English smocking. There are also two more stitches in regular smocking, the honeycomb or seed stitch and diamond or chevron stitch.

The fabric to use for regular smocking and the embroidery cotton are the same as for English smocking. After marking the smocking dots on the right side of fabric, either with a hot iron transfer, or by hand, start smocking (Fig. 1), on right side, working from left to right.

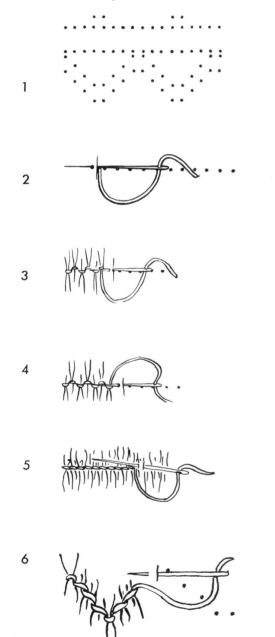

CABLE STITCH The thread passes alternately above and below the row of dots, gathering in the fold of fabric with each stitch. Figure 2 shows the first stitch with the needle facing from right to left, taking up a fold of fabric. The next two dots are then joined on the next stitch taken with the thread below the needle. Figure 3. The thread is passed above the needle and the needle passes through the next two dots gathering them together. Figure 4. Continue along the entire row.

OUTLINE STITCH With the needle always pointing to the left, adjoining dots are gathered with the thread always below the needle point. This is often used above or below a smocked section as a finish. Figure 5.

WAVE STITCH Designs often call for two step wave or three step wave. This describes the number of descending or ascending steps in the design. For this stitch use dots similar to those shown in Figure 1 left. There should be 6 dots for a three step wave. Knot thread, bring needle up to right side of material between first and second dots. Insert needle again, nearer the first dot, and bring up through first dot, pick up second dot having thread above the needle, and pull down together. With thread above needle pick up third dot. Keep thread above needle for 2nd, 3rd, 4th and 5th dots, but have thread below the needle for 6th, 7th, 8th dots, and the 1st dot of next wave. Pull up each time as in Figure 6. Continue along row in this way with thread above the needle when working down the wave, and below the needle when working up the wave.

HONEYCOMB OR SEED STITCH: This design is worked out with two or more rows of dots. Make a knot in the end of the thread and bring to the surface through 1st dot of top row. Join with dot 2 in anchoring stitch or buttonhole loop stitch. Pass under the fabric to dots 2 and 3 of row below, drawing them together. Pass thread under fabric again to upper row gathering together next 2 dots. Then alternate working up and down all the way across the rows of dots. This pattern is often worked out for deep areas using 4 or more rows of dots for the pattern. Figure 7.

DIAMOND OR CHEVRON STITCH This pattern is worked in the same way as the honeycomb stitch except the thread carries along the right side of the material instead of under the fabric to follow the folds of the fabric. Figure 8.

SHAPING YOKE OR COLLAR Sometimes you may wish to use your transfer pattern around a neck, to make a shaped yoke, or to form a curved collar line. To do this, carefully slash the transfer edges at even intervals and pin it together to form the desired shape. Then pin or baste to the material and press as for a straight transfer. Figure 9.

HOW TO PRESS SMOCKING You may press the smocking sections by steaming before making up the garment. Use a wet piece of thin fabric to make full steam when using the ordinary iron. If the finished work is narrower than desired it may be widened by pulling the smocking over the iron as if pressing flat, by pressing with the pleats from the top downward.

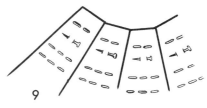

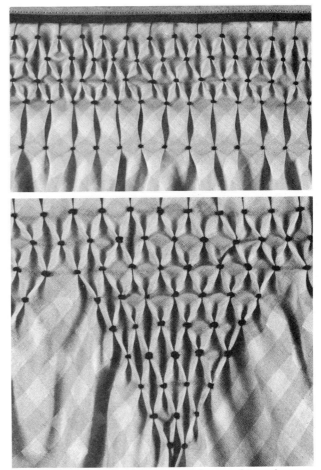

A typical example of a smocked yoke done in regular smocking. Practical and charming on children's clothes.

Actual-size details of honeycomb smocking show a straight band and typical pointed design.

83

Smocking: Lattice

Worked on corduroy and velvet, this kind of smocking is particularly suitable for making decorative pillows. Done by means of dots systematically placed on the wrong side of the fabric, the smocking produces deep, bold pleats on the right side of the fabric. If you wish, you may use satin or antique satin instead of a waled or napped fabric. Lattice smocking is easy to do, once you have learned the basic steps, and the smocking works up very quickly. Hats, handbags and even curtains may also be made in this type of smocking, using any fabric suited to the article.

Transfer patterns are made by McCall's for stamping the smocking dots used, but you can mark your own if you like. Use buttonhole twist, heavy-duty sewing thread or nylon sewing thread in the needle. Knot end of thread. All smocking is worked on wrong side of fabric. Stitches will not show on right side after smocking pleats are formed. After dots are marked on wrong side of fabric, start smocking at upper left. To pick up dots insert needle into fabric to right of dot and out through left side of same dot. Thread is carried from dot to dot on working side of fabric. Pick up dot 1 and make a second holding stitch as shown in Fig. 1. Then pick up dot 2, go back to first dot and pick up again as shown in Fig. 2. Pull dots 1 and 2 together and knot securely, Fig. 3. Pick up dot 3, then with thread above needle, slip needle under the thread between dots 1 and 3 as shown in Fig 4, pulling thread tightly at dot 3 to form knot. Be sure to keep fabric flat between dots 1 and 3. Pick up dot 4, then go back and pick up dot 3 again as shown in Fig. 5. Pull dots together and knot securely. Pick up dot 5 as shown in Fig. 6, slip needle under thread between dots 3 and 5 and knot as in Fig. 4. Continue down row of dots in this manner, starting with Fig. 2 and picking up dot 6 next.

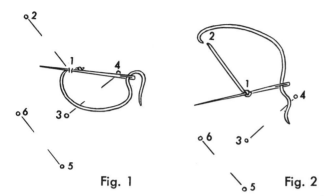

Fig. 1   Fig. 2

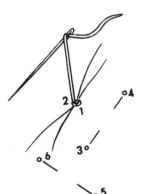   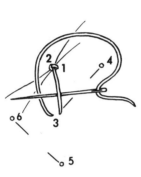

Fig. 3   Fig. 4

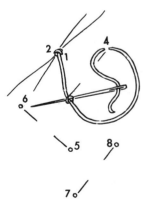   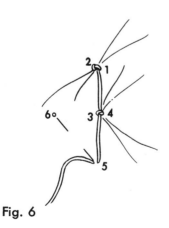

Fig. 5   Fig. 6

Lattice-smocked pillows made of rich materials can lend a refreshing note of elegance to almost any surroundings.

PILLOWS ARE A McCALL'S PATTERN

Smocking: On gingham

This is a fascinating and quick way to do smocking in the well-known honeycomb stitch. By working on gingham with one-inch square checks, you produce not only the classical honeycomb pattern, but an interesting light and dark effect when the gingham squares are brought together. This fabric smocking is particularly suitable for such useful household items as pillows. The stitch is easy to master and the large checks of the gingham are simple to follow. A puffy pineapple smocking can be produced in a similar manner by pulling the checks together in symmetrical instead of alternate rows. Smocking can also be done on plain material by using a transfer pattern to stamp guide dots on the fabric. Variations of the honeycomb smocking can also be done by leaving free rows, which form flat pleats, between smocking rows.

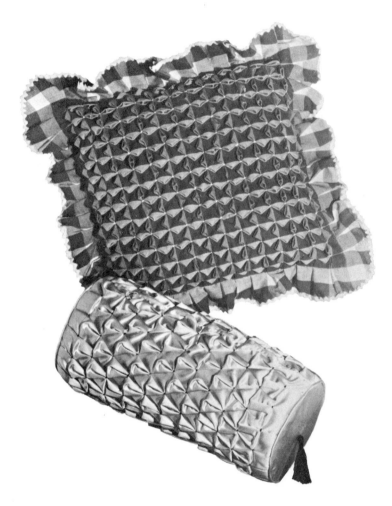

The illustration above shows a gingham pillow and a bolster of plain fabric, both smocked in the honeycomb stitch. The chair back and seat cushion are another example of honeycomb smocking on gingham, with pressed pleat ruffles formed by the smocking.

Honeycomb smocking stitch on gingham

Woven gingham with one-inch square checks is used for the smocking. To determine the amount of material required for honeycomb smocking, measure width of area to be smocked and allow double that amount of fabric. After measurements are taken, add seam allowances and hems as required. Use mercerized knitting and crochet cotton, or for a bolder effect and contrast, use six-strand embroidery cotton, the full six strands in needle. Smock on right side of gingham.

To start, make a knot in end of thread. To pick up corners of gingham checks, take a small stitch through fabric at corner of check. Thread is pulled up on right side only, and is kept flat between stitches on wrong side.

Bring needle up one inch in from upper and right edges, at lower right corner of a medium-tone check. See Fig. 1. Pick up lower left corner of same medium-tone check, Fig. 1. Pull thread up and take another stitch, bringing corners together so two dark checks meet, Fig. 2. Insert needle through fabric as in Fig. 3, bring it out at lower right corner of next medium-tone check, keeping thread flat on wrong side. Secure with another stitch taken in same corner, Fig. 4. Pick up lower left corner of same check and pull thread up, bringing the two dark checks together. Take another stitch to hold as shown in Fig. 6. Insert needle to wrong side as in Fig. 3 and continue across row to one inch from left side.

To make next row, bring needle up through fabric at lower right corner of second light check. Pick up lower left corner of same light check, Fig. 7. Pull up thread and take a stitch to hold, Fig. 8, bringing the two white checks together. Insert needle through fabric as in Fig. 9 and bring it out at lower right of next light check, keeping thread flat. Secure with another stitch and continue across row as for previous row. Repeat these two rows alternately. The margin of fabric across top and bottom naturally falls into pleats which can be tacked and used as ruffle. If pleated ruffle is desired at sides, separate pieces of gingham must be cut and pleated and seamed to sides.

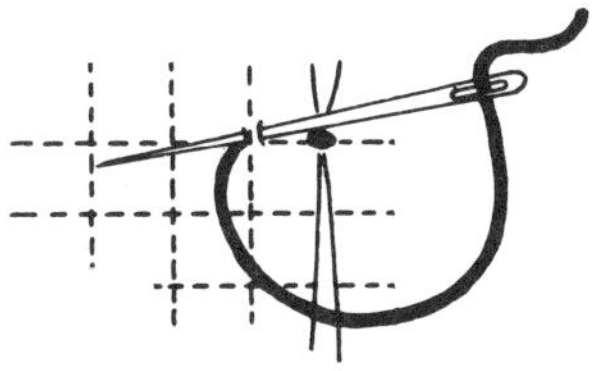

Fig. 1

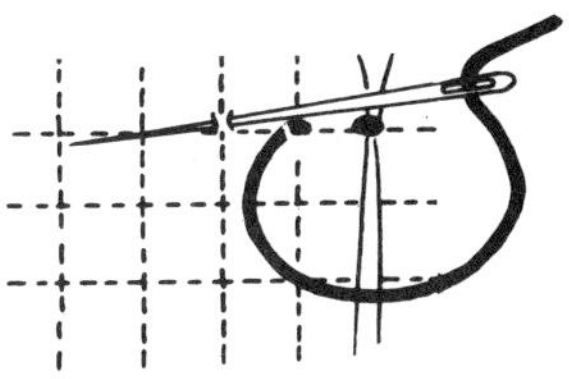

Fig. 2

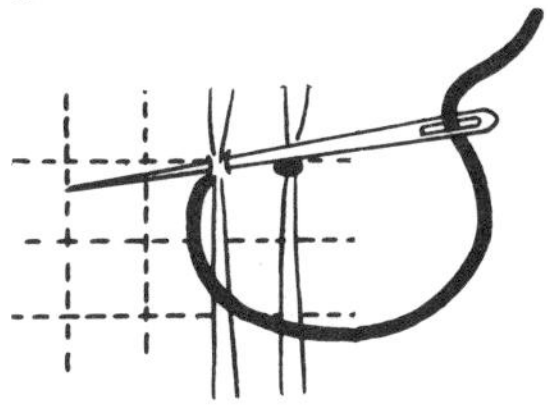

Fig. 3

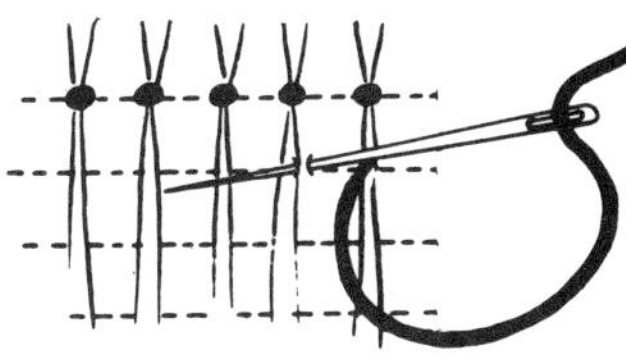

Fig. 4

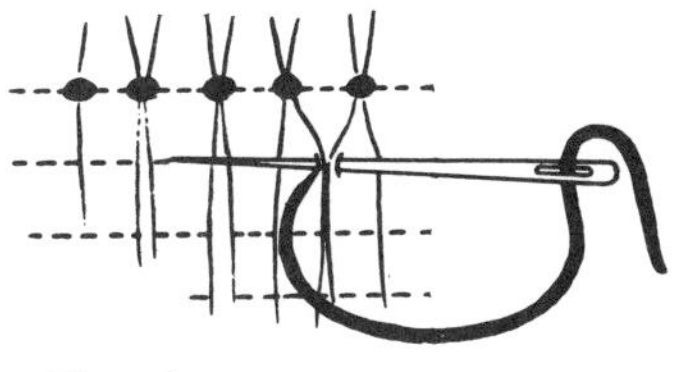

Fig. 5

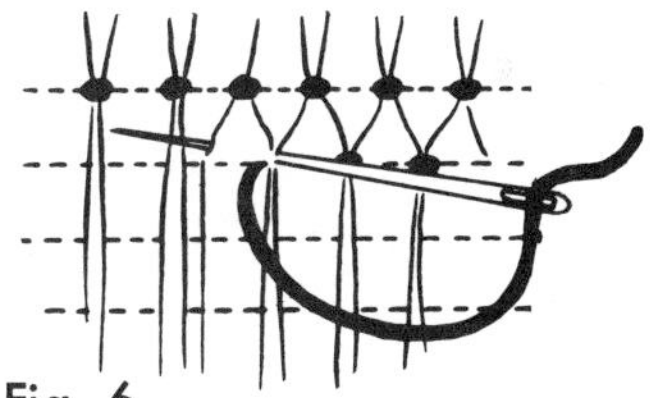

Fig. 6

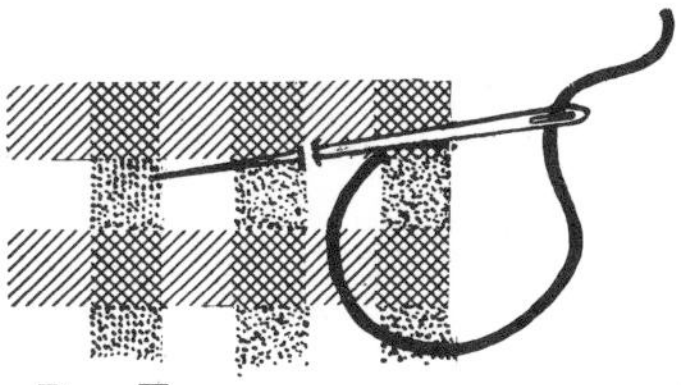

Fig. 7

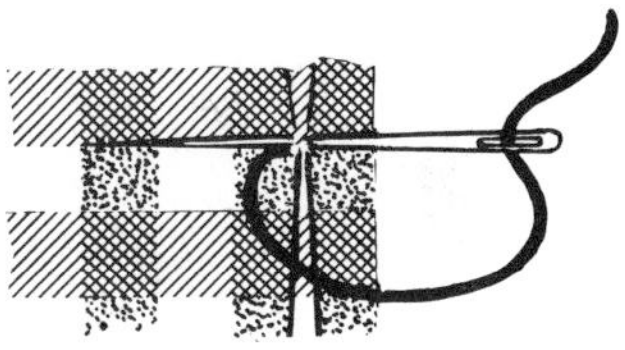

Fig. 8

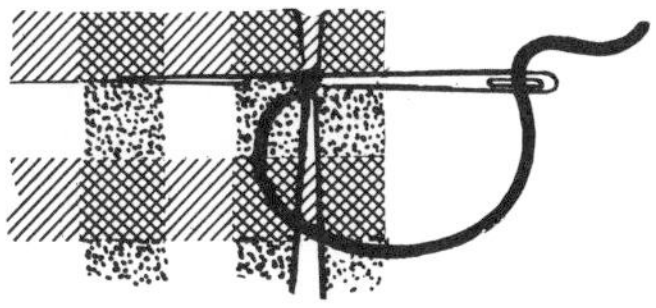

Fig. 9

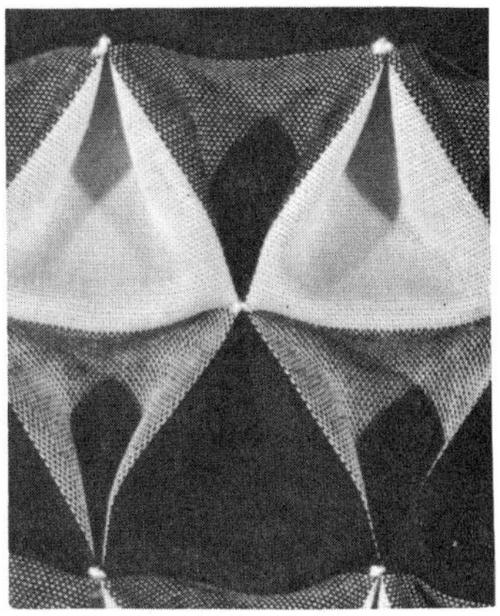

Actual-size detail shows honeycomb smocking.

Huck Embroidery

This type of embroidery gets its name from the fabric it is worked on, which is huck toweling, a textured fabric with the raised threads on both front and back. Huck embroidery is actually short for huckaback, and is also known erroneously as Swedish weaving. It can be done with six-strand cotton, pearl cotton, fine wool yarn, or other kinds of embroidery threads. The technique is simply running the thread under the pairs of raised threads on the wrong side of the huck. There are three main types of stitches, shown on this and the two following pages. A blunt needle is used so the pairs of threads can be picked up easily without going through the fabric. Knots should not be used; weave ends back into the same row of embroidery. Huck weaving can also be done on the right side of the fabric where prominent raised single threads appear. This method would be used if the length of the fabric was required. The pairs of raised threads on the back of the fabric are used across the width of the huck.

You can center a design on huck by starting the first row at the center and working to each side. If you are not centering the pattern, start at lower right corner and work across to left.

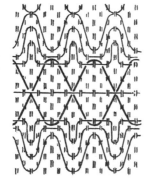

GOLD —
GRAY —

Chart shows one repeat of allover design of bag.

Bag is worked in basic stitch shown in enlarged detail.

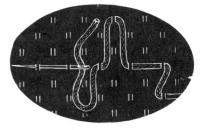

RED HUCK BAG

MATERIALS: ¾ yd. red huck toweling 17″ wide. ¼ yd. lining material 36″ wide. Fine yarn in gray; gold metallic yarn. 1 yd. ¼″ gold braid. Large-eyed embroidery needle. Red sewing thread.

DIRECTIONS: Work design on wrong side of huck under pairs of prominent threads.

To Cut: For bag front and back, cut 2 pieces 9½″ across huck and 6″ deep. For heading, cut 2 pieces 8″ across huck and 5½″ deep. For boxing strip around sides and bottom, cut 1 piece 3½″ across huck and 19″ long. Round off the 2 bottom corners of front and back pieces.

To Embroider: This design does not have to be centered, but it will be easier to begin the first row of front and back pieces at bottom in the center, ¼″ from lower edge, and work to both sides since bottom edge of front and back is curved and border design runs off material. With single strand of yarn in needle, work complete repeat border across huck following chart. Then start next border directly above with bottom of design going through same threads as top of first border design. Work 3 complete borders on front and back pieces. On boxing strip, work a wide border on right side of huck under single prominent threads, starting at lower right-hand corner with 3 top rows of chart; work all the way across. Then directly above, work one complete border across. End with first 3 rows of chart worked above complete border.

To Assemble: With embroidered sides together, baste boxing to sides and bottom of front and back pieces with ¼″ seams. Clip seam allowance at curves and stitch. Hem side edges of 2 heading pieces and fold in half lengthwise. Turn under top edges of bag and, centering headings, stitch one heading to inside of bag front and one heading to inside of bag back. About 1″ from folded edge of heading make a line of stitching across front and back for casing. Turn under and hem ends of boxing and raw edges at top of bag.

Cut a front, back and boxing from lining material, same as huck pieces, and stitch together. Place inside of bag with wrong sides of lining and bag together. Turn in raw edges of lining and blind stitch at bottom of heading. Make a 1″ tuck at ends of boxing on inside and tack. Run gold braid through casing twice around. Stitch ends of braid together. Pull cords of braid out on each side of bag to close top.

HOT-PLATE MAT

SIZE: 6″ x 8¾″.

MATERIALS: Red cotton huck toweling. 8″ x 11″, with 7½ pairs of prominent threads to the inch. White pearl cotton No. 5. Unbleached muslin. 14″ of round elastic. One piece heavy cardboard, ¼″ thick, or 2 pieces of thinner cardboard. White rickrack. White thread. Large-eyed embroidery needle.

DIRECTIONS: Entire mat is worked on every other row of pairs of prominent threads.

Work on wrong side of huck. Draw an oval 7½″ wide x 10½″ long on huck with prominent pairs of threads parallel to 10½″ length. Starting at lower right hand, embroider straight lines across with pearl cotton. Start squirrel design (see chart) about 2½″ from right side and 3″ from bottom, working straight lines of stitches on each side of design to edges of material. After completing squirrel, continue embroidering across in straight lines until work is completed. If coarser huck is used, squirrel design will be larger and must be centered on oval accordingly.

When embroidery is finished, make huck oval into slipcover as follows: Cut a bias strip of muslin 3″ wide and about 24″ long to fit around edge of huck for casing. Hem both ends. Fold muslin in half lengthwise and stitch both raw edges to edge of huck oval with ¼″ seam. At opening of muslin insert elastic with safety pin and pull all the way through casing to other end of opening. Overlap elastic ends and stitch. Cut cardboard oval 6″ x 8¾″. Put slip cover over cardboard. Center rickrack around edge, sew on.

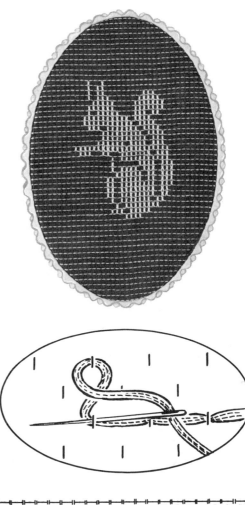

Squirrel design made into an oval hot mat and worked entirely in the figure eight stitch as shown in detail above. Follow chart to make squirrel motif with straight rows of thread filling in background.

Huck embroidery

CHILD'S APRON

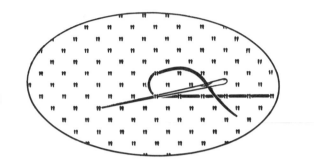

The looped stitch shown in detail above is worked in same manner as figure eight stitch. Embroider design, and fill in the background with straight rows of thread. The family of cats is an especially appropriate design for a child's apron.

MATERIALS: Turquoise huck toweling with seven pairs of prominent threads to the inch, a piece 17" wide and 15" long. Gray six-strand embroidery floss, 2 skeins. Turquoise sewing thread. Turquoise grosgrain ribbon 1" wide, 1½ yards. Large-eyed, blunt needle.

DIRECTIONS: Place huck flat, with pairs of prominent threads vertical; cut off a 2" wide piece across huck for waistband. Cut off end of waistband to make it 10½" long.

Using full six strands of embroidery floss in needle, weave six plain rows across waistband, leaving ½" seam allowance above and below. Turn in ½" all around waistband and baste.

For skirt of apron follow chart below. Embroider design across skirt, starting 2¼" from bottom.

If there are no selvages at sides of huck, make ¼" hems; make a ¼" hem across bottom. Gather top of skirt in to 9½". Baste waistband across gathers. Place grosgrain ribbon along back of waistband with even lengths at sides for ties. Stitch waistband to ribbon around all sides.

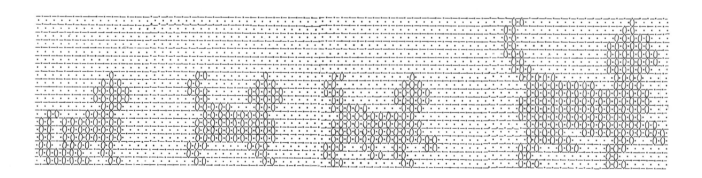

Huck embroidery in allover designs

Many articles not ordinarily thought of in connection with huck weaving can be made in attractive designs on huck fabric. The baby blanket and stole shown above combine a number of stitches and are worked to cover the huck completely. The outer portion of the baby blanket was worked in pink baby wool on pink huck fabric, while the center portion was done in white yarn. The stole, embroidered on white huck with green and gold metallic cotton thread, has long fringes at both ends.

Other fabrics for "huck" embroidery

Huck-style weaving done on a variety of smooth-textured fabrics opens up possibilities for designing many new patterns. The basic huck weaving stitch is used, with stitches being taken through the material, picking up a few threads of the fabric pattern to form the design. A wide range of effects can be achieved by using different materials—checks, dots, tiny-patterned fabrics. All designs shown are worked in six-strand cotton. General directions, here and on opposite page.

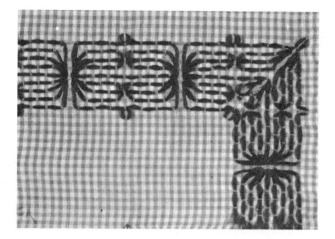

GENERAL DIRECTIONS: The technique used here for embroidering designs on various fabrics is basically the same as huck weaving. However, since the fabrics are generally smooth and have no raised threads to work through, the stitches are taken through the material, picking up a few threads of a dot, check or pattern for each stitch. In huck weaving, the stitches are taken through raised threads and not through the huck fabric. The embroidery thread between these tiny stitches forms the design. Good fabrics to use are diagonal or square checks, dotted Swiss or other dotted cottons, fabric with very close patterns in even or alternating lines, waffle piqué or monk's cloth.

Any huck weaving border chart can be used to embroider designs on checked fabrics, dotted Swiss, piqué, or other tiny-patterned material. On checked fabric like gingham, for instance, every other check represents one stitch as shown on the chart. On fabric with a pattern of smaller checks, every fourth check would represent one stitch. To work on dotted Swiss, use each dot, just as on the charts, because the dots are placed in the same position as the pairs of prominent threads on huck. On waffle piqué, the stitches go through the raised threads of the piqué, but not through the fabric, just as in regular huck weaving.

The border with the corner, below, is done on a fabric which looks like huck, but has no raised

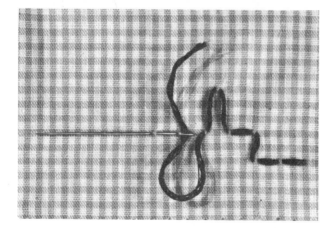

Detail shows huck weaving stitch used for all designs on these pages. Stitch goes through fabric, picking up the background check of the material as basis of pattern. It is interesting to note that the same design worked on two different fabrics produces different effects. On dotted Swiss fabric, the design is large and graceful. It is bolder and more striking worked on a fabric of small checks.

threads. Therefore, each stitch goes through the fabric.

One advantage of using patterned fabrics, rather than huck, is that because there are no vertical raised threads to work through, the stitches can be made in any direction. Therefore corners can be turned and designs worked both horizontally and vertically. Design your own corners to go with a straight huck weaving design.

The size of the finished design will vary depending on the size of the checks or dots of fabric used. When working on a two-colored check, the design can be made small and compact by working first row of stitches in each check of one color across and next row of stitches in alternate checks of other color in next row. To enlarge design work stitches in alternating squares of one color for the first row and in alternating squares of other color in next row. On one-color checks, work first row of stitches in every other square and second row of stitches in alternate squares of next row. Dotted fabrics usually have rows of alternate dots, but the size of the design will vary with the spacing of the dots. When planning a definite size for an article such as a place mat, there will be more or less repeats of the border design around all sides depending on the size of checks or spacing of dots in the fabric. Work the repeats of design and corner as nearly as possible to size planned.

Since it is difficult to determine the exact size to cut fabric for finished article with corner motifs, it is best to leave the fabric uncut until the first row of weaving is done. Begin weaving at lower right-hand corner of fabric. Follow the bottom row of chart from corner repeating design along side to next corner, turn chart and work corner. Continue around all sides or as many sides as required.

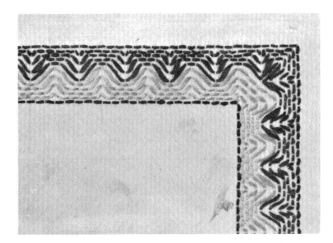

Fabric with a diagonal checked pattern can also be used. Here, as with regular checks, every other check, or more, would be skipped, depending upon the size of the checks. Small checks are shown above. A border with corner was worked on a white fabric with a tiny all-over pattern, similar in appearance to huck. The same design looks quite different (below) when worked on a checked gingham fabric.

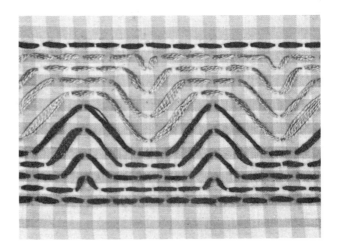

Applique

Appliqué is a very decorative embroidery done by laying pieces of fabric on a background fabric and stitching them in place. Its appeal lies in the colorful effect that can be obtained by using a variety of fabrics both print and plain to form the designs. In most cases embroidery stitches on the appliqué pieces are used to define and accent the design. But for the most part embroidery can be kept to a minimum, since the appliqué pieces themselves are the chief decorative element.

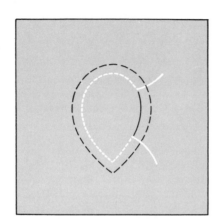

Fig. 1

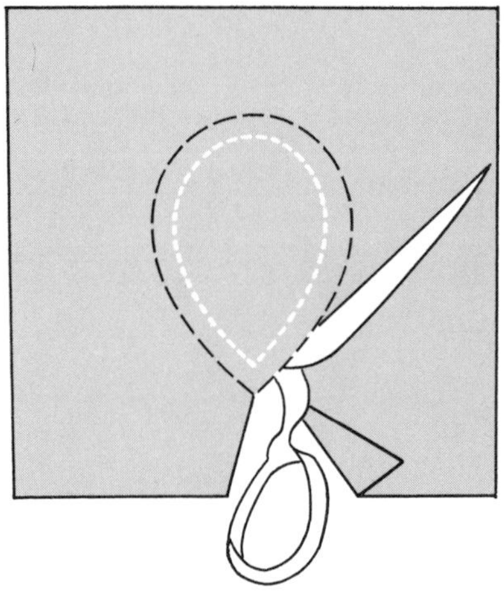

Fig. 2

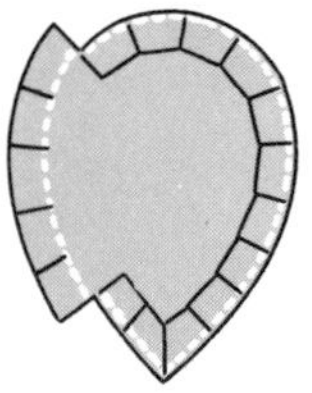

Fig. 3

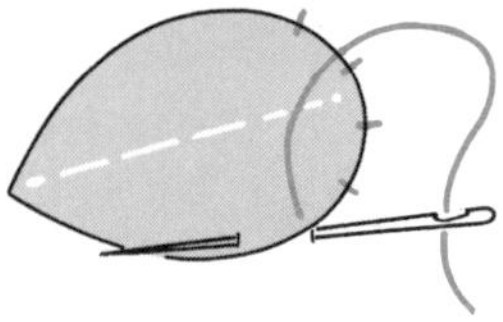

Fig. 4

Almost any material can be used for the background. Choose a fabric to suit the design and effect you want to achieve. A fine, matching thread can be used to sew the appliqué piece to the background, or an embroidery thread in a contrasting color may be used, if the appliqué is to be attached with decorative stitches. Appliqués are used on household linens, wearing apparel, quilts, and to make pictures for framing.

For the appliqué pieces themselves, many kinds of fabric may be used, but they should have a firm weave so a clean edge will be left after the pieces are cut. A cotton fabric like broadcloth is easiest to work with, but other materials such as linen, taffeta, velvet, cretonne and similar fabrics are also suitable. Several kinds of fabrics can be combined in one piece of work.

The best and most accurate method to use for appliquéing is to mark the complete design first on the background fabric. Then make a pattern piece for each part of the design. Taking each pattern piece in turn, mark the outline on the appliqué fabric, and mark a seam allowance all around the piece, usually ¼″ wide. Next, machine stitch on the design outline for a neat turning edge as shown in Fig. 1. Then cut out the appliqué on outer seam allowance line as shown in Fig. 2. For a smooth edge, clip curved edges and corners, then turn in seam allowance just inside machine stitching as shown in Fig. 3, and press. Pin the appliqué in place on the background and slip-stitch in place with tiny stitches as shown in Fig. 4.

If a decorative edging is desired on the appliqué piece, it can be topstitched in matching or contrasting color, or whipped in place. Or use a buttonhole stitch around the piece with stitches close together or spaced. Appliqué pieces may also be machine stitched in place, using a zigzag stitch either widely spaced, or closed for a satin stitch edge. A chain stitch may be used to embroider an appliqué to background.

An appliquéd picture done in shades of blue with appliqués of cotton broadcloth slip-stitched to a linen background. Note the touches of embroidery in outline stitch, running stitch, straight stitch, lazy daisy stitch and satin stitch. A pattern is given on the following page for reproducing this appliqué picture. Framed size, 18″ x 24″.

Pattern for blue appliqué picture

Above is the complete pattern for reproducing the Blue Appliqué Picture. To enlarge it to actual size, mark off a paper 21″ x 15″ in 1″ squares. Transpose the lines in each square onto your 1″ squares. Make a separate pattern for each appliqué piece and add 3/16″ seam allowance all around each. Carefully trace the complete design onto cream color linen background. Cut appliqué pieces from cotton broad-cloth in colors shown on previous page. Slip-stitch appliqué pieces to proper place on background putting down pieces first that appear underneath others. Embroider details with six-strand embroidery floss in outline stitch, running stitch, lazy daisy, satin stitch and French knot, using colors shown. Cut out long wide green stems on bias of fabric, in straight strips. These can then be curved and sewn in position.

San Blas "Appliqué"

Indian women on the picturesque San Blas Islands off Panama have a unique way of embroidering colorful blouses or "molas." The method used, which might be called "reverse appliqué," creates designs more by cutting out than by adding fabric. San Blas women start a blouse design with four or five thicknesses of cotton cloth—each layer a different, brilliant color—orange, red, green, blue—bottom layer sometimes black. Photos 1 to 3 on p. 98 illustrate cutting-away technique to reveal different colors and thus bring out the designs. The overall shape of the main design, such as a bird, is cut and edges sewn under; then the wing, tail and other large sections of design are treated in a similar way. Occasionally pieces of fabric are sewn on top, as in classic appliqué, to bring out small details (4), or a few embroidery stitches are added.

The designs reveal the ingenuity and imagination of these clever Indian women who copy from nature, from canned goods' labels—anything at all that interests them. Letters of the alphabet often appear with complete disregard for their meaning! The cloth used for the blouses, usually from England, is paid for with coconuts—the currency of San Blas. See "mola" designs below.

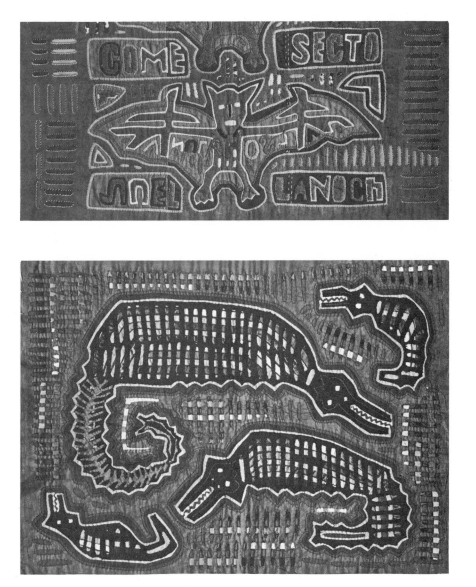

How to do San Blas (reverse) appliqué

The reverse appliqué technique involves sometimes as many as five or six layers of fabric all in different colors. Parts of the top layers are cut away to reveal the color below. If a central motif is to be used, the arrangement of the layers must be carefully planned before starting. You may have to cut through one, two or three layers at once to get to the color desired for some parts of the design. But if the colors are arranged well, it should not be necessary to cut through more than one layer at a time. It is also possible to arrange pieces of different colors of fabric under only some parts of the design.

To experiment with this type of appliqué, try using only three layers of fabric, and then using some small two-layer appliqués in open spaces. Embroidery may be used in simple stitches but should only accent the design. It should never detract from the strong, basic quality of the appliqué. In turning under edges of the fabric always use a slip stitch and matching thread. The illustrations show steps of reverse appliqué.

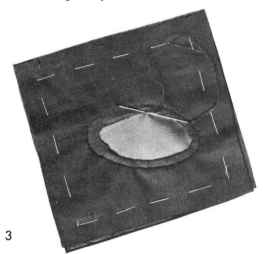

1

After number of colors and arrangement have been decided, baste fabrics all together around edge and also diagonally across to hold them securely.

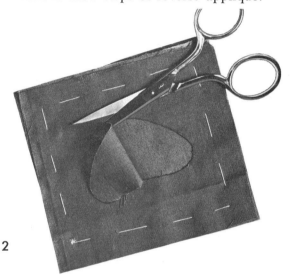

2

To reveal the first color under top layer, cut away a portion of top fabric in design desired, using a pair of sharp embroidery scissors.

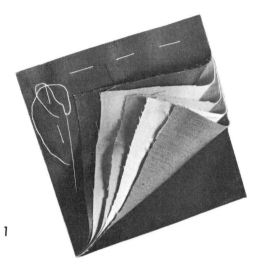

3

Clip the edge of fabric to be turned under on all curves or corners and turn in ⅛". Using matching sewing thread, slipstitch edge to layer below.

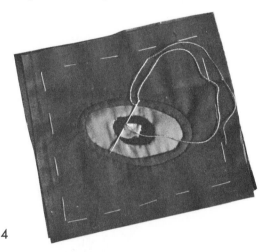

4

Small appliqués of another color may be added in one layer as shown above, or in two layers or more using same technique of cutting out to reveal color.

HANGING IS A McCALL'S NEEDLEWORK
& CRAFTS MAGAZINE LEAFLET.

*The hen in the wall hanging, in smart deco-
rator colors, exemplifies the bold, primitive
feeling of the San Blas art. Here six layers of
fabric are used and the hanging is backed
with one of the colors. A few lines of embroidery were added in outline stitch to accent the feathers and feet of the hen. The
small appliqués in cut-out spaces are in two
and three layers.*

99

Felt appliqué

For easy-to-do appliqué, use felt pieces. Since this material does not fray or ravel there is no need to turn the edges under. The pieces are merely pinned in place and slip-stitched to the background. Felt appliqués may be held in place while sewing by applying a few dabs of glue.

In keeping with the feeling of felt appliqués, a heavy, textured fabric should be chosen for the background. Burlap and most upholstery fabrics, for example, make attractive backgrounds for wall hangings. To add interest to the appliqués, use yarn embroidery alone or with rickrack.

A chart for making the wall hanging is given above. Enlarge it to actual size by copying it on paper ruled in 1″ squares.

Felt appliqués on a burlap background, designed for a modern setting, are especially suitable for a game room. The foam rubber-filled cushions double as game boards. The wall hanging is red burlap with white felt appliqués and wool yarn embroidery, with bits of white rickrack (flower outlines and base of plants). It was backed with white cotton fabric. The game cushions are also burlap with white felt appliqués and yarn embroidery. They are made with boxing and a zipper and white ready-made welting.

Sewing Machine Embroidery

These entrancing cats came to us from England, where their originator worked directly on the background fabric with a hand-operated sewing machine described as "by way of being an antique, so giving the interesting hoppity-hoppity line." However, you can duplicate these results without owning an antique machine.

This is an ideal type of embroidery for a sewing machine that does only straight stitching. The tension is loosened and a large stitch is used. A zigzag machine may be used, but a little experimenting will have to be done to produce this stitch effect.

Using a purely inspirational approach the cats can be stitched "freehand" on tailor's canvas or linen, adding detail and ornamentation ad lib. Or enlarge the drawings below to use as patterns. Creative readers will want to try original work in the same technique. For those who admire the whimsical results but lack their designer's light touch, we offer on the opposite page directions for embroidering and matting these pictures.

Detail shows wavy stitch line, which adds charm to the finished effect.

The chart below for the two cats and the stars is to be enlarged on ½″ squares to make actual size. Enlarge patterns on tracing paper, which is used in the process of doing sewing machine embroidery.

Sewing machine cat picture

MATERIALS: Pencils. Tracing paper. Ruler. Scissors. Sewing, beading, and embroidery needles. Sewing threads. Embroidery cottons. For fabric background, tailor's canvas or linen in white or eggshell; size specified below. Felt: dark gray or black for bodies, blue for eyes, contrasting color for flowers. Gauze or net in a contrasting color.

DIRECTIONS: Enlarge the patterns by copying on tracing paper ruled in ½" squares. When working the machine-stitched portions, if your machine does only straight stitch, use loose tension and longest possible stitch; if your machine does zigzig stitch, experiment to find a point part way between a straight stitch and a narrow zigzag stitch which approximates line shown in stitch detail opposite.

To make cats and flowers, pin paper patterns for cats to 5" x 9" piece of felt; cut out the two cats. Pin or baste cats in position on 10" x 14" fabric background, and machine stitch twice around each. Hand-embroider noses, mouths, whiskers, and eye outlines, using black embroidery cotton and straight stitches. Define eyes by adding felt pupils, seed beads and a few stitches in white embroidery cotton between pupil and outline of eye.

Stitch star flowers ad lib to fabric background; three sample shapes are shown on pattern. For each flower, use a circle of felt as a center and a larger gauze circle in a contrasting color over it.

Backing Pictures: To back finished picture, cut white cardboard 3" smaller all around than background fabric. Turn 1½" of background fabric over cardboard on all sides and glue.

Matting Picture: To mat picture, cut a mat-frame of desired size from mounting board. Cut an opening for picture ¼" smaller all around than cardboard-backed picture. To support picture in cutout opening, glue narrow strips of mounting board around edge of opening on back of mat-frame; place picture in position face down on mat-frame to gauge exactly where to place these strips. Build up thickness of mat-frame at outer edge so it equals thickness of inner edge: cut four long strips of mounting board and paste completely around back edge of mat-frame.

From mounting board or heavy cardboard, cut a backing same size as mounting board mat-frame. Place picture in position face down on mounting board mat-frame. Apply glue to built up strips. Press the backing firmly in place and allow to dry.

Zigzag sewing machine embroidery

The automatic sewing machines of today have brought a new embroidery art into the home. With the side-to-side swing of the needle, many interesting designs for borders and monograms can be produced in addition to the usual zigzag. Entire pictures can also be created. Some machines move the fabric back and forth while they stitch from side to side. Much interesting stitchery can be done on an automatic machine, and the manual accompanying it will explain this in detail.

Enlarged detail of machine embroidery shows satin stitch outlines and appliqués.

Below are patterns for butterfly wings and bodies, to be enlarged on 1″ squares.

1 RED   2 YELLOW   3 DARK YELLOW
4 GREEN   5 DARK GREEN   6 TURQUOISE
7 BLACK

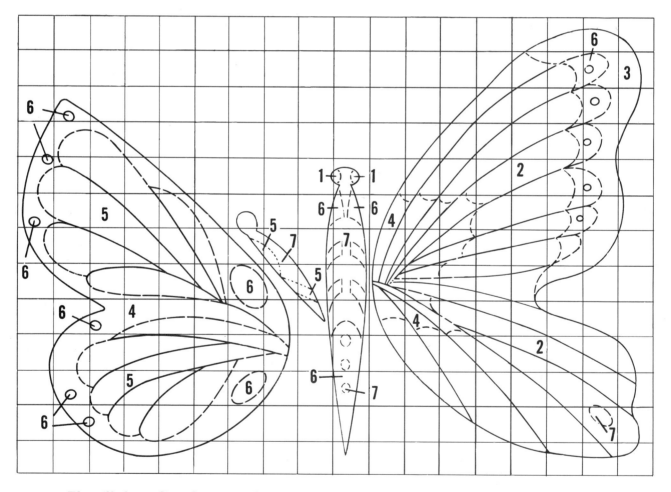

The silk butterflies shown on the opposite page can be done on a semi-automatic machine, a fully automatic one, or by using a zigzag attachment on a straight stitch machine. The zigzag stitch is worked very closely to produce satin stitch lines and dots to outline and accent the segments of the butterfly wings and bodies.

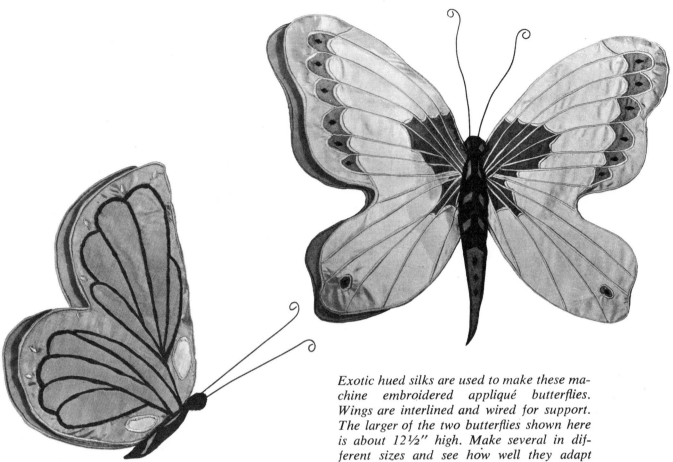

Exotic hued silks are used to make these machine embroidered appliqué butterflies. Wings are interlined and wired for support. The larger of the two butterflies shown here is about 12½″ high. Make several in different sizes and see how well they adapt themselves to a wall grouping.

MATERIALS: Silk fabric, various colors. Matching sewing thread. Heavy Pellon. Medium wire. Tracing paper. Hard and soft pencils. Pins. Small, pointed scissors. Automatic zigzag sewing machine.

DIRECTIONS: Enlarge patterns on opposite page for wings and bodies by copying on tracing paper ruled in 1″ squares.

With soft pencil trace along lines of pattern on wrong side. Pin background silk on Pellon. Using pattern as a guide, pin pieces of different colors of silk as indicated on pattern to top of background silk (dash lines show outline of appliqué pieces, solid lines are stitching lines). Cut appliqué pieces a little larger than sizes on pattern. (If background color is darker than color of appliqué, place a piece of Pellon between them to insure true color of appliqué.) Now pin pattern securely, right side up, on silk, being sure pattern matches placement of appliqué pieces, and all edges of silk and Pellon are secure. With hard pencil, trace around pattern on appliqué outlines and stitching lines to transfer design to silk. Remove pattern, cut away excess fabric and Pellon around butterfly, leaving a 1″ margin.

With a straight stitch, sew by machine around all solid lines and dash lines to hold silk in place. Trim off silk close to outside line of appliqués (leave extra fabric around butterfly). Set machine for satin stitch and stitch along straight stitching lines, changing width of stitch as you go to form solid lines of varying thickness. Do not satin stitch around outside of butterfly. When all designs inside butterfly have been satin stitched, pull ends of threads through fabric to back and tie. Lay a contrasting color of silk on back of Pellon, pin in place. Following first straight stitching on front of butterfly (outline), satin stitch around outside. Trim away excess silk and Pellon close to stitching. Make bodies in same manner.

For each butterfly, make an extra plain wing in darker color for shadow effect. Sew appliquéd wing to matching plain wing at body section; tack body to wings.

FINISHING: To stiffen wings, cut a tiny hole with small, pointed scissors at back of butterfly near inside edge of wing, about ¾ of the way from top, in silk only. Carefully insert wire in hole between silk and Pellon and push wire around top of wing and down other side to opposite point; bend wire to fit outline of wing. Bend a length of wire in half and shape into antenna; paint black. Tack antenna to back of butterfly body.

105

Beading: Fabric pictures

A McCALL'S NEEDLEWORK & CRAFTS MAGAZINE FEATURE.

Unique pictures to accent a room can be created by stitching colored glass beads on fabric. Sprinkle bead highlights on large design areas; use beads for color outlines, and enrich details with clusters of beads. Add depth by padding the wrong side of the printed fabric with absorbent cotton, and quilting on a backing. Beading instructions, together with details, are given below.

Many of today's printed fabrics—designed and sold primarily for other purposes—are eye-catching enough to be used as framed pictures. Some have individual motifs within squares or circles which can be cut apart to make small pictures. Others with a large central motif, even though surrounded by smaller designs, can be scissored to make most attractive pictures, as does the flower print on the opposite page.

The best kind of fabric to use for beading pictures is polished cotton. Large yardage departments carry designs suitable for any room in the house, from game room to nursery. All can be beaded to add richness.

Use either crystal glass seed beads, or opaque glass seed beads, depending on the kind of design being beaded. Small bugle beads, which are oblong, can be added if they suit your design. All these beads come in a great variety of colors, which can match or contrast with the color of the fabric design.

Before cutting the fabric, study it carefully to determine the best part to use for your picture, and be sure there is enough fabric left around it for mounting on a backing.

Some parts of the design will demand to be filled solidly with beads, while others call for only a sprinkling or an outline of beads. (See detail of bird's head, above.) Use a beading needle and fine thread and sew each bead on separately as shown in the beading details at right. Leaf veins and flower petal edges can be outlined in beads of a deeper tone than the fabric. Try using black or white beads as accents.

If you wish to pad any areas of your picture—individual flowers or figures, for instance—you will need a backing of thin material, such as lawn. Pad the area on back of picture sparingly with absorbent cotton and pin the backing to the wrong side of the picture to hold the padding in place. Then, with thread to match the area and a fine needle, take tiny running stitches around the padded area to make it look lightly puffed.

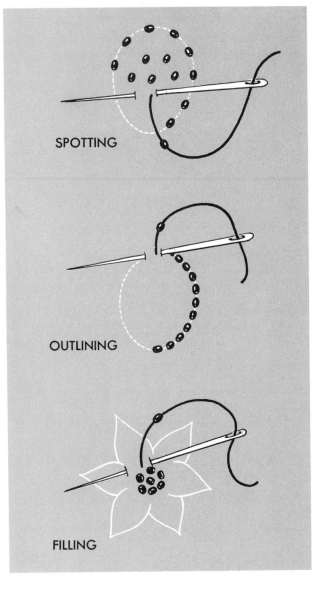

SPOTTING

OUTLINING

FILLING

Beading: As trimming

Combine seed and bugle beads with sequins for flattering and inexpensive glamor in your wardrobe. You can add chic to hostess slippers or an evening bag by sewing on pearls, sequins or rhinestones. Add them to a collar, or combine

This well-designed monogram for a knitted garment utilizes seed beads, bugle beads, sequins and pearls for massive effect.

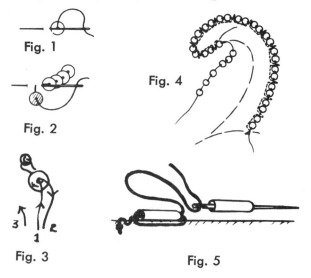

Fig. 1

Fig. 2

Fig. 3

Fig. 4

Fig. 5

them to make a bold, handsome monogram similar to the one shown here. Turn a sweater of simple design into an after-five favorite by couching metallic thread to make a flower stem with glittering jewel flowers. Directions given below.

HOW TO ATTACH A SEQUIN: To hide the stitch bring thread up through center of fabric and sequin, taking care to have the right side uppermost. Pass thread down to back of fabric and up through for next stitch as shown in Fig. 1. Thread a sequin on, and take a backstitch along the same line as shown in Fig. 2. This causes the sequins to overlap and thus hides the stitches. Continue around the outside of any area, then fill in the center.

TO ATTACH SEQUIN WITH BEAD IN THE CENTER: Bring thread up through fabric and center of sequin, then pass through the bead, then carry the thread down through the center of the sequin again. The bead acts as an anchor to hold the sequin in place. Pass needle through fabric to adjoining space for next sequin and bead, and repeat steps 1, 2 and 3 in Fig. 3.

TO SEW ON BEADS, PEARLS OR SMALL SHELLS: Pearls, round or faceted beads and some shells have two holes opposite each other. Choose a needle slim enough to slide through without splitting the bead and sew on with backstitch. Mercerized sewing cotton or nylon thread is recommended. Make each stitch just long enough to match the length of the bead. They will thus lie close together on the fabric. An alternate method is to string the beads or pearls and couch on with a second thread. Fig. 4.

Bugle beads are sewn on in the same manner, passing the thread through the hole in the bead as in Fig. 5, or stringing them to couch the strand to the fabric as in Fig. 4.

RHINESTONES OR FLAT FACETED JEWELS have a slot at the back, with sometimes another crossing it. Bring thread up through the fabric and pass through the slot at the back, sewing twice to fasten it firmly.

In sewing beads or sequins on fragile material or on sweaters, place a piece of firmer fabric or crisp muslin underneath to act as a stay support. A transfer design may be marked on tissue paper. Baste tissue in position on right side of material and sew the sequins along design through tissue, material and backing. When finished, tear tissue away close to edge of sequins.

Another method for sewing a bead design on a sweater is to stamp the design on organdy and baste it to right side of sweater. Then the beads are sewn in position through organdy and sweater with backstitch. When completed, cut away organdy.

Quilts

English and Dutch settlers brought quilt-making to America, where it developed into one of the greatest areas of folk art.

Our earliest bedcovers had prepared homespun backgrounds, pieced, embroidered, or appliquéd. The now rare wool-on-wool coverlets were worked in hooking or a combination of hooking and coarse needlework on wool blanketing. During the 18th century, motifs were cut from patterned chintzes, arranged to form new designs, and appliquéd in place. Simple mosaic patchwork grew into multi-block designs.

The old-time quilting bee was not only a party with a purpose, but a social event as well. Often girls would put their finished quilt tops away until the day friends were invited to a quilting bee—the equivalent of a formal engagement announcement! It was a charming custom for the bride's friends to stitch one block each to make up a "Bride's Quilt," using the best available materials and the finest needlework. They are a valuable source of information about the fabrics and needle arts of their times, and serve as inspiration to today's quilt designers. For quilts are still a favorite project of America's needleworkers, individually and in groups, and are one of the most popular items in art needlework departments.

The Garden Basket Quilt, a great favorite of other days, is featured here for ambitious and expert needleworkers to reproduce. This beautiful old quilt was made in New York State around 1835, and is unique in its delicate wool embroidery.

Copy an Old Quilt

The Garden Basket Quilt is a lovely combination of popular quilt-making techniques: piecing, appliqué, embroidery, and quilting. The nine baskets are pieced of red and green triangles and form a part of a square block with appliquéd and embroidered flowers. These colorful blocks are set diagonally with white blocks, quilted with Princess Feather wreaths. An appliquéd and embroidered flowering vine encircles the quilt top; a cable-pattern quilted border establishes the line for the scalloped edge. Patterns and directions for this quilt are on the following pages.

Above is a diagram showing one quarter of the Garden Basket Quilt, with placing for all applique, embroidery, and quilting. Note that diagonal quilting lines of border radiate at the corner.

111

KEY

PINK
MEDIUM RED
DARK RED*
LIGHT YELLOW
GOLD
LIGHT GREEN
DARK GREEN
LIGHT BLUE
VERY LIGHT GREEN
DIVISIONS IN EMBROIDERY
QUILTING STITCHES
SEAM LINES
* ALSO LEAVES AND BUDS
OF VERY LIGHT GREEN

Three embroidery stitches for Garden Basket Quilt:
Long and short, Satin, and Outline.

Garden basket quilt

SIZE: Approximately 80″ x 80″.

EQUIPMENT: Tracing paper. Heavy paper. Cardboard. Ruler. Pencils. Tailor's chalk. Scissors. Needles. Quilting frame.

MATERIALS: Cotton fabric, 36″ wide, such as muslin, percale, cambric, calico, broadcloth, in the following amounts: 5¾ yds. white for quilt top; 6 yds. white for quilt lining; ⅜ yd. red, 1½ yds. light green for basket pieces and appliqués. Crewel wool, six-strand cotton, or tapestry yarn in light yellow, gold, pink, medium red, dark red, very light green, dark green, and light blue. Mercerized sewing thread No. 50 in white, red, and light green. Cotton batting. Quilting thread.

DIRECTIONS: To Make Basket Blocks (Make nine: finished size, 10″ square): Using tracing paper and sharp pencil, trace patterns on pages 112-113, matching indications carefully to make one complete pattern. On back of tracing, go over lines with soft pencil. Place tracing, right side up, on cardboard and go over lines with sharp pencil to transfer.

Cut a piece of tracing paper exactly 10″ square. Place over cardboard pattern with bottom right point of basket at side edge of tracing paper. Trace all lines of basket (not flowers or quilting lines). Place ruler along each side edge of basket tracing; draw line straight up from each side of basket to edge of tracing paper. Block is now divided into its component pieces: one large 5-sided piece at top for flower embroidery and appliqué, eight triangles and one 4-sided piece for basket, two strips at sides of basket, and one triangle below.

Make cardboard patterns of these pieces (only one triangle for basket and one side strip are needed). Basket pieces are cut from red and light green fabric; all other pieces are white. Place cardboard patterns on wrong side of fabric, allowing ½″ between patterns. Mark around patterns lightly with pencil. Cut pieces ¼″ outside markings for seam allowance. Sew pieces together with running stitch to form 10½″ blocks (¼″ seam allowance on all sides). Press pieced sections with seams to one side; open seams weaken construction.

Go over lines on original tracing to make extra dark. Tape tracing to window pane; tape pieced fabric block in place over tracing. With sharp pencil, mark all embroidery and appliqué lines.

Use original tracing to make cardboard patterns for appliqués (two large red flowers at sides, and

Actual-size pattern for quilt block used diagonally in Garden Basket Quilt. Follow directions for using pattern. Color key indicates colors to be used for pieced basket, embroidery and for appliqué.

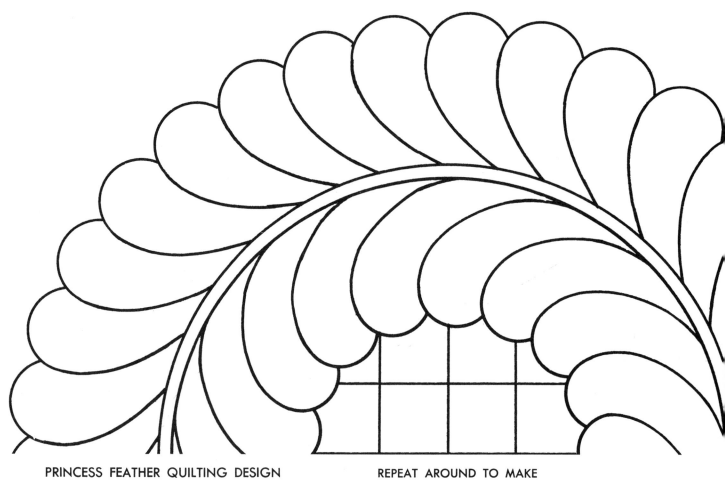

PRINCESS FEATHER QUILTING DESIGN

REPEAT AROUND TO MAKE
COMPLETE CIRCLE.

FLOWER MOTIF QUILTING DESIGN

light green leaves). Cut appliqué pieces from fabric, allowing ⅛″ for turning under. Sew appliqués (see Index) to blocks. Next, work embroidery, following color key. If cotton floss is used, work with all six strands in needle; if tapestry yarn, split yarn and work with two ply. Work stems in outline stitch, flowers in satin stitch and long and short stitch. Dotted lines on flowers indicate dividing lines between groups of stitches. Work satin stitch around edges and at center of left appliquéd flower.

To Cut and Join Quilt Top: Cut 10″ square piece of cardboard. Place on wrong side of white fabric; mark lightly around. Cut fabric block ¼″ outside markings; cut four. Cut cardboard pattern in half diagonally; cut eight white fabric triangles from pattern in same manner as blocks. Cut cardboard triangle in half; cut four small white fabric triangles.

Trace "Princess Feather" quilting design, opposite. Turn paper to complete pattern. Transfer to white fabric squares, triangles as for Basket Blocks.

Assemble center of quilt top, following placement of blocks and triangles as shown in diagram for quarter of quilt top, on page 111.

Make cardboard pattern of stylized flower motif, p. 114. Place on quilt top as indicated in diagram and mark lightly with pencil. Transfer small vine motifs on Basket Blocks.

Borders: Measure one side of assembled quilt top. Cut two strips that length and 18″ wide (cut 36″ wide fabric in half lengthwise). Sew strips to sides of quilt top. Cut two strips 80″ x 18″ for top and bottom borders. Sew to quilt top. Press seams.

To Embroider and Appliqué Serpentine Border: Enlarge the border pattern at right to actual size by copying on heavy paper, 20″ x 8″, ruled in 1″ squares.

First, plan placement of long curved appliquéd vine around border. Center of pattern is center of border. Repeat design to corners. Dotted lines across vine on pattern indicate corners. Pin paper pattern to border and, using longest stitch in sewing machine and no thread, stitch through vine. Repeat around border. Go over with tailor's chalk. Cut 1″ bias strips of light green fabric; fold in edges ¼″ on each side; appliqué strips over markings.

Placement of floral designs can be planned in same manner by perforating as many lines as necessary to place appliquéd leaves and embroidered flowers and stems. (Work same as for Basket Block.)

BORDER PATTERN

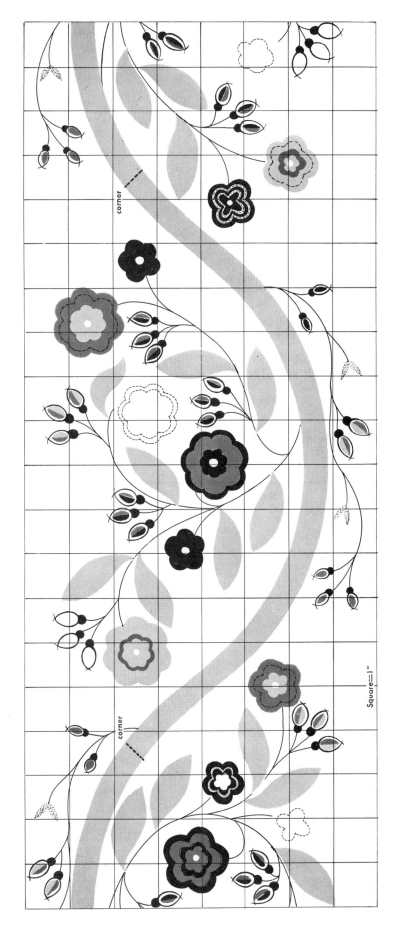

To Mark Border for Quilting: Transfer quilting lines of Cable-pattern Border, opposite, and Leaf motifs, below, in same manner as appliquéd vine, using sewing machine and tailor's chalk, following diagram on page 111.

Note that diagonal quilting lines of border radiate at the corner. To plan corner, continue line formed by bottom edge of quilt blocks straight out for 4″. Make a dot at this point. Mark inner edge of cable-pattern border every ½″. Radiate quilting from dot to half-inch marks on cable-pattern border until lines are parallel to quilting on sides.

To Line and Interline Quilt: Cut and sew lining material to make lining same size as top. Place inter-lining over lining; smooth out all wrinkles and creases. Baste together with long basting stitches, starting at center and sewing toward edge on all sides. Lay top over interlining and smooth. Then baste all three layers together through center horizontally, vertically, and diagonally. Baste near edges.

Quilting: Quilt in hand, or use a quilting frame. With quilting needle and thread, quilt Princess Feather, Flower, Leaf, Small Vine on Basket Blocks, and Cable-pattern Border motifs. In addition, quilt around lines of embroidery and quilt diagonal lines on border.

To Finish Edge: Cut scalloped edge ½″ beyond outer quilting line. Buttonhole-stitch around edge with white embroidery cotton, or bind edges with bias binding tape.

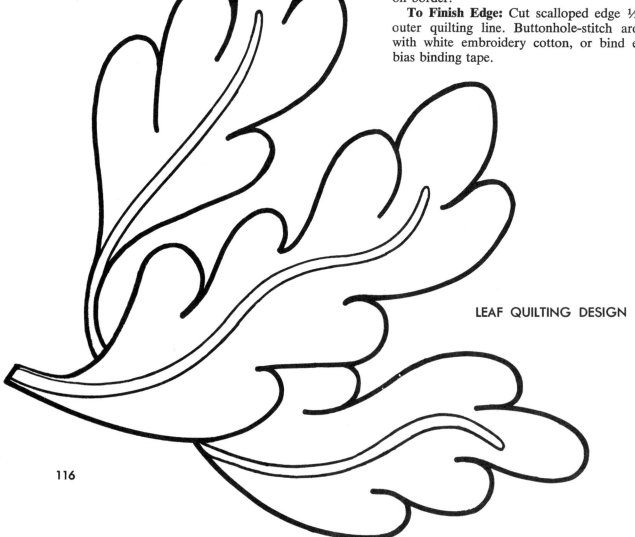

LEAF QUILTING DESIGN

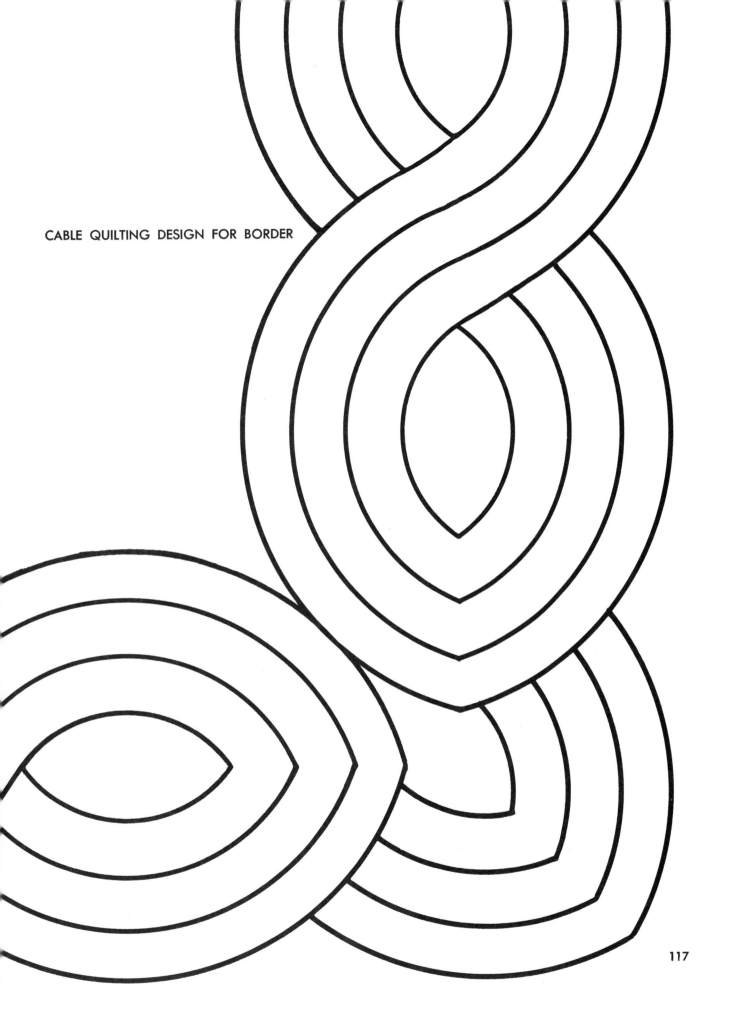

CABLE QUILTING DESIGN FOR BORDER

117

Patchwork Quilts

Patchwork has been practiced by industrious needlewomen ever since the first piece of cloth wore out, but not until the middle of the eighteenth century was it developed into the fine household art we know it to be. The diamond patch quilt is considered a patchworker's highest achievement. It requires accurate piecing so that the finished quilt will lie perfectly flat and even.

GENERAL DIRECTIONS: Cut master pattern pieces of thin cardboard; place on wrong side of fabric. Squares and oblongs must be cut with weave; diamonds and right-angle triangles need two sides on straight of goods.

Mark around edges on wrong side with hard pencil. Cut patches ¼″ outside penciled lines (seam allowance). Hold the patches firmly in place, face to face; seam together with small running stitches on penciled lines.

If the problem of sharp points and true meeting of seams proves difficult, cut from firm paper patterns exact size and shape of master pattern. Fit firm paper within penciled lines on wrong side of fabric patch and baste ¼″ seam allowance back over edges of paper. Whip patch pieces together with small over-and-over stitches. It will not matter if stitching goes through the paper; it can be removed as work progresses.

Press pieced sections with seams to one side; open seams weaken construction. When sewing blocks together, make sure all strips are even with one another. They must form a continuous line.

HARVEST SUN: Each of eight star points contains nine diamond patches, four dark and five light. Piece each point separately, then join four points for each half. Join halves, bringing all points together in center. Light and dark colors alternate in concentric circles. Stars are joined with squares and half-squares. Nine star units, three to a row, comprise body of quilt. Large squares (equal to four corner ones) and half-squares (equal to two, oblong in shape) fit into spaces made by nine pieced stars placed point to point. Smaller squares (size of corner square) fit diagonally into remaining spaces. The border is made of twenty-four pieced diamond patches, six to a side, placed point to point. The same diamond unit and arrangement is repeated as in points of star. For background and to even off border, patches half the size of pieced diamonds are fitted into spaces. Strips of calico, two inches wide, enclose border; four patches fill each corner. Baste quilt top, interlining, and lining together and place in frame. Quilt diagonally in both directions across each square, spacing about ¾″ apart. (Lines may be marked with ruler and white chalk pencil.) Trim edges around quilt and finish with a bias binding in color preferred.

Opposite: Harvest Sun's eight-point star is known by many names—Star of Bethlehem, Lone Star, Star of the West, Rising Sun, and others. The dividing squares are blue, brown, and a rose floral stripe. Tan, blue, red, and brown prints predominate in the border.

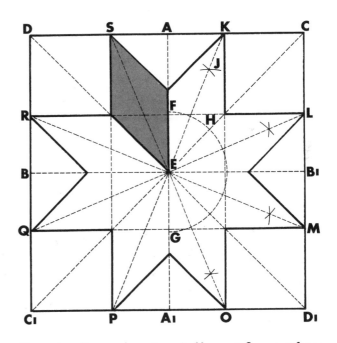

To make diamond pattern in Harvest Sun, cut from paper a square the size of desired center star (8″ in quilt shown). Quarter, draw diagonals with dotted lines. Compass on center (E), draw arc FG. With compass on F, then H, bisect angle at J. Repeat three times more on arc. Draw lines through bisection points and center (E) to opposite side. For star points, draw horizontal and vertical lines RL, QM, SP, KO; draw diagonal lines RO, SM, KQ, LP. (Colored areas are pattern pieces.)

The evolution of patchwork

The very first pieced quilts were arranged in a crazy quilt or hit-or-miss style, but quilt makers were soon trimming the shapeless scraps into uniform shapes. Hexagons were found to be especially adaptable in making one-patch quilts, and were used in the beautiful early "Mosaic" quilts. Another one-patch design, "Tumbler" contrasts light and dark colors for a cheerful effect.

Next developed was the two-patch design, with diagonally-cut squares or rectangles creating the first true quilt block. "Birds In The Air" is such a pattern. A well-known variation of it, and an example of a four-patch design, is "Flock of Geese." In "Broken Dishes," triangles are ar-

ranged in a four-patch block, then four of these are four-patched again.

The fundamental "Nine-Patch" is simply one block divided into nine equal squares. Variety is achieved by different arrangements of the dark and light squares, or by division of the individual squares. The old "Shoo Fly" pattern illustrates this, while even more intricate variations can be seen in "Duck and Ducklings" (known also as "Hen and Chicks").

Careful color placement and a greater variety of shapes resulted in more elaborate quilts.

By combining squares and diamonds of different shades, the effect of piled cubes is achieved

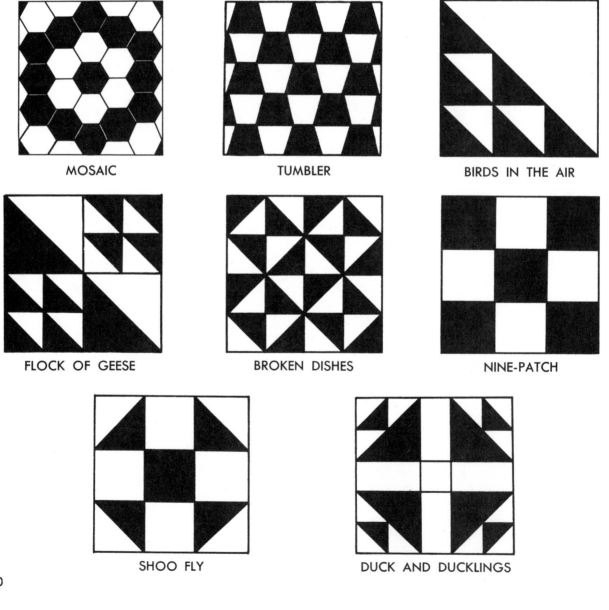

MOSAIC   TUMBLER   BIRDS IN THE AIR

FLOCK OF GEESE   BROKEN DISHES   NINE-PATCH

SHOO FLY   DUCK AND DUCKLINGS

in "Pandora's Box." (The same shapes in another shade arrangement produces "Heavenly Steps.") "World Without End" is more complicated in effect because colors are reversed in alternate blocks, although the shapes are simple triangles, squares, diamonds.

Light and dark squares with circular pieces cut out of corners and transposed create the very popular "Drunkard's Path" and "Steeplechase." "Rob Peter and Pay Paul" seems to "rob" a light square to piece a dark, and vice versa; actually the patches must be larger to allow for seams.

Contrasting rectangles around a central square form the "Log Cabin." Arranging the pieced blocks to form squares, stepping stones, or stairs results in three "different" quilts. No border is used.

A great favorite with experienced quilt makers is the deceptively simple "Double Wedding Ring." Using many different prints for the small wedge-shaped blocks which form the "rings," it is actually an involved arrangement of wedge, square, and melon shapes.

Perhaps the most difficult patchwork quilt is the "Clam Shell" because of its curved shapes. The effect can be obtained by overlapping circles, but traditionally it is made from shell-shaped patches in alternately light and dark rows.

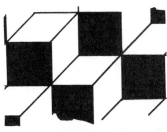

PANDORA'S BOX

WORLD WITHOUT END

STEEPLECHASE

DRUNKARD'S PATH

ROB PETER AND PAY PAUL

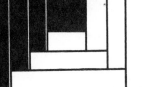

LOG CABIN

DOUBLE WEDDING RING

CLAM SHELL

Appliquéd Quilts

During the late 18th century quilts featuring intricate appliqués were made, but it was not appliqué as we think of it today. Motifs were carefully snipped from imported English chintzes and elegant French toiles—flowers, garlands, and birds—rearranged on a background, and stitched down to form lovely "picture quilts."

By 1850, appliquéd quilts using fabrics in shapes other than those suggested by prints had been developed and popularized. It is interesting to note, however, that flowers and birds continued to be a favorite theme for appliqué.

The Garden Bouquet appliquéd quilt shown here was adapted from a beautiful old quilt. It has been somewhat simplified in design and color in order to make it suitable for today's use.

PARAGON NEEDLECRAFT "GARDEN BOUQUET" QUILT TOP KIT WAS FEATURED IN McCALL'S NEEDLEWORK·&·CRAFTS.

Above: A Bride's Quilt, always the show-piece of a young woman's dower chest. This one is appliquéd of printed cottons on white blocks. No two of the prints are alike, but they all have the same soft red background. A block in the bottom row is inscribed, "Priscilla Halton's Work, 1849."

Left: Patterns for the lacy "snowflake" designs are made by folding a square of paper in half, then in quarters, and in eighths. Using sharp scissors, cut the folded paper as shown, being careful not to cut into the folds. Cut a variety and select the best ones.

Hawaiian Quilts

The first Hawaiian quilting bee took place in Honolulu harbor aboard the brig Thaddeus, when the wives of the New England missionaries gave the Hawaiian women their first sewing lesson. The Hawaiians learned how to sew small pieces together, Yankee fashion, using material from the ragbags which the provident missionary ladies had brought with them. It was not long, however, before they adapted the quilting technique to their own circumstances. Since they had worn only grass skirts and flower leis, they had no ragbag resources! Thus they cut their quilting patterns in one large piece from material bought new.

The Hawaiians drew upon their environment for inspiration, just as every other quilt maker has done, and the quilts reflect the beauty of the Islands. The original colors were turkey red on white, known as the "pai ula" or red pattern. The second development was cool green on white, used especially to depict waterfalls, leaves, and trees. Red and yellow were traditionally royal colors, because of the colors of the magnificent old feather capes, so red and yellow became favorite quilt colors.

The design is created in the same manner as for the Snowflake Bride's Quilt, except that only one large central motif is used. Appliqué the design and a border (if desired) to loosely woven cotton background material, line the quilt with cotton batting, and add the backing material. Devise a pattern of quilting that utilizes the curves and lines of the central motif.

Embroidered Quilts

Details of how to do cross-stitch to resemble gingham.

Old quilts often inspire designers, who adapt traditional motifs in bold, simple effects suited to the mood of today. Here you can see how motifs typical of early appliquéd quilts have been translated into an embroidered quilt. The five-to-the-inch cross-stitches give an effect of appliquéd gingham, while the simplified quilting design adds to the "old quilt look."

BUCILLA "BRIDE'S QUILT" WAS FEATURED IN McCALL'S NEEDLEWORK & CRAFTS MAGAZINE.

Above: Quilted White Coverlet made by Maria Kellogg and her sister as a gift for their mother, Lydia Bouton Kellogg, circa 1805.

Left: Detail from a coverlet, showing types of raised quilting. Trapunto quilting is used for fruit and leaf areas; Italian quilting makes lines of the basket and the stems.

Raised Quilting

Raised quilting uses two layers of fabric but no interlining. (If it is to be used for warmth, such as in a robe or quilt, a lining and interlining are added after quilting is completed.) There are two methods of doing this quilting. One is Trapunto quilting, in which the design areas are outlined with stitching and stuffed with cotton to make a puff padding. The other method is Italian quilting, in which two rows of stitching are used and a cotton cord or heavy wool yarn is drawn between the rows of stitching to make a raised line. The directions for both methods are given below.

Trapunto or padded quilting

It is best to use designs consisting of small areas, as a large area cannot be padded evenly. Baste together muslin for backing and a fabric such as silk for the top. Mark the design on the muslin backing. Outline all sections of design to be padded with small running stitches through both thicknesses, using matching thread. When design is completely outlined, pad each area separately. To pad, snip a tiny opening in muslin and stuff the area firmly with cotton, using a steel crochet hook or blunt end of a large needle (Fig. 1). Care must be taken to keep padding smooth and even.

Figure 1

Italian or corded quilting

Baste together muslin for backing and silk satin, or taffeta fabric for top. Mark design on muslin in double lines. (If cording is to be used for the padding, buy the cord first and plan the double rows of stitching to be spaced just far enough apart to hold cord firmly.) Working on the wrong side, stitch each line, using a fine running stitch through both thicknesses of fabric. When stitching is complete, run cord or heavy yarn through channels made by the double stitching, using a bodkin or large, blunt needle (Fig. 2). Take care not to catch top fabric or go through it, but keep padding in channel. (If using wool yarn, be sure sufficient yarn is used to raise design so it stands out well. It may be necessary to run yarn through channels a second time.) At angles or sharp curves, bring needle out on back, leave a small loop, and insert needle into channel again through same hole and continue (Fig. 3). This will prevent padding from shrinking and pulling when washed.

The work can be done from the right side, if desired, and the stitching may be done by machine. Using a thin fabric such as organdy or lawn for the top and bright-colored yarn for padding produces a lovely soft coloring in the design. (Be sure to use colorfast yarn.)

Figure 2

Figure 3

Corded coverlet with trapunto roses

EQUIPMENT: Tracing paper. Pencil. Carbon paper. Heavy paper for patterns. Scissors. Needles.

MATERIALS: Two white fabrics, one with a fairly firm weave and the other more open (for lining): about 4½ yards each. (Amount will vary, depending upon width of bed and of fabrics.) Cording, about 40 yards. Absorbent cotton. Sewing and quilting threads. Bias binding, about 8 yards.

DIRECTIONS: Top: Cut fabrics for coverlet and lining the same length and width as top of bed, plus ⅝″ all around for seams. Baste pieces together. Draw diagonals at 6″ intervals on lining. Quilt as directed page 129 for Italian or Corded Quilting.

Overhang: Measure one side of coverlet top. Cut two strips each of top and lining fabrics, that same length and 18″ wide. Baste pieces together and sew to sides of coverlet top. (For a more finished seam, use welting.) Measure width of coverlet, including overhang on each side. Cut one strip each of top and lining fabrics that same lengh and 18″ wide. Baste pieces together and sew across foot of coverlet and overhang pieces.

Trace pattern for rose, opposite. Using carbon paper, transfer to heavy paper; make several such patterns, so that you can keep designs clean and clear. Transfer one rose centered diagonally to each corner area, on under-side of overhang. Space and trace other roses as desired for size of bed. Quilt as directed for Trapunto or Padded Quilting on page 129.

Gentle scallops may be cut at edge of overhang to emphasize rose designs, or overhang may have a straight edge. Finish coverlet by binding outer edges.

Trace actual-size pattern for Trapunto Rose. Cross-line indications are guides for placing squarely on coverlet overhang and for enlarging or reducing (see Index) if desired for other purposes.

TOP

Candlewicking

Candlewick embroidery, first used in colonial days to decorate bedspreads, is truly American in origin. In its early period, it was always worked with natural cream-colored candlewick cotton—from which it took its name—on an unbleached background. At times during its development the French knot and backstitch were used in the embroidery; now the stitch generally associated with this work is a simple running stitch, clipped between stitches to form tufts. White-on-white is still popular, although other colors are also used. Curtains, pillows, bath mats and robes, as well as the traditional bedspreads, feature candlewicking. (Commercially produced chenille fabric closely resembles hand-tufted candlewicking.)

Candlewick cotton is a thick, loosely twisted multi-ply yarn; the background fabric should be firm but rather loosely woven, such as unbleached muslin, and not preshrunk—so that washing will tighten to secure candlewicking in fabric. Special candlewicking needles or large-eyed darning needles are used. A candlewicking needle has a thick shaft, large eye, and may be curved or slightly widened at the point. Double-eyed needles are used for extra-large, thick tufts.

Almost any kind of design is suitable, from flowers and scallops to geometric straight-line designs. Candlewicking may outline the design, fill in some areas, or cover the background solidly. Mark the pattern and work on the right side.

Thread a long length of candlewick cotton in the needle, pulling ends even so thread is double. To start, pick up a few threads of fabric on right side and draw candlewick through until a short end remains as a small tuft. Make even running stitches about ½″ apart, picking up only a few threads with each stitch, and leaving cotton between stitches loose. End with cotton on right side of fabric, clipping off to make small tuft. When stitching is completed, clip cotton at center between each stitch. The cut strands of cotton fluff up, making tufts. If stitches are taken close together, tufting will be in a continuous line; to spot tufts, space the stitches further apart and trim tufts to size.

Shrinking fabric to hold tufts securely is the finishing touch in candlewicking. If a washing machine is used, wash in warm, soapy water for at least twenty minutes. If washing by hand, let soak for three or four hours. Shake out; do not squeeze or wring. Hang in the sun to dry—if it is a windy day, so much the better. Lightly brush tufts before they are quite dry to fluff them. Do not iron a candlewick spread—the crinkly look is characteristic.

This beautifully designed bedspread is a handsome example of candlewick embroidery as it was done in 1825, when the tufts were often left uncut. Then, as now, the eagle of the Great Seal of the United States was a favorite motif of needleworkers.

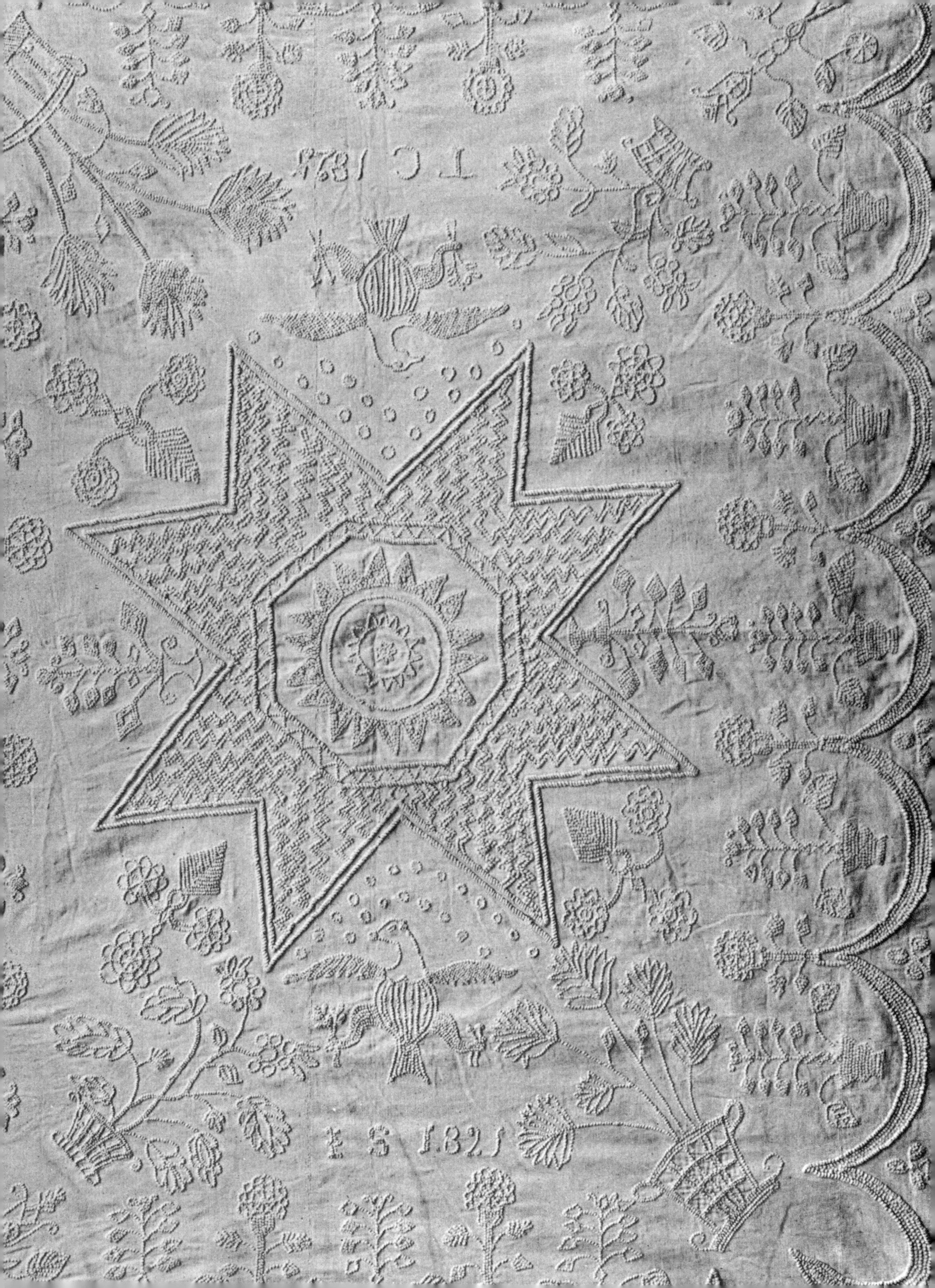

Homespun Blue Bedspread

Adapted from the heavy English Jacobean work of the same period, the American designs were airier and simpler to embroider—and more appropriate for today's interiors, too!

This "Homespun Blue" bedspread is typical of the old crewel designs, and is worked in comparatively inexpensive six-strand embroidery floss rather than the traditional crewel wools.

Crewel embroidery worked in blue-dyed lamb's wool on creamy homespun linen coverlets and valances decorated many an early colonial bed. New England homes often had an indigo tub in their rear kitchens, in which wool was tinted in a great variety of blue tones, inspired perhaps by the lovely Canton blues of the newly-arrived Oriental chinaware.

PARAGON NEEDLECRAFT "HOMESPUN BLUE" BEDSPREAD KIT WAS FEATURED IN McCALL'S NEEDLEWORK & CRAFTS MAGAZINE.

Quilting and Tufting

After the quilt top is finished, it is quilted or tufted. This serves the practical function of holding the layers of fabric and padding together, as well as providing additional decoration.

To prepare for quilting, spread the quilt top out carefully, face down, on a large, flat surface. Arrange wadding on top and tack at intervals. Add lining and smooth in place. Pin the three layers together, then baste at intervals of about 6″.

Select your quilting design carefully to suit the top. If you plan to follow the design of the piecing or appliqué, work from the right side. If there is a pattern to be drawn or transferred onto the lining, then work from the wrong side. The designs shown here are some of the more popular and some of the easiest ones to do. They should be enlarged to three or four times the size shown (see Index, "Enlarging or Reducing Designs"). Border designs are to be traced around the outside, with allover quilting in the center.

Quilting designs can be marked in several ways. Probably the simplest method is to make perforated patterns. Trace the pattern on wrapping paper and machine stitch along lines of the design, with the machine needle unthreaded. The design is marked on the quilt by laying the perforated pattern on the quilt lining, rough side down, and rubbing stamping powder or paste (or ground cinnamon, as our grandmothers did) through the perforations.

Quilting can be done in hand or using a quilting frame. If a frame is used, sew top and bottom edges of quilt to fabric strips attached to long parallel bars of frame. Sew securely with several rows of stitches, using strong thread, so that quilt will not pull away from frame when stretched taut.

The quilting stitch is a short even running stitch. There are two methods of making it. One is done in two separate motions, first pushing the needle down through the three thicknesses, then pushing it up again close to first stitch. One hand is always held under the quilt to guide the stitch; stitches should be of equal length on both sides. The second method is to take two or three little stitches before pulling needle through, holding quilt down at quilting line with thumb of one hand. (Tape this thumb to prevent soreness.) If you are a beginner, practice quilting a small piece in an embroidery hoop to find the easiest and best way for you to work.

The usual quilting needle is a short, sharp needle —No. 8 or 9—although some experienced quilters prefer a longer one. White sewing thread between Nos. 50 and 70 is best. Start quilting midway between the long parallel bars of frame, and sew toward you. To begin, knot end of thread. Bring needle up through quilt and pull knot through lining so it is imbedded in interlining. To end off, make a single backstitch and run thread through interlining.

If you wish to tuft rather than quilt, use several layers of wadding between the top and the lining. Mark evenly spaced points on the top surface with tailor tacks or pins. Thread a candlewick needle with candlewick yarn, or use a large-eyed needle with heavy Germantown or knitting worsted. Using thread double, push needle from top through layers to back, leaving thread end on top. Push needle back up again to surface, about ¼″ away. Tie yarn in firm double knot. Clip ends to desired length (at least ½″) to form tuft.

Simple quilting designs, to be enlarged three or four times size shown here.

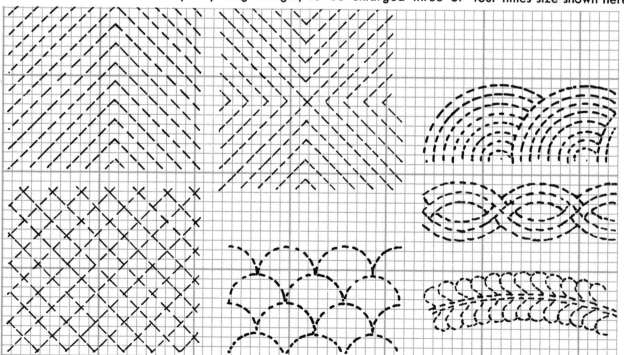

Rugs

Handmade floor coverings have beautified homes, be they tents or castles, for many centuries. Except for the Orient, where rug-making was a family craft, rugs were not made in the home until about two hundred years ago. Since that comparatively recent beginning, rug-making has become one of the most popular and most highly developed of the domestic arts. Now it is possible to produce just the right rug to accent any decorating style, to enhance any color scheme.

Rugs may be hooked, knotted, cross-stitched, worked in needlepoint, braided, crocheted, tufted—or worked in imaginative combinations of techniques. Color combinations are endless in their variety; some rug-makers dye the fabrics themselves in order to obtain the precise hues and tones design requires.

Many antique rugs are treasured in our museums; copy one of these to make your own heirloom. Or design a rug in the modern idiom — today's rugs may be as exciting and dramatic as abstract paintings. For the not-quite-so-adventurous, pre-stamped backgrounds and a wide selection of rug yarns are sold in needlework departments.

Hooked Rugs

Although hooked fabrics were in use in Egypt as early as the fifth century A.D. and they appeared in Spain and France shortly after, our hooked rugs seem to be more directly descended from the hooked clothing and bedcovers of Bronze Age Scandinavians. During the invasion of the British Isles, they introduced hooking to the Britons, and the Swedish word "rugge," meaning coarse or rough, became the English word "rug": a cloak or wrap. Hooking was used in the North of England and in Scotland for many centuries, and came to America with the Pilgrims. However, it was not until the colonial housewives began to hook floor-coverings similar to their bedcovers that "rugs" took on its modern meaning.

Today, there are three general types of hooked rugs, determined by the type of rug hook and the materials used with each hook.

One hook resembles a crochet hook and is used for the traditional method of hooking with rag strips, although yarn may be used if desired. Firmly woven burlap about 40″ wide is the usual foundation fabric; warp cloth is sometimes used instead. The design must be stamped on the right side of the fabric since work is done from top.

A second type of rug hook is the punch needle, which automatically makes loops of uniform height. Yarn is threaded through a needle eye in the point of the hook; there are usually different points supplied with the punch needle to accommodate various weights of yarn. Burlap or warp cloth is the usual foundation fabric, and must be stretched on a rug frame when a punch needle is used. The design is marked on the wrong side, for that is the side from which the needle is inserted. Surface may be sculptured or not; uncut pile may be contrasted with cut pile for an attractive effect. If desired, beveling may be used to emphasize certain areas or for shading.

Third, the latch hook is used for a knotted rug with a deep pile. Working from the right side of open weave canvas, the hook is passed through the canvas, latches onto the yarn, and ties a knot as it pulls up. Special canvas in a large mesh is used with the latch hook. A large rug may be worked in sections and the sections sewn together.

Antique rug, hand-hooked with wool rags in rich colors, has sculptured flowers

A McCALL'S NEEDLEWORK & CRAFTS·MAGAZINE FEATURE.

Before you start to hook

MARKING DESIGNS ON FOUNDATION FABRIC

Although art needlework departments feature many beautiful ready-to-hook rug designs, rug makers sometimes prefer to create their own designs or to copy antique rugs. Unless you are working from a chart, you will need to mark your design on the foundation material before you start hooking.

The material must be spread out flat on a large table or on the floor. Weight the edges with heavy objects—irons, large books, and so on—to keep the fabric taut, with the threads straight and true.

Before you start placing the design, mark the overall size and shape of the rug. When planning the placement of design elements, mark center lines vertically and horizontally with a soft pencil, in order to be able to center the main motif and arrange the border in a pleasing fashion.

There are several methods of marking a design on the foundation fabric. Some straight-line designs can be drawn directly on the foundation; for example, the Tile, Doodle, and Parquet rugs in this section.

A simple way of transferring a design is to make a tracing and mark it on the foundation using carbon paper. Go over the outlines of the large areas within the motifs, but work out the color-shading details as you hook.

If there are large leaves, scallops, bird or flower shapes, you may find it easier to cut the shapes out of stiff wrapping paper; these may then be laid on the foundation and drawn around. To make a symmetrical design, flop the paper shape and draw it in reverse. Grease pencils, felt-tipped marking pens, or crayons are excellent to use for drawing designs or indicating colors. If a wax crayon is used, cover completed design with paper towels and go over with a hot iron to set design and remove excess wax. Lines will be hidden when rug is hooked.

Another method of marking a design on the foundation fabric is to draw it first on a large sheet of wrapping paper; using the longest stitch on the sewing machine and no thread in the needle, stitch through all lines of the design. Lay this perforated pattern, rough side down, on the backing. Rub stamping powder or paste through the perforations, following manufacturer's directions.

Sometimes designs are painted on the background fabric, using oil paints thinned with naphtha or other cleaning fluids. This method makes it possible to indicate color placements and shadings. The fast-evaporating quality of the naphtha prevents "bleeding" of the color into surrounding areas. Since the oil paint is thinned, it will not stiffen the canvas or interfere with the hooking.

FINISHING EDGES

The finished edge must be planned before hooking is begun or, if using a frame, before the foundation fabric is placed in the frame.

One method is to stitch carpet tape at the edge of the rug design. Seam should be exactly on the edge of the design, with seam allowance of tape and backing extending beyond. When hooking is completed, turn carpet tape back over trimmed edge and hem to back of rug. This finish makes a firm, rounded pile at edge of rug. Another method is to finish the edges by turning under the foundation, hemming and pressing it when the work is complete. The entire rug is then lined with heavy cotton fabric.

Some rug makers (not using a frame) stitch around the edge, turn the fabric back about three inches, and press it in place using a hot iron; then hook through the two thicknesses to the outer edge. Rug binding is used to face the under edges.

Latch hook rug edges are usually finished by working first and last five rows with canvas turned over to front of rug; work these rows double thickness. Work sides to selvage or with excess turned back and edged with rug binding, depending upon the type of canvas and manufacturer's directions.

If foundation fabric is warp cloth, rug can be fringed at the ends. Before starting to hook, pull several threads along selvage edge. Using the threads and a darning needle, work buttonhole stitch in each mesh along outside line of pattern, working over three threads outside of line. To fringe ends of finished rug, cut warp cloth three to four inches from buttonholing and ravel cross threads. On long sides of rug, cut off warp cloth along buttonholing.

FRAMES

Although frames are not necessary for hooking all types of rugs, some rug makers prefer to use them. The easel frame tilts at any desired angle and stands in a frame at the usual table height of 30″. The adjustable roller bars at top and bottom make it easy to turn foundation fabric in order to work on one part of the design at a time, rolling up the finished work as it is completed.

To make a rug frame, simply fasten four strips of wood at the corners with carpenter's clamps. Or, using 1″ x 2″ lumber, cut two 4′ side pieces and two 1½′ cross pieces. Bore ½″ diameter holes at 3″ intervals; use wooden pegs in holes to adjust size of frame. The foundation material can be laced through remaining holes with heavy twine, or the wood can be wound with sheeting and the foundation material sewn securely to the sheeting.

Hand hooking

FABRICS

Hand-hooked rugs are usually made from fabric strips cut from discarded clothing or blankets, although new fabric may be used to supplement it, or even to make an entire rug. Try to use fabric of the same weight, thickness, and fiber content for the whole rug so that it will wear evenly. Wool strips wear exceedingly well, and do not show soil as much as silk, rayon, or cotton. Stocking or necktie strips may be used as highlights in wool rugs or to hook small ornamental mats.

If you wish to make your rag rug washable, it is important that your material be absolutely colorfast and it is a simple procedure to make it so. New or old, all material should be washed in hot water and borax to loosen and remove any excess dye. Wash each color separately, then rinse until no more dye comes out. (If the material is soiled, use naphtha soap.) Do not wring; hang in the sun to dry. The colors will not seem faded when hooked because color is entirely relative and depends upon your placement of adjacent colors for the overall effect.

DYEING

If material is to be dyed, follow carefully the directions on the dye package for boiling, exact timing, and setting. To get several shades of the same color, put the material for the darkest shade in the dye first; later, add the material for the next lighter shade, and finally that for the lightest. Dye more than you need. It is better to have too much than not enough, because it is almost impossible to match colors exactly. Allow from four to five pounds of material for a rug 24″ x 36″. This allows for ample material in the various colors. When cut into strips, 1½ to 2 square yards of wool or 2 square yards of cotton will hook about one square foot.

CUTTING INTO STRIPS

All strips should be cut in uniform widths, although strips to be used for fine detail in a small section may be cut narrower. A machine which cuts strips evenly is sold in art needlework departments. Most strips are cut on the straight of the fabric, but some workers prefer them cut slightly on the bias for more give. Cut firmly woven fabric in strips as narrow as ⅛″; more loosely woven material may be cut in strips 3/16″ to 5/16″ wide. Cotton strips should be ¼″ to ½″ wide.

HOOKING

If you have never hooked before, practice on a small square outside the edge of the rug design. Hold the hook above the foundation fabric in the right hand; hold the fabric strip underneath with the left. Push the hook through the fabric to draw a loop up through to the desired height; then reinsert the hook in the fabric close by and pull up another loop. Care must be taken to have all loops the same height; height is determined by the fabric used and the width of strip. If loops are to be cut, they should be no longer than usual. You will gauge how far apart your stitches should be by the width or thickness of the strands and the height of the loops; they should be close enough together to stay in place, yet far enough apart so that the rug will not buckle. Give hook a little clockwise twist as you pull the loops through. This makes a firmer and longer wearing pile. Pull ends through to top when starting and ending a strand; clip ends even with loops.

Swatch of burlap, the usual foundation material for working hand-hooked rugs. Actual size.

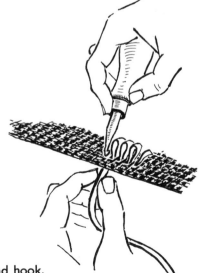

Process of hooking with traditional hand hook.

Hook with rags

HOOKED TILE RUG

EQUIPMENT AND MATERIALS: Rug hook. Scissors or rug stripping machine. Rug frame (optional). Burlap, 40″ wide, 1½ yards. Pencil. 5 yards rug binding.

Rug requires wool fabric of related shades of two contrasting colors. Original was made with green-and-black and red-and-black lumberjack plaid shirts.

DIRECTIONS: Mark corners of rug 30″ x 49″ on center of burlap. Draw soft pencil along grain of burlap to join corners. Divide rug into rectangles 6″ x 3½″—five on width of rug, fourteen on length. Rug may be worked in the hand or on a frame.

Cut fabric for hooking into working strands about ⅛″ wide. Using red, hook around outline of one rectangle. Work inside outline for two or three rows. Work outlines of adjacent rectangles in green. Fill in red rectangles. Fill in green rectangles, working adjacent red outlines first. Proceed in this manner until entire rug is hooked. Bind edges.

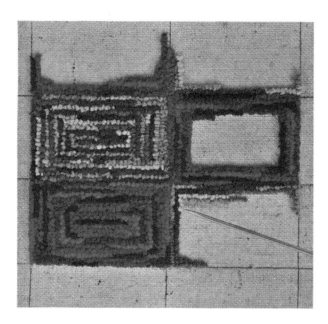

Detail of rug in work.

Hooked rug in simple tile arrangement adapts readily to any size. This original is 49″ x 30″.

Hook with yarn

HOOKED DOODLE RUG

EQUIPMENT AND MATERIALS: Hand rug hook. (This rug can also be made with a punch needle; see page 147). Rug frame (optional). Yardstick. Pencil. Compass.

Knitting worsted: Beige for background; black, blue, orange, green, and red for doodles. Burlap, 40" wide, 1⅝ yards.

DIRECTIONS: For rug shown, approximately 38" x 52" with 3½" doodles, mark burlap as follows: At center of width (20" from either selvage), draw a line between two threads from top to bottom of cloth. It is not necessary to use yardstick; pencil will follow grain. Draw four more parallel lines from top to bottom, two on either side of center line, spaced 6" apart. At center of length of burlap draw line across from edge to edge. Draw six more parallel lines, three on either side of center line, spaced 6" apart. Set compass for 1¾" radius. With point on intersection of two lines, describe a circle around each intersection—7 rows of 5 circles. Draw your own doodle lines in and around circles.

Work border to first row of doodles. For more interesting texture, do not follow threads of burlap exactly. Work first row of doodles; then work background around them. If desired, some doodles may be worked with longer loops than others. Continue working doodles and background until finished.

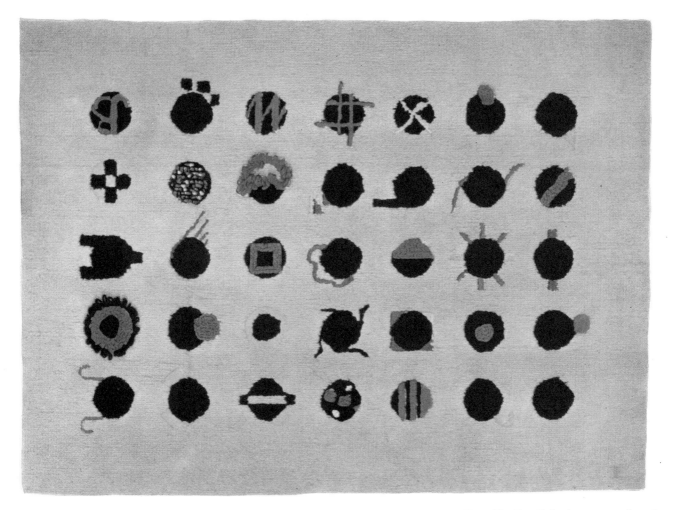

Amusing "Doodle Rug" is fun to make of many colors of yarn against a beige background. 38" x 52".

Shading

Lovely color effects can be obtained by shading areas. A group of shaded colors for making a motif is known as a swatch, and is made up of five or six 3″ x 12″ pieces of fabric, preferably wool, which shade from light to dark in the same hue. (We have described how to prepare material in related tones of a color in the directions for dyeing on page 141.)

To make the welcome mat illustrated, shades of blue, green, and rose are used against a beige background, with border, keys, and letters worked in dark gray, brown, or black. For more variety, combine colors from two or more related swatches; for example, you could take a light green from a yellow-green swatch, a medium value from a green swatch, and the darkest from a blue-green swatch. Colors are indicated with numbers running from 0 (light) to 5 or 6 (dark). The morning glory is worked in five shades of blue; note how the gradations are planned to give the flower roundness and form. The rose is worked in six shades of red ranging from a very pale pink through a deep wine. The leaf has five shades of green. In the original design, the leaves of the garland were veined along the center with strips of red plaid, indicated by symbols RP. They may instead be worked in deep green, brown, or black.

Foundation material, preferably burlap, should be about 26″ x 42″. Tack down firmly on a smooth, flat surface. Using soft pencil or charcoal, draw guide lines 2″ apart in each direction. With a grease pencil, draw the outline of the lower edge, then locate the top curve by marking the same shape in the corresponding squares of burlap. Next draw the leaf spray placing each leaf in the corresponding square. These leaves are all the same shape, so draw one and trace them all from it. Draw the stem for the central flower group and place the leaves. Draw the roses, then trace them in place. Add the lettering across the lower edge, place the keys, and the design is ready to be hooked.

For best effect in working the background, keep direction of stitches irregular. To keep each part of the flower clearly defined, always work first the shape which appears in front of the adjoining shapes, as rose center is "on top" of outer petals.

Work out similar arrangements of color shading when working other designs for other rugs.

Hand-hooked welcome mat, 22″ x 36″, features delicately shaded roses, morning glories, and leaves.

Above: Color indications for shading flowers and leaves.
Below: Chart for Welcome Mat. Enlarge on 2" squares.

146

Punch needle

The punch needle was designed to simplfy hand-hooking with a tool which would produce the same effect automatically. Most yarn companies now supply patented punch needles which punch yarn through the foundation fabric to deposit loops of measured height. There is usually an adjustment on the needle to regulate loop heights. Sketched on this page are some of the more common types of punch needles.

The foundation fabric is stretched on a rug frame with the underside, upon which the design is marked, up. To hook, thread needle with yarn, following manufacturer's directions. Plunge needle through fabric and pull end of yarn through to reverse side. Always hold needle in vertical position. Next, lift needle slightly above the fabric, bringing point just to surface and over to position where next loop is to be placed. Plunge needle in as far as it goes to make each stitch. Continue making loops evenly spaced. On last stitch, while needle is on reverse side, cut yarn halfway up needle.

Be sure yarn feeds freely over the back of the hand and through the needle; otherwise uneven loops or none at all will result. While hooking succeeding rows, hold loops of finished row away from row being worked, underneath frame, with fingertips of left hand. This will keep the work even and loops from meshing. Continue in this way. When moving rug to reach a new working area, tack finished portion to frame with upholstery tacks. These will hold hooked portion firmly on frame.

You may choose to contrast cut and uncut pile for an attractive effect. Complete the rug, then study the design and plan which areas you wish to trim to a velvety pile and which you wish to leave in the loop pile. Beveling may also be employed to emphasize design areas.

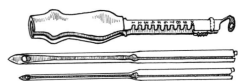

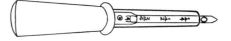

Patriotic 50-Star Rug is worked with a punch needle in only two colors of yarn—clipping and sculpturing adds subtle shading.

Three varieties of punch needles.

Parquet Rug to make with a punch needle and two colors of yarn. Outline loops are clipped to contrast with curly background loops. Complete rug measures 33" x 44".

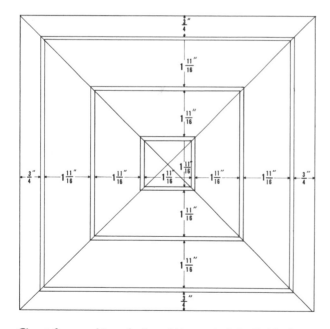

Chart for marking design. Warp cloth is divided into squares, diagonals drawn, inner squares added.

HOOKED "PARQUET" RUG

EQUIPMENT AND MATERIALS: Punch needle. Rug frame. Thumbtacks. Upholstering tacks. Yardstick. Pencil. Sharp scissors. Large darning needle. Lightweight rug yarn as recommended for use with your punch needle, about 42 ozs. each of medium beige and dark beige. Warp cloth, 36" wide, 1½ yards. Carpet thread.

PREPARING WARP CLOTH: Lay warp cloth on flat surface. Measure 1½" in from one selvage edge, draw line between two warp threads along complete length of cloth. Do not use yardstick; pencil will follow straight line between two threads. Measure 11" in from first pencil line, draw a second line parallel to first. Draw two more parallel lines in same manner, dividing warp cloth into three lengthwise sections 11" wide, with 1½" margin at each selvage edge.

About 5" from one cut end of warp cloth, draw line between two weft threads across width of cloth. Draw four more parallel lines, 11" apart, across warp cloth, thus dividing cloth into twelve 11" squares.

See chart for marking design, below, left. Thumbtack edges of warp cloth, outside pattern, to flat surface, making sure corners are square and warp cloth is as taut as possible. Mark each 11" square as follows: with yardstick on two opposite corners, draw diagonal line across square. Repeat diagonal line in opposite direction. Measure in ¾" from each side of square, draw line between two warp threads ending at diagonal lines. Draw another line two warp threads in from first line. Measure in 1-11/16" from second line, draw third line. Draw fourth line two warp threads in from third line. Measure in 1-11/16" from fourth line, draw fifth line. Draw sixth line two warp threads in from fifth line.

Each pattern square has two triangles worked in medium beige and two triangles worked in dark beige. See illustration of rug, top left, for placement of medium and dark triangles on rug. Mark each dark triangle with "D" for accurate placing of colors when working rug.

Dark lines forming three concentric squares on each pattern square are worked in the same color as the triangle in which they appear. They are worked in shorter loops than the rest of the rug; the loops are then clipped to give a darker tone.

HOOKING: Using point for thinner yarn, thread rug needle with rug yarn, following directions given with needle. Dark lines are worked first by making two rows of short loops along marked lines. To work short loops, set needle following manufacturer's directions. Work marked line, Fig. 1. On last stitch of row, while needle is on reverse side, cut yarn halfway up needle. Work second row on marked line two threads above. Work remaining marked lines in same way. Turn work to right side of rug. Pick up loops on blade of scissors and cut through center of each loop, Fig. 2.

Remainder of rug is worked with longer loops. When working outer edge of rug, hook two rows close together to give a firm edge where the wear is greatest. Work over every thread of the cloth for these two rows.

Fill in squares as follows: beginning at lower right-hand edge of triangle, * work over two threads of warp cloth for each stitch and continue across to left-hand edge of triangle. Work a second row directly above with one thread of warp cloth between. Skip two threads of warp cloth and repeat from *, Fig. 3.

FINISHING: Turn under selvages at sides of rug and hem to back of rug. Cut away all but 2″ of warp cloth on ends of rug, turn in ¼″, fold warp cloth back along edge of rug and hem to back.

MAKING LARGER RUGS: This design of 11″ squares may be repeated for larger rugs of any size provided that the dimensions are a multiple of 11″. For extra squares on the length of the rug, buy warp cloth in one piece long enough to accommodate extra squares (about one yard more than directions specify for three more squares). For extra squares on the width of the rug, buy double the length required. For more than three extra squares (seven, eight or nine squares across width of rug), buy triple the length required.

Mark additional squares on warp cloth as directed in Preparing Warp Cloth. On edges to be joined, machine-stitch ¾″ outside outline of pattern on both pieces, using fine stitches. Work design on each edge to within 1″ of pattern outline. After pieces have been hooked, cut off selvage edges just outside machine stitching. Lap unhooked edge of one piece over unhooked edge of other piece, pattern outline of top piece coinciding with pattern outline of bottom piece.

To lap edges accurately, use large pins; push pin down through pattern outline of top piece; raise edge so that you can see under it; push pin down through pattern outline of bottom edge. Pin edges together in this manner, then baste pieces together along both raw edges using threads raveled from cut-off selvages. Complete hooking of pattern, working through double thickness of warp cloth.

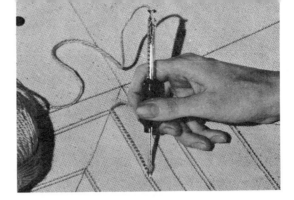

Fig. 1: Outlines being hooked.

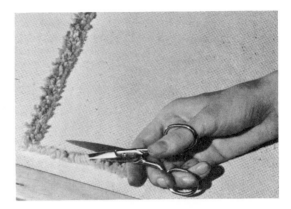

Fig. 2: Clipping outlines.

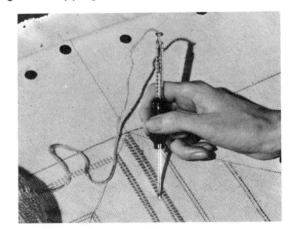

Fig. 3: Filling in background.

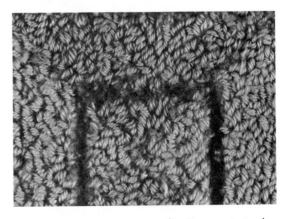

Detail of hooked rug square (half actual size).

Latch hook

A full, deep-piled rug texture is achieved by knotting short strands of yarn on canvas with a latch hook (also called latchet hook). Rugs of this construction may be vacuumed without danger of the strands coming loose. Yarn comes already cut into correct lengths, packaged according to color; or yarn from a ball or skein may be cut to the correct length (about 2½″) with easy-to-use automatic rug yarn cuttters. No frame is used in latch hooking.

Before starting to work knots, turn four or five rows at end of canvas over to front and work through this doubled canvas to form a finished end.

The drawings, right, illustrate how to make knots with a latch hook. Fold yarn over shank of hook; hold ends with left hand (Fig. 1). With hook in right hand, hold latch down with index finger; push hook down through mesh of canvas, under two horizontal threads, and up through mesh above (Fig. 2). Draw hook toward you, placing yarn ends inside hook. Be sure yarn is completely inside the hook when the latch closes, so that end of hook does not snag or split the yarn (Fig. 3). Pull hook back through the canvas, drawing ends of yarn through loop; tighten knot by pulling ends (Fig. 4).

Yarn must be knotted on the weft threads—those running across the canvas from selvage to selvage. For an evenly knotted rug, work completely across canvas before starting next row. If canvas is too wide, plan design from center of canvas and work first row from center out to edges of design. Trim edges to about 1½″; turn over at sides and work double. Or, turn back excess canvas at sides when rug hooking is completed and sew canvas to back; sew rug binding over those edges. When nearing the end of canvas, double it over to the front four or five rows and work through this doubled canvas as at the beginning.

Several completed sections may be fastened together to make a larger size rug. Turn back canvas along selvage edges to be joined. From wrong side, using curved upholsterer's needle and carpet thread, whip sections together, matching meshes. Trim canvas at side edges of rug to 1″, turn back, and baste to back of rug. Sew rug binding over joinings and margin.

After rug is completed, shake it well and rub the surface in one direction with your hand to remove loose fibers. Trim any uneven lengths.

Latch-hooked "Indian Summer" rug features vivid colors, lush pile.

A McCALL'S NEEDLEWORK & CRAFTS MAGAZINE FEATURE. YARN AND PAINTED CANVAS, SHILLCRAFT.

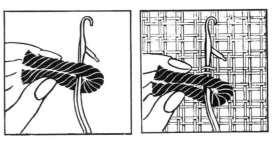

Fig. 1   Fig. 2

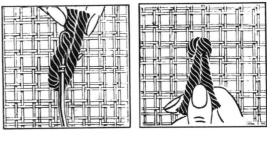

Fig. 3   Fig. 4

LATCH HOOK

Latch hook "Patchwork" rug

The charming repeat patterns of old patchwork quilts are fun to adapt to contemporary rugs. "Swing-in-the-Center" is 30" x 43", but may be repeated and joined to make larger sizes. Chart may also be used to make rug in cross-stitch or needlepoint, although sizes will vary according to mesh count of foundation material.

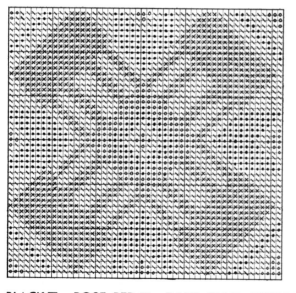

BLACK ⊡   ROSE RED ◎   DARK OLIVE GREEN ⊠
WHITE ◹

SWING-IN-THE-CENTER RUG

EQUIPMENT AND MATERIALS: Latch (or latchet) hook. Tapestry or upholsterer's needle. 30" wide rug canvas with approximately 3½ meshes to the inch, about 1⅓ yards. Rug yarn: Rose red, 2 packs (31 yds.); Dark olive, 6 packs (153 yds.); White, 6 packs (137 yds.); Black, 3 packs (76 yds.). (If yarn is not pre-cut, a yarn cutter is necessary.) Rug binding.

DIRECTIONS: Place one end of canvas and the chart in front of you on table. To begin, fold four or five rows of canvas over to right side; work over doubled canvas, following chart for design and repeating design across chart. When nearing end of canvas, double it over and work as for beginning. Turn under selvages and baste to back; sew rug binding over canvas edges on back.

Cross-Stitch on Burlap

Anyone who can do cross-stitch can make attractive, long-wearing rugs. They are usually worked in rug wool on burlap, and no frame is required. In making cross-stitch, the ends are run in along the back of the work. Do not attempt to run them in on the front; a noticeable thickening would result.

The diagonal technique used for needlepoint is employed for the first half of the cross-stitch, when making a rug. This produces an interwoven texture on the back which is more durable than cross-stitch worked in the usual manner. To work in the diagonal technique, start at upper right, leaving a 2″ end of yarn at the back of the burlap. Follow Figures 1, 2, 3, and 4, working over the end of the yarn. These are the four steps of the diagonal method. When working diagonal rows upward, the needle is horizontal (4); when working rows downward, needle is upright (2). To start new rows, hold needle at angle (1 and 3). Figure 5 shows stitches as work progresses. To cross stitches, work back and forth, as in Figure 6. It is very important that all stitches cross in the same direction. Avoid turning the rug as you work, or the whole effect may be spoiled.

Use good quality burlap in a width to suit your needs; allow at least 3″ on all sides of the design. A chenille needle No. 14 is a good size to use. Cross-stitching is done over squares of burlap threads, approximately three cross-stitches to the inch (burlap varies slightly). To make sure that all stitches are the same size, mark up the entire design surface into squares, four threads by four threads. Using a soft pencil, draw lines between the threads so that each square will contain four threads vertically and horizontally.

To block, thumbtack embroidered piece face down on a flat surface, pulling into shape and making sure corners are square. Dampen back of piece; let dry. Turn under 3″ allowance and bind.

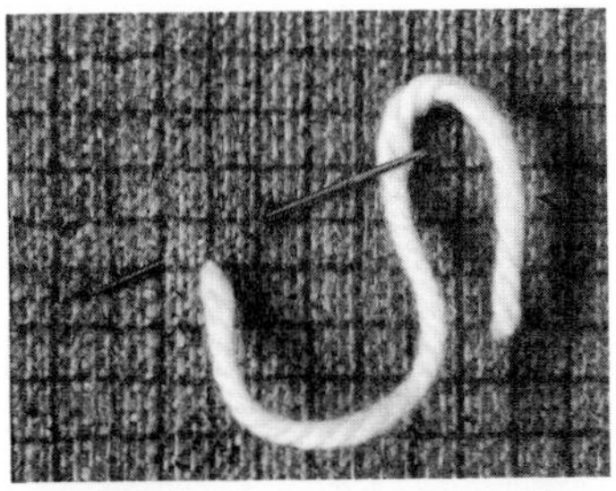

Figure 1

Figure 2

Figure 3

Figure 4

Figure 5

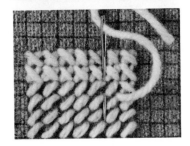

Figure 6

Cross-stitch rug

Keyed to contemporary design and color, this rug may be worked in colors suggested —white, light yellow green, and medium green—or in other shades to suit your taste and decor. Rug shown is approximately 31″ x 46″, but can be made larger by repeating the pattern square. Chart is also suitable for a needlepoint or latch hook rug.

Chart for rug design shown above. Square is repeat section, approximately 15″ x 15″. Work medium green lines first, then solid diamonds, fill in background last.

WHITE □   YELLOW-GREEN ⊠   MED. GREEN ■

SQUARE-ON-SQUARE CROSS-STITCH RUG

EQUIPMENT AND MATERIALS: Chenille needle No. 14. Burlap, 36″ wide, 1½ yards. Rug yarn: 26 skeins white, 9 skeins yellow-green, 7 skeins medium green. Rug binding, 4½ yards.

DIRECTIONS: Mark burlap into 4-thread squares, using soft pencil and drawing between threads. Allowing 3″ all around design for turnover, work in diagonal cross-stitch, following chart. The design is repeated twice for width of rug, three times for length of rug. Work two rows of medium green crosses all around.

To block, thumbtack face down on a flat surface. being careful corners are square; dampen; let dry. Turn under edges and finish with rug binding.

Needlepoint Rug

UNDER-THE-SEA RUG

EQUIPMENT AND MATERIALS: Large-eyed, blunt-pointed rug needle. Latch hook. Scissors and cardboard or rug yarn cutter. 40″ wide rug canvas, approximately five meshes to the inch, 1¾ yds. Rug yarn, 24-yd. skeins: 4 antique white, 6 maroon, 12 dark green-blue, 14 light turquoise, 15 medium blue-green. Rug binding, 5 yds.

DIRECTIONS: To work rug in sections: Cut canvas in half lengthwise; cut each strip into three pieces, one 32″ long, the other two 15″ long. Mark one end of each as top. Selvage edge is side edge.

The six sections to be worked separately are clearly outlined by heavy dark lines on the chart. Start needlepoint for each section 2″ inside top and right side edge of canvas. Be sure to have marked edge of canvas at top. Do not work design shown in the joining strips. Following chart, work needlepoint in continental or diagonal stitch (see Index). Diagonal stitch is preferred for rugs.

When six sections have been worked, block each piece separately. Mark proper size on brown paper. Thumbtack needlepoint face down to flat surface over paper guide; be sure corners are square. Wet thoroughly with cold water; let dry.

To join sections, first join three sections to make one long strip for half of rug. Carefully cut away all but four rows of unworked mesh on one of the two edges to be joined; lap cut edge over corresponding edge so that the four rows of meshes on top coincide with the four rows of meshes below. Be sure pieces line up correctly. Pin together through centers of lapped edges. Following chart for design between sections, work needlepoint over double thickness of canvas. Repeat for third piece of that half. Join second half in same manner, then join the two halves.

To work rug in one piece: Mark one end of canvas as top; selvage edge is side edge. Disregard heavy lines on chart; work entire chart in continental or diagonal stitch (see Index). Block as directed above.

To make fringe: Cut yarn into 2½″ lengths with rug yarn cutter; or wind around 1¼″ cardboard and cut with scissors. Place rug on table, right side up, with edge to be fringed toward you and extending off table. Work four rows of knots with latch hook (see Index), making first row of knots over double threads along edge of needlepoint, using yarn same color as needlepoint. Work other three sides in same manner; fill in corners. Trim.

To bind rug: Turn under margin of canvas and baste to back. Sew rug binding over canvas edges.

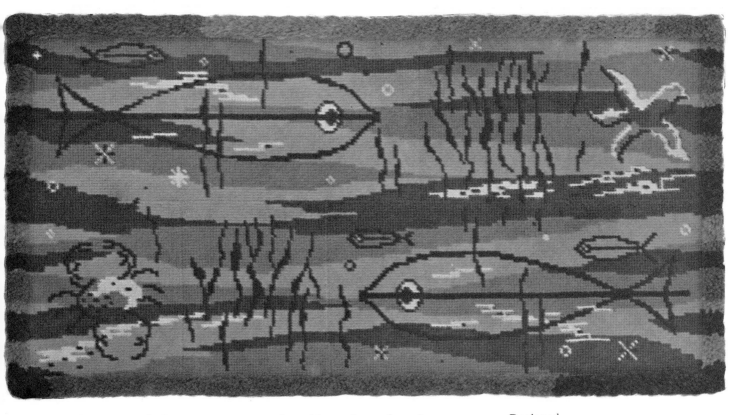

Needlepoint worked on rug canvas makes this cool-toned contemporary rug. Designed in six sections for easy handling, it can also be made in one piece; directions for both methods and latch hook edge are given. Chart for 51″ x 26″ rug is on following pages.

155

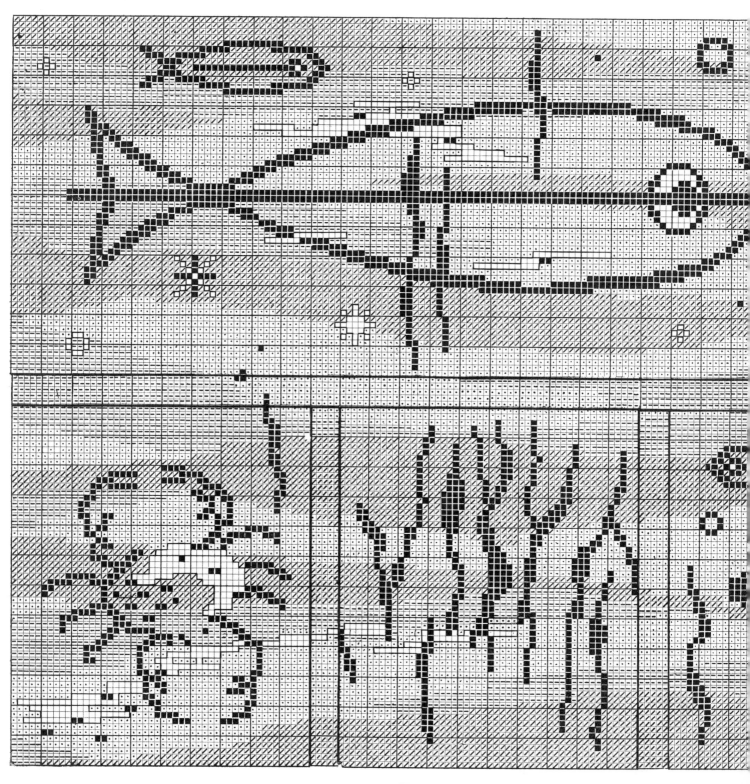

□ ANTIQUE WHITE   ⊡ LT. TURQUOISE

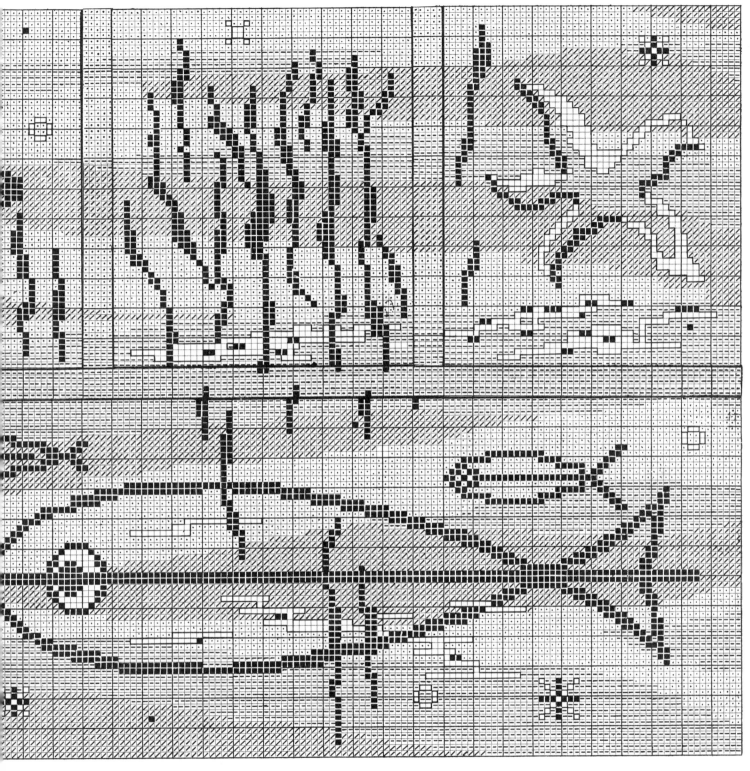

☑ MED. BLUE-GREEN   ⊟ DK. GREEN-BLUE   ■ MAROON

Braided Rugs

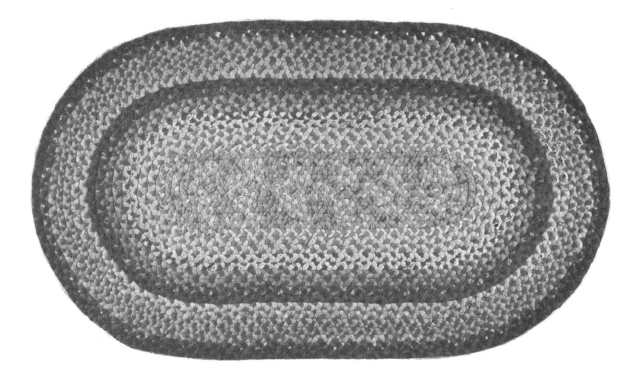

A fine example of an oval braided rug.

Braided rugs in the Westport, Conn., home of artist Amos Sewell, blend beautifully with Early American antiques.

Although rushes were plaited into mats as early as 6,000 B.C., and cornhusks were used by the Pilgrims to make their earliest recorded floor coverings, the braiding of rags into rugs is a comparatively recent and apparently native American craft. Certainly braided rag rugs are a remarkable reflection of the qualities for which their originators are famous: thrift, durability, and colorful personalities! As such, they are appropriate for all our periods of home decoration, from colonial to contemporary.

Start by collecting the materials in an old-fashioned "rag bag." Generally, wool makes the best rugs; it works up easily, wears well, and does not show soil. Other fabrics may be used, but do not combine different types of fabrics in one rug—they will wear unevenly. Cotton is practical for rugs which will need frequent washing; silks and synthetics may be used alone for small mats or for bedroom rugs. If you need additional fabric, it may be purchased from remnant counters or mill end shops. Plan your colors before you begin to braid; if you lack a desired color, the fabric may be dyed. It is simple to dye rags for braiding, for any unevenness of color serves to add to the rug's beauty!

Make your rug in any size and shape suitable for the area in which it will be used. It may be scatter-size or room-size, rounded or rectangular. The photographs on opposite page and sketches on this page show some of the possibilities and their effect in room settings. The size must be decided before you start any shape other than round, for the starting strip will determine the finished size. For example, to find the proper length for the starting braid of an oval rug, subtract the width of the desired size of the finished rug from the length.

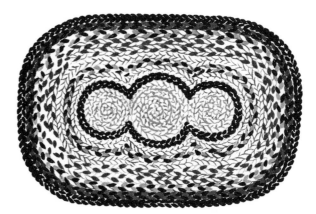

Braided rugs in a variety of shapes and techniques.

159

How to braid

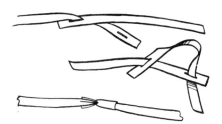

Figure 1: Splicing

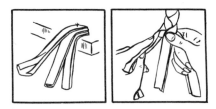

Figure 2: Starting a Three-Strand Braid

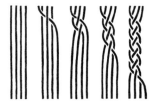

Figure 3: Four-Strand Braiding

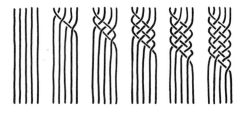

Figure 4: Five-Strand Braiding

MATERIALS: Cotton, wool, and silk fabrics are all suitable for braiding, but should not be combined in one rug because of the difference in their wearing qualities. Generally, wools make the best rugs. A wool rug requires about ¾ pound of material for each square foot, so that a 2′ x 3′ rug will take four to five pounds. When the desired color is not obtainable in rag bag or store, the fabric may be dyed. All fabric should be washed, each color separately, in warm water with borax or naphtha soap, rinsed without wringing and hung in sunlight to dry. This insures a colorfast, washable rug.

BRAIDING STRIPS: Cut or tear strips on the lengthwise grain of fabric, the width determined by the weight of the fabric in relation to the thickness of the braid. For a large wool rug, the finished braid is usually ¾″ or 1″ wide. Cut strip, therefore, should be 1½″ to 2″ wide for medium-weight wool. To make strips desired length, join pieces by sewing together on the bias by hand or machine. Start with strips of different lengths in order to avoid joinings all in same place.

Strips may also be spliced. Splicing is a simplified method of joining braiding strips which eliminates having to sew strips together. It does not make as smooth a braid as sewn strips, but it is quick and simple to do. Cut a 1″ slit lengthwise in the end of each strip. Pass slit end of strip being braided through slit of new strip. Pass other end of new strip through slit of strip being braided. Pull together (Fig. 1).

To gauge the amount of strips needed, estimate the desired length of the finished braid and multiply by 1½. Prepare the strips for braiding by folding in the raw edges so that they almost meet at center, then fold the strip in half lengthwise. This may be done by hand as you braid, or by using braiding aids which fold the strip automatically.

Three-Strand Braid: The simplest type of braid is made with three strands. Pin or sew ends of three folded strands together. Anchor ends firmly. Begin braiding by folding right-hand strand over middle strand, then fold left-hand strand over middle strand keeping folded-in edges to center. Continue braiding, always folding alternate outside strand over middle strand (Fig. 2).

Four-Strand Braid: In four-strand braiding, the outer left hand strand is carried each time over the next strand, under the following strand, and over the opposite outside strand (Fig. 3).

Five-Strand Braid: For five-strand braid, it may help to baste the folded strands for ease in handling. Pin the five folded strands together. With folded-in edges to the left, anchor end firmly. In your mind number strands 1 to 5 from left to right. Fold 1 over 2, put it under 3, over 4, under 5, folding 5 over 1 for a smooth edge. Strand 2 now becomes strand 1; continue in same manner, always weaving strand furthest to left over and under to right (Fig. 4).

JOINING BRAIDS: Braids can be sewed together through touching edges with doubled heavy carpet thread, or laced through the braid loops. Work on a flat surface to keep rug flat and even. When sewing, take stitches at center sides of braids using a curved upholstery needle. To lace, fasten doubled carpet thread to a loop in braid on right, using blunt needle or lacer; push needle through loop of adjacent braid, then into next loop of first braid. Pull thread tightly to lock loops into each other.

Interbraiding may be used instead of sewing to join the braids as they are braided. Use a rug hook. The outer strip—after passing over, under, and above the other strips—is hooked through the loop of the finished braid adjoining. In rounding curves, two succeeding strips are hooked through the same loop.

Braids may be made in a continuous rope and sewn around in a spiral or oblong. In this method, the change in color combinations is usually made one strip at a time, at staggered intervals to achieve a gradual blending of color.

If the rug is made with a continuous braid strip spiraling around until the end is reached, the ending may come at any point convenient: at one end, or along the curved side. If the rug is oblong, it will usually be more satisfactory to end at a corner. Taper trim each strip to a bias cut and braid right to the end, making the braid very small. Then sew this into place along the edge. Or braid as far as desired without tapering and lay the flat strips over to the wrong side of the rug to sew flat.

Butting: Many rug makers prefer to butt each row. Butting is used to form a perfect circle, oval, or square, or to make sharp color changes. It eliminates the jogging out of the pattern. Leave both ends of the braid unfinished. Sew braid to rug within 6″ of the point of butting. Cut strips of both unfinished ends diagonally, tapering to a point. Braid strips almost to end. Fold points of strips to back of braid, tuck underneath the loops neatly, and spread braid to normal width, keeping square at end for neat joining. Sew finished ends together. If braids are butted at different points the joinings will be unnoticeable.

FRINGING: If you wish to fringe the ends of a rectangular braided rug, make each braid the length desired; hold each end with safety pin as strips are sewn together. When rug is complete, sew across ends of rug at point where you wish fringe to begin. Unravel ends of braids and trim evenly.

Figure 5:   Joining by Sewing

Figure 6:   Joining by Interbraiding

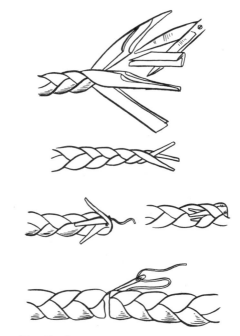

Figure 7:   Butting

Figure 8:   Fringing

SUGAR AND SPICE RUG

MATERIALS: About 7½ pounds medium-weight wool fabric, pink, brown-and-white check, and brown. Heavy brown carpet thread. Lacer. Sewing needle.

Center of rug is five-strand braids 1¼″ wide; wide border is three-strand braids ¾″ wide. Cut fabric 1¼″ to 1½″ wide. Sew strips together, using one color for each strand.

CENTER: Place five strands for first braid on pin with folded-in edges to left as follows: Two strands pink, one strand brown-and-white check, one strand brown, one strand brown-and-white check. Make 30″ five-strand braid. Make ten more braids same length, changing color sequence on pins by shifting strands one color over to the right for each successive braid. To lace braids together, place braids with starting pins pointing downward to right and folded-in edges upward. Match colors of first and second braids; attach thread to end loop of second braid, push lacer up into matching loop of first braid, down into next loop of second braid and continue. Lace third braid to second, etc. When braids are all joined, stitch straight across each end, remove pins, cut away fabric outside stitching. Bind ends with a 1¼″ strip of brown fabric and miter neatly at corners.

BORDER: Braids are attached all around center and corners are braided square. Start making three-strand braid in brown, 2″ shorter than length of one side of center section. Turn center to wrong side, lace braid just made to long right-hand edge, starting 2″ from bottom and lacing to top corner with folded-in edges of braid facing up. Turn work around so braid is on left-hand side and braid corner as follows: Place left strand 1 over 2, 2 over 1, 1 over 2 again; pull strand 3 very tight and braid in usual way thus turning corner. Continue braiding in usual manner to next corner. Make all corners the same. Sew braid to bound ends of center. Butt ends of braid together. Make one more brown round same. For border, put folded strands of wool on pin as follows: Round 3, two brown-and-white, one pink; rounds 4 and 5, two pink, one brown-and-white; rounds 6 and 7, two brown-and-white, one pink; rounds 8 and 9, two pink, one brown-and-white; round 10, two brown-and-white, one pink; round 11, two brown-and-white, one brown; round 12, two brown, one brown-and-white; round 13, two brown-and-white, one brown; rounds 14 and 15, three brown. Turn corners; butt ends of each round.

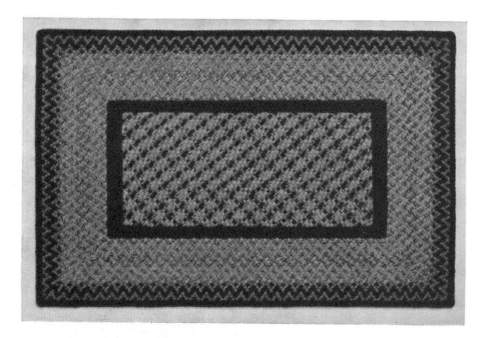

Rectangular braided rug with square braided corners is unusual and attractive. 30″ x 45½″.

Crocheted Rugs

OLD COLONY RUG

EQUIPMENT AND MATERIALS: Aluminum crochet hook size G or 5. Cotton rug yarn in any desired combination of colors for block centers and in brown, dark brown, light green, emerald green, dark green, and wine for block borders.

DIRECTIONS: Block (13″ square): **Center:** Ch 29, making sts a little looser than usual. **Row 1:** Sk first ch and working tightly, sc in remaining 28 ch. **Row 2:** Ch 1, turn, sc in first sc, * sc down at base of next sc into row below (long sc made), sc in next sc. Repeat from * across, alternating a long sc with a sc. End row with a long sc. **Row 3:** Ch 1, turn, sc in first long sc, * a long sc over next sc, sc in next long sc. Repeat from * across. End row with a long sc. ** Cut off yarn leaving 3″ end. **Row 4:** Leaving 3″ end of next color, draw yarn through the lp on hook (ch-1 made). Tie 3″ ends of 2 colors tog in a hard, double knot and let ends hang on edge. Turn, sc in first long sc, (1 long sc, 1 sc) repeated across. End row with a long sc. Repeat row 3 once, twice or more times. Continue in same way, repeating from **, using a few or many colors, making from one to four or more rows of each color and putting blending colors tog until work is square (about 42 rows).

Border: Rnd 1: Join brown, turn, * 2 sc in first long sc, (a long sc over next sc, sc in next long sc) 13 times, 3 sc in end sc; working down side make (sc in next 2 rows, 2 sc in next row) 6 times, working over the yarn ends which were left hanging and covering them up. Sc in next 2 rows, 3 sc in corner. Repeat from * around, end with 1 more sc in first corner, join with sl st in first sc and cut off yarn, leaving 3″ end. **Rnd 2:** Turn, join dk. green and make sc in each sc around with 3 sc in center sc of 3 sc at corners, working over end left from last row and being careful to have the same number of sc on each side. Joint and cut yarn as before. **Rnd 3:** Turn, and with lt. green, make 2 sc in center sc at one corner, (a long sc over next sc, sc in next sc) repeated around with 3 sc in center sc at each corner, working over end left from last rnd. End with 1 sc in starting corner, join with sl st in first sc. **Rnd 4:** Ch 1, turn, 2 sc in same place with sl st, (a long sc over next sc, sc in next long sc) repeated around with 3 sc in center sc at each corner. End as in last rnd. Cut yarn as before. Repeat rnds 3 and 4 with brown, then with emerald green, then make 1 row each in wine and dk. brown. Fasten off.

Repeat blocks for required size of rug, making centers all alike or in different color arrangements, as desired. Sew blocks tog in strips, going through 1 lp of each sc, turning blocks so rows in centers are alternately crosswise and lengthwise. Sew strips tog, being careful to match corners exactly.

Steam rug on back with a hot iron and wet cloth, then press dry through a cloth.

Crocheted in 13″ squares, this handsome rug can be made room size or as a color accent.

CROCHETED BRICK RUG

EQUIPMENT AND MATERIALS: Steel crochet hook No. 00. Rayon and cotton rug yarn, 12 70-yd. skeins red, 8 70-yd. skeins gray. Carpet thread, 2 spools gray.

DIRECTIONS: Rug background is in filet crochet. Spaces (sps) are shown on chart by open squares; blocks (bls) by black squares.

To Make Bls: Dc in each of 3 sts (1 bl); dc in each of next 2 sts for each additional bl.

To Make Sps: Dc in 1 st, ch 1, sk 1 st, dc in next st (1 sp); ch 1, sk 1 st, dc in next st for each additional sp.

With red yarn, ch 85, dc in 5th ch from hook, * ch 1, skip next ch, dc in next ch, repeat from *

across for first row of sps on chart, ch 3, turn. Dc in 2nd dc for sp, make 7 bls (14 dc), 1 sp, continue across, following chart. Continue in this manner, working complete section shown on chart, then repeat from arrow 3½ times more. Work one row of spaces and fasten off.

Make 736 gray pompons: cut a piece of carpet thread about 6″ long, place along edge of pencil. Wind rug yarn around pencil and carpet thread 16 times, winding in three layers. Cut off rug yarn, tie ends of carpet thread very tightly in a knot over wound yarn, slip yarn off pencil and cut loops opposite knot. Trim pompon ends evenly to about ½″ length. Tie a pompon on each bar between spaces with ends of carpet thread, making three or four tight knots.

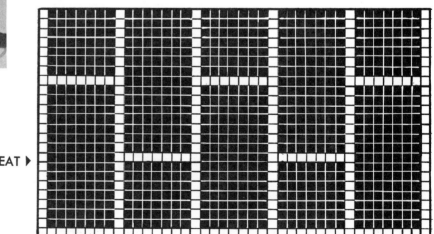

Crocheted Brick Rug, 25½″ x 43″, has "mortar" made of tied-on gray pompons.

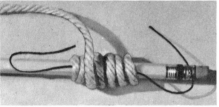

Method of making pompon

REPEAT ▶

164

Tufted Rugs

There are various methods of tufting: stitched and knotted, made in pompons, fringe or strip tufting. Combinations of colors or of shades of one color may be used; however, the pile is so deep a detailed pattern would not show up.

POODLE RUG

Cut circle of heavy muslin 2″ larger than size desired for finished rug. Mark off concentric circles every ½″ or ¾″ between center and outer edge. (Half-inch rows make a very full rug, but require more yarn.) Turn under 1″ hem and baste.

Cut several pieces of yarn at once, about 8″ or 10″ long. Use a long piece of yarn in rug needle, knot at end. Draw thread through to right side of

Deep pile rugs may be made from cotton rug yarn, from wool rug yarn, or from string. Tufts require a firm foundation of canvas or strong unbleached muslin, may be attached to rug mesh foundation or to a crocheted backing.

cloth at rug center. Double one of the pieces of yarn and sew it down firmly with a short stitch. Knot doubled strand over the stitch. Continue to work out from center, following marked circles and making knots about ¼″ apart.

When stitching thread ends, knot it on right side and leave end equal to length of knotted loops.

Rug may be backed with another muslin circle, backstitched to rug edge. Finish with a row of tufting around edge.

Tufted rug made in the stitched and knotted method.

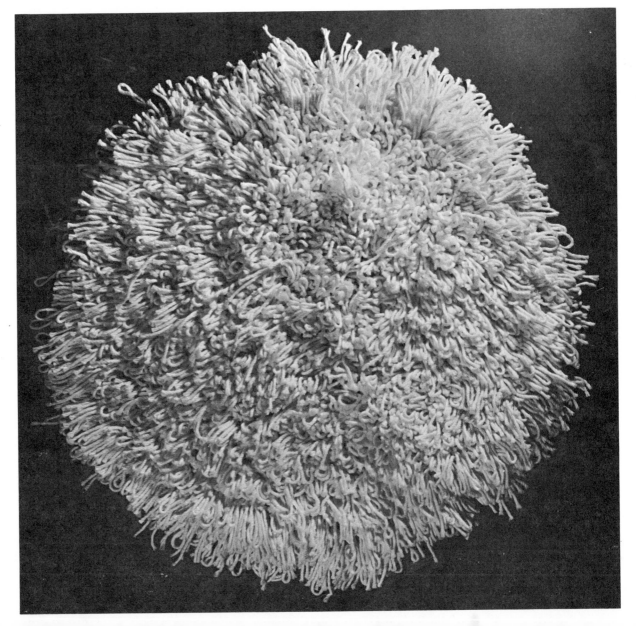

Fringe or strip tufts

For fringe or strip tufts, yarn is wrapped around a rectangular strip of cardboard, wide enough to have a stitching slot at center and an area for winding at both sides. A 4″ wide strip will have ½″ stitching slot and produce tufting 1½″ to 1¾″ deep.

Wind cardboard form with yarn (Fig. 1). Sew along center by hand with firm backstitch or on machine; use heavy duty thread. Cut along edges (Fig. 2); remove from form. Starting at outer edge and working toward center, stitch fringe to foundation (Fig. 3). Repeat until whole foundation is covered with closely placed strips of fringe.

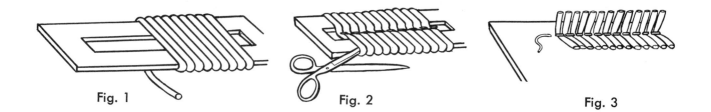

Fig. 1   Fig. 2   Fig. 3

Pompon tufts

For pompon tufts, yarn is wrapped around a doughnut-shaped piece of cardboard until the form is full, the size of "doughnut" determining depth of tufts. A 4½″ circle with ¾″ center hole is a good working size, but try variations of it to determine the size you prefer.

Wind form with yarn. Be sure to wind each pompon the same number of times so all tufts will be the same density. Tie cord around center by passing it through with yarn needle; tie cord (Fig. 1). Cut around edge (Fig. 2). Pull pompon from form. With yarn needle still attached to center anchoring cord, sew pompon to foundation, starting at outer edge and working toward center (Fig. 3).

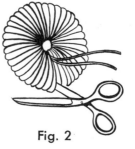

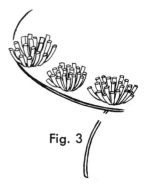

Fig. 1   Fig. 2   Fig. 3

Knitting

The origin of knitting, the art of pulling up loops of yarn from one needle to another, is lost in antiquity. Shepherds tending their flocks in ancient times were probably knitters. Many centuries ago, Arab traders knitted as they rode on their donkeys leading camel caravans east to India and west to Egypt. But in Europe, knitting was unknown before the 15th century. The invention of the process is generally attributed to the Spaniards though the Scots claim it and perhaps devised it independently.

Knitting was man's work until the invention of a commercial knitting machine in England in 1589 made it impractical for men to knit by hand. Women then became the hand knitters and have been plying their needles ever since. Today, women in many countries knit for a livelihood, each area producing designs and patterns which are distinctive. Some examples are shown in this knitting section in the authentic Tyrolean, Aran Isles and Norwegian sweaters. In America, women for the most part knit for themselves and their families for the sheer joy of knitting, for the sense of accomplishment that all creative handwork provides.

Knitting Needles and Accessories

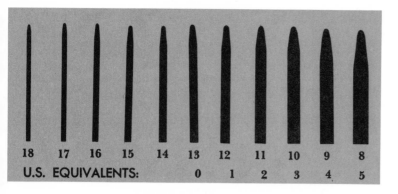

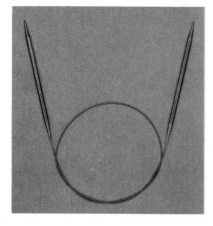

Single-pointed needles of aluminum, plastic, steel or wood, are used in pairs to knit back and forth in rows. For ease in working, choose a color to contrast with the yarn. Colored aluminum and plastic needles come in 7½", 10", 12", and 14" lengths in sizes varying from 1 to 5 in the shorter lengths, and 1 to 10½, 13 and 15 in the longer lengths. Colored aluminum needles also come in size 0. Wood needles, 14" long, come in sizes 10½ to 15; steel in 0 to 3. Flexible "jumper" needles, of nylon or nylon and aluminum, are available in 18" lengths in sizes 4 to 15.

Double-pointed (dp) needles are used in sets of four for tubular knitting, such as socks, mittens, or gloves. Of plastic, aluminum or nickel-plated steel, they come in 5", 7", and 10" lengths. Plastic dp needles come in sizes 1 to 15, aluminum in 0 to 8. Steel dp needles are measured on an English gauge and run from a high number, 18, for the finest to a low number, 8, for the largest. Single 3" needles in sizes 1 to 4 are available for making cable stitch.

Circular knitting needles of plastic, nylon or metal come in 9" lengths in sizes 0 to 4; 11" to 36" lengths are available in sizes 0 to 10½; the 36" length is also made in sizes 11, 13 and 15. Circular needles are used for knitting skirts without seams, circular yokes and other tubular pieces, but may be used for knitting back and forth in flat knitting, too.

Many accessories are available to the knitter: stitch holders to keep one section of knitting from ravelling while another section is being worked; counters to keep track of increases, decreases, stitches and rows; needle point guards to keep knitting on needles when not in use; bobbins or snap yarn holders to use when knitting in small areas of color; little ring markers; needle gauges to determine correct sizes of needles.

Knitting Lesson for Beginners

Knitting is based on two stitches, KNIT STITCH and PURL STITCH. Many knitted articles can be made with these two stitches alone. Before starting any knitted piece, it is necessary to CAST ON a certain number of stitches; that is, to place a series of loops on one needle so that you can work your first row of knitting. After you have finished your piece of knitting, it is necessary to BIND OFF your stitches so that they will not ravel out. On the following pages, in step-by-step illustrations and directions, you will be shown how to cast on, knit, purl and bind off.

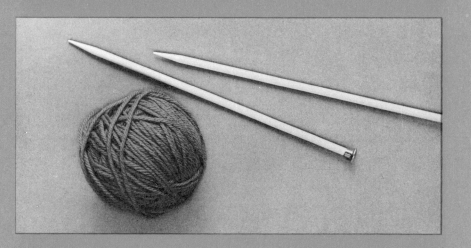

TO CAST ON
WITH ONE NEEDLE

For your practice piece, use a ball of knitting worsted and a pair of knitting needles No. 8.

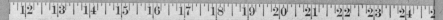

With a tape measure or yardstick, measure off about 20 inches from end of yarn to cast on 20 stitches.

At this point, bring yarn end from ball over left index finger. Bring yarn end under and over thumb.

Hold one needle in right hand. Insert point of needle from left to right through the loop on thumb.

Grasp both yarn strands with three fingers of left hand. Insert needle under strand on index finger.

With needle, bring this strand toward you and through loop on thumb. Remove thumb from loop.

Place thumb under strand which is nearest to you. Pull gently until slipknot is close to needle.

With thumb back, bring needle in front of thumb and to left of the strand, forming a loop on thumb.

Still grasping both strands of the yarn, insert needle from left to right up through loop on thumb.

172

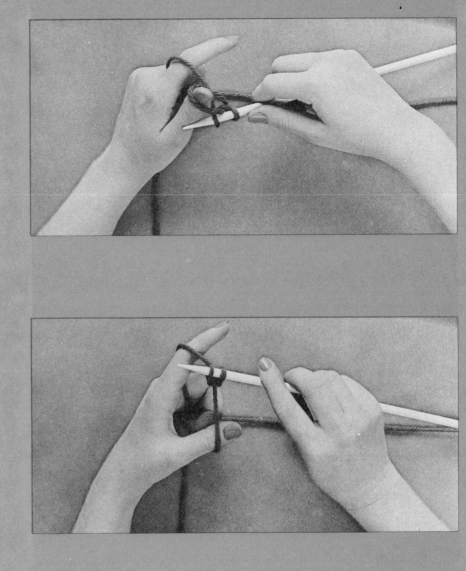

Pick up strand on index finger, bring it through loop on thumb, removing thumb at the same time.

Place thumb under front strand as before and tighten second stitch close to first stitch on needle.

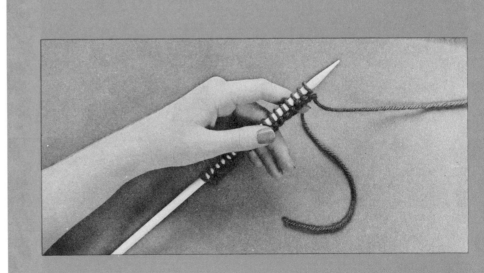

Repeat this procedure until you have cast on 20 stitches. Place the casting-on needle in left hand.

TO KNIT

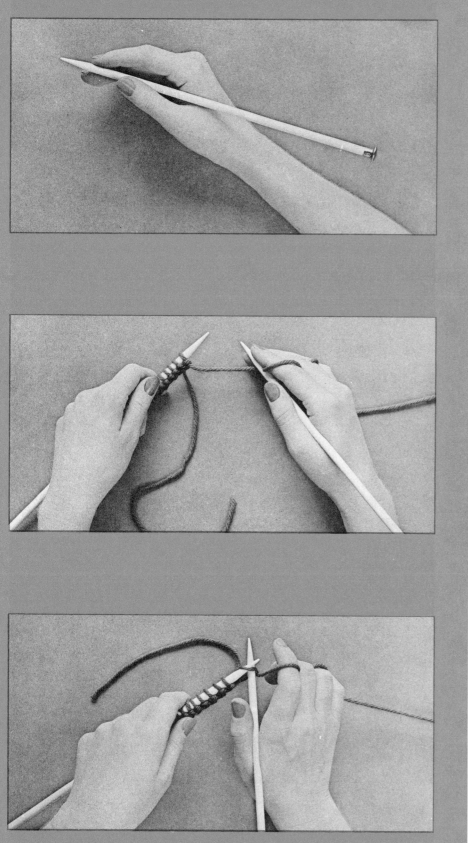

The needle with which you will knit the stitches should be held in the right hand like a pencil.

Weave yarn over index finger of right hand, under middle finger, over third, under little finger.

To knit the first stitch, insert right needle ·into front of stitch on left needle from left to right.

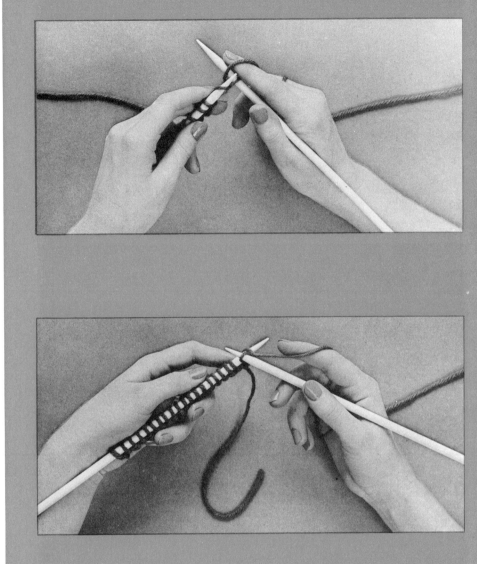

Point of right needle is now behind left point. Bring yarn under and over point of right needle.

Bring point of right needle down and under left needle to front, thus drawing yarn through stitch.

Slip the loop through which you drew yarn off left needle. One knit stitch is now on right needle.

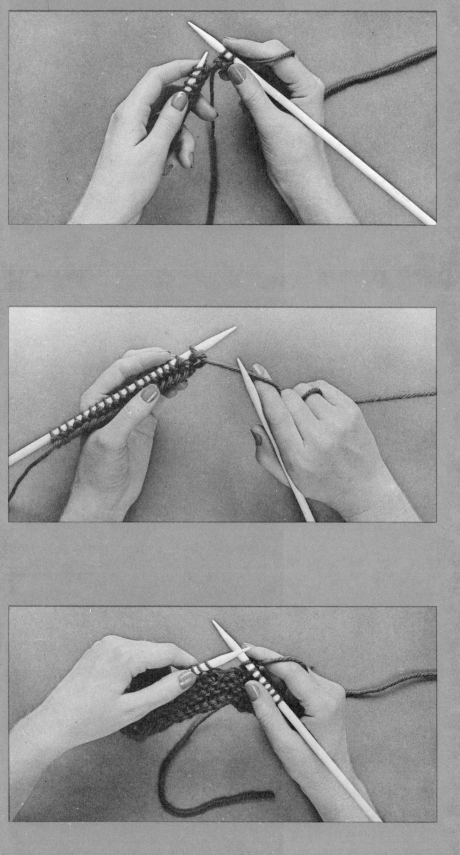

Insert right needle into the next stitch and knit another stitch. Knit all 20 stitches in same way.

When row is finished, turn work around and place it in left hand. Work another row of knit stitch.

Continue to knit rows of stitches. Plain knitting is called garter stitch and has a ridged effect.

TO PURL

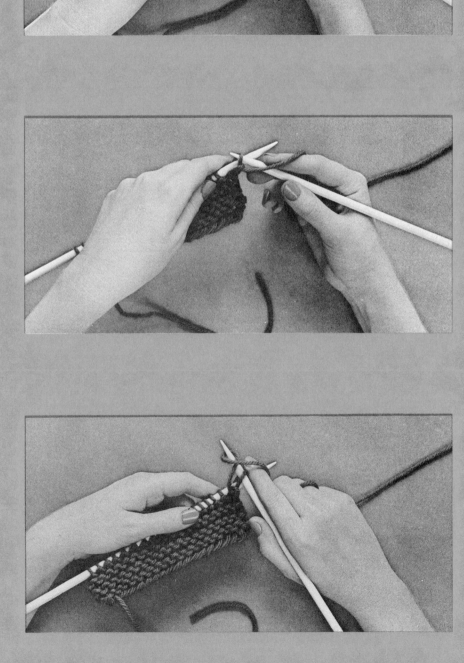

To make a purl stitch, bring yarn which comes from first stitch to the front of your right needle.

Insert point of right needle from right to left through the front of first stitch on left needle.

Bring yarn back between points of needles, then bring it down under point of right needle to front.

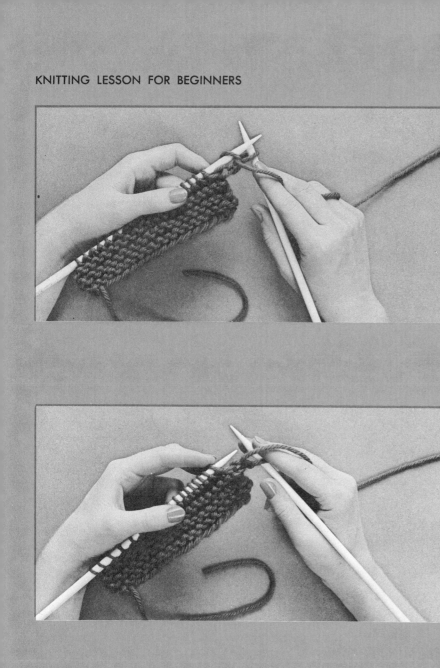

Bring point of right needle back through the first stitch. Right needle is now behind left needle.

Slip the loop through which you drew yarn off left needle. One purl stitch is on right needle.

Continue across row until you have purled all 20 stitches. Work the following row in knit stitch.

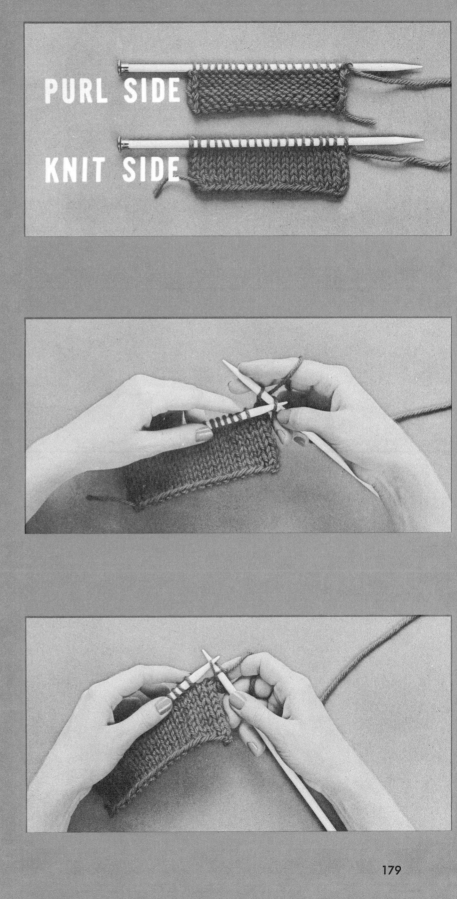

Make a practice piece of stockinette stitch, alternating one row
of knitting, one row of purling.

TO BIND OFF

Knit the first two stitches. Insert
left needle from left to right
through front of first stitch.

Lift the first stitch over the second stitch and over tip of needle.
One stitch has been bound off.

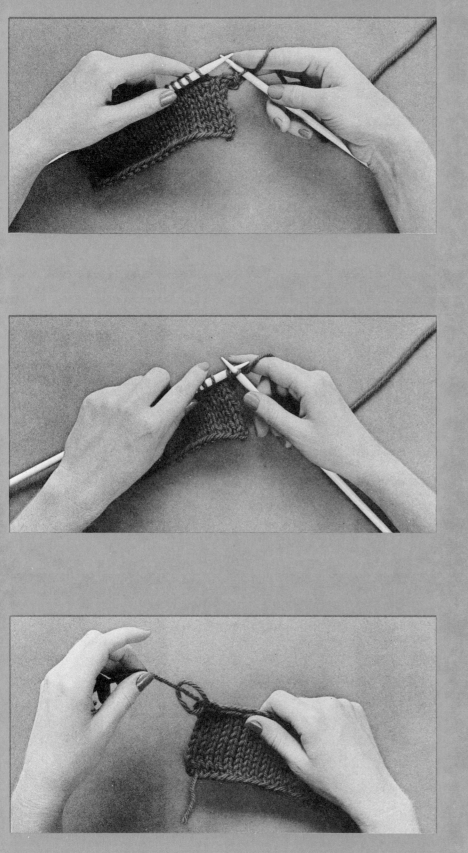

One stitch remains on right needle. To bind off this stitch, knit another stitch onto right needle.

Again lift first stitch over second stitch and off right needle. Two stitches have been bound off.

Continue across until all stitches are bound off. One loop remains. Cut yarn, pull end through loop.

OTHER METHODS OF CASTING ON STITCHES: There are several ways to cast on in addition to the method given in the Knitting Lesson for Beginners.

The simplest one-needle method is shown in Figures 1-5. Make a slip loop on needle; Fig. 1. Loop yarn around left thumb; Fig. 2. Insert needle in loop; Fig. 3. Remove thumb; Fig. 4. Pull yarn to tighten stitch; Fig. 5. This method is suitable if the cast-on edge will not show or receive wear.

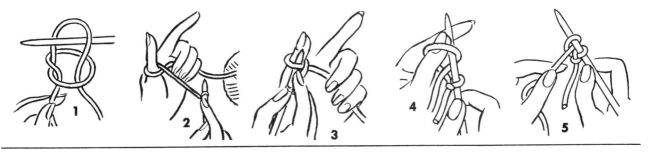

Another one-needle method is shown in Figures 6 and 7. Start with a slip loop the same number of inches from end of yarn as number of stitches to be cast on; e.g. 30 stitches, 30″ from end of yarn. Hold needle with slip loop in right hand. * With short end of yarn make a loop on left thumb by bringing yarn up around thumb from left to right; Fig. 6. Insert needle in this loop from left to right; Fig. 7. Bring yarn from ball under and over needle, draw through loop on thumb, tighten short end with left hand. Repeat from * for required number of stitches. This method gives the same sturdy edge as method shown in Knitting for Beginners.

The two-needle method for casting on makes a firm knitted edge. First make a slip loop over left needle. * Pass right needle through loop from left to right, yarn under and over right needle. Draw yarn through loop and transfer loop on right needle to left needle by inserting left needle in loop from right to left; Fig. 8. Repeat from * for desired number of stitches. This method is used when stitches must be added to the side of your knitting as, for example, when sleeves are knitted with the body of the garment. In this case, the first added stitch is made in the end stitch of your knitting.

TO CAST ON STITCHES LOOSELY: For most garments, it is best to cast on stitches loosely. If you tend to cast on tightly, use a larger needle for casting on than for knitting the garment.

TO BIND OFF STITCHES: Binding off is usually done in the pattern stitch of the garment; that is, each stitch to be bound off is worked in the way it would be if you were not binding off. Unless the directions read "bind off tightly," or "bind off loosely," the bound-off edge should be the same tension as the knitting. If you tend to bind off too tightly, use a larger needle for binding off than for knitting the garment. On a high ribbed neckline, it is absolutely essential to bind off loosely.

6

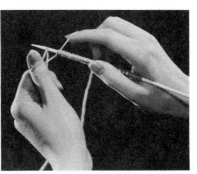

7

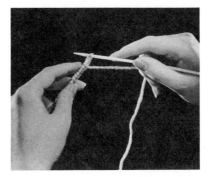

8

TO INCREASE ONE STITCH: Method 1: Knit 1 stitch in the usual way but do not slip it off left needle. Bring right needle behind left needle, insert it from right to left in same stitch (called "the back of the stitch") and make another knit stitch. Slip stitch off left needle. To increase 1 stitch on the purl side, purl 1 stitch in the usual way but do not slip it off left needle. Bring yarn between needles to back, knit 1 stitch in back of same stitch.

Method 2: Pick up horizontal strand between stitch just knitted and next stitch, place it on left needle. Knit 1 stitch in back of this strand, thus twisting it.

Method 3: Place right needle behind left needle. Insert right needle in stitch *below* next stitch, knit this stitch; then knit stitch above it in the usual way.

YARN OVER: This is an increase stitch. It is used primarily in lace patterns or for the openwork increases on raglan sleeve shapings.

To Make a Yarn Over When Knitting: Bring yarn under right needle to front, then over needle to back, ready to knit next stitch.

To Make a Yarn Over When Purling: Bring yarn up over right needle to back, then under needle to front, ready to purl next stitch.

TO SLIP A STITCH: Insert needle in stitch as if to knit stitch (unless directions read "as if to purl") and slip stitch from left needle to right needle without knitting or purling it.

TO DECREASE ONE STITCH: On the right side of work, knit 2 stitches together either through the front of the stitches (the decrease slants to the right) or through the back of the stitches (the decrease slants to the left). On the purl side, purl 2 stitches together.

PSSO (pass slip stitch over) is a decrease stitch. When directions say "sl 1, k 1, psso," slip first stitch, knit next stitch, bring slip stitch over knit stitch as in binding off.

ABBREVIATIONS USED IN KNITTING DIRECTIONS

k—knit	psso—pass slip stitch over
p—purl	inc—increase
st—stitch	dec—decrease
sts—stitches	beg—beginning
yo—yarn over	pat—pattern
sl—slip	lp—loop
sk—skip	MC—main color
tog—together	CC—contrasting color
rnd—round	dp—double-pointed

THE USE OF ASTERISKS IN DIRECTIONS: The asterisk (*) is used in directions to mark the beginning and end of any part of the directions that is to be repeated one or more times. For example, "* k 9, p 3, repeat from * 4 times" means to work directions after first * until second * is reached, then go back to first * 4 times more. Work 5 times in all.

THE USE OF PARENTHESES IN DIRECTIONS: When parentheses ( ) are used to show repetition, work directions in parentheses as many times as specified. For example "(k 9, p 3) 4 times" means to do what is in ( ) 4 times altogether.

TO TIE IN A NEW STRAND OF YARN: Join a new ball of yarn at beginning of a row by making a slipknot with new strand around working strand. See illustration. Move slipknot up to edge of work and continue with new ball. If yarn cannot be joined at beginning of row, splice yarn by threading new yarn into a tapestry needle and weaving it into the end of the old yarn for about 3″, leaving short end on wrong side to be cut off after a few rows have been knitted. If the yarn cannot be spliced (e.g. nubby yarn), leave a 4″ end of yarn, work next stitch with new yarn leaving a 4″ end. Work a few rows, tie ends together and weave them into work.

MULTIPLE: In pattern stitches, multiple means the number of stitches required for one pattern. The number of stitches on needle should be evenly divisible by the multiple. If pattern is a multiple of 6 stitches, number of stitches to be worked might be 180, 186, 192, etc. If directions say "multiple of 6 sts plus 2," 2 extra stitches are required: 182, 188, 194, etc.

TYING IN A NEW STRAND

GAUGE: All knitting directions for garments include a stitch gauge. The stitch gauge gives the number of stitches to the inch with the yarn and needles recommended in the pattern stitch of the garment. The directions for each size are based on the given gauge. The gauge (or tension) at which you work controls the size of each finished piece. It is therefore essential to work to the gauge given for each garment if you want the garment to fit. To test your gauge, cast on 20 or 30 stitches, using the needles specified. Work in the *pattern stitch* for 3″. Smooth out your swatch and pin it down. Measure across 2″ and place pins 2″ apart as shown. Count number of stitches between pins. If you have *more* stitches to the inch than directions specify, you are knitting too tightly; use larger needles. If you have *fewer* stitches to the inch, you are knitting too loosely; use smaller needles.

Most patterns give a row gauge too. Although the proper length of a finished garment does not usually depend upon the row gauge (directions usually give lengths in inches rather than rows), in some patterns it is important to have the proper row gauge too.

TO PICK UP DROPPED STITCH: Use a crochet hook. In stockinette stitch, from knit side of work, insert hook through loop of dropped stitch from front to back of work, hook facing upward. *Pull horizontal thread of row above stitch through loop on hook; repeat from * to top.

TO RAVEL OUT KNITTING: When it is necessary to ravel work and then pick up stitches again, remove needles from work. Rip down to row of error. Rip this row stitch by stitch, placing each stitch (as if to purl) on a fine needle. Then knit these stitches onto correct size needle.

TO PICK UP AND KNIT STITCHES ALONG EDGE: From right side of work, insert needle into edge of work, put yarn around needle, finish as a knit stitch. When picking up on bound-off or cast-on edge, pick up and knit 1 stitch in each stitch (going through 2 loops at top of each bound-off stitch). On front or side edges, pick up and knit 1 stitch in each knot formed on edge of each row.

TO CHANGE FROM ONE COLOR TO ANOTHER: When changing from one color to another, whether working on right or wrong side, pick up the new strand from underneath dropped strand. This prevents a hole in your work. Carry the unused color loosely across back of work. Illustration shows wrong side of work with light strand being picked up under dropped strand in position to be purled.

MEASURING YOUR GAUGE

TO COUNT STITCHES WHEN BINDING OFF: At the beginning of a row, when directions read "bind off 7 sts," knit 2 stitches; * insert left needle under first stitch on right needle and lift it over the second stitch. This is 1 stitch bound off. Knit 1 more stitch and repeat from * 6 times—7 stitches bound off (8 stitches have been knitted to bind off 7 stitches but 1 stitch, already knitted, is on right needle).

When binding off within a row (as for buttonholes), knit the required number of stitches to point of binding off, then knit next 2 stitches to bind off first stitch. Bind off required number of stitches (1 stitch is already knitted after bound-off stitches). When directions read "knit until 7 sts after bound-off stitches," this means to knit 6 more stitches or until there are 7 stitches after bound-off stitches.

TO INSERT MARKERS: When directions read "sl a marker on needle," put a small safety pin, paper clip, or commercial ring marker on needle. In working, always slip marker from one needle to another. To mark a row or stitch, tie contrasting thread around end of row or stitch.

TO MEASURE WORK: Spread piece on flat surface to require width, measure length at center.

WORK EVEN: This term means to work in same stitch without increasing or decreasing.

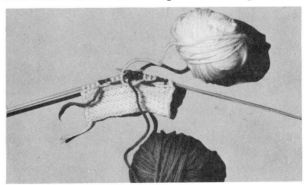

CHANGING COLORS

KNITTING LEFT-HANDED

HINTS FOR THE LEFT-HANDED: There is no simple answer to the question asked by left-handed people, "How can I learn to knit?" Here are some suggestions:

If you are not strongly left-handed and can do some things with your right hand, you should first try to knit in the way shown in "Knitting Lesson for Beginners." Since knitting is basically a two-handed process, you may be able to master knitting by the conventional method. The awkwardness you experience may well be simply that of a beginner, rather than caused by your left-handedness. If you can learn to knit by this method, you will be spared some difficulties in reading directions.

If this method does not work for you, you might try the so-called "German" method. This is right-handed knitting too, in the sense that the needle in the right hand knits the stitches from the needle in the left hand. The difference is that the *yarn* is held by the left hand. The yarn is not thrown around the needle as it is in the "Knitting Lesson for Beginners," but is pulled through the stitch by the right needle. To hold the yarn in your left hand, weave it through your fingers as follows: under the little finger, over the ring finger, under the middle finger, over the index finger and once more around the index finger. Grasp both needles the same, with your hands over the needles. To make a knit stitch, insert right needle in stitch from left to right as shown in "Knitting Lesson for Beginners," put needle over strand which comes from left index finger and pull loop through stitch. To make a purl stitch, insert right needle in stitch from right to left as shown in "Knitting Lesson for Beginners," bring strand over and under point of right needle to front, place right thumb on strand to keep it from sliding off needle and push right needle under left needle to back. Many right-handed knitters use this method. It is faster than the method usually taught today because there is less motion of the hands involved. The disadvantages are: the tension is not as easy to control. Flat ribbon knitting cannot be done by this method.

If you find the "German" method too awkward for you, you can learn to knit left-handed by placing a mirror to each step given in the "Knitting Lesson for Beginners" and substituting the word "left" for "right" and "right" for "left" in every case.

Some left-handed knitters have learned to knit by sitting opposite a right-handed knitter and copying all motions with the hand directly opposite.

In reading directions, the following problems will arise: Wherever the word "left" is used, substitute the word "right" and vice versa. When a garment has two fronts, therefore, and directions are given for the left front, you will be working on the right front. In a misses' cardigan or coat, where there are button-holes on the right front, you will either have to figure out from the right front directions how to make the buttonholes, or have them made after the garment is finished.

In men's cardigans, directions for the right front are usually given first. You will be working on the left front, on which the buttonholes should be made.

If the sleeves of a garment are shaped differently (if the back of the sleeve is different from the front), when directions are given for the right sleeve, you will be working on the left sleeve.

If a pattern stitch forms a diagonal pattern, your diagonal lines will run counter to the stitch pictured.

INTERCHANGING YARNS

TO SUBSTITUTE ONE YARN FOR AN-OTHER: When a knitted garment is designed, the yarn in which it is made is an integral part of the design. The thickness of the yarn in relation to the pattern stitch is important: the same pattern stitch would not be used for a bulky jacket and a light-weight cardigan. The texture of the yarn in relation to the pattern stitch is also important: pattern stitches for hairy, looped, slubbed, or tweed yarns tend to be simpler than pattern stitches for the smooth yarns. In general, therefore, it is advisable to use the yarn called for in the directions.

If you wish to substitute a yarn choose one as similar as possible to the specified yarn. Be sure you can work to the proper gauge in the substitute yarn. If your gauge is not correct, the garment will be too big or too small. Be sure you like the texture of the pattern stitch in the new yarn. It may be too limp or too stiff even though the gauge is correct.

Yarns have different degrees of elasticity, depending upon the fiber content. Care should be taken in substituting cotton or linen for wool as these fibers have less elasticity and additional stitches are needed.

Generally, the thicker a yarn is the less yardage it has per ounce and the more ounces it takes to cover the same area. That is why more ounces of bulky yarn are required to make a sweater than ounces of finer yarn. If you wish to substitute a thicker yarn than pattern calls for, even though you can work to the stitch gauge, you will need more ounces of yarn. Yarns of the same type, thickness and fiber content have approximately the same yardage per ounce. In interchanging these yarns, the same number of ounces is usually required.

If you wish to make a garment in an entirely different weight of yarn, this is, in effect, a new design. The design should be re-planned and the directions rewritten to the new stitch gauge.

RIBBING: Most knitted sweaters use ribbing around cuffs, lower edge and neckline. Ribbing holds in these edges to fit more snugly than the rest of the sweater. Ribbing combines knitting and purling in the same row. For example, cast on a multiple of 4 sts. * K 2, p 2, repeat from * across row. Repeat this row. Various multiples of knit and purl stitches may be used to form different rib patterns.

1. RIBBING VARIATION (Multiple of 2 sts):
Row 1: * Yo, sl 1 as if to p, k 1, repeat from * across.

Row 2: * Yo, sl 1 as if to p, k 2 tog (sl-st and yo-st of last row), repeat from * across. Repeat row 2 for pattern.

To Bind Off: Omit yo, p 1, k 2 tog as you bind off.

2. "MISTAKE STITCH" RIBBING (Multiple of 4 sts plus 3):
Row 1: * K 2, p 2, repeat from * across, end k 2, p 1. Repeat this row for pattern. Bind off in pattern.

3. SLIPPED STITCH RIDGES (Multiple of 6 sts plus 5):
Row 1 (right side): K 5, * yarn in back, sl 1 as if to p, k 5, repeat from * across.

Row 2: P 5, * yarn in front, sl 1 as if to p, p 5, repeat from * across.

Row 3: Repeat row 1.

Row 4: Purl. Repeat these 4 rows for pattern. Bind off on last row of pattern.

SEED STITCH or MOSS STITCH is worked on an uneven number of stitches. On the first row, * k 1, p 1, repeat from * across, end k 1. Repeat this row.

4. DOUBLE SEED STITCH (Multiple of 4 sts):
Rows 1 and 2: * K 2, p 2, repeat from * across.

Rows 3 and 4: * P 2, k 2, repeat from * across. Repeat these 4 rows for pattern. Bind off in pattern.

RIBBING VARIATION

"MISTAKE STITCH" RIBBING

SLIPPED STITCH RIDGES

DOUBLE SEED STITCH

SEED AND STOCKINETTE STITCH RIBS

BASIC CABLE STITCH

5. SEED AND STOCKINETTE STITCH RIBS (Multiple of 5 sts):
Row 1 (right side): Knit.
Row 2: * K 2, p 3, repeat from * across. Repeat these 2 rows for pattern. Bind off in pattern.

6. GULL STITCH (Multiple of 7 sts plus 1):
Row 1 (right side): P 1, * k 6, p 1, repeat from * across.
Row 2 (wrong side): K 1, * p 6, k 1, repeat from * across.
Row 3: P 1, * k 2, yarn in back, sl next 2 sts as if to p, k 2, p 1, repeat from * across.
Row 4: K 1, * p 2, yarn in front, sl next 2 sts as if to p, p 2, k 1, repeat from * across.
Row 5: P 1, * sl as if to p next 2 sts to dp needle, hold in back, k next sl-st, then k sts from dp needle (right cross st made), sl next sl-st to dp needle, hold in front, k next 2 sts, then k st from dp needle (left cross st made), p 1, repeat from * across. Repeat rows 2-5 for pattern.
To Bind Off: Omit pat, k the k sts, p the p sts as you bind off; work all other sts in pattern.

7. BASIC CABLE STITCH (Multiple of 11 sts plus 5): Row 1 (right side): P 5, * k 6, p 5, repeat from * across.
Row 2: K 5, * p 6, k 5, repeat from * across.
Rows 3-10: Repeat rows 1 and 2.
Row 11 (cable row): P 5, * sl next 3 sts on a dp needle, hold dp needle in back of work, k next 3 sts; k the 3 sts from the dp needle without twisting sts (see detail drawing), p 5, repeat from * across. Repeat rows 2-11 for pattern. Repeat rows 2-10 after last cable row. Bind off on next row, knitting the k sts and purling the p sts.

8. SIMPLE CABLES AND RIBBING (Multiple of 12 sts plus 2):

Rows 1, 3, 5 (right side): * K 2, p 2, k 6, p 2, repeat from * across, end k 2.

Rows 2, 4, 6: * P 2, k 2, p 6, k 2, repeat from * across, end p 2.

Row 7: * K 2, p 2, sl next 3 sts as if to p on a dp needle, hold in front, k next 3 sts, then k sts from dp needle (cable made), p 2, repeat from * across, end k 2. Repeat rows 2-7 for pattern. Bind off in pattern.

9. PLAIT STITCH (Multiple of 12 sts plus 3):

Row 1 (right side): * P 3, k 9, repeat from * across row, end p 3.

Row 2: * K 3, p 9, repeat from * across, end k 3.

Row 3: * P 3, sl 3 sts on dp needle, hold in back of work, k next 3 sts, then k 3 sts from dp needle, k 3, repeat from * across row, end p 3.

Row 4: Repeat row 2.

Row 5: Repeat row 1.

Row 6: Repeat row 2.

Row 7: * P 3, k 3, sl 3 sts on dp needle, hold in front of work, k 3 sts, then k 3 sts from dp needle, repeat from * across row, p 3.

Row 8: Repeat row 2.

Row 9: Repeat row 1.

Row 10: Repeat row 2. Repeat rows 3-10 for pattern. Bind off in pattern.

10. DOUBLE CABLES (Multiple of 12 sts plus 4): Rows 1, 3, 5, 7 (right side): * P 4, k 8, repeat from * across, end p 4.

Rows 2, 4, 6, 8: * K 4, p 8, repeat from * across, end k 4.

Row 9: * P 4, sl next 2 sts as if to p on a dp needle, hold in back, k next 2 sts, then k sts from dp needle, sl next 2 sts on a dp needle, hold in front, k next 2 sts, then k sts from dp needle, repeat from * across, end p 4. Repeat rows 2-9 for pattern. Bind off in pattern.

11. MOCK CABLE PATTERN (Multiple of 8 sts plus 3):

Rows 1 and 3 (right side): P 3, * k 2, p 1, k 2, p 3, repeat from * across.

Rows 2 and 4: K 3, * p 2, k 1, p 2, k 3, repeat from * across.

Row 5: P 3, * sk 1 st, k in front lp of next st, k in front lp of skipped st (cable), sl both sts off needle, p 1, cable on next 2 sts, p 3, repeat from * across. Repeat rows 2-5 for pattern. Bind off in pattern.

SIMPLE CABLES AND RIBBING

PLAIT STITCH

DOUBLE CABLES

MOCK CABLE PATTERN

BASKET WEAVE STITCH

HERRINGBONE STITCH

POPCORNS ON STOCKINETTE STITCH

TRINITY STITCH

12. BASKET WEAVE STITCH (Multiple of 10 sts plus 3):

Row 1 (right side): * K 3, p 7, repeat from * across row, end k 3.

Row 2: * P 3, k 7, repeat from * across row, end p 3.

Row 3: Repeat row 1.

Row 4: P across row.

Row 5: P 5, * k 3, p 7, repeat from * across to last 8 sts, k 3, p 5.

Row 6: K 5, * p 3, k 7, repeat from * across row to last 8 sts, p 3, k 5.

Row 7: Repeat row 5.

Row 8: P across row. Repeat rows 1-8 for pattern. Bind off in pattern.

13. HERRINGBONE STITCH (Multiple of 7 sts plus 1):

Row 1 (wrong side): P across row.

Row 2: * K 2 tog, k 2, inc 1 st in next st (to inc, place point of right needle behind left needle, insert point of right needle from top down through st below next st, k this st, then k st above it), k 2, repeat from * across, end k 3.

Row 3: P across row.

Row 4: K 3, * inc 1 st in next st as in row 2, k 2, k 2 tog, k 2, repeat from * across, end k 2 tog. Repeat these 4 rows for pattern.

14. POPCORNS ON STOCKINETTE STITCH (Multiple of 4 sts plus 3):

Row 1 (right side): Knit.

Row 2: Purl.

Row 3: Knit.

Row 4 (wrong side): P 3, * in next st (k 1, p 1, k 1, p 1) loosely, p 3, repeat from * across.

Row 5: K 3, * sl next 3 sts as if to p, k next st, pass separately 3rd, 2nd and first of the sl sts over last k st, k 3, repeat from * across.

Rows 6 and 7: Repeat rows 2 and 3.

Row 8: P 1, * in next st (k 1, p 1, k 1, p 1) loosely, p 3, repeat from * across, end last repeat p 1.

Row 9: K 1, * sl next 3 sts as if to p, k next st, pass the sl sts over k st (as in row 5), k 3, repeat from * across, end last repeat k 1. Repeat rows 2-9 for pattern. Bind off on k or p row.

15. TRINITY STITCH (Multiple of 4 sts):

Row 1 (right side): Purl.

Row 2: * (K 1, p 1, k 1) all in one st, p next 3 sts tog, repeat from * across.

Row 3: Purl.

Row 4: * P 3 sts tog, (k 1, p 1, k 1) in next st, repeat from * across. Repeat these 4 rows for pattern. Bind off on the right side.

16. HONEYCOMB STITCH (Multiple of 2 sts):
Row 1 (right side): Purl.
Row 2: Purl.
Row 3: * Yo, sl 1, k 1, psso, repeat from * across.
Row 4: Purl. Repeat these 4 rows for pattern. Bind off on a purl row.

17. THREE-DIMENSIONAL HONEYCOMB (Multiple of 2 sts): When slipping sts, hold yarn in back, sl all sts as if to p.
Row 1 (wrong side): * K 1, yo, sl 1, repeat from * across. Yo and sl st count as 1 st.
Row 2: K 1, * sl yo st, k 2, repeat from * across, end sl yo st, k 1.
Row 3: * Yo, sl 1, k tog the yo and next k st of last row as 1 st, repeat from * across.
Row 4 (right side): * K 2, sl yo st, repeat from * across.
Row 5: * K tog the yo and next k st of last row as 1 st, yo, sl 1, repeat from * across.
Row 6: K 1, * sl yo st, k 2, repeat from * across, end sl yo st, k 1. Repeat rows 3-6 for pattern stitch. To bind off, bind off in k on wrong side of pattern, knitting tog the yo and k 1 of last row as 1 st. Or, bind off in k on right side of pattern, knitting tog the k 1 and yo of last row as 1 st.

18. QUAKER STITCH OR RIDGING: This stitch forms horizontal ribs. It consists of stripes of stockinette stitch alternated with stripes (ridges) of reverse stockinette stitch. For example:
Row 1 (right side): Knit.
Row 2: Purl.
Row 3: Knit.
Row 4: Purl.
Row 5 (right side): Purl.
Row 6: Knit.
Row 7: Purl.
Row 8: Knit. Repeat rows 1-8 for pattern stitch.

19. GARTER STITCH AND LACE RIBS:
Rows 1-6: Knit.
Row 7: * K 1, yo, repeat from * across, end k 1.
Row 8: * K 1, drop yo off needle, repeat from * across, end k 1.
Row 9-14: Knit. Repeat rows 7-14 for pattern. Bind off on last row of pattern.

HONEYCOMB STITCH

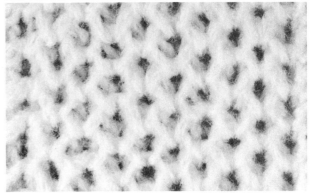

THREE-DIMENSIONAL HONEYCOMB

QUAKER STITCH OR RIDGING

GARTER STITCH AND LACE RIBS

EYELET PATTERN STITCH

SMALL-PATTERNED LACE STITCH

LACE STRIPES

OPENWORK DIAMONDS

20. EYELET PATTERN STITCH (Multiple of 8 sts): Row 1 (right side): Knit.

Row 2 and All Even Rows: Purl.

Row 3: * K 6, yo, k 2 tog, repeat from * across. **Row 5:** Knit.

Row 7: K 2, * yo, k 2 tog, k 6, repeat from * across, end last repeat k 4. **Row 8:** Purl. Repeat rows 1-8 for pattern. Bind off on a purl row.

21. SMALL-PATTERNED LACE STITCH (Multiple of 6 sts plus 2): Sl all sl sts as if to k.

Row 1 and All Odd Rows (wrong side): Purl.

Row 2 (right side): * Yo, k 3, yo, sl 1 as if to k, k 2 tog, psso, repeat from * across, k 2.

Row 4: * Yo, sl 1, k 1, psso, k 1, k 2 tog, yo, k 1, repeat from * across, end yo, sl 1, k 1, psso.

Row 6: K 1, * yo, sl 1, k 2 tog, psso, yo, k 3, repeat from * across, end last repeat k 4.

Row 8: * K 2 tog, yo, k 1, yo, sl 1, k 1, psso, k 1, repeat from * across, end last repeat k 3.

Row 10: K 4, * yo, sl 1, k 2 tog, psso, yo, k 3, repeat from * across, end last repeat k 1. Repeat rows 3-10 for pattern. Bind off on a purl row.

22. LACE STRIPES (Multiple of 11 sts plus 3):
Row 1 (right side): * K 3, yo, sl 1, k 2 tog, psso, yo, p 2, yo, sl 1, k 2 tog, psso, yo, repeat from * across, end k 3.

Row 2: P 6, k 2, * p 9, k 2, repeat from * across, end p 6.

Row 3: K 6, p 2, * k 9, p 2, repeat from * across, end k 6. **Row 4:** Repeat row 2. Repeat these 4 rows for pattern. Bind off on last row of pattern.

23. OPENWORK DIAMONDS (Multiple of 10 sts): Row 1 and All Odd Rows (wrong side): Purl.

Row 2 (right side): K 3, * yo, sl 1 as if to p (throughout pattern), k 2 tog, psso, yo, k 7, repeat from * across, end last repeat k 4.

Row 4: K 2 tog, k 2, * yo, k 1, yo, k 2, sl 1, k 1, psso, k 1, k 2 tog, k 2, repeat from * across to last 6 sts, yo, k 1, yo, k 2, sl 1, k 1, psso, k 1.

Row 6: * K 2 tog, k 1, yo, k 3, yo, k1, sl 1, k 1, psso, k 1, repeat from * across.

Row 8: K 2 tog, * yo, k 5, yo, sl 1, k 1, psso, k 1, k 2 tog, repeat from * across to last 8 sts, yo, k 5, yo, sl 1, k 1, psso, k 1.

Row 10: K 1, yo, * k 7, yo, sl 1, k 2 tog, psso, yo, repeat from * across to last 9 sts, k 7, yo, sl 1, k 1, psso—1 extra st.

Row 12: K 1, * yo, k 2, sl 1, k 1, psso, k 1, k 2 tog, k 2, yo, k 1, repeat from * across.

Row 14: K 2 tog, * yo, k 1, sl 1, k 1, psso, k 1, k 2 tog, k 1, yo, k 3, repeat from * across, end last repeat k 2. Extra st taken off.

Row 16: K 2, * yo, sl 1, k 1, psso, k 1, k 2 tog, yo, k 5, repeat from * across, end last repeat k 3. Repeat these 16 rows for pattern. Bind off on p row.

24. LEAF-PATTERNED LACE STITCH (Multiple of 12 sts plus 1):
Row 1 and All Odd Rows (wrong side): Purl.
Row 2 (right side): * K 1, yo, sl 1, k 1, psso, k 7, k 2 tog, yo, repeat from * across, end k 1.
Row 4: * K 1, yo, k 1, sl 1, k 1, psso, k 5, k 2 tog, k 1, yo, repeat from * across, end k 1.
Row 6: * K 1, yo, k 2, sl 1, k 1, psso, k 3, k 2 tog, k 2, yo, repeat from * across, end k 1.
Row 8: * K 1, yo, k 3, sl 1, k 1, psso, k 1, k 2 tog, k 3, yo, repeat from * across, end k 1.
Row 10: * K 1, yo, k 4, sl 1, k 2 tog, psso, k 4, yo, repeat from * across, end k 1.
Row 12: K 4, k 2 tog, * yo, k 1, yo, sl 1, k 1, psso, k 7, k 2 tog, repeat from * across to last 7 sts, yo, k 1, yo, sl 1, k 1, psso, k 4.
Row 14: K 3, k 2 tog, k 1, * yo, k 1, yo, k 1, sl 1, k 1, psso, k 5, k 2 tog, k 1, repeat from * across to last 7 sts, yo, k 1, yo, k 1, sl 1, k 1, psso, k 3.
Row 16: K 2, k 2 tog, k 2, * yo, k 1, yo, k 2, sl 1, k 1, psso, k 3, k 2 tog, k 2, repeat from * across to last 7 sts, yo, k 1, yo, k 2, sl 1, k 1, psso, k 2.
Row 18: K 1, k 2 tog, k 3, * yo, k 1, yo, k 3, sl 1, k 1, psso, k 1, k 2 tog, k 3, repeat from * across to last 7 sts, yo, k 1, yo, k 3, sl 1, k 1, psso, k 1.
Row 20: K 2 tog, k 4, * yo, k 1, yo, k 4, sl 1, k 2 tog, psso, k 4, repeat from * across to last 7 sts, yo, k 1, yo, k 4, sl 1, k 1, psso. Repeat these 20 rows for pattern. Bind off on a purl row.

25. SHELL LACE PATTERN (Multiple of 11 sts plus 5):
Row 1 and All Odd Rows (wrong side): Purl.
Row 2 (right side): * K 1, yo, k 2, sl 1, k 2 tog, psso, k 5, yo, repeat from * across to last 5 sts, k 1, yo, k 2, sl 1, k 1, psso.
Row 4: K 2, * yo, k 1, sl 1, k 2 tog, psso, k 4, yo, k 3, repeat from *, end yo, k 1, sl 1, k 1, psso.
Row 6: K 3, * yo, sl 1, k 2 tog, psso, k 3, yo, k 5, repeat from * across, end yo, sl 1, k 1, psso.
Row 8: Yo, k 3, * sl 1, k 2 tog, psso, k 2, yo, k 1, yo, k 5, repeat from * across, end sl 1, k 1, psso.
Row 10: Yo, k 3, * sl 1, k 2 tog, psso, k 1, yo, k 3, yo, k 4, repeat from *, end sl 1, k 1, psso.
Row 12: * Yo, k 3, sl 1, k 2 tog, psso, yo, k 5, repeat from * across, end yo, k 3, sl 1, k 1, psso. Repeat these 12 rows. Bind of on a purl row.

26. ALLOVER LACE PATTERN (Multiple of 6 sts plus 3): Yarn in back, sl all sl sts as if to p.
Row 1 (right side): K 2, * yo, sl 1, k 1, psso, k 1, k 2 tog, yo, k 1, repeat from * across, end last repeat k 2. **Row 2:** Purl.
Row 3: K 3, * yo, sl 1, k 2 tog, psso, yo, k 3, repeat from * across.
Row 4: Purl. Repeat these 4 rows for pattern.

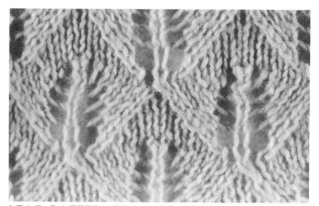
LEAF-PATTERNED LACE STITCH

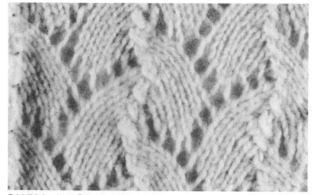
SHELL LACE PATTERN

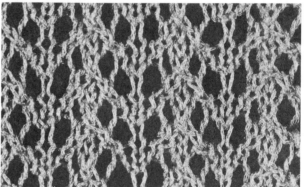
ALLOVER LACE PATTERN

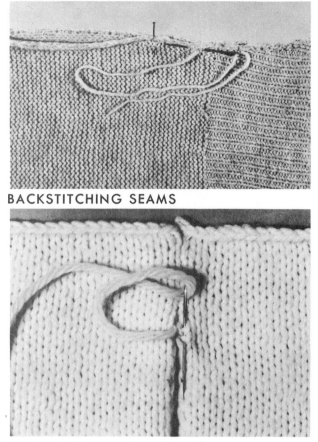

BACKSTITCHING SEAMS

WEAVING VERTICAL SEAMS

WEAVING STOCKINETTE STITCH

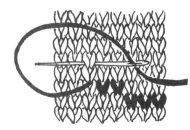

DUPLICATE STITCH

FINISHING STITCHES

TO SEW SEAMS WITH BACKSTITCH: Most seams should be sewn with backstitch. Pin right sides of pieces together, keeping edges even and matching rows or patterns. Thread matching yarn in tapestry needle. Run end of yarn through several stitches along edge to secure: backstitch pieces together close to edge. Do not draw yarn too tight. See illustration.

TO SEW IN SLEEVES: Place sleeve seam at center underarm and center of sleeve cap at shoulder seam. Ease in any extra fullness evenly. Backstitch seam.

TO WEAVE SEAMS TOGETHER: Straight vertical edges, such as those at the back seam of a sock, can be woven together invisibly from the right side. Thread matching yarn in tapestry needle. Hold edges together, right side up. Bring needle up through first stitch on left edge. Insert needle down through center of first stitch on right edge, pass under 2 rows, draw yarn through to right side. Insert needle in center of stitch on corresponding row of left edge, pass under 2 rows as before, draw yarn through to right side. Continue working from side to side, matching rows. Keep seam flat and elastic.

TO WEAVE TOP EDGES OF STOCKINETTE STITCH: Two equal top edges of stockinette stitch can be joined by an invisible seam. In this case, the stitches are not bound off, but are kept on the needles or stitch holders until they are ready to be woven. Thread yarn in tapestry needle. Lay the two pieces together so that the edge stitches match. Draw up yarn in first stitch of upper piece, inserting needle from wrong side; insert needle from right side in first stitch on lower piece, bring up through next stitch on lower piece, from wrong side. Draw up yarn, * insert needle from right side in same stitch as before on upper piece, bring up through next stitch on upper piece from wrong side. Draw up yarn, insert needle in same stitch as before on lower piece. Repeat from * until all stitches are joined.

DUPLICATE STITCH: When an additional color is desired for a small area it is advisable to work it in with duplicate stitch rather than to knit it in. Thread a tapestry needle with yarn of contrasting color and work as follows: Draw yarn from wrong side of work to right side through center of lower point of stitch. Insert needle at top right hand side of same stitch. Then holding needle in horizontal position draw through top left hand side of stitch and insert again into base of stitch to left of where needle came out at start of stitch. Keep yarn loose enough to lie on top of work and cover knitted stitch.

Body Measurements

How to Take Measurements

Directions for the knitted and crocheted items on the following pages are based on body measurements given in the tables on this page.

To take body measurements for misses', women's, and teens' sizes, measure around fullest part of bust (with bra), natural waistline, and fullest part of hip. Find the column of measurements in the tables which approximates the measurements taken. The size at the top of the column is the size to make. Necessary allowance has been made in the directions for the proper fit of each garment according to style, stitch, and yarn type. The blocked, or finished, bust measurement of the knitted or crocheted garment is given with the directions.

To take body measurements for children's sizes, measure around fullest part of child's chest over underwear, holding tape comfortably, neither snugly nor loosely. Find the chest measurement in table, then find size to make directly above in same column. Other measurements in table will help you decide whether your child differs in build from the average so that adjustments can be made easily as you work. Children's garments are designed for a casual, easy fit and allow for a child's growth. The chest, or breast, measurement, not the child's age is your guide in choosing the correct size to knit. This is the most important measurement in fitting a child's knitted garment. Shoulders are in proportion to chest.

Adjusting to Larger and Smaller Sizes

There is a 2″ difference in bust, waist, and hip between each misses' and each women's size, except for size 10. To make a garment one size larger than given in directions, add the number of stitches equaling 1″ to both back and front for a pullover, 1″ to back and ½″ to each front for a cardigan or jacket, 2″ to a skirt. Subtract the same number for a smaller size. For size 10, subtract only half these amounts from size 12. When stitch is a repeat pattern, add or subtract the number of stitches equal to one or more multiples.

There is a ½″ difference across back and front at shoulders for each misses' and each women's size, 1″ for each men's size. To obtain desired width at shoulders, decrease more or less stitches at armhole shaping, dividing evenly between armholes. There is a ¼″ difference at wrist and ½″ at underarms for each size.

The length of sweaters, jackets, dress waists, and sleeves is changed by adding or subtracting required number of inches before armhole is reached.

MISSES' BODY MEASUREMENTS

SIZE	10	12	14	16	18	20	
BUST	31	32	34	36	38	40	ins.
WAIST	23	24	26	28	30	32	”
HIP	33	34	36	38	40	42	”

WOMEN'S BODY MEASUREMENTS

SIZE	36	38	40	42	44	46	
BUST	38	40	42	44	46	48	ins.
WAIST	30	32	34	36	38	40	”
HIP	40	42	44	46	48	50	”

TEENS' BODY MEASUREMENTS

SIZE	10	12	14	16	
BUST	30	31	33	35	ins.
WAIST	23	24	26	28	”
HIP	32	33	35	37	”

MEN'S BODY MEASUREMENTS

SIZE	34	36	38	40	42	44	
CHEST	34	36	38	40	42	44	ins.
WAIST	30	32	34	36	38	40	”

INFANTS' AND GIRLS' BODY MEASUREMENTS

SIZE	6 mos.	1	2	3	4	6	8	10	12	
BREAST	19	20	21	22	23	24	26	28	30	ins.
WAIST	19	19½	20	20½	21	22	23	24	25	”
HIP	20	21	22	23	24	26	28	30	32½	”
HEIGHT*	22	25	29	31	33	37	41	45	49	”

BOYS' BODY MEASUREMENTS

SIZE	1	2	3	4	6	8	10	12	14	16	
CHEST	20	21	22	23	24	26	28	30	32	34	ins.
WAIST	19½	20	20½	21	22	23	24	25½	27	29	”
NECK					11	11½	12	12½	13½	14	”
HIP	20	21	22	23	25	27	29	31	33	35½	”
HEIGHT*	25	29	31	33	37	41	45	49	53	55	”

* The height for girls and boys (wearing shoes) is measured from socket bone at back of neck to floor.

An allover raised motif and doubled V neck-line vary this classic pullover.

194

Raised diamond slip-on

SIZES: Directions for size 10-12. Changes for size 14-16 in parentheses.

Body Bust Size: 31"-32" (34"-36").

Blocked Bust Size: 34" (38").

MATERIALS: Knitting worsted, 8 (9) 2-oz. skeins. Set of dp needles No. 5 for neckband; 14" knitting needles Nos. 5 and 7. (Or English sizes 8 and 6.) One stitch holder.

GAUGE: 5 sts=1"; 20 rows=3" (pat before blocking, No. 7 needles).

PATTERN (multiple of 10 sts plus 5):

Row 1 (right side): K 5, * p 5, k 5, repeat from * across row.

Row 2: P 5, * k 5, p 5, repeat from * across row.

Row 3: P 1, k 4, * p 4, k 1, p 1, k 4, repeat from * across row.

Row 4: P 4, k 1, * p 1, k 4, p 4, k 1, repeat from * across row.

Row 5: P 2, k 3, * p 3, k 2, p 2, k 3, repeat from * across row.

Row 6: P 3, k 2, * p 2, k 3, p 3, k 2, repeat from * across row.

Row 7: P 3, k 2, * p 2, k 3, p 3, k 2, repeat from * across row.

Row 8: P 2, k 3, * p 3, k 2, p 2, k 3, repeat from * across row.

Row 9: P 4, k 1, * p 1, k 4, p 4, k 1, repeat from * across row.

Row 10: P 1, k 4, * p 4, k 1, p 1, k 4, repeat from * across row.

Row 11 (right side): P 5, * k 5, p 5, repeat from * across row.

Row 12: K 5, * p 5, k 5, repeat from * across row.

Row 13: K 1, p 4, * k 4, p 1, k 1, p 4, repeat from * across row.

Row 14: K 4, p 1, * k 1, p 4, k 4, p 1, repeat from * across row.

Row 15: K 2, p 3, * k 3, p 2, k 2, p 3, repeat from * across row.

Row 16: K 3, p 2, * k 2, p 3, k 3, p 2, repeat from * across row.

Row 17: K 3, p 2, * k 2, p 3, k 3, p 2, repeat from * across row.

Row 18: K 2, p 3, * k 3, p 2, k 2, p 3, repeat from * across row.

Row 19: K 4, p 1, * k 1, p 4, k 4, p 1, repeat from * across row.

Row 20: K 1, p 4, * k 4, p 1, k 1, p 4, repeat from * across row. Repeat these 20 rows for pat.

SLIP-ON: BACK: With No. 5 needles, cast on 84 (94) sts. Work in ribbing of k 1, p 1 for 1½", inc 1 st at end of last row—85 (95) sts. Change to No. 7 needles. Work in pat (**note,** beg with pat row 1 when working back; beg with pat row 11 when working front) until piece measures 15" from start or desired length to underarm, end wrong side.

Shape Armholes: Bind off in pat 4 (5) sts at beg of next 2 rows. Dec 1 st each side every other row 3 (5) times—71 (75) sts. Work even until armholes measure 7½" (8") above first bound-off sts.

Shape Shoulders: Bind off in pat 5 sts at beg of next 8 rows, 3 (5) sts next 2 rows. Put remaining 25 sts on a holder for neckband.

FRONT: Work as for back (see note) until piece measures ½" less than back to underarm, end on wrong side.

Divide Sts for Neck: Work first 42 (47) sts, drop yarn, put next st on a safety pin, join another skein of yarn and work last 42 (47) sts.

Shape V Neck and Armholes: Working on both sides at once, dec 1 st at each neck edge every 4th row 12 times; **at same time,** when piece measures same as back to underarm, bind off 4 (5) sts at beg of each arm side once, then dec 1 st at each arm side every other row 3 (5) times. When neck decs are completed, work even on 23 (25) sts of each side until armholes measure same as back.

Shape Shoulders: Bind off in pat 5 sts at beg of each arm side 4 times, 3 (5) sts once.

SLEEVES: With No. 5 needles, cast on 38 (40) sts. Work in ribbing of k 1, p 1 for 2½", inc 7 (5) sts evenly spaced across last row—45 sts. Change to No. 7 needles. Beg with pat row 1, work in pat and inc 1 st each side every ¾" 1 (10) times, every 1" 11 (5) times, working added sts into pat—69 (75) sts. Check gauge: piece above last inc row should be 14" (15") wide. Work even until piece measures 17½" from start or desired length to underarm.

Shape Cap: Bind off in pat 4 (5) sts at beg of next 2 rows. Dec 1 st each side every other row 15 (17) times. Bind off 3 sts at beg of next 6 rows. Bind off remaining 13 sts.

FINISHING: Run in yarn ends on wrong side. Block pieces and sew seams with backstitch as follows: Sew shoulder seams. Sew in sleeves. Sew side and sleeve seams; weave cuffs and waistband ribbing from right side. Steam-press seams.

Neckband: Put back of neck sts on dp needle. Dividing sts on 3 dp needles, from right side, join yarn, k across back of neck sts, pick up and k 58 (60) sts on left neck edge to center front, put a marker on needle, k center st from safety pin, put a marker on needle, pick up and k 58 (60) sts on right neck edge to shoulder—142 (146) sts. Join, work in ribbing of p 1, k 1 and dec 1 st before first and after 2nd marker on every other rnd 4 times, keeping center st in k. Work even for 4 rnds. Inc 1 st in st before first and in st after 2nd marker on next rnd, then every other rnd 3 times. Work 1 rnd even. Bind off loosely in ribbing. Fold neckband in half to wrong side; sew loosely in place, matching center k st.

Classic vest

Features knitted-in pockets, short rows

SIZES: Directions for size 36, changes for sizes 38 and 40 in parentheses.

MATERIALS: Sport Yarn, 4 ply, 4 2-oz. balls. Knitting needles Nos. 1 and 2. (Or English sizes 12 and 11.) Six buttons.

GAUGE: 8 sts=1"; 11 rows=1".

BACK: With No. 2 needles cast on 120 (128-136) sts. Work in stockinette st, inc 1 st each side every ¾" 10 times—140 (148-156) sts. Work even until 9" from beg.

Armholes: Bind off 5 sts at beg of next 8 rows. Dec 1 st each side every 2nd row 4 times—92 (100-108) sts. Work even until armholes measure straight up from underarm 9½" (10"-10½") including bound-off rows. **Shoulders:** Bind off 7 (8-9) sts at beg of next 8 rows. Bind off remaining 36 sts.

RIGHT FRONT POCKET LININGS (make 2): With No. 2 needles cast on 28 sts.

Row 1: K 4, turn. Sl 1 st, p 3.

Row 3: K 8, turn. Sl 1 st, p 7. Continue to work short rows, working 4 sts more at end of every k row until all sts are worked. Work even until 3" from beg, measured on longest side. Break off; sl sts to holder.

LEFT FRONT POCKET LININGS (make 2): Cast on 28 sts.

Row 1: P 4, turn. Sl 1 st, k 3.

Row 3: P 8, turn. Finish to correspond to right front pocket linings, purling 4 sts more at end of every p row until all sts are worked.

RIGHT FRONT: With No. 2 needles cast on 60 (64-68) sts.

Row 1: K 4, turn. Sl 1, p 3.

Row 3: K 8, turn. Sl 1, p 6, inc 1 st in last st at front edge.

Row 5: K 13, turn. Sl 1 st, p to front edge.

Continue short rows, working 4 sts more at end of every k row until all sts are worked, at the same time repeating inc at front edge every 4th row 7 times—68 (72-76) sts. Work stockinette st for 1¾", keeping front edge even and shaping underarm edge as for back—70 (74-78) sts, end with p row.

Pocket: K 24 sts and place on holder, bind off next 4 sts, finish row. Continuing to shape underarm edge as on back throughout, bind off 4 sts at beg of next 6 k rows for pocket opening, end at underarm edge; place remaining sts on another holder, break yarn. Beg at front edge and working from right side of both pieces, take up and k 24 front sts from holder, k 28 sts of right pocket lining to same needle. Work 11 more rows on these 52 sts. On next row, k 52 sts, k sts from holder to end of row. Work until same length as back, measured at underarm edge to armhole, end at underarm edge—78 (82-86) sts.

Armhole and Pocket: Bind off 5 sts at beg of next row for underarm, finish row. On next row, k 24 sts and place on holder, bind off next 4 sts for pocket, finish row. Complete pocket as before, at the same time working armhole as on back to end of armhole shaping, end at front edge—54 (58-62) sts.

Neck Shaping: * Dec 1 st at front edge, finish row. Work 1 row even. Dec 1 st at front edge, finish row. Work 3 rows even. Repeat from * 8 (6-4) times. Dec 1 st at front edge on next row and repeat dec every 4th row 7 (11-15) times—28 (32-36) sts. Work even until armhole is same length as on back, end at armhole edge. Shape shoulder the same as on back.

LEFT FRONT: With No. 2 needles cast on 60 (64-68) sts.

Row 1: P 4, turn. Sl 1, k 3.

Row 3: P 8, turn. Sl 1, k 6, inc 1 st in last st at front edge. Continue to work short rows and inc to correspond to right front until 3 rows above last inc at front edge, end with p row.

BUTTONHOLE: K to within 5 sts of front edge, bind off 3 sts, k to end. Cast on 3 sts over buttonhole on next row. Repeat buttonhole every 2″, including last buttonhole, 5 times; 6th buttonhole will be at about beg of neck shaping. Finish to correspond to right front, binding off for pockets on p side and shaping neck edge at beg of p row.

BORDER: With No. 1 needles, working from right side, pick up and k 36 sts on back of neck. K 5 rows to form 3 garter st ridges. Bind off as to k. Beg at shoulder from right side, pick up and k sts on left front and on lower edge, having 3 sts to 4 rows on front edge and 1 st in each st on lower edge; work border as on back of neck.

Work border on right front to correspond. Sew shoulder seams. Work border on lower edge of back. Sew underarm seams. Work border around armholes and on 28 bound-off sts of each pocket.

FINISHING: Sew side edges of pocket borders to front. Sew pocket linings to wrong side. Finish buttonholes. Steam.

Raglan pullover

Fisherman's rib is the stitch for this boat-necked pullover quickly made of knitting worsted on big needles.

SIZES: Directions for size 38. Changes for sizes 40 and 42 in parentheses.

Fits Chest Size: 38″ (40″-42″).

Loosely fitted garment.

MATERIALS: Nylon and wool knitting worsted, 9 (10-10) 2-oz. skeins. 14″ knitting needles Nos. 7 and 10½. (Or English sizes 6 and 2.)

GAUGE: 7 sts=2″; 6 rows (or 3 long k sts)=1″ (unstretched pat, No. 10½ needles).

PATTERN (multiple of 2 sts): **Row 1:** * P 1, k 1 in row below next st, repeat from * across, end p 2. Repeat this row for pattern.

Note: To k 1 in row below next st, insert needle from front to back through st **under** needle, yarn around needle, pull yarn through st, slip st above knitted st off needle.

BACK: With No. 7 needles, cast on 70 (74-78) sts. Work in ribbing of p 1, k 1 for 3″. Change to No. 10½ needles and work even in pat until piece measures 14½″ (15″-15½″) from start or desired length to underarm. Put a marker on work each side of last row for underarms.

Shape Raglan Armholes: Row 1: Work in pat on 4 sts, p 3, work in pat to last 6 sts, p 3, k 1 in row below next st, p 2.

Row 2 (mark this row as right side of work): P 1, k 1 in row below next st, p 1, sl 1, k 2 tog, psso, work in pat to last 7 sts, sl 1, k 2 tog, psso, p 1, k 1 in row below next st, p 2—2 sts dec each side.

** Work in pat for 4 rows, repeat rows 1 and 2 of armholes. Repeat from ** 8 (8-9) times more—30 (34-34) sts remain. Work even for 0 (3-0) rows.

Neckband: Change to No. 7 needles. Work in ribbing of p 1, k 1 for 2½″. Bind off loosely in ribbing.

FRONT: Work same as back.

SLEEVES: With No. 7 needles, cast on 34 (38-42) sts. Work in ribbing of k 1, p 1 for 3″. Change to No. 10½″ needles. Work in pat, inc 1 st each side every 1½″ 8 times, working added sts into pat. Work even on 50 (54-58) sts until piece measures 18″ (19″-20″) or desired length from start to underarm.

Shape Raglan Armholes: Work as for back—10 (14-14) sts remain. Work even for 0 (3-0) rows.

Neckband: Work as for back.

FINISHING: With right sides tog, sew raglan sleeves to front and back armholes, using backstitch, so that a p rib appears each side of seam on right side. Sew neckband seams. Fold neckband in half and sew bound-off edge to wrong side of pullover. With right sides tog, sew side and sleeve seams in backstitch. Do not press pullover as pat will stretch to fit.

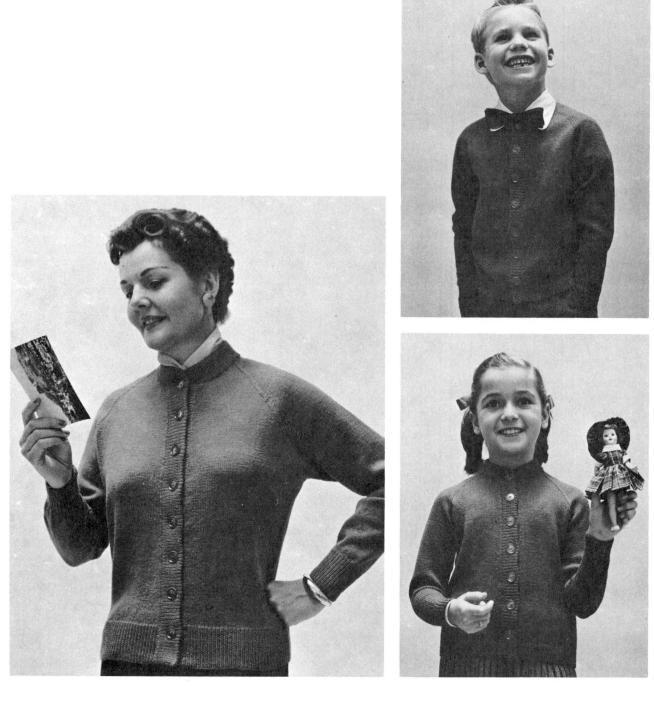

In these comfortable cardigans, back, fronts and sleeves are worked separately from the bottom up, then joined for the knitted-in-one raglan yoke. Also knitted-in-one are the front borders and neckband, folded double for extra wear. Directions for childrens' cardigans, opposite; women's, page 200.

198

Boys' and Girls' raglan sleeve cardigans

SIZES: Directions for size 4. Changes for sizes 6, 8, 10, 12 and 14 in parentheses.

Body Chest Size: 23″ (24″-26″-28″-30″-32″).

Blocked Chest Size: 26″ (27″-29″-31″-33″-35″).

MATERIALS: Fingering Yarn, 3 ply, 6 (7-7-8-9-10) 1-oz. pull skeins. Straight knitting needles and 29″ circular needles Nos. 1 and 2. (Or English sizes 12 and 11.) Five stitch holders. Seven or eight (size 12 and 14) buttons.

GAUGE: 8 sts=1″; 12 rows=1″ (stockinette st, No. 2 needles).

BACK: Beg at lower edge, with No. 1 straight needles, cast on 104 (108-116-124-132-140) sts. Work in ribbing of k 1, p 1 for 1½″ (1½″-1½″-2″-2″-2″). Change to No. 2 straight needles. Work in stockinette st (k 1 row, p 1 row) until piece is 9″ (10″-11″-12″-13″-14″) from start, end p row.

Shape Underarms: Bind off 6 sts at beg of next 2 rows, end p row. Sl remaining 92 (96-104-112-120-128) sts on a holder for raglan shaping later.

LEFT FRONT: With No. 1 straight needles, cast on 50 (52-56-60-64-68) sts. Work as for back to underarm, end p row.

Shape Underarm: Bind off 6 sts at beg of next row. P 1 row. Sl last 44 (46-50-54-58-62) sts on a holder.

RIGHT FRONT: Work as for left front to underarm, end k row.

Shape Underarm: Bind off 6 sts at beg of next row, finish row. Sl last 44 (46-50-54-58-62 sts on a holder.

SLEEVES: Beg at wrist edge, with No. 1 straight needles cast on 46 (48-50-52-54-56) sts. Work in ribbing of k 1, p 1 for 2″ (2″-2″-2½″-2½″-2½″). Change to No. 2 straight needles. Work in stockinette st, inc 1 st each side every 6th row 14 (16-18-20-22-24) times. Work even on 74 (80-86-92-98-104) sts until piece measures 11″ (12″-13½″-15″-16″-17″) from start or desired length to underarm, end p row.

Shape Underarms: Bind off 6 sts at beg of next 2 rows, end p row. Sl remaining 62 (68-74-80-86-92) sts on a holder.

RAGLAN YOKE: From right side of each piece, with No. 2 circular needle, k sts of right front, sl a marker on needle, k sts of one sleeve, sl a marker on needle, k sts of back, place marker, k sts of other sleeve, place marker, k sts of left front—304 (324-352-380-408-436) sts. P 1 row, slipping markers.

Shape Raglan: Row 1 (right side): * K to within 2 sts of marker, k 2 tog, sl marker, sl 1, k 1, psso, repeat from * 3 times, k to end of row.

Row 2: Purl, slipping markers. Repeat these 2 rows until 20 (22-24-26-28-30) dec rows have been worked—144 (148-160-172-184-196) sts on needle, end p row.

Shape Neck: Still shaping raglan every k row 8 (8-9-10-11-12) times more, bind off 9 sts at beg of next 2 rows (neck edges), dec 1 st at each neck edge every p row 7 (7-8-9-10-11) times. Bind off remaining 48 (52-54-56-58-60) sts for neck edge.

BORDER: From right side, with No. 1 circular needle, pick up and k 110 (122-134-146-158-170) sts on right front edge to neck shaping, sl a marker on needle, pick up and k 92 (96-100-104-110-116) sts around neck edge; sl a marker on needle, pick up and k 110 (122-134-146-158-170) sts on left front edge—312 (340-368-396-426-456) sts on needle.

Row 1 (wrong side): Work in ribbing of k 1, p 1, slipping markers.

Row 2 (right side): * Work in ribbing to within 1 st of marker, inc 1 st in next st, sl marker, inc 1 st in next st, repeat from * once, work in ribbing to end of row.

Row 3: Work in ribbing as established, slipping markers.

Rows 4-7: Repeat rows 2 and 3, ending at lower edge of right front for girls' cardigan. For boys' cardigan, repeat row 2 once more, ending at lower edge of left front.

Buttonholes: Rib first 4 (10-16-16-14-12) sts, * bind off next 4 sts, rib until 13 (14-15-17-16-18) sts, repeat from * until 7 (7-7-7-8-8) buttonholes are made; finish row, increasing each side of markers on girls' cardigan.

Next Row: Cast on 4 sts over each set of buttonholes, inc each side of markers on boys' cardigan. Continue in ribbing for 6 rows more, inc each side of markers on right side.

Facing: Work in ribbing for 6 rows, dec 1 st each side of markers (sl 1, k 1, psso before marker, k 2 tog after marker) on right side. Continue to dec 1 st each side of markers on right side, working buttonholes as follows:

Buttonholes: Beg at lower edge of right front for girls', left front for boys' cardigan, work the 2 rows for buttonholes, as before. Working in ribbing for 7 rows more, dec 1 st each side of markers on right side. For boys' cardigan, work 1 row more. Bind off in ribbing.

FINISHING: Sew side, sleeve, and underarm seams. Fold border in half to wrong side, buttonholes meeting; hem in place. Reinforce buttonholes. Steam-press cardigan to size, using steam iron or dry iron and damp cloth. Sew on buttons.

Woman's raglan sleeve cardigan

SIZES: Directions for size 48. Changes for sizes 50, 52 and 54 in parentheses.

Body Chest Size: 50″ (52″-54″-56″).

Blocked Chest·Size: 53″ (55″-57″-59″).

MATERIALS: Fingering Yarn, 3 ply, 15 (16-16-17) 1-oz. pull skeins. Straight knitting needles and 29″ circular needles Nos. 1 and 2. (Or English sizes 12 and 11.) Five stitch holders. Nine buttons.

GAUGE: 8 sts = 1″; 12 rows = 1″ (stockinette st, No. 2 needles).

BACK: Beg at lower edge, with No. 1 straight needles, cast on 212 (220-228-236) sts. Work in ribbing of k 1, p 1 for 3″. Change to No. 2 straight needles. Work in stockinette st (k 1 row, p 1 row) until piece measures 15″ (15″-15″-15½″) from start, end p row.

Shape Underarms: Bind off 8 sts at beg of next 2 rows, end p row. Sl remaining 196 (204-212-220) sts on a holder for raglan shaping later.

LEFT FRONT: With No. 1 straight needles, cast on 104 (108-112-116) sts. Work as for back to underarm, end p row.

Shape Underarm: Bind off 8 sts at beg of next row. P 1 row. Sl last 96 (100-104-108) sts on a holder.

RIGHT FRONT: Work as for left front to underarm, end k row.

Shape Underarm: Bind off 8 sts at beg of next row, finish row. Sl last 96 (100-104-108) sts on a holder.

SLEEVES: Beg at wrist edge, with No. 1 straight needles, cast on 78 (80-82-84) sts. Work in ribbing of k 1, p 1 for 3″, inc 14 sts evenly spaced across last row. Change to No. 2 straight needles. Work in stockinette st, inc 1 st each side every 5th (5th-4th-4th) row 33 (34-35-36) times. Work even on 158 (162-166-170) sts until piece measures 18½″ from start or desired length to underarm, end p row.

Shape Underarms: Bind off 8 sts at beg of next 2 rows, end p row. Sl remaining 142 (146-150-154) sts on a holder.

RAGLAN YOKE: From right side of each piece, with No. 2 circular needle, k sts of right front, sl a marker on needle, k sts of one sleeve, sl a marker on needle, k sts of back, place marker, k sts of other sleeve, place marker, k sts of left front—672 (696-720-744) sts. P 1 row, slipping markers.

Shape Raglan: Row 1 (right side): * K to within 2 sts of marker, k 2 tog, sl marker, sl 1, k 1, psso, repeat from * 3 times, k to end of row.

Row 2: Purl, slipping markers. Repeat these 2 rows until 47 (48-49-50) dec rows have been worked —296 (312-328-344) sts on needle, end p row.

Shape Neck: Still shaping raglan every k row 18 (19-20-21) times more, bind off 14 (15-16-17) sts at beg of next 2 rows (neck edges), dec 1 st at each neck edge every p row 17 (18-19-20) times. Bind off remaining 90 (94-98-102) sts for neck edge.

BORDER: From right side, with No. 1 circular needle, pick up and k 206 (208-210-216) sts on right front edge to neck shaping, sl a marker on needle, pick up and k 168 (172-176-180) sts around neck edge; sl a marker on needle, pick up and k 206 (208-210-216) sts on left front edge—580 (588-596-612) sts on needle. Work in ribbing of k 1, p 1 for 9 rows, inc 1 st in st each side of each marker every other row (right side).

Buttonholes: Beg at lower edge of right front, rib first 10 (12-14-12) sts, * bind off next 4 sts, rib until 20 (20-20-21) sts, repeat from * until 9 buttonholes are made; finish row, increasing 1 st each side of markers.

Next Row: Cast on 4 sts over each set of buttonholes. Continue in ribbing for 8 rows more, inc each side of markers on right side.

Facing: Work in ribbing for 8 rows, dec 1 st each side of markers (sl 1, k 1, psso before marker, k 2 tog after marker) on right side.

Next 2 Rows: Work buttonholes as before, dec 1 st each side of markers on right side. Work in ribbing for 9 rows more, dec 1 st each side of markers on right side. Bind off loosely in ribbing.

FINISHING: Sew side, sleeve, and underarm seams. Fold border in half to wrong side, buttonholes meeting; hem in place. Reinforce buttonholes. Steam-press cardigan to size, using steam iron or dry iron and damp cloth. Sew on buttons.

A pair of raglan-sleeved sweaters for the younger set. Both the cardigan and the pullover are worked from the neck down in red, white and blue stripes, in knitting worsted. Directions start page 202.

Striped cardigan

SIZES: Directions for size 6. Changes for sizes 8 and 10 are in parentheses.

Body Chest Size: 24″ (26″-28″).

Blocked Chest (closed): 27″ (29″-31″).

MATERIALS: Knitting worsted, 2 4-oz. skeins royal blue (B), 1 skein each of white (W) and red (R). 14″ knitting needles Nos. 4 and 8. (Or English sizes 9 and 5.) Three stitch holders. Five buttons.

GAUGE: 5 sts=1″; 7 rows=1″ (stockinette st, No. 8 needles).

STRIPED PATTERN: Work in stockinette st (k 1 row, p 1 row) as follows: 3 rows B, 2 rows W, 3 rows B, 13 rows R. Break off colors; join as needed. Repeat these 21 rows for striped pat.

Note: Cardigan is worked from neck to lower edge.

Inc Notes: Before marker, k the st but do not drop it off needle, k in lp behind this st in row below, then drop st off left-hand needle (1 inc made), sl marker. **After marker,** k in lp behind next st in row below, then k the st above and drop st off left-hand needle (1 inc made).

NECKBAND: With B and No. 4 needles, cast on 75 sts. Work back and forth in ribbing as follows:

Row 1 (right side): P 1, * k 1, p 1, repeat from * across.

Row 2: K 1, * p 1, k 1, repeat from * across. Repeat these 2 rows for ¾″, end on right side and dec 1 st at center of last row—74 sts.

YOKE: Next Row (wrong side): Work in ribbing on first 7 sts, cut off B, sl these sts on a safety pin to be worked later for right center band; change to No. 8 needles and W, p next 11 sts for right front, put a marker on needle, p 8 for right sleeve, put a marker on needle, p 22 sts for back, put a marker on needle, p 8 sts for left sleeve, put a marker on needle, p 11 sts for left front, sl last 7 sts on a safety pin to be worked later for left front center band—60 sts on needle. Work wih W for entire yoke as follows:

Shape Raglan: Row 1 (right side): Knit, inc 1 st (see Inc Notes) before and after each marker—8 incs. **Row 2:** Purl. Repeat these 2 rows 20 (22-24) times, end on k row. There are 32 (34-36) sts on each front, 50 (54-58) sts on each sleeve and 64 (68-72) sts on back—228 (244-260) sts. Armholes should measure 6″ (6½″-7″) straight up from neckband.

Divide Work (wrong side): Removing markers, p first 32 (34-36) sts, sl these sts on a holder for right front; p next 50 (54-58) sts, sl these sts on a holder for right sleeve; p next 64 (68-72) sts, sl these sts on a holder for back; p to end of row. Drop W. Sl last worked 32 (34-36) sts on a holder for left front; leave remaining 50 (54-58) sts on needle for left sleeve.

LEFT SLEEVE: Beg on right side, with No. 8 needles, join W, work in stockinette st (k 1 row, p 1 row), casting on 1 st for underarm at beg of next 2 rows—52 (56-60) sts. Cut off W. Join B, work in

striped pat, dec 1 st each side every 1″ 7 times—38 (42-46) sts. Continue in striped pat until piece measures 10½″ from underarm, ending with first 8 rows of striped pat. Change to No. 4 needles. With B, work in ribbing of k 1, p 1 for 1″ (1½″-2″) or work until desired sleeve length. Bind off loosely in ribbing.

RIGHT SLEEVE: Sl sts from holder to No. 8 needle. Work as for left sleeve.

BODY: From wrong side, sl to No. 8 needle sts of right front, back and left front (leave center band sts on safety pins).

Next Row: From right side, pick up W left at beg of left front, k across sts of left front, cast on 2 sts for underarm, k across sts of back, cast on 2 sts for underarm, k across sts of right front—132 (140-148) sts. With W, p 1 row. Cut off W. Join B, work in striped pat for 10½″ from underarm, ending on right side with first 8 rows of striped pat (same amount of stripes as on sleeves). With B, p 1 row, inc 1 st at center of row—133 (141-149) sts. Leave sts on needle. Cut off B.

With pins, mark position of 4 buttonholes on center edge of left front for boys' cardigan; right front for girls' cardigan: first one at start of yoke (5th buttonhole to be made ½″ (¾″-1″) above body in waistband).

BUTTONHOLES: From right side, p 1, k 1, bind off in ribbing next 3 sts, finish row. **Next Row:** Cast on 3 sts over bound-off sts.

RIGHT CENTER BAND: Sl 7 sts from safety pin to No. 4 needle. From right side, join B at inside edge, with No. 4 needles, work in ribbing as established, forming buttonholes opposite markers for girls' cardigan only, until piece when slightly stretched is same length as right front edge; end at inside edge, cut off B and sl these sts on a holder.

LEFT CENTER BAND: Sl 7 sts from safety pin to No. 4 needle. From wrong side, join B at inside edge. Work in ribbing as established, forming buttonholes opposite markers on boys' cardigan, until piece when slightly stretched is same length as left front edge; end at inside edge. Work as follows:

WAISTBAND: From right side, with No. 4 needle of left center band sts, work in ribbing of k 1, p 1 across sts of body and right center band—147 (155-163) sts. Beg with row 2, work in ribbing as for neckband for ½″ (¾″-1″). Form 5th buttonhole on same center band as before. Continue in ribbing until waistband measures 1″ (1½″-2″) from start. Bind off in ribbing same tension as sts.

FINISHING: Sew center bands to front edges. Sew underarm and sleeve seams. With B, work buttonhole stitch around buttonholes. From right side, with B, work 1 row sc on each front edge.

Steam-press cardigan. Do not press neckband, cuffs and waistband. Sew on buttons.

HOW TO INCREASE ONE STITCH BEFORE MARKER

HOW TO INCREASE ONE STITCH AFTER MARKER

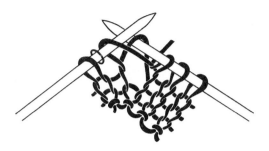

Striped slip-on

SIZES: Directions for size 6. Changes for sizes 8 and 10 are in parentheses.

Body Chest Size: 24″ (26″-28″).

Blocked Chest Size: 26″ (28″-30″).

MATERIALS: Knitting worsted, 2 4-oz. skeins white (W); 1 skein each of royal blue (B) and red (R). Set of dp needles Nos. 4 and 8; 24″ circular needles Nos. 4 and 8. (Or English sizes 9 and 5.) Three stitch holders.

GAUGE: 5 sts=1″; 7 rows=1″ (stockinette st, No. 8 needles).

STRIPED PATTERN: Note: Always change colors on wrong side, picking up new strand from under dropped strand. Knit 3 rnds B, 2 rnds W, 3 rnds B, 13 rnds R. Break off colors; join as needed. Repeat these 21 rnds for striped pat.

Note: Slip-on is worked from neck to lower edge.

NECKBAND: With B, cast on very loosely 20 sts on each of 3 No. 4 dp needles—60 sts. Join, work around in ribbing of k 1, p 1 for ¾″. Cut off B.

YOKE: Next Rnd: Change to No. 8 dp needles and W, k first 22 sts for back (put a marker on work to keep track of back sts), put a marker on needle for raglan shaping, k 8 sts for right sleeve, put a 2nd marker on needle, k 22 sts for front, put a 3rd marker on needle, k last 8 sts for left sleeve, put a 4th marker on needle (end of rnd). Work with W for entire yoke.

Shape Raglan: Rnd 1: Knit, inc 1 st at beg of rnd (this is after 4th marker, see Inc Notes in directions for Striped Cardigan), inc 1 st before and after each of next 3 markers, then inc 1 st before 4th marker— 8 incs. **Rnd 2:** K all sts. Repeat these 2 rnds 20 (22-24) times. Change to No. 8 circular needle when sts get crowded. There are 64 (68-72) sts on each of back and front, 50 (54-58) sts on each sleeve—228 (244-260) sts on needle. Armholes should measure 6″ (6½″-7″) straight up from neckband. Cut off W.

Divide Work: Removing markers, from right side, sl on separate holders 64 (68-72) sts of back, 50 (54-58) sts of right sleeve, 64 (68-72) sts of front; leave last 50 (54-58) sts of left sleeve on needle.

SLEEVES: Beg with left sleeve still on needle and working back and forth on circular needle, work sleeves as for Striped Cardigan.

BODY: From wrong side, sl sts of front then back to circular needle. From right side, join W at left underarm of back, k across sts of back, cast on 2 sts for underarm, k across sts of front, cast on 2 sts for underarm—132 (140-148) sts. From right side, continue around back and front for 1 rnd. Mark end of rnd. Cut off W. Join B, work around in striped pat for 10½″ from underarm, ending with first 8 rnds of striped pat (same number of stripes as on sleeves). Change to No. 4 circular needle. With B, work in ribbing of k 1, p 1 for 1″ (1½″-2″) or work for desired body length. Bind off in ribbing.

FINISHING: Weave in all yarn ends on wrong side. Sew underarm and sleeve seams. Steam-press slip-on, using steam iron or damp cloth and dry iron. Do not press ribbing.

Knitting With Four Needles

Socks, mittens, gloves, hats, helmets, sleeves and necklines can all be knitted on four double-pointed needles in a tubular fashion. Stitches are cast on loosely and divided as evenly as possible on three needles; the fourth is used for the actual knitting. Stitch gauge is as important as in flat knitting; be sure the gauge agrees with that of the model for proper fit. As in flat knitting, shaping is accomplished by increasing or decreasing. Pattern stitches, including cables, are adaptable to

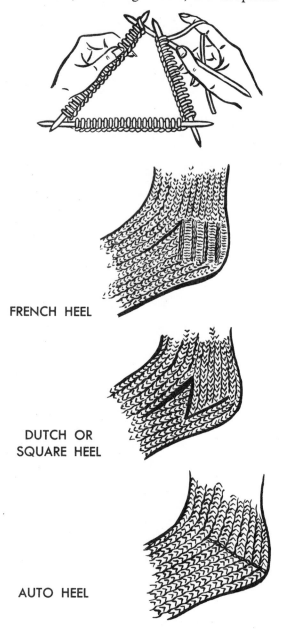

FRENCH HEEL

DUTCH OR SQUARE HEEL

AUTO HEEL

four needle knitting. For twisting cables, an additional needle is required. Ribbing is worked by knitting over the knit stitches and purling over the purl stitches. Working round and round in plain knit stitch produces a seamless stockinette tube. Toes, fingers, etc. are finished by drawing the stitches together and sewing them securely or by weaving them in Kitchener stitch.

Socks are probably the most popular item made on four needles. A properly knitted sock fits well and wears well.

CUFFS: Cast on cuff stitches loosely so they will not bind or be broken in putting on the sock. Leave an extra long end in casting on. Carry this end with yarn and knit with a double strand for first row of ribbing. To insure a snug fit, an elastic thread may also be carried along with yarn for the first few rows. Cuffs are always ribbed and are usually 1″ to 2″ deep for the shorter lengths of men's socks and 2½″ to 4″ deep for regulation length.

LEGS: Slack length socks for men are about 4½″ from top of sock to top of heel; regulation length are 8″ to 9″ from top of sock to top of heel. When making these lengths, no decreases are necessary from top to heel to insure a smooth fit. If longer socks are made, more stitches must be cast on to fit the calf. These extra stitches are decreased 2 at a time at even intervals down center back of leg. The center 2 stitches are marked and decreases are made either side of the marked stitches.

HEELS: Reinforce the heels by carrying a matching nylon thread along with yarn unless sock is knitted of nylon or nylon and wool yarn.

French Heel: This is the most popular heel for men's and women's socks because it wears well and provides "cushion comfort." The heel stitches are worked in alternate rows of k 1, sl 1, repeated across, and purl, producing a ribbed effect.

Dutch or Square Heel is similar to the French Heel, but without the ribbed effect.

Auto or Easy Heel is often suggested for children's socks. When the heel is reached, the yarn is dropped and the heel stitches are knitted across with a contrasting strand of yarn. These stitches are then slipped back on the left-hand needle and knitted again with the dropped yarn. The sock is continued until the toe is completed. The heel stitches are then slipped on two needles as the contrasting yarn is pulled out. One needle will have one stitch less then the other. This stitch is picked up on the first round. The heel is then completed in the same manner as a toe, weaving the remaining stitches together after the shaping is completed.

Foot Length: Sizes for socks are measured in inches from center back of heel to tip of toe. A size 11 sock, for instance, is 11″ from front to back of foot. Tapering the toe section requires 2″ in length for men's and women's socks, 1½″ for children's socks; therefore, in making a size 11 sock, knit evenly around foot section until piece measures 9″ from back of heel straight forward to needles, then start toe decreases. When knitting a sock the same size as a ready-made one, mark off 2″ from toe. Measure back from this point to heel to determine how long foot should be before starting toe decreases.

TOES: Reinforce toes in same way as heels.

Round Toe: Stitches, evenly divided on three needles, are gradually decreased to a few stitches at the end which are drawn up and sewed together.

Pointed Toe: Instep and sole stitches are gradually decreased at sides. When sufficiently tapered, remaining stitches are woven together in Kitchener stitch.

Replacing Heels and Toes

If the heels or toes of hand-knitted socks wear out and the rest of the socks are still in good condition, replace them as follows:

Toes: Run a line of basting thread through each stitch at the point where the toe shaping begins. Cut out worn area and ravel back the toe to the basting line, leaving a 2 to 3 inch yarn end. Using same size needles and weight of yarn as the original sock, pick up the stitches from the basting thread. Re-knit toe following any toe directions.

Heels: Run a line of basting around area to be replaced, carefully catching each stitch. Cut out the worn area and ravel the uneven edge up to the line of basting. Pick up the stitches along the back of the heel at the top and knit a new heel section, shaping the same as original heel. When the heel is long enough to join rest of sock, do not cast off stitches, but weave them together using Kitchener stitch. Weave together the sides of the instep and edges of the heel replacement, working from wrong side.

KITCHENER STITCH

Stitches are evenly divided on two needles and held parallel. To weave them together, proceed as follows: Break off yarn, leaving about 12″ end on work. Thread this into a tapestry needle. Working from right to left, * pass threaded needle through first st on front needle as if to knit and slip st off needle; pass yarn through 2nd st on front needle as if to purl but leave st on needle; pass yarn through first st on back needle as if to purl and slip st off needle; pass yarn through 2nd st on back needle as if to knit but leave st on needle. Repeat from * until all sts are woven together. Fasten off yarn.

MEASURING FOR START
OF TOE DECREASES

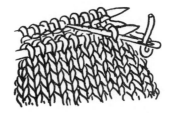

KITCHENER STITCH

Heelless socks for men or women

SIZES: 9 to 12. Slack or regulation length.

MATERIALS: Sock and sweater yarn, 3 1-oz. balls for sizes 9 and 10; 4 balls for sizes 11 and 12. Set of dp needles No. 2. (Or English size 11.)

GAUGE: 7 sts=1"; 12 rnds=1".

CUFF: Cast on 64 sts loosely. Divide on 3 needles and join, being careful not to twist sts. Work in ribbing of k 2, p 2 for 1" for slack length, 2" for regulation length. Work in pattern as follows:

Rnds 1-3: * K 2, p 2, repeat from * around.

Rnd 4: * Sk first st, k next st on left-hand needle but do not take it off; k the skipped st and sl both sts off left-hand needle at one time, p 2; repeat from * around.

Rnds 5-7: * K 1, p 2, k 2, repeat from * around, end k 1.

Rnd 8: K 1, * p 2, sk next st, k following st but do not take it off; k the skipped st and sl both sts off left-hand needle at one time; repeat from * around.

Rnds 9-11: * P 2, k 2, repeat from * around.

Rnd 12: * P 2, sk next st, k next st but do not take it off; k the skipped st and sl both sts off left-hand needle at one time; repeat from * around.

Rnds 13-15: P 1, * k 2, p 2, repeat from * around, end p 1.

Rnd 16: P 1, * sk next st, k next st but do not take it off; k the skipped st and sl both sts off left-hand needle at one time, p 2; repeat from * around, end p 1. Repeat rnds 1-16 for pat. Work in pat until piece measures in all:

For Slack Length: 11½" (size 9); 12" (size 10); 12½" (size 11); 13" (size 12).

For Regulation Length: 18½" (size 9); 19" (size 10); 19½" (size 11); 20" (size 12).

SHAPE TOE: Divide sts so there are 16 sts on first needle; 32 sts on 2nd needle; 16 sts on 3rd needle.

Rnd 1: On first needle, k across to last 3 sts, k 2 tog, k 1; on 2nd needle, k 1, sl 1, k 1, psso, k to last 3 sts, k 2 tog, k 1; on 3rd needle, k 1, sl 1, k 1, psso, k to end of rnd.

Rnd 2: K around. Repeat last 2 rnds until 12 sts remain on rnd. Weave sts tog in Kitchener stitch.

Simplest socks to knit are spiral-patterned tubes, made without heel shapings.

Socks with French heels for men

MATERIALS: For lightweight socks: 3-ply sock and sport yarn, 3 1-oz. skeins. Set of dp needles No. 1. (Or English size 12.) **For medium-weight socks:** 4-ply sport yarn, 2 2-oz. balls. Set of dp needles No. 2. (Or English size 11.)

GAUGE: 17 sts=2″ (3-ply yarn). 15 sts=2″ (4-ply yarn).

Directions are written for lightweight yarn. Changes for medium-weight yarn are in parentheses.

CUFF: Cast on loosely 68 (64) sts; divide on 3 needles. Join, work in ribbing of k 2, p 2 for 4″. K 1 rnd, inc 1 st in every 17th st 4 times—72 sts (keep 64 sts for medium-weight yarn).

K even in stockinette st for 5½″. Mark space between first and last st of rnd as center back.

Dec Rnd: K 1, k 2 tog, k to within 3 sts of end of rnd, sl 1, k 1, psso, k 1. Work 1″ even. Repeat dec rnd—68 (60) sts. Work even until 12″ from beg or desired length to top of heel, end at center back.

FRENCH HEEL: K 18 (15), sl last 36 (30) sts worked to one needle for heel, hold remaining 32 (30) sts on 2 needles for instep.

Row 1: Working from wrong side, sl first st of heel needle as if to p, p to end.

Row 2: * Sl 1 as if to p, k 1, repeat from * to end of row. Repeat last 2 rows until there are 40 (32) rows on heel. Begin to turn heel on wrong side: sl 1, p 20 (16), p 2 tog, p 1, turn; sl 1, k 7 (5), sl 1, k 1, psso, k 1, turn; sl 1, p 8 (6), p 2 tog, p 1, turn; sl 1, k 9 (7), sl 1, k 1, psso, k 1, turn; sl 1, p 10 (8), p 2 tog, p 1, turn; sl 1, k 11 (9), sl 1, k 1, psso, k 1, turn; sl 1, p 12 (10), p 2 tog, p 1, turn; sl 1, k 13 (11), sl 1, k 1, psso, k 1, turn. Continue in this way to work towards sides of heel, having 1 st more before dec on each row until there are 22 (18) sts left, end k row.

GUSSETS AND FOOT: With free needle, pick up and k 20 (16) sts on side edge of heel; k 32 (30) instep sts to one needle; with free needle, pick up and k 20 (16) sts on other side of heel and k 11 (9) sts of heel to same needle. Sl remaining 11 (9) heel sts to first needle. There will be 31 (25) sts on first and 3rd needles; 32 (30) sts on 2nd or instep needle. K 1 rnd.

Next Rnd: K to within 3 sts of end of first needle, k 2 tog, k 1; k across instep needle; on 3rd needle, k 1, sl 1, k 1, psso, k to end of rnd. Repeat last 2 rnds until 18 (13) sts remain on each of first and 3rd needles—68 (56) sts. K until foot is 9″ or desired length from tip of heel allowing 2″ for toe.

TOE: Beg at center of sole, place 17 (14) sts on first needle, 34 (28) sts on 2nd needle, 17 (14) sts on 3rd needle.

First Dec Rnd: K to within 3 sts of end of first needle, k 2 tog, k 1; on 2nd needle, k 1, sl 1, k 1, psso, k to last 3 sts, k 2 tog, k 1; on 3rd needle, k 1, sl 1, k 1, psso, k to end. K 1 rnd even. Repeat these last 2 rnds until 20 (16) sts remain. K 5 (4) sts of first needle to 3rd needle. Break off leaving an end. Weave 10 (8) sts of sole and 10 (8) upper sts tog in Kitchener st. Steam-press socks.

Plain stockinette stitch is used for these basic socks to make in any length, any size, in lightweight or medium-weight yarns.

Argyle socks

SIZE: Adjustable length, men's sizes.

MATERIALS: Fingering yarn, 3 ply, 3 1-oz. skeins oxford, main color (MC), 1 skein each of scarlet, white and black. Straight knitting needles Nos. 1 and 2; set of dp needles No. 2. (Or English sizes 12 and 11.) Set of bobbins.

GAUGE: 15 sts=2"; 11 rows=1" (stockinette st, No. 2 needles).

Pattern Note: Use a separate bobbin for each white, MC and scarlet diamond. Use separate bobbin wound with MC between diamond panels. Use separate strands of black for diamond outline sts. Always change colors on wrong side, picking up new strand from under dropped strand. Following chart, work pat in stockinette st (k 1 row, p 1 row). **On K Rows** (right side): Read chart from A to B. **On P Rows:** Read chart from B to A.

CUFF AND LEG: With MC and No. 1 needles, cast on loosely 64 sts. Work in ribbing of k 2, p 2 for 2½". Change to No. 2 straight needles. Work in pat (see Pat Note) to top of chart. With MC bobbin at edge, k 1 row. With dp needle, p 1 row. Break off all bobbins.

Divide Sts for Heel: Sl first and last 16 sts on one dp needle, having back seam at center of heel; divide and leave center 32 sts on 2 dp needles for instep.

HEEL: From right side, join MC at beg of heel sts, work back and forth on 32 heel sts as follows: **Row 1** (right side): * K 1, sl 1, repeat from * across.

Row 2: Purl. Repeat these 2 rows until 33 rows are completed, ending k row.

Turn Heel: P 17 sts, p 2 tog, p 1, turn; sl 1, k 3, sl 1, k 1, psso, k 1, turn; sl 1, p 4, p 2 tog, p 1, turn; sl 1, k 5, sl 1, k 1, psso, k 1, turn; sl 1, p 6, p 2 tog, p 1, turn. Continue in same way, working 1 st more before dec on each row until all sts are worked, ending k row—18 sts.

INSTEP: With same heel needle, pick up and k 16 sts on side of heel piece; with 2nd dp needle, k across 32 instep sts; with 3rd dp needle, pick up and k 16 sts on other side of heel piece and with same needle k 9 sts from heel needle. Mark last st for end of rnd. There are 25 sts on each of first and 3rd needles, 32 sts on 2nd needle. K around as follows:

Shape Gussets: Rnd 1: K to last 3 sts on first needle, k 2 tog, k 1; k across 2nd needle; on 3rd needle, k 1, sl 1, k 1, psso, k to end of rnd.

Rnd 2: K even. Repeat these 2 rnds until 16 sts remain on each of first and 3rd needles. Work even on 64 sts until foot measures 2" less than desired finished length from center back of heel.

Shape Toe: Rnd 1: K to last 3 sts on first needle, k 2 tog, k 1; on 2nd needle, k 1, sl 1, k 1, psso, k to last 3 sts, k 2 tog, k 1; on 3rd needle, k 1, sl 1, k 1, psso, k to end of rnd. **Rnd 2:** K even. Repeat these 2 rnds until 20 sts remain in rnd. With 3rd needle, k across first needle. Break off yarn, leaving about 12" end on work. Thread this into a tapestry needle and, holding needles parallel, weave sole and instep sts together in Kitchener stitch (see index). Sew back seam. Steam-press, using steam iron or damp cloth and dry iron.

Argyle-patterned socks, unlike most socks, are worked back and forth on two needles until diamonds are completed; then socks are finished in four-needle knitting. Each colorful diamond is knitted from a separate bobbin of yarn as described in directions.

B   A

◢ BLACK   ⊡ SCARLET   ☐ MC   ⊠ WHITE

Cable trim gloves for men

SIZE: 7½-8 (for hand 7½" around measured below four fingers).

MATERIALS: 4-ply sport yarn, 1 2-oz. ball. Set of dp needles No. 1. (Or English size 12.) Crochet hook or cable stitch holder.

GAUGE: 8 sts=1"; 11 rnds=1".

RIGHT GLOVE: CUFF: Cast on 56 sts, divide on 3 needles. Join, work in ribbing of k 2, p 2 for 3"; mark last st as end of rnd.

HAND: Rnd 1: K 4, * p 1, k 6, p 1, k 4, p 1, k 6, p 1 *; k 6, k 3 sts in next st (first inc for thumb), k to end of rnd.

Rnds 2 and 3: K 4, repeat from * to * of rnd 1, k to end of rnd.

Rnd 4: K 4, repeat from * to * of rnd 1, k 6, inc 1 st in next st (first thumb st), k 1, inc 1 st in next st (last thumb st), k to end of rnd.

Rnds 5-7: Repeat rnd 2.

Rnd 8 (cable row): K 4, p 1, sl next 3 sts as if to p to a crochet hook, hold in front of work, k next 3 sts, slide sts on hook to end of hook and without twisting sts k 3 sts from end of hook, p 1, k 4, p 1, sl next 3 sts to hook and hold in front, k next 3 sts, k 3 sts from hook, p 1, k 6; inc 1 st in next st, k 3, inc 1 st in next st, k to end of rnd. Repeat these 8 rnds for pat, inc 1 st in first and last thumb sts every 4th rnd, having 2 sts more in thumb gore after each successive inc rnd and repeating cable twist every 8th rnd, until there are 9 incs at each side of thumb gore. There will be 19 sts in thumb gore. Work 1 rnd after last inc, end in st before first thumb st. Sl 19 thumb sts to a thread, cast on 5 sts for inner side of thumb, work to end of rnd, end in st before 5 cast-on sts—60 sts. Work 18 rnds even, continuing cable pat. Work 6 rnds, discontinuing cable pat, end in st before 5 cast-on sts.

FIRST FINGER: Sl last 10 sts to a free needle; with another needle k next 5 sts (over 5 cast-on sts), k 2 more sts to last needle; sl remaining 43 sts to a thread (to be held for other 3 fingers); cast on 4 sts on 2nd needle. Divide 21 sts on 3 needles; join, k around for 3".

Next Rnd: K 2 tog, k to end of rnd. K 1 rnd even.

First Dec Rnd: * K 2 tog, k 3, repeat from * to end of rnd—16 sts. K 1 rnd even. * K 2 tog, k 2, repeat from * to end of rnd—12 sts. K 1 rnd even. K 2 tog 6 times; break off and draw end twice through remaining 6 sts. Darn in end.

2ND FINGER: Sl 7 sts from thread on back of hand to needle, pick up and k 4 sts on the 4 cast-on sts on side of first finger, k 7 sts from other end of thread (palm side) to a needle, cast on 3 sts for other side of finger. Place these 21 sts on 3 needles. K around for 3¼". Finish as for first finger.

3RD FINGER: Sl 7 sts from end of thread on back of hand, pick up and k 3 sts on 3 cast-on sts on 2nd finger, k 7 sts from other end of thread to a needle, cast on 3 sts. On these 20 sts, work same as for first finger. Dec as for first finger, beg with first dec rnd.

4TH FINGER: Sl remaining 15 sts from thread to needles; pick up and k 3 sts on 3 cast-on sts on 3rd finger. Work even on these 18 sts for 2¼". Dec as follows: * K 2 tog, k 1, repeat from * 5 times—12 sts. K 1 rnd even. K 2 tog 6 times; break yarn and draw end twice through remaining 6 sts. Darn in end.

THUMB: Sl 19 thumb sts from thread to 2 needles, pick up and k 5 sts on 5 cast-on sts and an extra st at each end—26 sts. K 2 rnds even. * **Next Rnd:** Dec 1 st at center of 5 cast-on sts. K 1 rnd even. Repeat from * 3 times. Work even on remaining 22 sts until thumb measures 2¼" on inner side.

Next Rnd: * K 2 tog, k 9, repeat from * once. K 1 rnd even. Finish as for first finger beg with first dec rnd.

LEFT GLOVE: Work cuff as for right glove.

HAND: Rnd 1: K 25, k 3 sts in next st, k 6, * p 1, k 6, p 1, k 4, p 1, k 6, p 1*; k 4. Work to correspond to right glove to first finger.

FIRST FINGER: Begin first finger 2 sts **before** the 5 sts cast on over thumb, k 5 sts cast on over thumb, k next 10 sts, cast on 4 sts for inside of finger. Complete as for right glove. Steam-press gloves.

Of all four-needle projects, gloves are most fascinating to knit. Directions tell how to make thumb gusset, fingers; how to work left glove to correspond to right; how to use crochet hook for twisting cables.

Reversible double-thick mittens for men

SIZE: Men's medium size.

MATERIALS: 6 ozs. knitting worsted. Knitting needles No. 6. (Or English size 7.)

GAUGE: 4 k sts=1″.

MITT: Cast on 48 sts. Work in ribbing of k 2, p 2 for 4″.

Inc Row: (Inc 1 st in each of 2 k sts, p 2) 5 times, (inc 1 st in each of 2 k sts, inc 1 st in each of 2 p sts) twice, inc 1 st in 2 k sts, p 2) 5 times—76 sts.

Double Knitting Pat: Row 1: * K 1, yarn in front of work, sl 1 as if to p allowing yarn to cross in front of st, repeat from * across. Repeat row 1 for pat. This pat forms a double thickness of knitting.

Work in pat for 10 rows (looks like 5 rows).

First Inc for Thumb: Work in pat on 35 sts, put marker on needle, inc 1 st in each of next 2 sts, work in pat on 2 sts, inc 1 st in each of next 2 sts, put a marker on needle, work in pat on 35 sts. Work in pat for 3 rows, slipping markers.

2nd Inc for Thumb: Work in pat to marker, sl marker, inc 1 st in each of next 2 sts, work in pat on 6 sts, inc 1 st in each of next 2 sts, sl marker, work in pat to end. Work in pat for 3 rows, slipping markers. Continue in this manner, increasing 2 sts after first marker and 2 sts before 2nd marker every 4th row until there are 30 sts between markers for thumb. Work in pat for 3 rows.

Thumb: Work in pat on 35 sts, place these sts on a holder. Inc 1 st in first st of thumb, work in pat to last st of thumb, inc 1 st—32 sts for thumb. Place remaining 35 sts on a holder. Work even in pat on 32 thumb sts for 2½″.

First Dec Row: * Work pat on 4 sts, k 2 tog twice, repeat from * across. Work back in pat.

2nd Dec Row: * Work pat on 2 sts, k 2 tog twice, repeat from * across. Work back.

3rd Dec Row: K 2 tog across row. Break yarn leaving end for sewing. Draw end through sts; fasten. Sew thumb seam.

HAND: Place sts from first holder on needle, join yarn, pick up and k 6 sts under thumb, work pat on 35 sts of 2nd holder. Work even in pat on these 76 sts for 4″.

First Dec Row: * Work pat on 6 sts, k 2 tog twice, repeat from * across, work pat on 6 sts. Work 3 rows in pat—62 sts.

2nd Dec Row: * Work pat on 5 sts, k 2 tog twice, repeat from * across to last 8 sts, work pat on 4 sts, k 2 tog twice. Work 3 rows in pat—48 sts.

3rd Dec Row: * Work pat on 4 sts, k 2 tog twice, repeat from * across. Work 3 rows in pat—36 sts.

4th Dec Row: * Work pat on 3 sts, k 2 tog twice, repeat from * across, sl last st. Work 1 row in pat—26 sts.

5th Dec Row: * Work pat on 2 sts, k 2 tog twice, repeat from * across, k 1, sl 1. Work 1 row in pat—18 sts. K 2 tog across next row. Break yarn leaving end for sewing. Draw end through sts. Sew side seam.

Reversible double-thick mittens are worked in double-knitting pattern, an ingenious stitch that forms two layers of knitting.

211

Snowflake pattern gloves for women

Colored patterns can be worked in four-needle knitting, as in these authentic Norwegian gloves. Pattern color forming large snowflakes on backs and smaller motifs on fingers and palms is carried around with background color.

SIZE: 8-8½.

MATERIALS: Sport yarn, 2 2-oz. balls blue, main color (MC); 2 balls white, contrasting color (CC). One set of dp needles No. 2. (Or English size 11.) One stitch holder.

GAUGE: 15 sts=2″ (pat).

Pattern Note: Always change colors on wrong side, picking up new strand from under dropped strand. Carry colors across loosely; when there are more than 5 sts, twist colors every 3rd st.

RIGHT GLOVE: CUFF: With MC, cast on 45 sts, divide sts evenly on 3 needles. Mark end of rnd. Join, working in ribbing of k 2, p 1 for 7 rnds.

Striped Pat: Rnds 1-10: Continue in ribbing, working 1 rnd CC, 1 rnd MC alternately. Break off CC. With MC, continue in ribbing for 6 rnds.

HAND: Work in stockinette st (k each rnd) for 4 rnds, inc 12 sts evenly spaced on last rnd—57 sts.

Thumb Gore: Rnd 1: Following Chart 1 from right to left, k first 37 sts, put a marker on needle, with MC, k in front and back of next st (thumb inc made), put a marker on needle, k 2 CC, continue in pat to end of rnd.

Rnd 2: Following Chart 1, work rnd 2 of pat, having 2 MC sts in thumb gore and 2 CC sts each side of thumb gore.

Rnd 3: Following Chart 1, work rnd 3 of pat to first marker, with MC, k 1, inc 1 st in next st, k 2 CC, continue in pat to end of rnd.

Rnd 4: Following Chart 1, work rnd 4 of pat, having 3 MC sts in thumb gore and 2 CC sts each side of thumb gore.

Rnds 5-11: Continue to inc 1 st in st after first and before 2nd marker on next rnd, then every other rnd 3 times as shown on chart—11 sts between markers for thumb gore, 67 sts.

Rnds 12-14: Following Chart 1, work even.

Rnd 15: Following Chart 1, work to within 2 sts of first marker, sl next 15 sts on a holder for thumb, with MC, cast on 15 sts, work in pat to end of rnd. Remove markers.

Rnd 16: Following Chart 1, k first 33 sts, with MC, k 2 tog, work in pat to end of rnd—66 sts.

Rnds 17-27: Following Chart 1, work in pat.

Rnd 28: Following Chart 1, sl first 22 sts on a colored thread for back of hand side of other fingers, break off yarn; join MC and k next 19 sts as shown on chart for first finger, with MC, cast on 5 sts on inner side, sl remaining 25 sts on another colored thread for palm side of other fingers.

First Finger: Divide these 24 sts on 3 needles. Join, following Chart 2 from right to left for right glove (from left to right for left glove). K around in pat to end of rnd 20.

Shape Tip: Rnd 21: Following Chart 2, k to after first CC stripe, sl 1, k 1, psso, k to last 4 sts of rnd, k 2 tog, k 2 CC.

Rnds 22-24: * Sl 1, k 1, psso, k to within 2 sts of CC stripe, k 2 tog, k 2 CC, repeat from * once—10 sts remain at end of rnd 24.

Rnd 25: * With MC, sl 1, k 2 tog, psso, k 2 CC, repeat from * once—6 sts. Break off MC.

Rnd 26: With CC, k 2 tog 3 times—3 sts.

Rnd 27: With CC, sl 1, k 2 tog, psso. End off last st. Break off CC, pull CC strand to wrong side and fasten securely.

Second Finger: Sl next 6 sts from back of hand to needle. From right side, join MC at beg of back finger, k sts on needle, pick up and k 5 sts on cast-on sts of last finger, sl next 8 sts of palm on a spare needle, on palm needle, (k 3 MC, k 1 CC) twice, with MC, cast on 5 sts. Divide these 24 sts on 3 needles.

Join, following Chart 2, k around in pat to end of rnd 20. Shape tip as for first finger.

Third Finger: Work as for second finger.

Fourth Finger: Sl last 10 sts from back of hand to needle. From right side, join CC, at beg of back finger, k 2 CC, k 8 MC, with MC, pick up and k 5 sts on cast-on sts of last finger, sl last 9 sts of palm on a spare needle, on palm needle, (k 3 MC, k 1 CC) twice, k 1 MC. Divide these 24 sts on 3 needles. Join, following Chart 2, k around in pat to end of rnd 14.

Shape Tip: Rnds 15-18: Following Chart 2, work rnds 15-18, shaping tip as for rnds 21-24 of directions on first finger.

Rnds 19-21: Work as for rnds 25-27 of directions on first finger.

THUMB: Sl 15 sts from holder to 2 needles, join MC, pick up and k 15 sts on cast-on sts. Divide these 30 sts on 3 needles. Join, with CC, k 2 CC sts, mark last st for end of rnd. Following Chart 3 from right to left, k around in pat to end of rnd 12.

Shape Tip: Rnds 13 and 14: Following Chart 3, k to after first CC stripe, sl 1, k 1, psso, k to last 4 sts

of rnd, k 2 tog, k 2 CC (these 2 CC sts are part of back sts)—26 sts.

Rnds 15-18: Following Chart 3, work rnds 15-18, shaping tip as for rnd 22 of directions on first finger —10 sts.

Rnds 19-21: Work as for rnds 25-27 of first finger.

LEFT GLOVE: Work as for right glove to thumb gore.

Thumb Gore: Rnd 1: Following Chart 1, from left to right, k first 19 sts, put a marker on needle, with MC, k in front and back of next st (thumb inc made), put a marker on needle, k 2 CC, work in pat to end of rnd.

Rnds 2-27: Repeat rnds 2-27 as for right glove.

Rnd 28: Following Chart 1, sl first 25 sts on a colored thread for palm, break yarn; join CC, k next 19 sts as shown on chart for first finger, with MC, cast on 5 sts on inner side, sl remaining 22 sts on another colored thread for back of hand.

Work fingers as for right glove, beg fingers from palm side; work thumb as for right glove. Steam-press gloves; stretch fingers if necessary.

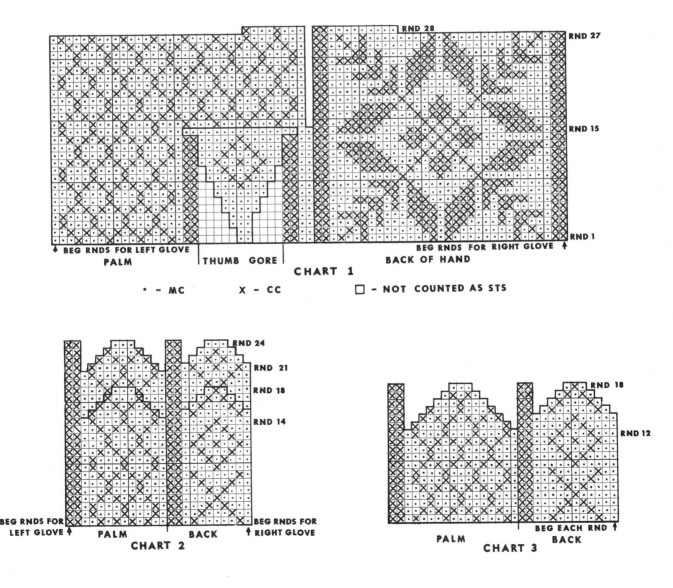

CHART 1

• – MC   X – CC   □ – NOT COUNTED AS STS

CHART 2

CHART 3

Lace patterns are frequently used for late-day sweaters. The "yarn over" and decrease stitches present in all lace knitting can be combined in a wide variety of arrangements to produce exquisite openwork effects. In the women's cardigan shown here, a relatively simple lace pattern is used and accented with sewn-on beads and pearls.

Women's beaded cardigan

SIZES: Directions for size 34. Changes for sizes 36, 38, 40, 42 in parentheses.

Fits Bust Size: 36" (38"-40"-42"-44"). Easy-fit garment.

MATERIALS: Fingering yarn, 8 (9-10-11-12) 1-oz. skeins. Plastic knitting needles Nos. 2 and 3. (Or English sizes 11 and 10.) Bugle beads and pearls for trimming (optional). Four pearl buttons. Two stitch holders.

GAUGE: 15 sts=2"; 11 rows=1" (lace pat, No. 3 needles).

LACE PATTERN (multiple of 10 sts plus 1):
Note: Yarn in back, sl all sl sts as if to p.

Row 1 and all odd rows (wrong side): Purl.

Row 2: K 1, * yo, sl 1, k 1, psso, k 5, k 2 tog, yo, k 1, repeat from * across.

Row 4: K 2, * yo, sl 1, k 1, psso, k 3, k 2 tog, yo, k 3, repeat from * across, end last repeat k 2.

Row 6: K 3, * yo, sl 1, k 1, psso, k 1, k 2 tog, yo, k 5, repeat from * across, end last repeat k 3.

Row 8: K 4, * yo, sl 1, k 2 tog, pass sl st over the k 2 tog, yo, k 7, repeat from * across, end last repeat k 4. Repeat these 8 rows for lace pat.

To Bind Off: Bind off in p at beg of odd pat rows, bind off in k (omitting pat) at beg of even pat rows. When sts are bound off on even pat rows, st remaining on right-hand needle counts as first st of pat row.

CARDIGAN: BACK: With No. 2 needles, cast on 121 (121-131-131-141) sts.

Ribbing: Row 1 (wrong side): P 1, * k 1, p 1, repeat from * across.

Row 2: K 1, * p 1, k 1, repeat from * across. Repeat these 2 rows for 2", end on right side and inc 10 sts evenly spaced across last row—131 (131-141-141-151) sts. Change to No. 3 needles. Work in lace pat until piece measures 12" (12"-12½"-12½"-13") from start, end on right side. Keep track of pat row ended.

Shape Armholes: Bind off (see To Bind Off) 10 sts at beg of next 2 rows, then dec 1 st each side every p row 5 (5-6-4-7) times—101 (101-109-113-117) sts. Work even in lace pat until armholes measure 7½" (7¾"-8"-8¼"-8½") above first bound-off sts, end on right side of work.

Shape Shoulders: Bind off 5 (5-4-6-3) sts at beg of next 2 rows, 10 sts next 4 rows, 5 (5-9-8-13) sts next 2 rows. Bind off remaining 41 (41-43-45-45) sts for back of neck.

LEFT FRONT: With No. 2 needles, cast on 79 (89-89-99-99) sts.

Ribbing: Row 1 (wrong side): P 13, k 1, put a marker on needle (facing and center band), p 1, * k 1, p 1, repeat from * across.

Row 2: K 1, * p 1, k 1, repeat from * to marker, sl marker, p 1, k 6 (center band), sl 1 as if to p, k 6 (facing). Repeat these 2 rows for 2", end on right side and inc 6 sts evenly spaced across ribbing only—85 (95-95-105-105) sts. Keeping center band and facing sts as established, work in lace pat until piece measures 3½" above ribbing, end with lace pat row 7.

Shape Front Edge: Next Row: Work in lace pat to within 2 sts of marker, k 2 tog (front dec), sl marker, work center band and facing. Keeping center band and facing sts as established, continue in lace pat, dec 1 st inside of center band and facing sts on right side as before every 6th row 24 (5-13-2-2) times, every 4th row 1 (30-18-37-35) times; **at same time,** when piece measures same as back to underarm, end same lace pat row as back at underarm. Work 1 row more on left front to end at arm side.

Shape Armhole: Still shaping front edge, bind off 10 sts at beg of arm side once, then dec 1 st at arm side every p row 5 (5-6-7-7) times. When front decs are completed, 44 (44-47-48-50) sts remains. Work even until armhole measures same as back.

Shape Shoulder: Bind off 5 (5-4-3-3) sts at beg of arm side once, 10 sts twice, 5 (5-9-11-13) sts once. Work even on remaining 14 sts of center band and facing for 2½" (2½"-2¾"-3"-3"). Sl sts on a holder. Break yarn; on left front leave a long end for weaving center band and facing sts.

RIGHT FRONT: With No. 2 needles, cast on 79 (89-89-99-99) sts.

Ribbing: Rows 1 and 3 (wrong side): P 1, * k 1, p 1, repeat from * across to last 14 sts, put a marker on needle, k 1, p 13 (center band and facing).

Rows 2 and 4: K 6, sl 1 as if to p, k 6, p 1, sl marker (facing and center band), k 1, * p 1, k 1, repeat from * to end of row.

Row 5: Repeat row 1.

Buttonhole Row (right side): K 2 sts at beg of front edge, bind off next 2 sts, work until 5 sts from bound-off sts, bind off next 2 sts, finish row.

Next Row: Cast on 2 sts over each group of bound-off sts. Continue to work as for left front to start of front edge shaping, repeating buttonholes on every 17th and 18th rows 3 times.

Shape Front Edge: Next Row (right side): Work facing and center band sts, sl marker, sl 1, k 1, psso (front dec), beg with k 2 instead of k 4, work row 8 of lace pat to end of row. Keeping facing and center band sts as established, complete right front as for left front.

SLEEVES: With No. 2 needles, cast on 65 (70-75-80-85) sts. Work in ribbing as for back for 2", end on right side and inc 16 (11-16-11-16) sts evenly spaced across last row—81 (81-91-91-101) sts. Change to No. 3 needles. Work in lace pat, inc 1 st each side every 10th row 10 times, working added sts into pat—101 (101-111-111-121) sts. Work even until piece measures 12" (12"-12½"-12½"-13") from start, end same pat row as back at underarm.

Shape Cap: Bind off 10 sts at beg of next 2 rows. Dec 1 st each side every other row 20 (22-22-24-24) times, every row 10 (8-12-10-14) times. Bind off remaining 21 (21-23-23-25) sts.

FINISHING: Steam-press pieces lightly. Sew shoulder seams. Matching pat, sew in sleeves; sew side and sleeve seams. Weave ends of neckband tog with Kitchener stitch (see Index). Sew inside edge of neckband to back of neck. Fold facing to wrong side at sl st (buttonholes meeting); hem in place. Work buttonhole stitch around double buttonholes. Steam-press seams. Sew on buttons. If desired, trim every other row of "eyelets" on fronts and sleeves with bugle beads and pearls as pictured.

Sequin lace jacket

Opalescent sequins are knitted right into the lace pattern of this evening jacket. Modified dolman sleeves are worked in one with the back and fronts.

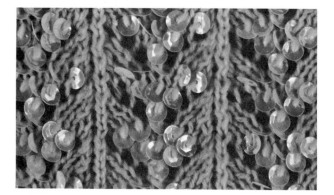

SIZES: Directions are for small size (10-12). Changes for medium (14-16) and large (18-20) are in parentheses.

Fits Bust: 31″-32″ (34″-36″; 38″-40″).

MATERIALS: Fingering yarn, 3 ply, 9 (10-10) 1-oz. skeins. Straight knitting needles No. 0; 29″ circular needle No. 3. (Or English sizes 13 and 10.) Cup sequins No. 6, about 13 (13-14) strings (1000 sequins to each string). Stitch holders.

GAUGE: 7 sts=1″; 10 rows=1″ (lace pat, No. 3 needle).

GENERAL DIRECTIONS: To String Sequins on Yarn: With inside of cup (right side) facing yarn, tie sequin thread around yarn (never tie yarn around sequin thread). Slide sequins carefully over knot onto yarn (right side going on first).

PLAIN LACE PATTERN (multiple of 9 sts):

Row 1 (right side): * K 2 tog, k 2, yo, k 1, yo, k 2, k 2 tog, repeat from * across row.

Rows 2 and 4 (wrong side): Purl.

Row 3: * K 2 tog, k 1, yo, k 3, yo, k 1, k 2 tog, repeat from * across row.

Row 5: * K 2 tog, yo, k 5, yo, k 2 tog, repeat from * across row.

Row 6: Purl. Repeat these 6 rows for plain lace pat.

SEQUIN LACE PATTERN: Rows 1, 3, 5 (right side): Work as for plain lace pat, keeping sequins right side up and at bottom of k st in last row on right side of work.

Row 2 (sequin row worked from wrong side): * P 4, **for sequin p st,** with yarn in front of work, insert needle in next st as if to p, slide right side of sequin up close to st, complete p st bringing both sequin (wrong side of sequin facing you) and yarn through st to right side (thus placing sequin right side up at bottom of st on right side of work), p 4, repeat from * across.

Row 4: * P 3, make 3 sequin p sts, p 3, repeat from * across row.

Row 6: * P 2, make 5 sequin p sts, p 2, repeat from * across row. Repeat these 6 rows for sequin lace pat.

JACKET: BACK: Beg at lower edge with No. 3 circular needle, cast on 117 (126-135) sts. Work back and forth in plain lace pat for 6 rows. Break off yarn; put aside for use later. String sequins on another skein of yarn (see General Directions). Tie sequin-strung yarn to yarn end close to side of last row. Work in sequin lace pat until piece measures 10″ from start or desired length to underarm, end on pat row 5. Put a marker on work each side of last row for underarms. Check gauge; piece should be 16¾″ (18″-19¼″) wide.

Shape Sleeves: * Cast on 9 sts each side of pat row 6 for sleeves. Work last group of 9 cast-on sts at each arm side in plain lace pat (since this will go under arm) and all other sts in sequin lace pat for 5 rows. Repeat from * 7 times—261 (270-279) sts. Check gauge; piece should be 37¼″ (38½″-39¾″) wide across last 5 rows. Cast on 5 sts for sleeve bands each side of pat row 6—271 (280-289) sts. Put a marker on needle 5 sts from each sleeve edge. Work 5 sts at each sleeve edge in stockinette st (k on right side, p on wrong side) and all other sts in sequin lace pat until piece measures 8½″ (9″-9½″) above underarm markers, end on pat row 5.

Next Row: P first 122 sts, sl these sts on a holder for left shoulder, bind off in p next 27 (36-45) sts for back of neck, sl last 122 sts (including st left on right-hand needle) on another holder for right shoulder.

RIGHT FRONT: With plain yarn and No. 3 circular needle, cast on 59 (68-77) sts.

Row 1: K first 5 sts for center band, put a marker on needle, work row 1 of plain lace pat to end of row. Work center bands sts in stockinette st (p on wrong side, k on right side) and all other sts in plain lace pat for 5 rows more. Break off yarn; put aside for use later. String sequins as before and join to yarn end close to side of last row. Keeping center band as established, work in sequin lace pat until piece measures same as back to underarm markers, end on pat row 5. Put a marker on work at arm side of last row for underarm. Check gauge; piece inside of center band should be 7¾″ (9″-10¼″) wide.

Shape Sleeves: * Cast on 9 sts at beg of pat row 6 for sleeve, p to end of row. Work last group of 9 cast-on sts at arm side in plain lace pat (since this will go under arm), sts inside of marker in sequin lace pat and center band sts as established for 5 rows more. Repeat from * 7 times—131 (140-149) sts. Piece inside of center band should be 18″ (19¼″-20½″) wide across last 5 rows. Cast on 5 sts for sleeve band at beg of pat row 6, p to end of row—136 (145-154) sts. Work 5 sts at sleeve edge in stockinette st (k on right side, p on wrong side), sts inside of marker in sequin lace pat and center band sts as established until piece measures 4″ (4½″-5″) above underarm marker, end at center edge.

Shape Neck: Work 5 center band sts, sl these sts on a safety pin for neckband, work to end of row. Continue in pat as established, bind off 9 sts at beg of center edge 1 (2-3) times—122 sts. Work even until piece measures 8½″ (9″-9½″) above underarm

marker, end at neck edge with pat row 6 for right front (**note,** end at neck edge with pat row 5 when working left front). Break yarn, leaving a long end for joining shoulder seam. Sl these sts on a stitch holder.

LEFT FRONT: Work as for right front, reversing center band (work center band at end of row 1 of front) and sleeve shaping (cast on sts for sleeve and sleeve band at end of pat row 6.)

FINISHING: Run in yarn ends on wrong side. To block, dip each piece in cold water. Smooth pieces out, right side up, on a padded surface. Using rust-proof pins, pin pieces to measurements given. When completely dry, remove pins. Do not press sequins with an iron.

Beg at sleeve edges, sl sts of right back shoulder to one No. 0 needle, sl sts of right front shoulder to another No. 0 needle. Join right shoulder seam as follows: With right sides touching, hold sts of right back shoulder (toward you) parallel with sts of right front shoulder and points of needles at neck edge. Beg at neck edge, from wrong side with circular needle, * k tog 1 st of back shoulder with 1 st of front shoulder as 1 st, repeat from * to end of row (work loosely so that shoulder seam does not pull). **Next Row:** Bind off seam sts loosely in k. Beg at sleeve edges, sl sts of left front shoulder to one No. 0 needle, sl sts of left back shoulder to another No. 0 needle. Join left shoulder seam as for right shoulder seam, holding left front shoulder toward you, working from neck edge to end of row.

From wrong side, sew sleeve seams with backstitch, matching each group of cast-on sts. Sew side seams with backstitch, matching pat. Steam-press seams open flat on wrong side.

Neckband: Sl sts of right front holder to No. 3 circular needle. Join plain yarn at inside edge, continue in stockinette st on 5 sts to center back of neck. Bind off. Work neckband on left front neck in same way. Weave ends of neckband tog; sew inside edge around neck edge.

BORDERS: With plain yarn and No. 0 needles, cast on 17 sts. **Row 1** (right side): K 8, sl 1 as if to p, k 8.

Row 2: Purl. Repeat these 2 rows until border fits entire outside edge of jacket. Bind off. Weave ends of border tog. With right sides tog, sew one edge of border to inside edge (along 5th k st) of center bands, neckband and across 6th row of plain lace pat at lower edge of jacket, catching in flat ends of side seams. Turn border to wrong side on sl st over edge of jacket; sew inside edge (tuck in one st) of border in place, covering seam of border. Make two more borders to fit sleeve edges. With seam of border at sleeve seams, sew borders to sleeve edges in same manner as on edge of jacket. Steam-press borders being careful to avoid touching sequins with iron.

Tyrolean cardigan

Authentic Tyrolean cardigans combine lace patterns, raised patterns and touches of brightly colored embroidery. Necklines and front edges are often crocheted in a contrasting color.

SIZES: Directions for size 12. Changes for sizes 14, 16 and 18 are in parentheses.

Body Bust Size: 32″ (34″-36″-38″).

Blocked Bust Size: 34″ (37″-38″-41″).

MATERIALS: Featherweight knitting worsted, 6 (7-7-8) 2-oz. skeins white, main color (MC); 1 skein dark green, contrasting color (CC). Small amounts of blue, yellow and red for embroidery. 14″ knitting needles Nos. 2 and 4. (Or English sizes 11 and 9.) Steel crochet hook No. 2. Large-eyed tapestry needle. Six buttons. One yard 1″ grosgrain ribbon.

GAUGE: 7 sts=1″; 9 rows=1″ (lace pat, No. 4 needles).

LACE PATTERN (multiple of 8 sts plus 3): **Rows 1, 3, 5** (right side): P 4, * sl 1, k 2 tog, psso, p 5, repeat from * across, end last repeat p 4. These rows have fewer sts.

Rows 2, 4, 6 (wrong side): K 2, yo, * k 5, yo, k 1, yo, repeat from * across, end k 5, yo, k 2. These rows restore original number of sts.

Row 7: Repeat row 1.

Rows 8, 10, 12, 14: Shift pat as follows: K 4, * yo, k 1, yo, k 5, repeat from * across, end last repeat k 4. These rows restore original number of sts.

Rows 9, 11, 13, 15: P 1, k 2 tog, * p 5, sl 1, k 2 tog, psso, repeat from * across, end p 5, k 2 tog, p 1. These rows have fewer sts. Repeat rows 2-15 for lace pat.

To Bind Off: Bind off in p on right side, in k on wrong side. The st that remains on right-hand needle after binding off is next st of pat. When shaping garment, omit a yo or psso after a k 2 tog at edges to keep correct number of sts.

BACK: With MC and No. 2 needles, cast on 114 (122-130-138) sts. Work in ribbing of k 1, p 1 for 3½″, inc 1 st at end of last row—115 (123-131-139) sts. Change to No. 4 needles. Work in lace pat until piece is 13½″ (14″-14″-14½″) from start or desired length to underarm, end on the wrong side.

Shape Armholes: Bind off (see To Bind Off) 4 sts at beg of next 2 rows, end wrong side. Dec 1 st each side every 3rd row 4 (5-6-7) times, end wrong side. Work even in pat on 99 (105-111-117) sts until armholes measure 7¼″ (7½″-7¾″-8″) above first bound-off sts, end wrong side.

Shape Shoulders: Bind off 11 (12-12-13) sts at beg of next 4 rows, 10 (10-12-12) sts next 2 rows. Bind off remaining 35 (37-39-41) sts for back of neck.

LEFT FRONT: With MC and No. 2 needles, cast on 67 (75-75-83) sts.

Ribbing: Row 1 (right side): K 1, * p 1, k 1, repeat from * across.

Row 2: P 1, * k 1, p 1, repeat from * across. Repeat these 2 rows for 3½″, end wrong side. Change to No. 4 needles.

Pattern: Row 1 (right side): Work in lace pat to last 8 sts, (p 1, k 1) 4 times for center seed st band.

Row 2: (K 1, p 1) 4 times, work in pat to end of row. Repeat these 2 rows until piece is same as back to underarm, end arm side.

Shape Armhole: Bind off (see To Bind Off) 4 (4-4-6) sts at beg of arm side, finish row. Dec 1 st at arm side every 3rd row 6 (8-8-8) times, end wrong side. Work even on 57 (63-63-69) sts until armhole measures 4¾″ (5″-5¼″-5½″) above first bound-off sts.

Shape Neck: Bind off 9 (9-9-10) sts at beg of center edge once, 3 sts 5 (6-6-7) times, 1 st 1 (2-0-0) times, end wrong side. Work even on 32 (34-36-38) sts until armhole measures same as back.

Shape Shoulder: Bind off 11 (12-12-13) sts at beg of arm side twice, 10 (10-12-12) sts once.

With pins, mark position of 6 buttons evenly spaced on center band of left front: first one ½″ from lower edge, last one ½″ below neck edge.

BUTTONHOLES: Work 3 sts at beg of center edge, bind off next 3 sts, finish row. **Next Row:** Cast on 3 sts over bound-off sts.

RIGHT FRONT: Cast on and work ribbing as for left front, forming buttonhole opposite marker. Change to No. 4 needles.

Pattern: Row 1 (right side): (K 1, p 1) 4 times for center seed st band, work in lace pat to end of row.

Row 2: Work in lace pat to last 8 sts, (p 1, k 1) 4 times. Repeating these 2 rows for pat, complete right front as for left, form buttonholes opposite markers.

SLEEVES: With MC and No. 2 needles, cast on 52 (54-60-62) sts. Work in ribbing of k 1, p 1 for 4½″, inc 7 (5-7-5) sts evenly spaced across last row —59 (59-67-67) sts. Change to No. 4 needles. Put a marker on needle each side of last row. Work in lace pat between markers, casting on 1 st each side every 7th row 4 times and working added sts in reverse stockinette st (p on right side, k on wrong side), end row 15 of pat. Move markers out to each side of last row. Continue with pat and shaping, working lace pat between markers and added sts in reverse stockinette st, as follows:

Alternate Lace Pat: On Pat Rows 2, 4, 6: Work original pat repeating from first * to 2nd * across row, end k 5. There will be 2 extra sts because of pat after first row—69 (69-77-77) sts on needle.

On Pat Rows 3, 5, 7: P 1, sl 1, k 2 tog, p 5, then repeat original pat from first * to 2nd * across row, end sl 1, k 2 tog, p 1; cast on 1 st each side of row 7.

On Pat Rows 8, 10, 12, 14: K 3, yo, k 5, then repeat original pat from first * to 2nd * across row, end yo, k 3; cast on 1 st each side of row 14.

On Pat Rows 9, 11, 13, 15: Work the original pat and repeat from first * to 2nd * across row, end p 5. Repeat first 5 rows of alternate lace pat—73 (73-81-81) sts. Remove markers.

Next Row: Cast on 1 st, repeat row 7 of original lace pat across entire row, end last repeat p 3; cast on 1 st. Put markers on needle each side of last row. Beg with row 8, work original lace pat between markers;

cast on 1 st each side every 7th row 4 times, working added sts in reverse stockinette st, ending row 7 of pat. Remove markers.

Next Row: Work row 8 of alternate lace pat on all sts. There will be 2 extra sts on row because of pat— 85 (85-93-93) sts on needle. Beg with row 9, work even in alternate lace pat, omitting cast-on sts (there will be no extra sts because of pat), until sleeve measures 17″ (17½″-17½″-18″) from start or desired length to underarm, end wrong side.

Shape Cap: Bind off (see To Bind Off) 4 (4-4-6) sts at beg of next 2 rows, end wrong side. Dec 1 st each side every 3rd row 6 (6-8-9) times, every row 22 (20-23-21) times, end wrong side. Bind off remaining sts in p.

FINISHING: Sew shoulder seams. Sew in sleeves. Sew side and sleeve seams. Beg at lower edge of right front, from right side, with CC, work 1 row sc on front and neck edges. End off.

Neckband: Row 1: With CC, make a lp on crochet hook. Beg right side of right front neck edge, make sc in 6th sc on neck, * ch 1, sk 1 sc, sc in next sc, repeat from * across neck to last 5 sts of left front edge. Ch 1, turn.

Row 2: Sc in first sc, * ch 7, sc in next ch-1 sp, repeat from * across, end sl st in last sc. Ch 7, turn.

Row 3: Sc in 2nd sc from end, * ch 7, sc in next sc, repeat from * across. End off.

Steam-press cardigan, being careful not to flatten lace pat. Face front edges with grosgrain ribbon. Cut through ribbon and reinforce buttonholes. Sew on buttons.

EMBROIDERY: Thread tapestry needle with single strand of CC and make 2 fly sts 3 rows apart to form stem and leaves (see st detail). Work vertical satin st buds with double strand of yellow, blue or red yarn, beg with small sts for padding and increasing in size to cover space between fly sts and form plump raised bud.

Work vertical row of buds each side of center band, alternating blue and yellow. Scatter red, blue and yellow buds on fronts and top of sleeves.

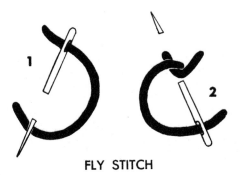

FLY STITCH

SATIN STITCH

Aran Isles cardigan

The Irish-knit sweater is distinguished for its variety of raised pattern stitches set side by side in vertical panels. In this cardigan, open cables, rope cables, raised diamonds and "tree" panels are juxtaposed and seed stitch borders added for more texture interest. The adventurous knitter can substitute her own pattern favorites for these; some possibilities are shown on pages 185-188, Knitted Pattern Stitches.

SIZES: Directions for size 12. Changes for sizes 14 and 16 are in parentheses.

Body Bust Size: 32″ (34″-36″).

Blocked Bust Size: 36″ (38″-40″).

MATERIALS: Knitting worsted, 7 (7-8) 4-oz. skeins. Knitting needles Nos. 6 and 10. (Or English sizes 7 and 3.) One dp needle. Six buttons.

GAUGE: 11 sts=2″; 6 rows=1″ (pat before blocking, No. 10 needles).

ARAN PATTERN: Row 1 (right side): **Side rib-** bing, (k 1 in b lp [back lp] of st, p 1) 1 (2-3) times; **k panel,** k 4; **open cable panel,** p 1, k 1 in b lp, p 3, k 1 in b lp, p 1; **rope cable panel,** k 1 in b lp, p 1, k 6, p 1, k 1 in b lp; **tree panel,** p 5, k 3, p 5; **diamond panel,** k 1 in b lp, p 1, k 2, p 8, k 2, p 1, k 1 in b lp; **tree panel,** p 5, k 3, p 5; **rope cable panel,** k 1 in b lp, p 1, k 6, p 1, k 1 in b lp; **open cable panel,** p 1, k 1 in b lp, p 3, k 1 in b lp, p 1; **k panel,** k 4; **side ribbing,** (p 1, k 1 in b lp) 1 (2-3) times.

Row 2: Side ribbing, (p 1, k 1) 1 (2-3) times; **p**

panel, p 4; **open cable panel**, k 1, p 1, k 3, p 1, k 1; **rope cable panel**, p 1, k 1, p 6, k 1, p 1; **tree panel**, k 5, p 3, k 5; **diamond panel**, p 1, k 1, p 2, k 8, p 2, k 1, p 1; **tree panel**, k 5, p 3, k 5; **rope cable panel**, p 1, k 1, p 6, k 1, p 1; **open cable panel**, k 1, p 1, k 3, p 1, k 1; **p panel**, p 4; **side ribbing**, (k 1, p 1) 1 (2-3) times.

Row 3: Side ribbing, (k 1 in b lp, p 1) 1 (2-3) times; **k panel**, k 4; **open cable panel**, p 1, k 1 in b lp, p 3, k 1 in b lp, p 1; **rope cable panel**, k 1 in b lp, p 1, k 6, p 1, k 1 in b lp; **tree panel**, p 4, sl 1 st to dpn (dp needle), hold in back, k 1 in b lp, p 1 from dpn, k 1 in b lp, sl 1 st to dpn, hold in front, p 1, k 1 in b lp from dpn, p 4; **diamond panel**, k 1 in b lp, p 1, sl 2 sts to dpn, hold in front, p 1, k 2 sts from dpn, p 6, sl 1 st to dpn, hold in back, k 2 sts, p 1 from dpn, p 1, k 1 in b lp; **tree panel**, p 4, sl 1 st to dpn, hold in back, k 1 in b lp, p 1 from dpn, k 1 in b lp, sl 1 st to dpn, hold in front, p 1, k 1 in b lp from dpn, p 4; **rope cable panel**, k 1 in b lp, p 1, k 6, p 1, k 1 in b lp; **open cable panel**, p 1, k 1 in b lp, p 3, k 1 in b lp, p 1; **k panel**, k 4; **side ribbing**, (p 1, k 1 in b lp) 1 (2-3) times.

Row 4: Side ribbing, (p 1, k 1) 1 (2-3) times; **p panel**, p 4; **open cable panel**, k 1, p 1, k 3, p 1, k 1; **rope cable panel**, p 1, k 1, p 6, k 1, p 1; **tree panel**, k 4, (p 1, k 1) twice, p 1, k 4; **diamond panel**, p 1, k 2, p 2, k 6, p 2, k 2, p 1; **tree panel**, k 4, (p 1, k 1) twice, p 1, k 4; **rope cable panel**, p 1, k 1, p 6, k 1, p 1; **open cable panel**, k 1, p 1, k 3, p 1, k 1; **p panel**, p 4; **side ribbing**, (k 1, p 1) 1 (2-3) times.

Row 5: Side ribbing, (k 1 in b lp, p 1) 1 (2-3) times; **k panel**, k 4; **open cable panel**, p 1, sl 1 st to dpn, hold in front, sk 3 p sts, yarn in front, k in front lp of next st and leave st on left-hand needle, p the 3 skipped sts, sl the st already worked off left-hand needle, k 1 in b lp from dpn, p 1; **rope cable panel**, k 1 in b lp, p 1, sl next 3 sts to dpn, hold in back, k 3, then k 3 sts from dpn, p 1, k 1 in b lp; **tree panel**, p 3, sl 1 st to dpn, hold in back, k 1 in b lp, p 1 from dpn, p 1, k 1 in b lp, p 1, sl 1 st to dpn, hold in front, p 1, k 1 in b lp from dpn, p 3; **diamond panel**, k 1 in b lp, p 2, sl 2 sts to dpn, hold in front, p 1, k 2 sts from dpn, p 4, sl 1 st to dpn, hold in back, k 2 sts, p 1 st from dpn, p 2, k 1 in b lp; **tree panel**, p 3, sl 1 st to dpn, hold in back, k 1 in b lp, p 1 from dpn, p 1, k 1 in b lp, p 1, sl 1 st to dpn, hold in front, p 1, k 1 in b lp from dpn, p 3; **rope cable panel**, k 1 in b lp, p 1, work rope cable on next 6 sts, p 1, k 1 in b lp; **open cable panel**, p 1, work open cable on next 5 sts, p 1; **k panel**, k 4; **side ribbing**, (p 1, k 1 in b lp) 1 (2-3) times.

Row 6: Side ribbing, (p 1, k 1) 1 (2-3) times; **p panel**, k 4 (ridge made); **open cable panel**, k 1, p 1, k 3, p 1, k 1; **rope cable panel**, p 1, k 1, p 6, k 1, p 1; **tree panel**, k 3, (p 1, k 2) twice, p 1, k 3; **diamond**

panel, p 1, k 3, p 2, k 4, p 2, k 3, p 1; **tree panel**, k 3, (p 1, k 2) twice, p 1, k 3; **rope cable panel**, p 1, k 1, p 6, k 1, p 1; **open cable panel**, k 1, p 1, k 3, p 1, k 1; **p panel**, k 4 (ridge made); **side ribbing**, (k 1, p 1) 1 (2-3) times.

Row 7: Side ribbing, (k 1 in b lp, p 1) 1 (2-3) times; **k panel**, p 4 (ridge made); **open cable panel**, p 1, k 1 in b lp, p 3, k 1 in b lp, p 1; **rope cable panel**, k 1 in b lp, p 1, k 6, p 1, k 1 in b lp; **tree panel**, p 2, sl 1 st to dpn, hold in back, k 1 in b lp, p 1 from dpn, p 2, k 1 in b lp, p 2, sl 1 st to dpn, hold in front, p 1, k 1 in b lp from dpn, p 2; **diamond panel**, k 1 in b lp, p 3, sl 2 sts to dpn, hold in front, p 1, k 2 sts from dpn, p 2, sl 1 st to dpn, hold in back, k 2 sts, p 1 st from dpn, p 3, k 1 in b lp; **tree panel**, p 2, sl 1 st to dpn, hold in back, k 1 in b lp, p 1 from dpn, p 2, k 1 in b lp, p 2, sl 1 st to dpn, hold in front, p 1, k 1 in b lp from dpn, p 2; **rope cable panel**, k 1 in b lp, p 1, k 6, p 1, k 1 in b lp; **open cable panel**, p 1, k 1 in b lp, p 3, k 1 in b lp, p 1; **k panel**, p 4 (ridge made); **side ribbing**, (p 1, k 1 in b lp) 1 (2-3) times.

Row 8: Side ribbing, (p 1, k 1) 1 (2-3) times; **p panel**, p 4; **open cable panel**, k 1, p 1, k 3, p 1, k 1; **rope cable panel**, p 1, k 1, p 6, k 1, p 1; **tree panel**, k 2, p 1, (k 3, p 1) twice, k 2; **diamond panel**, p 1, k 4, p 2, k 2, p 2, k 4, p 1; **tree panel**, k 2, p 1, (k 3, p 1) twice, k 2; **rope cable panel**, p 1, k 1, p 6, k 1, p 1; **open cable panel**, k 1, p 1, k 3, p 1, k 1; **p panel**, p 4; **side ribbing**, (k 1, p 1) 1 (2-3) times.

Row 9: Side ribbing, (k 1 in b lp, p 1) 1 (2-3) times; **k panel**, k 4; **open cable panel**, p 1, k 1 in b lp, p 3, k 1 in b lp, p 1; **rope cable panel**, k 1 in b lp, p 1, k 6, p 1, k 1 in b lp; **tree panel**, p 1, sl 1 st to dpn, hold in back, k 1 in b lp, p 1 from dpn, p 3, k 1 in b lp, p 3, sl 1 st to dpn, hold in front, p 1, k 1 in b lp from dpn, p 1; **diamond panel**, k 1 in b lp, p 4, sl 2 sts to dpn, hold in front, p 1, k 2 sts from dpn, sl 1 st to dpn, hold in back, k 2 sts, p 1 from dpn, p 4, k 1 in b lp; **tree panel**, p 1, sl 1 st to dpn, hold in back, k 1 in b lp, p 1 from dpn, p 3, k 1 in b lp, p 3, sl 1 st to dpn, hold in front, p 1, k 1 in b lp from dpn, p 1; **rope cable panel**, k 1 in b lp, p 1, k 6, p 1, k 1 in b lp; **open cable panel**, p 1, k 1 in b lp, p 3, k 1 in b lp, p 1; **k panel**, k 4; **side ribbing**, (p 1, k 1 in b lp) 1 (2-3) times.

Row 10: Side ribbing, (p 1, k 1) 1 (2-3) times; **p panel**, p 4; **open cable panel**, k 1, p 1, k 3, p 1, k 1; **rope cable panel**, p 1, k 1, p 6, k 1, p 1; **tree panel**, k 1, p 1, (k 4, p 1) twice, k 1; **diamond panel**, p 1, k 5, p 4, k 5, p 1; **tree panel**, k 1, p 1, (k 4, p 1) twice, k 1; **rope cable panel**, p 1, k 1, p 6, k 1, p 1; **open cable panel**, k 1, p 1, k 3, p 1, k 1; **p panel**, p 4; **side ribbing**, (k 1, p 1) 1 (2-3) times.

Row 11: Side ribbing, (k 1 in b lp, p 1) 1 (2-3) times; **k panel**, k 4; **open cable panel**, p 1, k 1 in b lp, p 3, k 1 in b lp, p 1; **rope cable panel**, k 1 in b lp, p 1, k 6, p 1, k 1 in b lp; **tree panel,** p 5, k 3, p 5; **diamond panel,** k 1 in b lp, p 5, sl 2 sts to dpn, hold in front, k 2 sts, k 2 sts from dpn, p 5, k 1 in b lp; **tree panel,** p 5, k 3, p 5; **rope cable panel,** k 1 in b lp, p 1, k 6, p 1, k 1 in b lp; **open cable panel,** p 1, k 1 in b lp, p 3, k 1 in b lp, p 1; **k panel,** k 4; **side ribbing,** (p 1, k 1 in b lp) 1 (2-3) times.

Row 12: Side ribbing, (p 1, k 1) 1 (2-3) times; **p panel,** p 4; **open cable panel,** k 1, p 1, k 3, p 1, k 1; **rope cable panel,** p 1, k 1, p 6, k 1, p 1; **tree panel,** k 5, p 3, k 5; **diamond panel,** p 1, k 5, p 4, k 5, p 1; **tree panel,** k 5, p 3, k 5; **rope cable panel,** p 1, k 1, p 6, k 1, p 1; **open cable panel,** k 1, p 1, k 3, p 1, k 1; **p panel,** p 4; **side ribbing,** (k 1, p 1) 1 (2-3) times.

Row 13: Side ribbing, (k 1 in b lp, p 1) 1 (2-3) times; **k panel,** k 4; **open cable panel,** p 1, k 1 in b lp, p 3, k 1 in b lp, p 1; **rope cable panel,** k 1 in b lp, p 1, k 6, p 1, k 1 in b lp; **tree panel,** p 4, sl 1 st to dpn, hold in back, k 1 in b lp, p 1 from dpn, k 1 in b lp, sl 1 st to dpn, hold in front, p 1, k 1 in b lp from dpn, p 4; **diamond panel,** k 1 in b lp, p 4, sl 1 st to dpn, hold in back, k 2 sts, p 1 from dpn, sl 2 sts to dpn, hold in front, p 1, k 2 sts from dpn, p 4, k 1 in b lp; **tree panel,** p 4, sl 1 st to dpn, hold in back, k 1 in b lp, p 1 from dpn, k 1 in b lp, sl 1 st to dpn, hold in front, p 1, k 1 in b lp from dpn, p 4; **rope cable panel,** k 1 in b lp, p 1, k 6, p 1, k 1 in b lp; **open cable panel,** p 1, k 1 in b lp, p 3, k 1 in b lp, p 1; **k panel,** k 4; **side ribbing,** (p 1, k 1 in b lp) 1 (2-3) times.

Row 14: Side ribbing, (p 1, k 1) 1 (2-3) times; **p panel,** p 4; **open cable panel,** k 1, p 1, k 3, p 1, k 1; **rope cable panel,** p 1, k 1, p 6, k 1, p 1; **tree panel,** k 4, (p 1, k 1) twice, p 1, k 4; **diamond panel,** p 1, k 4, p 2, k 2, p 2, k 4, p 1; **tree panel,** k 4, (p 1, k 1) twice, p 1, k 4; **rope cable panel,** p 1, k 1, p 6, k 1, p 1; **open cable panel,** k 1, p 1, k 3, p 1, k·1; **p panel,** p 4; **side ribbing,** (k 1, p 1) 1 (2-3) times.

Row 15: Side ribbing, (k 1 in b lp, p 1) 1 (2-3) times; **k panel,** k 4; **open cable panel,** p 1, sl 1 st to dpn, hold in front, sk 3 p sts, yarn in front, k in front lp of next st and leave st on left-hand needle, p the 3 skipped sts, sl the st already worked off left-hand needle, k 1 in b lp from dpn, p 1; **rope cable panel,** k 1 in b lp, p 1, sl next 3 sts to dpn, hold in back, k 3, then k 3 sts from dpn, p 1, k 1 in b lp; **tree panel,** p 3, sl 1 st to dpn, hold in back, k 1 in b lp, p 1 from dpn, p 1, k 1 in b lp, p 1, sl 1 st to dpn, hold in front, p 1, k 1 in b lp from dpn, p 3; **diamond panel,** k 1 in b lp, p 3, sl 1 st to dpn, hold in back, k 2 sts, p 1 st from dpn, p 2, sl 2 sts to dpn, hold in front, p 1, k 2 sts from dpn, p 3, k 1 in b lp; **tree panel,** p 3, sl 1 st to dpn, hold in back, k 1 in b lp, p 1 from dpn, p 1, k 1 in b lp, p 1, sl 1 st to dpn, hold in front, p 1, k 1 in b lp from dpn, p 3; **rope cable panel,** k 1 in b lp, p 1, work rope cable on next 6 sts, p 1, k 1 in b lp; **open cable panel,** p 1, work open cable on next 5 sts,

p 1; **k panel,** k 4; **side ribbing,** (p 1, k 1 in b lp) 1 (2-3) times.

Row 16: Side ribbing, (p 1, k 1) 1 (2-3) times; **p panel,** k 4 (ridge made); **open cable panel,** k 1, p 1, k 3, p 1, k 1; **rope cable panel,** p 1, k 1, p 6, k 1, p 1; **tree panel,** k 3, (p 1, k 2) twice, p 1, k 3; **diamond panel,** p 1, k 3, p 2, k 4, p 2, k 3, p 1; **tree panel,** k 3, (p 1, k 2) twice, p 1, k 3; **rope cable panel,** p 1, k 1, p 6, k 1, p 1; **open cable panel,** k 1, p 1, k 3, p 1, k 1; **p panel,** k 4 (ridge made); **side ribbing,** (k 1, p 1) 1 (2-3) times.

Row 17: Side ribbing, (k 1 in b lp, p 1) 1 (2-3) times; **k panel,** p 4 (ridge made); **open cable panel,** p 1, k 1 in b lp, p 3, k 1 in b lp, p 1; **rope cable panel,** k 1 in b lp, p 1, k 6, p 1, k 1 in b lp; **tree panel,** p 2, sl 1 st to dpn, hold in back, k 1 in b lp, p 1 from dpn, p 2, k 1 in b lp, p 2, sl 1 st to dpn, hold in front, p 1, k 1 in b lp from dpn, p 2; **diamond panel,** k 1 in b lp, p 2, sl 1 st to dpn, hold in back, k 2, p 1 from dpn, p 4, sl 2 sts to dpn, hold in front, p 1, k 2 sts from dpn, p 2, k 1 in b lp; **tree panel,** p 2, sl 1 st to dpn, hold in back, k 1 in b lp, p 1 from dpn, p 2, k 1 in b lp, p 2, sl 1 st to dpn, hold in front, p 1, k 1 in b lp from dpn, p 2; **rope cable panel,** k 1 in b lp, p 1, k 6, p 1, k 1 in b lp; **open cable panel,** p 1, k 1 in b lp, p 3, k 1 in b lp, p 1; **k panel,** p 4 (ridge made); **side ribbing,** (p 1, k 1 in b lp) 1 (2-3) times.

Row 18: Side ribbing, (p 1, k 1) 1 (2-3) times; **p panel,** p 4; **open cable panel,** k 1, p 1, k 3, p 1, k 1; **rope cable panel,** p 1, k 1, p 6, k 1, p 1; **tree panel,** k 2, p 1, (k 3, p 1) twice, k 2; **diamond panel,** p 1, k 2, p 2, k 6, p 2, k 2, p 1; **tree panel,** k 2, p 1, (k 3, p 1) twice, k 2; **rope cable panel,** p 1, k 1, p 6, k 1, p 1; **open cable panel,** k 1, p 1, k 3, p 1, k 1; **p panel,** p 4; **side ribbing,** (k 1, p 1) 1 (2-3) times.

Row 19: Side ribbing, (k 1 in b lp, p 1) 1 (2-3) times; **k panel,** k 4; **open cable panel,** p 1, k 1 in b lp, p 3, k 1 in b lp, p 1; **rope cable panel,** k 1 in b lp, p 1, k 6, p 1, k 1 in b lp; **tree panel,** p 1, sl 1 st to dpn, hold in back, k 1 in b lp, p 1 from dpn, p 3, k 1 in b lp, p 3, sl 1 st to dpn, hold in front, p 1, k 1 in b lp from dpn, p 1; **diamond panel,** k 1 in b lp, p 1, sl 1 st to dpn, hold in back, k 2 sts, p 1 from dpn, p 6, sl 2 sts to dpn, hold in front, p 1, k 2 sts from dpn, p 1, k 1 in b lp; **tree panel,** p 1, sl 1 st to dpn, hold in back, k 1 in b lp, p 1 from dpn, p 3, k 1 in b lp, p 3, sl 1 st to dpn, hold in front, p 1, k 1 in b lp from dpn, p 1; **rope cable panel,** k 1 in b lp, p 1, k 6, p 1, k 1 in b lp; **open cable panel,** p 1, k 1 in b lp, p 3, k 1 in b lp, p 1; **k panel,** k 4; **side ribbing,** (p 1, k 1 in b lp) 1 (2-3) times.

Row 20: Side ribbing, (p 1, k 1) 1 (2-3) times; **p panel,** p 4; **open cable panel,** k 1, p 1, k 3, p 1, k 1; **rope cable panel,** p 1, k 1, p 6, k 1, p 1; **tree panel,** k 1, p 1, (k 4, p 1) twice, k 1; **diamond panel,** p 1, k 1, p 2, k 8, p 2, k 1, p 1; **tree panel,** k 1, p 1, (k 4, p

1) twice, k 1; **rope cable panel,** p 1, k 1, p 6, k 1, p 1; **open cable panel,** k 1, p 1, k 3, p 1, k 1; **p panel,** p 4; **side ribbing,** (k 1, p 1) 1 (2-3) times. Repeat these 20 rows for pat.

CARDIGAN: BACK: With No. 6 needles, cast on 72 (76-80) sts. Work in ribbing of k 2, p 2 for 3", inc 16 sts evenly spaced across last row—88 (92-96) sts. P 1 row, k 1 row, p 1 row. Change to No. 10 needles. Work in Aran Pat, inc 1 st each side every 1" 6 times, working added sts as for side ribbing—100 (104-108) sts. Work even until piece measures 13" (13½"-14") from start or desired length to underarm.

Shape Armholes: Keeping to pat, bind off 5 sts at beg of next 2 rows, then dec 1 st each side every other row 5 (6-7) times—80 (82-84) sts. Work even until armholes measure 7½" (8"-8½") above first bound-off sts.

Shape Shoulders: Bind off 10 sts at beg of next 4 rows, 10 (10-11) sts next 2 rows. Bind off remaining 20 (22-22) sts for back of neck.

LEFT FRONT: With No. 6 needles, cast on 43 (47-51) sts.

Ribbing: Row 1 (right side): K 2, * p 2, k 2, repeat from * to last 9 sts, k 1, (p 1, k 1) 4 times (seed st border).

Row 2: K 1, (p 1, k 1) 4 times (seed st border), p 2, * k 2, p 2, repeat from * across row. Repeat these 2 rows for 3", end wrong side.

Next Row: Inc 9 (7-5) sts evenly spaced across ribbing only—52 (54-56) sts. Keeping seed st border as established, p 1 row, k 1 row, p 1 row. Change to No. 10 needles.

Pattern: Row 1 (right side): Following row 1 of directions for Aran Pat, work side ribbing on first 4 (6-8) sts, work rope cable panel, tree panel, diamond panel; work seed st border.

Row 2: Work seed st border; following row 2 of directions for Aran Pat, work diamond panel, tree panel, rope cable panel and side ribbing on last 4 (6-8) sts. Continue to work Aran Pat panels in this manner, inc 1 st at side edge every 1" 6 times, working added sts as for side ribbing—58 (60-62) sts. Work even until piece measures same as back to underarm.

Shape Armhole: Keeping to pat, bind off 5 sts at beg of arm side, then dec 1 st every other row 5 (6-7) times—48 (49-50) sts. Work even until armhole measures 5½" (6"-6½") above first bound-off sts.

Shape Neck: Bind off 10 (11-11) sts at beg of center edge, then dec 1 st every row 8 times—30 (30-31) sts. Work even until armhole measures same as back.

Shape Shoulder: Bind off 10 sts at beg of arm side twice, 10 (10-11) sts once.

With pins, mark position of 6 buttons evenly spaced on border of left front: first one ½" from lower edge, last one ½" below neck edge.

BUTTONHOLES: Work 3 sts at beg of center edge, bind off next 2 sts, finish row. **Next Row:** Cast on 2 sts over bound-off sts.

RIGHT FRONT: With No. 6 needles, cast on 43 (47-51) sts.

Ribbing: Row 1 (right side): K 1, (p 1, k 1) 4 times (seed st border), k 2, * p 2, k 2, repeat from * across.

Row 2: P 2, * k 2, p 2, repeat from * across to last 9 sts, k 1, (p 1, k 1) 4 times (seed st border). Repeat these 2 rows for 3", forming first buttonhole (see Buttonholes) opposite marker, end wrong side.

Next Row: Inc 9 (7-5) sts evenly spaced across ribbing only—52 (54-56) sts. Keeping seed st border as established, p 1 row, k 1 row, p 1 row. Change to No. 10 needles.

Pattern: Row 1 (right side): Work seed st border; following row 1 of directions for Aran Pat, work diamond panel, tree panel, rope cable panel and side ribbing on last 4 (6-8) sts.

Row 2: Following row 2 of directions for Aran Pat, work side ribbing on first 4 (6-8) sts, rope cable panel, tree panel, diamond panel and seed st border. Continue to work Aran Pat panels in this manner, forming buttonholes opposite markers and inc 1 st at side edge every 1" 6 times, working added sts as for side ribbing—58 (60-62) sts. Work even until piece measures same as back to underarm. Shape armhole and complete right front as for left front.

SLEEVES: With No. 6 needles, cast at 32 (36-40) sts. Work in ribbing of k 2, p 2 for 3", inc 14 sts evenly spaced across last row—46 (50-54) sts. P 1 row, k 1 row, p 1 row. Change to No. 10 needles.

Pattern: Row 1 (right side): Following row 1 of directions for Aran Pat, work side ribbing on first 2 (4-6) sts, work tree panel, diamond panel, tree panel, side ribbing on last 2 (4-6) sts. Continue to work Aran Pat panels in this manner, inc 1 st each side every 1" 8 times, working added sts as for side ribbing—62 (66-70) sts. Work even until piece measures 17" (17½"-18") from start or desired length to underarm.

Shape Cap: Keeping to pat, bind off 5 sts at beg of next 2 rows, then dec 1 st each side every other row until 28 sts remain. Bind off 2 sts at beg of next 6 rows. Bind off remaining 16 sts.

FINISHING: Steam-press pieces. Sew shoulder seams. Sew in sleeves. Sew side and sleeve seams. Reinforce buttonholes. Sew on buttons.

Collar: Beg in 8th st from center edge of right front, from right side, with No. 6 needles, pick up and k 59 (61-63) sts around neck edge to within 7 sts from left front edge. Work in seed st for 3 rows. Keeping to seed st, dec 1 st at beg of next 6 rows. Bind off loosely in seed st.

Knitting with ribbon

Ribbon for knitting is available in silk, rayon, combinations of silk and rayon, and wool; any of these may also be woven with metallic threads. The texture may be either soft or crisp. Ribbon is adaptable to most conventional knitting techniques and stitches. It may be worked alone or in combination with other yarns.

Ribbon, unlike any other knitting material, can be knitted flat to produce a fabric with a woven-like texture. As flat ribbon knitting is quite different from ordinary knitting, the technique is illustrated below in the plain flat knitting stitch. Three other pattern stitches, Peak Stitch, Woven Stitch, Twisted Stockinette Stitch also shown.

In all flat knitting, the ribbon must never be twisted and the same side of the ribbon must always be laid against the needle. To prevent twisting, keep the spool of ribbon on a spindle or in a small box. Unwind sufficient ribbon to keep tension loose. Drop ribbon and readjust after each stitch.

PRACTICE PIECE: With No. 10 needles, cast on 16 sts and work for about 4" in plain flat knitting or any of the other pattern stitches. Bind off and block before measuring. The gauge should be 4 sts to 1". Change needle size if necessary to obtain proper gauge. For practice piece, it is helpful to mark one side of ribbon with a pencil.

TO BLOCK: Block each piece of garment separately before assembling. Lay piece right side up on a padded surface. First, examine for any imperfect stitches and straighten by placing plain end of crochet hook under imperfect stitch to hold it straight. Apply steam to set the straightened stitch. Smooth piece right side up on padded surface and pin enough to control curling at edges; do not stretch. Place pressing cloth over piece and press, using steam and slight pressure on iron to flatten stitches and set pattern. Do not use ironing motion. Then, unpin piece and repin, stretching to desired measurements. Cover with dry pressing cloth and block with steam iron.

SEAMS: Allow ⅜" to ½" for seams. Sew all seams by machine with mercerized sewing cotton, using a loose tension and a long stitch, or use a zig-zag stitch. Seams may also be made by hand with a running backstitch. Press seams flat open.

PLAIN FLAT KNITTING: Cast on loosely by any method.

TO KNIT

Insert right needle in *back* of stitch on left needle from right to left. Throw ribbon around point of right needle, passing it under needle, then over, keeping ribbon flat.

Form loop by pulling right needle through stitch toward you.
Flip stitch off left needle, then pull ribbon held in right hand up slightly to loosen stitch.

TO PURL

Insert point of right needle through front of stitch on left needle from right to left. Bring ribbon back between needles, then to left of right needle.

Keep ribbon flat, loop it under right needle and up. Push this loop through stitch to back and slip stitch off left needle, keeping ribbon in front of work.

PEAK STITCH

BEFORE BLOCKING   **AFTER BLOCKING**

PEAK STITCH: Work in garter stitch laying ribbon over needle from front to back.

WOVEN STITCH

In this stitch, ribbon twists as it comes off spool on knit row and straightens as it unwinds for purl row. Same side of ribbon is always against needle and must be shifted over finger after each stitch.

WOVEN STITCH: On knit rows, insert needle through *back* of stitch. Place ribbon over needle from front to back. Pull loop through. Slip stitch off the left needle.

On purl rows, insert needle through front of stitch from right to left. Place ribbon over needle from back to front. Pull loop through. Slip stitch off left needle.

TWISTED STOCKINETTE STITCH

Be sure to put same side of ribbon against needle for all stitches.

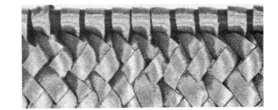

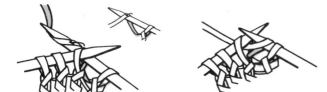

TWISTED STOCKINETTE STITCH: On knit rows, insert needle through *back* of stitch. Place ribbon over needle from back to front. Pull loop through. Slip stitch off left needle.

On purl rows, insert needle through front of stitch from right to left. Place ribbon over needle from front to back. Pull loop through. Slip stitch off left needle.

Knitting with More Than One Color

Boat-neck pullovers

The Boat-Neck Pullovers shown opposite get their distinction from "Swedish Weave" stripes which are made by weaving in yarn as you knit. For directions, see page 228.

Novelty stitch pullover

A Novelty Stitch Pullover to make for a young miss depends on tone-on-tone for its unusual effect. Make the sweater and hat following the instructions on page 229.

Boat-neck pullovers

SIZES: Directions for size 32-34. Changes for sizes 36-38 and 40-42 are in parentheses.

Blocked Bust or Chest Size: 36″ (40″; 44″).

MATERIALS: Bear Brand or Fleisher's Shetland and Wool or Bear Brand or Fleisher's Spice, 6 (7-8) 2-oz. skeins main color (MC); Bear Brand or Fleisher's Shetland and Wool or Bear Brand or Fleisher's Spice, 1 2-oz. skein, contrasting color (CC). 14″ knitting needles Nos. 6, 8 and 10½. (Or English sizes 7, 5, 2.)

GAUGE: 5 sts=1″; 7 rows=1″ (stockinette st, No. 8 needles).

Pattern Notes: Note 1: Carry MC strand loosely across wrong side of work so that work does not pull. Carry double CC strand loosely across front or back of work where necessary to form pat. Carry yarn not in use loosely up side. **Note 2:** Sl all sl sts as if to p.

PATTERN STRIPE (multiple of 5 sts plus 2): Work with No. 10½ needles and double strand of CC throughout pat stripe only. **Row 1** (right side): K 1 MC, * drop MC to wrong side (join a 2nd skein of CC on wrong side on first row only), pick up double CC yarn from under dropped MC yarn and bring CC to front of work, sl next 3 sts (see Notes); keeping CC yarn loosely side by side in front of sl sts so that work does not pull, bring CC to back of work and drop †; k 2 MC *, repeat from first * to 2nd * across row, end last repeat k 3 MC.

Row 2: P 1 MC, * drop MC to wrong side; pick up double CC yarn from under dropped MC yarn and bring CC to back of work, sl next 3 sts; keeping CC yarn loosely side by side in back of sl sts so that work does not pull, bring CC to front of work and drop †; p 2 MC *, repeat from first * to 2nd * across, end last repeat p 3 MC.

Row 3: K 4 MC, work from first * to 2nd * of row 1 across, end last repeat at †.

Row 4: Pick up MC from under CC yarn, p 4 MC; beg at first *, work as for row 2 across, end last repeat at †.

Row 5: Pick up MC from under dropped CC yarn, k 1 MC; beg at first *, work as for row 1 across, end last repeat at † with 1 sl st (instead of 3).

Row 6: Pick up MC from under CC yarn, p 2 MC; work from first * to 2nd * as for row 2 across row.

Rows 7-11: Repeat rows 5, 4, 3, 2 and 1 (picking up MC from wrong side and under CC yarn at beg of each row). Cut off CC strands, fasten securely on wrong side. Pat stripe completed.

PULLOVER: BACK: With MC and No. 6 needles, cast on 90 (100-110) sts. **Hem:** (P 1 row, k 1 row) for 5 rows. Drop MC. Change to No. 8 needles. Join CC, work in garter st (k each row) for 4 rows (2 ridges). Drop CC. Pick up MC, (k 1 row, p 1 row)

for 4 rows; cast on 1 st each side on 4th row—92 (102-112) sts. Change to No. 10½ needles. Work the 11 rows of pat stripe (see Pattern Stripe). Change to No. 8 needles. With MC, p 1 row and dec 1 st each side—90 (100-110) sts. Drop MC. Join 1 strand CC, work in garter st for 4 rows (2 ridges). Cut off CC. With MC; work in stockinette st (k 1 row, p 1 row) until piece measures 14″ (15″-16″) above hem or desired length to underarm, end on p row. Check gauge; piece above pat stripe should be 18″ (20″-22″) wide.

Shape Armholes: Bind off 5 (6-7) sts at beg of next 2 rows. Dec 1 st each side every k row 4 (5-7) times, end on p row—72 (78-82) sts. Drop MC. With 1 strand CC, work in garter st for 4 rows (2 ridges). Drop CC. With MC, (k 1 row, p 1 row) for 4 rows, dec 1 st at end of last row on size 36-38 only—72 (77-82) sts. Change to No. 10½ needles. Work the 11 rows of pat stripe. Change to No. 8 needles. With MC, p 1 row. Drop MC. Join 1 strand CC, work in garter st for 4 rows (2 ridges). Cut off CC. With MC, work in stockinette st (k 1 row, p 1 row) until armholes measure 8″ (9″-9½″) above first bound-off sts, end on p row.

Shape Shoulders: Bind off 10 (11-12) sts at beg of next 4 rows, ending p row—32 (33-34) sts. K next 2 rows for turning ridge.

Neck and Shoulder Facings: Continue in stockinette st (k 1 row, p 1 row), cast on 10 (11-12) sts at beg of next 4 rows (shoulders)—72 (77-82) sts. Work even for 6 rows. Bind off loosely.

FRONT: Work as for back.

SLEEVES: With MC and No. 6 needles, cast on 40 (46-50) sts. Work in ribbing of k 1, p 1 for 2″, inc 12 (9-10) sts evenly spaced across last row—52 (55-60) sts. Change to No. 8 needles. Work in stockinette st for 12 rows. Inc 1 st each side of next row, then every 10th row 8 (9-9) times—70 (75-80) sts. Check gauge; piece above last inc row should be 14″ (15″-16″) wide. Work even until piece measures 17″ (19″-20″) from start or desired length to underarm, end on p row.

Shape Cap: Bind off 5 (5-6) sts at beg of next 2 rows. Dec 1 st each side every k row 15 (18-21) times. Bind off 3 (3-2) sts at beg of next 4 rows. Bind off loosely remaining 18 (17-18) sts.

FINISHING: Run in yarn ends on wrong side. Block pieces and sew seams with backstitch as follows: Sew shoulder seams. Weave shoulder facing seams from right (k) side. Turn neck and shoulder facing to wrong side on turning ridge; sew loosely in place. Sew in sleeves. Sew sleeve seams. Sew side seams up to hems; weave hem seams from right side. Steam-press seams open flat on wrong side. Turn and sew hem to wrong side at lower edge.

Novelty stitch pullover

SIZES: Directions for small size (4-6). Changes for medium size (8-10) and large size (12-14) in parentheses.

Body Chest Size: 23″-24″ (26″-28″; 30″-32″).

Blocked Chest Size: 27″ (31″-34″).

MATERIALS: Knitting worsted, 3 (4-4) 4-oz. skeins Bittersweet, main color (MC), 2 skeins Pink, contrasting color (CC). Knitting needles Nos. 7 and 10. (Or English sizes 6 and 3.) Set of dp needles No. 8. (Or English size 5.) Stitch holders.

GAUGE: 5 sts=1″; 6 rows=1″.

PATTERN STITCH (multiple of 8 sts plus 2):

Row 1 (right side): Keeping both colors to back of work, * k 2 CC, k 6 MC, repeat from *, end k 2 CC.

Row 2 (wrong side): Keeping MC to front of work and CC to back of work, k 2 CC, * p 6 MC, k 2 CC, repeat from *.

Row 3: Keeping both colors to back of work, k 4 MC; * place point of right needle under long CC strand of previous row, (k next st in CC catching in CC strand) twice, k 6 MC, repeat from * across to last 6 sts, k 2 CC catching in CC strand, k 4 MC.

Row 4: Bring CC yarn under needle to back of work before purling first st. Keeping MC to front of work and CC to back of work, p 4 MC (catching in CC at edge), * k 2 CC, p 6 MC, repeat from * across to last 6 sts, k 2 CC, p 4 MC.

Row 5: Bring CC yarn under needle to back of work. Keeping both colors to back of work, place point of right needle under CC strand into first st, k 1 CC catching in CC strand, work next st the same, * k 6 MC, k 2 CC catching in long CC strand of previous row, repeat from * across to last 8 sts, k 6 MC, k 2 CC catching in long CC strand.

Repeat rows 2-5 for pat.

BACK: With MC and No. 7 needles, cast on 66 (74-82) sts. Work in ribbing of k 1, p 1 for 2″. Change to No. 10 needles. Work in pat until piece measures 9″ (10″-11½″) from start or desired length to underarm.

Shape Armholes: Keeping to pat, bind off 3 sts at beg of next 2 rows, then dec 1 st each side every other row 3 times—54 (62-70) sts. Work even in pat until armholes measure 5″ (6″-6¾″) from first bound-off sts.

Shape Shoulders: Bind off 5 (6-7) sts at beg of next 6 rows. Place remaining 24 (26-28) sts on a holder for neck.

FRONT: With MC and No. 7 needles, cast on 66 (82-90) sts. Work as for back to armholes.

Shape Armholes: Keeping to pat, bind off 3 (4-4) sts at beg of next 2 rows, then dec 1 st each side every other row 3 (4-4) times—54 (66-74) sts. Work even in pat until armholes measure 4½″ (5½″-6¼″) from first bound-off sts; end wrong side.

Shape Shoulders and Neck: Work across first 21 (26-29) sts. Place next 12 (14-16) sts on a holder for front of neck; join another ball of MC and CC, finish row. Working on both sides at once, bind off 3 sts at beg of each neck edge every other row twice, 0 (2-2) sts once; **at same time,** when armholes measure same as back, bind off 5 (6-7) sts at arm side every other row 3 times.

SLEEVES: With MC and No. 7 needles, cast on 34 (42-42) sts. Work in ribbing of k 1, p 1 for 2″. Change to No. 10 needles. Work in pat, inc 1 st each side every 8th row 8 (8-10) times, working added sts into pat—50 (58-62) sts. Work even until sleeve measures 12″ (14½″-16½″) from start or desired length to underarm.

Shape Cap: Bind off 5 sts at beg of next 2 rows. Then dec 1 st each side every other row until 24 (26-28) sts remain. Bind off remaining sts.

FINISHING: Steam-press pieces lightly. Sew shoulder seams.

Collar: Place back of neck sts on one No. 8 dp needle, place front of neck sts on another dp needle. From right side, beg at right shoulder seam, join MC, work in ribbing of k 1, p 1 across 24 (26-28) sts for back of neck. With another dp needle, pick up and k 15 (16-17) sts along left front neck edge; with same dp needle work in p 1, k 1 (k 1, p 1—p 1, k 1) ribbing across 12 (14-16) sts for front of neck. With third dp needle, pick up and k 15 (16-17) sts along right front neck edge—66 (72-78) sts. Divide sts evenly on 3 dp needles, work around loosely in k 1, p 1 ribbing for 3½″ (3½″-4½″). Bind off loosely in ribbing.

Sew in sleeves. Sew side and sleeve seams.

HAT: With MC and No. 7 needles, cast on 82 (82-90) sts. Work in ribbing of k 1, p 1 for 3″. Change to No. 10 needles. Work in pat until piece measures 7½″ (8½″-9½″) from start, ending with row 5 of pat. Break off CC.

First Dec Row: With MC, p 4, (p 2 tog, p 6) 9 (9-10) times, p 2 tog, p 4—10 (10-11) decs.

2nd Dec Row: K 4, (k 2 tog, k 5) 9 (9-10) times, k 2 tog, k 4—10 (10-11) decs.

3rd Dec Row: P 4, * p 2 tog, p 4, repeat from * across—10 (10-11) decs.

4th Dec Row: K 4, (k 2 tog, k 3) 9 (9-10) times, k 2 tog, k 4—10 (10-11) decs.

Next Row: P 2 tog across row—21 (21-23) sts. Break yarn, leaving long end for sewing seam. Draw end through sts on needle, pull sts tog. Sew back seam.

Pompon: Wind MC 125 (125-150) times around a 5″ (5″-6″) cardboard. Remove from cardboard, tie all strands securely tog at center, cut through loops at both ends. Trim into shape. Sew to hat.

Jack or Jill cardigan

No charts are needed for this unusual sweater for the very young. Patterned fronts are combined with ribbed sleeves and backs of a single color.

SIZES: Directions for size 1. Changes for sizes 2 and 3 are in parentheses.
Body Chest Size: 20″ (21″-22″).
Blocked Chest Size: 22″ (23″-24″).
MATERIALS: Nylon and wool knitting worsted: **For Girl,** 2 4-oz. skeins pink, main color (MC); 1 skein each of white (A) and light blue (B). **For Boy,** 2 4-oz. skeins light blue, main color (MC); 1 skein each of white (A) and pink (B). Knitting needles Nos. 4 and 8. (Or English sizes 9 and 5.) Steel crochet hook No. 0. Five buttons.
GAUGE: 5 sts=1″ (pat, No. 8 needles). 11 sts= 2″; 8 rows=1″ (ribbing before blocking, No. 8 needles).

CARDIGAN: BACK: With MC and No. 8 needles, cast on 59 (61-65) sts.

Ribbing: Row 1 (right side): P 1, * k 1, p 1, repeat from * across.

Row 2: K 1, * p 1, k 1, repeat from * across. Repeat these 2 rows for 7½" (8"-9").

Shape Armholes: Bind off in ribbing 3 sts at beg of next 2 rows, then dec 1 st each side every other row twice—49 (51-55) sts. Work even in ribbing until armholes measure 4½" (4½"-4¾") above first bound-off sts.

Shape Shoulders: Bind off in ribbing 5 sts at beg of next 4 rows, 4 (5-6) sts next 2 rows. Bind off remaining 21 (21-23) sts for back of neck.

Buttonhole Note: For Girls' Cardigan, work left front first; **for Boys' Cardigan,** work right front first. When first front is completed, with pins mark position of 5 buttons evenly spaced on center band: first one 1" above hemline, last one ½" below neck edge. When working 2nd front, form double buttonholes opposite markers as follows:

Double Buttonholes: Beg at center edge, work first 2 sts, bind off next 2 sts, work until 5 sts from bound-off sts, bind off next 2 sts, finish row. **Next Row:** Cast on 2 sts over bound-off sts.

Pattern Note: Sl all sl sts as if to p, holding yarn on wrong side. Carry unused colors loosely up side, twisting colors every other row.

LEFT FRONT: With A and No. 8 needles, cast on 24 (28-28) sts. Work in stockinette st for 5 rows (hem). **Next Row:** Cast on 13 sts for center band at beg of row and k across this row (wrong side) for hemline—37 (41-41) sts. K 1 row, p 1 row. See Buttonhole Note. Work as follows:

Pattern (multiple of 4 sts plus 1): **Row 1** (right side): With MC, k 1, * sl 1, k 1, repeat from * across.

Row 2: With MC, purl.

Row 3: With B, repeat row 1.

Row 4: With B, p 1, * sl 1, p 1, repeat from * across.

Rows 5 and 6: With MC, k 1 row, p 1 row.

Row 7: With A, repeat row 1.

Rows 8-10: With A, p 1 row, k 1 row, p 1 row.

Row 11: With MC, k 1, * sl 3, k 1, repeat from * across.

Row 12: With MC, p 2, * sl 1, p 3, repeat from * across, end sl 1, p 2.

Row 13: With A, sl 1, * k 3, sl 1, repeat from * across.

Row 14: With A, purl.

Row 15: With B, sl 2, * k 1, sl 3, repeat from * across, end k 1, sl 2.

Row 16: With B, sl 1, * p 3, sl 1, repeat from * across.

Row 17: With A, k 2, * sl 1, k 3, repeat from * across, end sl 1, k 2.

Row 18: With A, purl.

Rows 19-22: Repeat rows 11-14.

Rows 23 and 24: With A, k 1 row, p 1 row. Repeating these 24 rows for pat, work even until piece measures same as back to underarm above hemline.

Shape Armhole: Note: Bind off in k on right side; bind off in p on wrong side, working in pat on all other sts. Bind off 3 sts at beg of arm side, then dec 1 st every other row 2 (3-2) times—32 (35-36) sts. Work even until armhole is 3" (3¼"-3½") above first bound-off sts.

Shape Neck: Bind off 14 (15-15) sts at beg of center edge once, finish row. Dec 1 st at center edge every row 4 (5-5) times—14 (15-16) sts. Work even until armhole measures same as back.

Shape Shoulder: Bind off 5 sts at beg of arm side twice, 4 (5-6) sts once.

RIGHT FRONT: Work as for left front, casting on 13 sts for center band at end of hemline row (on next row above hem). See Buttonhole Note.

SLEEVES: With MC on No. 4 needles, cast on 35 (37-39) sts. Work in ribbing as for back for 1" (cuff). Change to No. 8 needles. Continue in ribbing, inc 1 st each side of next row, then every ¾" 6 times, working added sts into ribbing—49 (51-53) sts. Work even until piece measures 8" (9"-10") from start or desired length to underarm.

Shape Cap: Bind off 3 sts at beg of next 2 rows, then dec 1 st each side every other row until 29 sts remain. Bind off 2 sts at beg of next 4 rows. Bind off 21 sts.

COLLAR: With MC and No. 8 needles, cast on 77 sts. For girls' cardigan, work in ribbing as for back for 3", 2½" for boys' cardigan. Bind off loosely in ribbing.

FINISHING: Steam-press pieces lightly, keeping to gauge on ribbing of back and sleeves. Do not press cuffs. Sew shoulder seams. Sew in sleeves. Sew side and sleeve seams. Turn under hems at lower edge of fronts; sew to wrong side.

Fold center bands in half to wrong side (buttonholes meeting); sew in place. Sew tog lower and top edges of center bands and facings. Work buttonhole st around double buttonholes. From right side, with MC, work 1 row sc on each front edge and across top edges of center bands. Sew cast-on edge of collar to neck ½" from each front edge. Steam-press seams. Sew on buttons.

Girls' Fair Isle sweater and cap

Characteristic of Fair Isle knitting is the horizontal pattern stripe worked in stockinette stitch of two or more colors. Each stripe may be a different pattern repeat, as in child's pullover shown here. Stripes may all vary in color, too.

SIZES: Directions for size 6. Changes for sizes 8 and 10 are in parentheses.

Body Chest Size: 24″ (26″-28″).

Blocked Chest Size: 26″ (28″-30″).

MATERIALS: Knitting worsted, 6 (7-7) 2-oz. balls white, main color (MC); 1 ball each red (R), light blue, and black. Knitting needles Nos. 2 and 5. Sets of dp needles Nos. 2 and 5. (Or English sizes 11 and 8.)

GAUGE: 5 sts=1″; 6 rows=1″.

Pattern Note: Always change colors on wrong side, picking up new strand from underneath dropped strand. Carry colors loosely across; when more than 5 sts, twist colors every 3rd st.

BACK: With MC and No. 2 needles, cast on 64 (68-72) sts. Work in ribbing of k 2, p 2 for 2½″ (3½″-4″), inc 0 (0-2) sts evenly spaced across last row—64 (68-74) sts. Change to No. 5 needles.

Pattern: Work from Chart 1, following key to colors: **Odd Rows** (right side), work from A to B once, from B to C twice, from C to D once. K all odd rows except rows marked "P" on chart; purl these rows. **Even Rows,** p from D to C once, from C to B twice, from B to A once. When top of chart is reached, with MC, bind off in purling.

FRONT: Work as for back.

Mark 13 (15-17) sts each side at top edge of back and front for shoulders. Sew shoulder seams. Place markers 6½″ (7″-7½″) down from shoulders on each side of back and front for armholes.

SLEEVES: From right side, with MC and No. 5 needles, pick up and k 64 (68-74) sts on armhole edge between markers. P 1 row.

Pattern: Work as for back from top of chart down through row 39; **at same time,** dec 1 st each side every 3rd row 7 times (mark dec sts off on chart—50 (54-60) sts. At end of row 39, sk next 18 rows on chart, work from row 20 to row 1; dec 10 (10-12) sts evenly spaced across last row—40 (44-48) sts. Change to needles No. 2. With MC, work in ribbing of k 2, p 2 for 3″ (3″-4″) or desired sleeve length. Bind off in ribbing same tension as sts.

FINISHING: Matching pat, sew side and sleeve seams.

Collar: From right side, with MC and dp needles No. 2, pick up and k 38 (38-40) sts each on neck edge of front and back; divide on 3 needles. Join, working in ribbing of k 2, p 2 on 76 (76-80) sts for 4″. Bind off very loosely in ribbing.

Steam-press sweater to size, using steam iron or damp cloth and dry iron.

232

CAP: With MC and No. 5 dp needles, cast on 72 (80-80) sts; divide on 3 needles. Put and keep a marker on needle between last and first st of rnd.

Pattern: Join, being careful not to twist sts. Working from Chart 2 and following key for colors, k all rnds except rnds marked "P" on chart. P these rnds. Work to top of chart; dec 2 (0-0) sts evenly on rnd 8.

Shape Top: Rnd 1: K 1 MC, * k 1 R, k 9 MC, repeat from * around, end k 8 MC.

Rnd 2: * Sl 1, k 1 MC, psso, k 1 R, k 7 MC, repeat from * around—63 (72-72) sts.

Rnd 3: K 1 MC, * k 2 R, k 7 MC, repeat from * around, end k 6 MC.

Rnd 4: * Sl 1, k 1 MC, psso, k 2 R, k 5 MC, repeat from * around—56 (64-64) sts. **Rnd 5:** K 1 MC, * k 3 R, k 5 MC, repeat from * around, end k 4 MC.

Rnd 6: * Sl 1, k 1 MC, psso, k 3 R, k 3 MC, repeat from * around—49 (56-56) sts. **Rnd 7:** K 1 MC, * k 4 R, k 3 MC, repeat from * around; end k 2 MC.

Rnd 8: * Sl 1, k 1 MC, psso, k 4 R, k 1 MC, repeat from * around—42 (48-48) sts.

Rnd 9: * Sl 1, k 1 MC, psso, k 4 R, repeat from * around—35 (40-40) sts.

Rnd 10: * Sl 1, k 1 MC, psso, k 3 R, repeat from * around—28 (32-32) sts.

Rnd 11: * Sl 1, k 1 MC, psso, k 2 R, repeat from * around—21 (24-24) sts.

Rnd 12: * Sl 1, k 1 MC, psso, k 1 MC, repeat from * around—14 (16-16) sts remain in rnd.

Rnd 13: * With MC, k 2 tog around—7 (8-8) sts. Break MC, leaving 10" end; draw through sts and fasten securely.

EARLAPS: From right side, sk 5 (6-6) cast-on sts from beg of rnd (center back) at bottom of cap; with MC and needles No. 5, pick up and k 1 st in each of next 20 (22-22) sts. Work in stockinette st, dec 1 st at beg of each row until 2 sts remain. Bind off. Sk next 20 (24-24) cast-on sts (front) at bottom edge of cap, with MC, pick up and k 1 st in each of next 20 (22-22) sts. Work as for first earlap. Make two 20" twisted cords (see Index), sew to ends of earlaps.

Chart 1

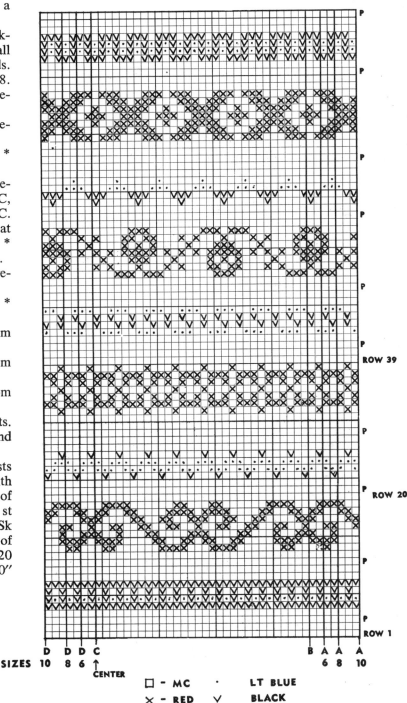

SIZES 10 8 6 ↑ CENTER   B A A A   6 8 10

□ - MC   ·   LT BLUE
× - RED   V   BLACK

On Child's Sweater chart, above, knit all odd rows except those marked "P", which are purled. Rows purled on right side form garter stitch ridge.

Start each rnd of Child's Cap chart at arrow; repeat across rnd. Purl rnds marked "P"; knit other odd rnds.

Chart 2

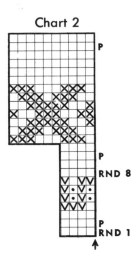

233

Scandinavian ski sweater

Camel color background with white snow-flakes is completely worked in tubular knit-ting. Circular yoke and sleeve borders in red, white, black and oxford feature an easy repeat pattern.

SIZES: Directions for size 12. Changes for sizes 14 and 16 are in parentheses.

Body Bust Size: 32″ (34″-36″).

Blocked Bust Size: 35″ (37″-39″).

MATERIALS: Knitting worsted, 4 (4-5) 4-oz. skeins camel, main color (MC), 1 skein white (W); 1 2-oz. skein each of red, black, oxford. Set of dp needles No. 2; 24″ circular needles Nos. 2 and 5; 11″ circular needle No. 5. (Or English sizes 11 and 8.)

GAUGE: 5 sts=1″; 7 rows=1″ (No. 5 needles).

Pattern Note: Always change colors on wrong side, picking up new strand from underneath dropped strand. Carry colors loosely across.

SNOWFLAKE PATTERN (multiple of 4 sts):

Rnd 1: K 1 MC, * k 1 W, k 3 MC, repeat from * around, end k 1 W, k 2 MC.

Rnds 2 and 3: With MC, knit.

Rnd 4: * K 3 MC, k 1 W, repeat from * around.

Rnds 5 and 6: With MC, knit. Repeat these 6 rnds for snowflake pat.

BODY: Beg at lower edge, with MC and 24″ circular needle No. 2, cast on 140 (148-156) sts. Put and keep marker on needle between last and first st of rnd. Join, being careful not to twist sts; work in ribbing of k 2, p 2 for 3″. Change to 24″ circular needle No. 5.

Next Rnd: With MC, (k 3, inc 1 st in next st) 32 (32-24) times, * k 2 (4-4), inc 1 st in next st, repeat from * 3 (3-11) times—176 (184-192) sts. Work in snowflake pat until piece measures 14″ from start or desired length to underarm, end on row 1 or 4 of pat. Keep track of pat row ended.

Next Rnd: With MC, bind off 8 sts (underarm), k until 72 (76-80) sts (front), bind off next 16 sts (underarm), k until 72 (76-80) sts (back), bind off next 8 sts. End off. Leave sts on needle.

SLEEVES: With MC and dp needles, cast on 44 (48-52) sts; divide evenly on 3 needles. Put and keep a marker on needle between last and first st of rnd. Join; work in ribbing of k 2, p 2 for 3″. Change to 11″ circular needle No. 5.

Next Rnd: (K 3, inc 1 st in next st) 8 times, * k 2 (3-4), inc 1 st in next st, repeat from * 3 times—56 (60-64) sts. With MC, k 1 rnd.

Design: Following chart 1, work design in stockinette st (k each rnd) from rnd 16 down to rnd 1 on chart. Break off all colors but MC.

Next 2 Rnds: With MC, k. Work in snowflake pat until piece is 15″ from start or 3½″ less than desired length to underarm. Keeping to snowflake pat, inc 1 st each side of marker on next rnd, then every 8th rnd 3 times more—64 (68-72) sts, end same pat rnd as for back at underarm.

Next Rnd: With MC, bind off 8 sts, k until 48 (52-56) sts, bind off last 8 sts. End off. Matching pat, sl these sts at end of rnd on needle of body sts. Make other sleeve in same manner. End off, leave sts on sleeve needle.

YOKE: From right side, join MC at beg of front on needle of body sts, k across front, k sts from sleeve needle, k sts of back and other sleeve—240 (256-272) sts. Put marker on needle between last and first st of rnd. Join; work 1 more snowflake rnd. With MC, k 2 rnds.

Design: Rnds 1-17: Following chart 1, work design in stockinette st.

Rnd 18: With MC, * k 2, k 2 tog, repeat from * around. Work design on 180 (192-204) sts through rnd 23.

Rnd 24: With MC, * k 3 (2-2) sts, k 2 tog, repeat from * 7 (7-15) times, (k 3, k 2 tog) 28 (32-28) times. Work design on 144 (152-160) sts through rnd 33. Change to 11″ circular needle No. 5.

Rnd 34: With MC, * k 2 (1-2) sts, k 2 tog, repeat from * 7 times, (k 2, k 2 tog) 28 (32-32) times. Work design on 108 (112-120) sts through rnd 39.

Rnd 40: With MC, * k 2, k 2 tog, repeat from * around. Work design on 81 (84-90) sts through rnd 42. Turn to wrong side.

Short Rows: Using chart 2, work as follows: **Row 1** (wrong side): P and repeat from B to A on 49 (51-55) sts, turn.

Row 2: K and repeat from A to B on 43 (43-46) sts, turn.

Row 3: P and repeat from B to A on 40 (40-43) sts, turn.

Row 4: K and repeat from A to B on 37 (37-40) sts, turn.

Rows 5-8: Repeat rows 3 and 4, keeping to design on chart and working 3 sts less at end of each row—25 (25-28) sts worked in row 8 of pat on back of neck. Break off all colors. Do not turn.

COLLAR: Next Rnd (right side): Join MC, work tightly in ribbing of k 2, p 2 on all sts and dec 1 (0-2) sts on rnd. Work tightly in ribbing on 80 (84-88) sts for 2″, then work loosely for 2″ more. Bind off very loosely in ribbing. Sew bound-off sts tog at underarms. Steam-press sweater.

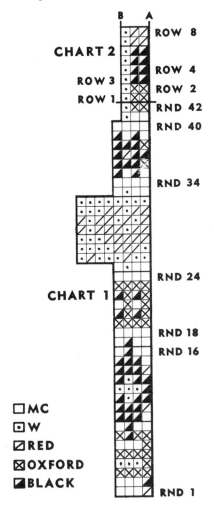

☐ MC
☐ W
☑ RED
☒ OXFORD
◼ BLACK

Norwegian cardigan

Typical of the Norwegian cardigan is a deep round yoke, radiant with pattern and color. In this style, completely seamless, knitting is worked back and forth on a circular needle except for the sleeves, knitted tubular on double-pointed needles.

SIZES: Directions are for size 14-16.
Body Bust Size: 34″-36″.
Blocked Bust Size: 38″.
Easy-fit garment.

MATERIALS: Sport yarn, 7 2-oz. balls white, main color (MC); 3 balls black (B), 1 ball each of red (R) and gold (G). Set of dp needles No. 2; 24″ circular needles Nos. 2 and 4; 11″ circular needle No. 4. (Or English sizes 11 and 9.) One stitch holder. Tapestry needle. Nine silver buttons.

GAUGE: 13 sts=2″; 17 rows=2″ (stockinette st, No. 4 needle).

Pattern Note: Always change colors on wrong side of work, picking up new strand from under dropped strand. Carry colors across loosely. Carry unused colors loosely up side, twisting strands every other row.

CARDIGAN: BODY: Beg at lower edge of fronts and back with B and 24″ circular needle No. 2, cast on 220 sts. Work back and forth in ribbing of k 1, p 1 for 3″. Change to 24″ circular needle No. 4.

Inc Row: With B, k 11, * inc 1 st in next st, k 5, repeat from * 33 times, end last repeat k 10—254 sts.

Zigzag Stripe: Rows 1 and 3 (wrong side): Following Chart 1, p from D to C once, from C to B 31 times, from B to A once.

Rows 2 and 4: Following Chart 1, k from A to B once, from B to C 31 times, from C to D once.

Row 5: Repeat row 1.

Snowflake Pat: Row 1 and All Odd Rows (right side): Following Chart 2, k from A to B to last 2 sts, k from B to C.

Row 2 and All Even Rows: Following Chart 2, p from C to B once, p from B to A to end of row. Work and repeat these 12 rows of snowflake pat until piece measures 12″ from start or desired length to underarm, end row 7 or 1 of snowflake pat.

Shape Armholes: Keeping to snowflake pat, p first 64 sts (left front); join another ball of MC and bind off next 6 sts for underarm, p until 114 sts from bound-off sts (back); join another ball of MC and bind off next 6 sts for underarm, p last 64 sts (right front). Working fronts and back at same time, dec 1 st at arm side of each front and at each arm side of back every k row twice, end with a snowflake row—62 sts remain on each front and 110 sts on back. Break off B. Discontinue snowflake pat. With MC, k 1 row, p 1 row, k 1 row. Leave sts on needle. Break off MC on right front and back only.

SLEEVES: With B and dp needles, cast on 56 sts; divide evenly on 3 needles. Put and keep a marker on needle between last and first st of rnd. Join; work in ribbing of k 1, p 1 for 3″. Change to 11″ circular needle No. 4.

Inc Rnd: (K 2, inc 1 st in next st) 8 times, (k 1,

inc 1 st in next st) 16 times—80 sts.

Zigzag Stripe: Rnds 1-5: Following Chart 1, k and repeat from B to C on each rnd.

Snowflake Pat: Following Chart 2, k and repeat these 12 rnds of pat, working each rnd from A to B to last 2 sts, end from B to C; **at same time,** inc 1 st in st each side of marker every 6th rnd 16 times, working added sts into snowflake pat—112 sts. Work even until piece measures 18″ from start or desired length to underarm. End same pat row as body at underarms.

Shape Armholes: Next Row: With MC, bind off first 3 sts, k to last 3 sts, bind off last 3 sts. End off. Join MC at right side edge of sleeve; working back and forth on needle, dec 1 st each side every k row twice, end with a snowflake row—102 sts. Break off B. Discontinue snowflake pat. With MC, k 1 row, p 1 row, k 1 row. Break off yarn, sl these sts on a holder. Make other sleeve in same manner. Break off yarn, leave these sts on sleeve needle.

YOKE: From wrong side, pick up MC strand at left front, p left front sts and dec 1 st at center of row, p sleeve sts from sleeve needle, p sts of back and dec

1 st at center of row, p other sleeve, p right front sts and dec 1 st at center of row—435 sts.

Next Row: With MC, k 6, * k 2 tog, k 8, repeat from * across, end k 2 tog, k 7—392 sts. P 1 row.

Yoke Pattern: Row 1 (right side): Following Chart 3, k from A to B once, from B to C 27 times, from C to D once.

Row 2: Following Chart 3, p from D to C once, from C to B 27 times, from B to A once.

Rows 3-25: Repeat rows 1 and 2 alternately.

Row 26 (wrong side): With MC, p 10, (p 2 tog, p 7) 41 times, p 2 tog, p 11—350 sts. Break off B, G and R, join as needed.

Row 27: With MC, knit.

Rows 28 and 30 (wrong side): Following Chart 3, p from D to C once, from C to B 24 times, from B to A once.

Rows 29 and 31 (right side): Following Chart 3, k from A to B once, from B to C 24 times, from C to D once.

Row 32 (wrong side): With MC, p 10, (p 2 tog, p 5) 47 times, p 2 tog, p 9—302 sts.

CHART 1

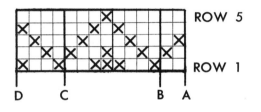

ROW 5

ROW 1

D C B A

CHART 2

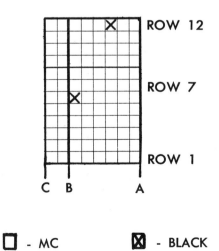

ROW 12

ROW 7

ROW 1

C B A

☐ - MC   ☒ - BLACK

CHART 3

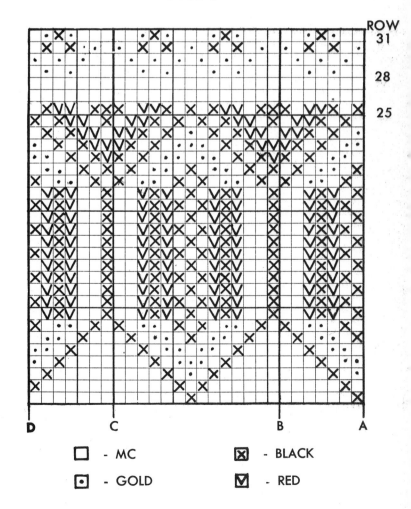

ROW 31

28

25

D C B A

☐ - MC   ☒ - BLACK

⊡ - GOLD   ⱽ - RED

Row 33: With MC, knit.

Rows 34-36: Following Chart 4, p 1 row, k 1 row, p 1 row.

Row 37 (right side): With MC, k 3, (k 2 tog, k 4) 49 times, k 2 tog, k 3—252 sts.

Row 38: With MC, purl.

Rows 39-43: Following Chart 4, work pat in stockinette st.

Row 44 (wrong side): With MC, p 2, (p 2 tog, p 4) 41 times, p 2 tog, p 2—210 sts.

Row 45: With MC, knit.

Row 46: With R, purl.

Rows 47-54: Following Chart 4, work pat in stockinette st.

Row 55 (right side): With MC, k 1, (k 2 tog, k 3) 41 times, k 2 tog, k 2—168 sts.

Row 56: With MC, purl.

Rows 57-61: Following Chart 4, work pat in stockinette st.

Row 62 (wrong side): With MC, p 11, (p 2 tog, p 3) 29 times, p 2 tog, p 10—138 sts.

Rows 63-66: Following Chart 4, work pat in stockinette st.

Row 67 (right side): K 10, (k 2 tog, k 2) 29 times, k 2 tog, k 10—108 sts.

Row 68: With MC, purl.

Row 69: With R, k and dec 6 sts evenly spaced around—102 sts.

Rows 70-73: Following Chart 4, work pat in stockinette st. Break off all colors except B.

Facing: Work with B hereafter. **Row 1** (wrong side): P 1, * p 2 tog, yo, repeat from * across, end p 1 (turning-row)—102 sts. Beg with k row, work in stockinette st for 8 rows.

Next Row: K first 20 sts, join another ball of B and bind off next 62 sts (neck), finish row. Working on both sides at once, continue in stockinette st, dec 1 st at each neck edge every other row 10 times— 10 sts remain each side. Work even until piece measures same as front edges to first row above ribbing. Bind off.

FINISHING: With right sides together, sew outside edges of facing to front edges; turn facings to wrong side of front edges, sew in place. With B and tapestry needle, sew buttonloops to fit buttons on right front edge as follows: one buttonloop at bottom and one at top of ribbing, one at neck edge, then 6 more evenly spaced between ribbing and buttonloop at neck. To make buttonloop, take stitch allowing yarn to loop; work over loop with buttonhole stitch. Sew armhole seams. Steam-press cardigan, using steam iron or damp cloth and dry iron. Sew on buttons.

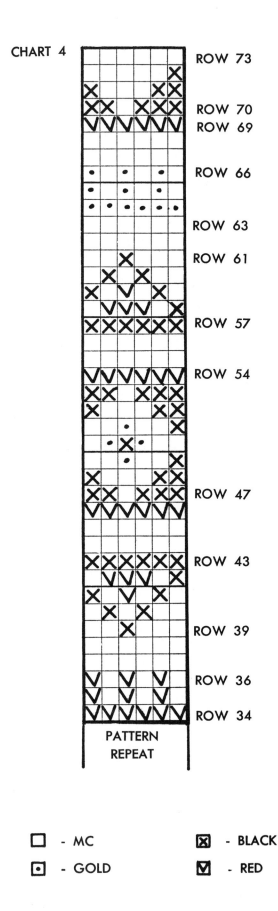

CHART 4

ROW 73

ROW 70

ROW 69

ROW 66

ROW 63

ROW 61

ROW 57

ROW 54

ROW 47

ROW 43

ROW 39

ROW 36

ROW 34

PATTERN REPEAT

□ - MC   ☒ - BLACK

⊡ - GOLD   ☑ - RED

No beginner's project, the knitted doily with its intricate lace patterns in circular knitting is a challenge even to the experienced knitter. Directions for Aster Doily, page 240, include helpful hints for making doily.

239

Knitted aster doily

Size: 20″ diameter.

Materials: Six Cord Mercerized Crochet Cotton, size 30, 3 220-yd. balls. Five dp aluminum needles No. 1. (Or English size 12.) Steel crochet hook No. 13.

Note: Circular needles may be substituted for dp needles after Rnd 21 as follows: Rnd 22 (11″ needle), Rnd 28 (16″ needle), Rnd 38 (24″ needle).

Stitches and additional abbreviations:

C 2—Cross 2 Stitches: Sk 1 st, k in front lp of next st, k in front lp of skipped st, sl both sts from left-hand needle.

T 1—Turn 1 Stitch: K in back lp of st.

D 1—Butterfly Drop Stitch: With crochet hook, sl st off left-hand needle and unravel it for 5 or 3 rows as specified, place this st back on left-hand needle; with hook in back of work, pick up the 5 or 3 strands and place them on left-hand needle, then k the st and 5 or 3 strands off tog.

R 2 decs—Reverse 2 Decreases: Sl 1, k 1, psso (1 dec), sl remaining k st to left-hand needle and pass next st on left-hand needle over this slipped st (1 dec), then sl the slipped st back to right-hand needle.

DOILY: Beg at center, cast on 12 sts. Divide on 3 needles (4 sts on each needle) and work with 4th needle.

Rnd 1: Join, k around. Sl and keep a marker on needle between last and first st of rnd.

Rnd 2: Knit.

Rnd 3 and all odd rnds: Knit.

Rnd 4: (Yo, k 1) 12 times—24 sts.

Rnd 6: (Yo, C 2) 12 times—36 sts.

Rnd 8: (Yo, k 1, C 2) 12 times—48 sts.

Rnd 10: (Yo, k 2, C 2) 12 times—60 sts.

Rnd 12: (Yo, k 1, C 2 twice) 12 times—72 sts.

Rnd 14: (Yo, k 1, C 2, k 1, C 2) 12 times—84 sts.

Rnd 16: (Yo, k 1, C 2, k 2, C 2) 12 times—96 sts.

Rnd 18: (Yo, k 1, C 2, k 3, C 2) 12 times—108 sts.

Rnd 20: (Yo, k 1, C 2, k 4, C 2) 12 times—120 sts.

Rnd 22: (Yo, k 1, C 2, k 5, C 2) 12 times—132 sts.

Rnd 24: (Yo, sl 1, k 1, psso, C 2, k 5, C 2) 12 times—132 sts.

Rnd 26: (Yo, k in back and front of next st, yo, sl 1, k 1, psso, C 2, k 4, C 2) 12 times—156 sts.

Rnd 28: (Yo, k 4, yo, sl 1, k 1, psso, C 2, k 3, C 2) 12 times—168 sts.

Rnd 30: * (Yo, p 3, pass the first p st over 2 remaining p sts) twice, yo, sl 1, k 1, psso, C 2, k 2, C 2, repeat from * 11 times more—168 sts.

Rnd 32: * Yo, k 2, yo, p 3, pass first p st over 2 remaining p sts, yo, k 2, yo, sl 1, k 1, psso, C 2, k 1, C 2, repeat from * 11 times more—192 sts.

Rnd 34: * Yo, k 2, (yo, p 3, pass first p st over remaining 2 p sts) twice, yo, k 2, yo, sl 1, k 1, psso, C 2 twice, repeat from * 11 times more—216 sts.

Rnd 36: * Yo, k 2, (yo, p 3, pass first p st over 2 remaining p sts) 3 times, yo, k 2, yo, sl 1, k 1, psso, k 1, C 2, repeat from * 11 times more—240 sts.

Rnd 38: * Yo, C 2, (yo, p 3, pass first p st over 2 remaining p sts) 4 times, yo, C 2, yo, sl 1, k 1, psso, C 2, repeat from * 11 times more—264 sts. Divide sts on 4 needles and work with 5th needle.

Rnd 40: * (Yo, k 2 tog) 4 times, yo, sl 2, k 1, pass 2 sl sts over k st, yo, (sl 1, k 1, psso, yo) 4 times, sl 1, k 1, psso, k 1, repeat from * 11 times more—252 sts.

Rnd 42: * (Yo, k 2 tog) 4 times, yo, sl 2, k 1, pass 2 sl sts over k st, yo, (sl 1, k 1, psso, yo) 4 times, C 2, repeat from * 11 times more—252 sts.

Rnd 44: * K 2 tog, (yo, k 2 tog) 3 times, yo, k 3, yo, (sl 1, k 1, psso, yo) 3 times, sl 1, k 1, psso, C 2, repeat from * 11 times more—252 sts.

Rnd 46: Remove marker, sl 1 st, insert marker, * k 2 tog, (yo, k 2 tog) twice, yo, k 5, yo, (sl 1, k 1, psso, yo) twice, sl 1, k 1, psso, C 2 twice, repeat from * 11 times more—252 sts.

Rnd 48: Remove marker, sl 1, insert marker, * (yo, k 2 tog) twice, yo, k 3, yo, D 1 for 5 rows, yo, k 3, yo, (sl 1, k 1, psso, yo) twice, sl 1, k 1, psso, C 2, k 2 tog, repeat from * 11 times more—276 sts.

Rnd 50: * K 2 tog twice, yo, k 5, yo, k 1, yo, k 5, yo, (sl 1, k 1, psso) 3 times, k 2 tog, repeat from * 11 times more—252 sts.

Rnd 52: Remove marker, sl 2 sts, insert marker, * yo, k 3, yo, D 1 for 5 rows, yo, k 3, yo, T 1, yo, k 3, yo, D 1 for 5 rows, yo, k 3, yo, sl 1, k 1, psso, k 2, k 2 tog, repeat from * 11 times more—324 sts.

Rnd 54: * Yo, k 5, yo, k 1, yo, k 5, yo, T 1, yo, k 5, yo, k 1, yo, k 5, yo, sl 1, k 1, psso, k 2 tog, repeat from * 11 times more—396 sts.

Rnd 56: * Sl 1, k 1, psso, k 11, k 2 tog, yo, T 1, yo, sl 1, k 1, psso, k 11, k 2 tog, C 2, repeat from * 11 times more—372 sts.

Rnd 58: * Sl 1, k 1, psso, k 9, k 2 tog, yo, k 1, yo, T 1, yo, k 1, yo, sl 1, k 1, psso, k 9, k 2 tog, yo, C 2, yo, repeat from * 11 times more—396 sts.

Rnd 60: * Sl 1, k 1, psso, k 7, k 2 tog, yo, k 3, yo, T 1, yo, k 3, yo, sl 1, k 1, psso, k 7, k 2 tog, yo, sl 1, k 1, psso, k 2 tog, yo, repeat from * 11 times more—396 sts.

Rnd 62: * Sl 1, k 1, psso, k 5, k 2 tog, yo, k 2, yo, D 1 for 3 rows, yo, k 2, yo, T 1, yo, k 2, yo, D 1 for 3 rows, yo, k 2, yo, sl 1, k 1, psso, k 5, k 2 tog, yo, sl 1, k 1, psso, k 2 tog, yo, repeat from * 11 times more —444 sts.

Rnd 64: * Sl 1, k 1, psso, k 3, k 2 tog, yo, k 9, yo, T 1, yo, k 9, yo, sl 1, k 1, psso, k 3, k 2 tog, yo, sl 1, k 1, psso, k 2 tog, yo, repeat from * 11 times more—444 sts.

Rnd 66: * Sl 1, k 1, psso, k 1, k 2 tog, yo, sl 1, k 1, psso, k 7, k 2 tog, yo, k 1, yo, sl 1, k 1, psso, k 7, k 2 tog, yo, sl 1, k 1, psso, k 1, k 2 tog, yo, k 2 tog, yo, sl 1, k 1, psso, yo, repeat from * 11 times more—408 sts.

Rnd 68: * Sl 1, k 2 tog, psso, yo, k 1, yo, sl 1, k 1, psso, k 5, k 2 tog, yo, k 3, yo, sl 1, k 1, psso, k 5, k 2 tog, yo, k 1, yo, R 2 decs, yo, k 2 tog, yo, k 1, yo, sl 1, k 1, psso, yo, repeat from * 11 times more—408 sts.

Rnd 70: Remove marker, sl 1, insert marker, * yo, k 2 tog, yo, k 1, yo, sl 1, k 1, psso, k 3, k 2 tog, yo, k 2 tog, yo, k 1, (yo, sl 1, k 1, psso) twice, k 3, k 2 tog, yo, k 1, yo, (sl 1, k 1, psso, yo) 3 times, k 1, (yo, k 2 tog) twice, repeat from * 11 times more—432 sts.

Rnd 72: * (Yo, k 2 tog) twice, yo, k 1, yo, sl 1, k 1, psso, k 1, k 2 tog, yo, k 2 tog, (yo, k 1) 3 times, yo, sl 1, k 1, psso, yo, sl 1, k 1, psso, k 1, k 2 tog, yo, k 1, yo, (sl 1, k 1, psso, yo) 4 times, k 1, (yo, k 2 tog) twice, repeat from * 11 times more—480 sts.

Rnd 74: * (K 2 tog, yo) 3 times, k 1, yo, sl 1, k 2 tog, psso, (yo, k 2 tog) twice, yo, k 3, yo, (sl 1, k 1, psso, yo) twice, R 2 decs, yo, k 1, (yo, sl 1, k 1, psso) 5 times, yo, k 1, yo, (k 2 tog, yo) twice, repeat from * 11 times more—504 sts.

Rnd 76: * (Sl 1, k 1, psso, yo) 7 times, sl 2, k 1, pass 2 sl sts over k st, (yo, k 2 tog) 9 times, yo, k 3, yo, (sl 1, k 1, psso, yo) twice, repeat from * 11 times more—504 sts.

Rnd 78: * (Sl 1, k 1, psso, yo) 5 times, (sl 1, k 1, psso) twice, k 1, (k 2 tog) twice, (yo, k 2 tog) 7 times, yo, k 5, yo, (sl 1, k 1, psso, yo) twice, repeat from * 11 times more—480 sts.

Rnd 80: * (Sl 1, k 1, psso, yo) 4 times, (sl 1, k 1, psso) twice, k 1, (k 2 tog) twice, (yo, k 2 tog) 6 times, yo, k 3, yo, D 1 for 5 rows, yo, k 3, yo, (sl 1, k 1, psso, yo) twice, repeat from * 11 times more—480 sts.

Rnd 82: Remove markers, sl 1, insert marker, * (k 2 tog, yo) 3 times, k 1, yo, sl 1, k 1, psso, k 1, k 2 tog, yo, k 1, (yo, sl 1, k 1, psso) 7 times, k 5, (k 2 tog, yo) 4 times, repeat from * 11 times more—480 sts.

Rnd 84: Remove marker, sl 1, insert marker, * (k 2 tog, yo) twice, k 3, yo, sl 2, k 1, pass 2 sl sts over k st, yo, k 3, (yo, sl 1, k 1, psso) 7 times, k 3, (k 2 tog, yo) 5 times, repeat from * 11 times—480 sts.

Rnd 86: Remove markers, sl 1, insert marker, * k 3, yo, sl 1, k 2 tog, psso, yo, (k 1, yo) 3 times, sl 1, k 2 tog, psso, yo, k 3, (yo, sl 1, k 1, psso) 6 times, k 1, (k 2 tog, yo) 6 times, repeat from * 11 times more—504 sts.

Rnd 88: Remove marker, sl 2, insert marker, * k 1, k 2 tog, (yo, k 1, yo, k 3) twice, yo, k 1, yo, sl 1, k 1, psso, k 1, k 2 tog, (yo, sl 1, k 1, psso) 5 times, yo, sl 2, k 1, pass 2 sl sts over k st, yo, (k 2 tog, yo) 5 times, sl 1, k 1, psso, repeat from * 11 times more—528 sts.

Rnd 90: Remove marker, sl 1, insert marker, * (k 3, yo, sl 1, k 2 tog, psso, yo) 3 times, k 1, yo, (sl 1, k 1, psso, yo) 4 times, sl 1, k 1, psso, k 1, k 2 tog, (yo, k 2 tog) 4 times, yo, k 1, yo, sl 1, k 2 tog, psso, yo, repeat from * 11 times more—528 sts.

Rnd 92: * (Yo, sl 1, k 2 tog, psso, yo, k 3) 3 times, (yo, k 1) twice, yo, (sl 1, k 1, psso, yo) 4 times, sl 2, k 1, pass 2 sl sts over k st, (yo, k 2 tog) 4 times, yo, (k 1, yo) twice, k 3, repeat from * 11 times more—576 sts.

Rnd 94: * K 3, yo, sl 1, k 2 tog, psso, yo, (k 1, yo) 3 times, (sl 1, k 2 tog, psso, yo, k 3, yo) twice, (k 1, yo) twice, (sl 1, k 1, psso, yo) twice, (sl 1, k 1, psso) twice, k 1, (k 2 tog) twice, (yo, k 2 tog) twice, yo, (k 1, yo) twice, k 3, yo, sl 1, k 2 tog, psso, yo, repeat from * 11 times more—624 sts.

Rnd 96: * Yo, sl 1, k 2 tog, psso, yo, k 3, (yo, k 1, yo, k 3) twice, (yo, sl 1, k 2 tog, psso, yo, k 3) twice, (yo, k 1) twice, yo, (sl 1, k 1, psso) 3 times, k 1, (k 2 tog) 3 times, yo, (k 1, yo) twice, k 3, yo, sl 1, k 2 tog, psso, yo, k 3, repeat from * 11 times more—672 sts.

Rnd 98: Sl last st of rnd on crochet hook, * sl first 3 sts from left-hand needle on crochet hook, yo and through 3 lps on hook, yo and through 2 lps on hook (sc on 3 sts tog), ch 8, sc next 3 sts tog as before, ch 9, sc next 3 tog, (ch 10, sc next 3 tog) twice, ch 9, sc next 3 tog, ch 8, sc next 3 tog, ch 7, sc next 3 tog, ch 6, sc next 3 tog, ch 5, sc next 3 tog, ch 4, sc next 3 tog, ch 3, sc next 2 tog, ch 3, (sc 1 st off at a time, no ch between) 7 times, ch 3, sc 2 tog, ch 3, sc 3 tog, ch 4, sc 3 tog, ch 5, sc 3 tog, ch 6, sc 3 tog, ch 7, repeat from * around, end last repeat sc 2 tog, ch 7, sl st in first sc. End off. If desired, draw cast-on sts tog at center. Wash, starch and pin out to size, let dry.

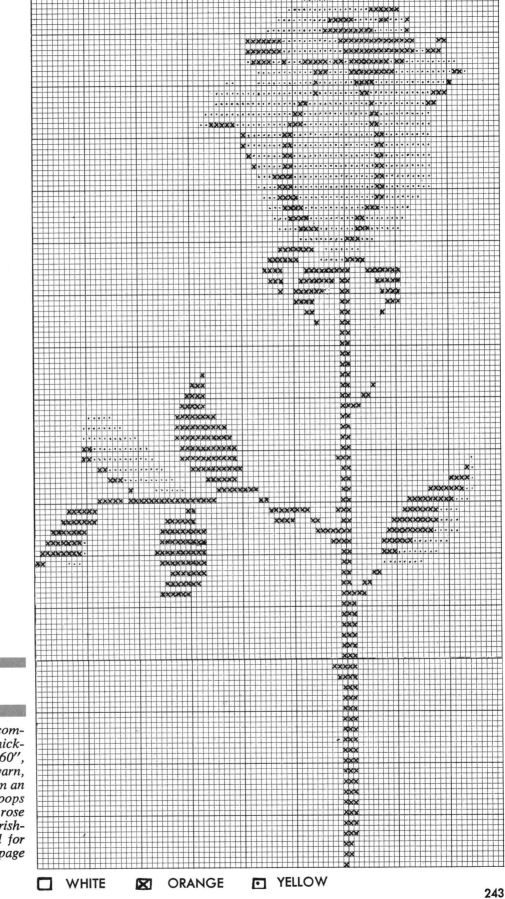

Rose rug

Knitting and knotting are combined in a wonderfully soft, thick-piled rug. Base of rug, 40" x 60", is knitted in ridges. Loops of yarn, knotted through the ridges, form an allover fringed texture when loops are cut. Directions for making rose rug are on page 244. For Irish-crochet motif and edging used for bedspread and pillow, see page 296.

☐ WHITE   ⊠ ORANGE   ⊡ YELLOW

Knitted rose rug

Figure 1

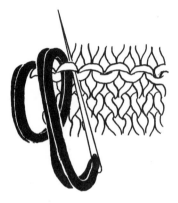

Figure 2

Figure 3

SIZE: About 40″ x 60″.

MATERIALS: Heavy cotton rug yarn, 55 70-yard skeins white, 3 skeins orange, 2 skeins light yellow. 14″ or "jumper" knitting needles No. 10, or circular needle No. 10. (Or English size 3.) Aluminum crochet hook size G. Three large-eyed yarn needles.

GAUGE: 3 sts=1″; 7 rows=1″.

RUG FOUNDATION: With white, cast on 120 sts. **Row 1:** Knit.

Row 2: Purl.

Rows 3-5: Knit. Repeat rows 2-5 for pattern until there are 100 ridges (formed by row 4 of the pattern). Work row 5 of the last repeat. Purl 1 row. Bind off in knitting on next row.

EDGING: With white and crochet hook, work 1 row of single crochet around rug, working 1 sc in each st at ends of rug, 1 sc in every other row at sides of rug and 3 sc in each corner. Join; cut yarn. Weave in ends.

FRINGE: Thread a 6-yard length of white in yarn needle. Bring ends together to form a double strand. Working from left to right in first ridge row, draw yarn up through first st, leaving 1¼″ ends.

Insert needle up through same st and to the right of hanging ends, pull yarn through until there is a small loop, draw yarn from right to left through small loop; tighten knot.

* Insert needle from bottom up through ridge of next st; figure 1. Pull yarn through, holding 1¼″ loop under thumb.

Insert needle to right of loop up through same st; figure 2. Pull yarn through leaving a loop.

Put needle through this loop; figure 3. Tighten knot. Repeat from * across row.

Cut through loops. Loops may be cut after each row or after entire rug is completed.

Work 5 rows of white fringe at bottom of rug. On 6th ridge row (first row at bottom of chart, page 243), work 79 loops of white, skip 1 st, finish row with 40 loops of white. In skipped st, knot orange, leaving ends as for beginning of row. Cut off orange 1¼″ from knot.

Continue to work from chart, making loops in every st of every ridge row. Each square across chart equals 1 st. Every other row of squares on chart represents one ridge row of rug. There are 20 loops of white to left of chart and 15 loops of white to right of chart which are not shown.

When top of chart is reached, work remaining ridge rows in white.

Quick-knit afghan

An easy two-color pattern is knitted of bulky yarns on big needles. Except for garter stitch borders at sides, afghan is worked entirely in one piece. Directions, page 246, suggest what to do when needles are crowded.

Quick-knit afghan

SIZE: About 48" x 60" plus fringe.

MATERIALS: Wool and nylon knitting worsted, 16 2-oz. skeins main color (MC). Bulky wool and nylon yarn, 8 2-oz. skeins contrasting color (CC). Two pairs of 18" "jumper" knitting needles or 36" circular needle No. 13. (Or English size 0.) Aluminum crochet hook size K.

GAUGE: 3 sts=1"; 11 rows=2" (pat).

Notes: Use double strand of knitting worsted (MC) and single strand of bulky yarn (CC) throughout afghan. If sts are too crowded on one 18" needle, keep sts on two needles, knit with third and fourth needles. If circular needle is used, work back and forth on needle.

PATTERN (multiple of 2 sts): Sl all sl sts as if to purl. **Row 1** (right side): With CC, * k 1, yarn in back, sl 1, repeat from * across.

Row 2: With CC, * yarn in front, sl 1, yarn to back, k 1, repeat from * across.

Rows 3 and 4: With MC, knit.

Row 5: With CC, * yarn in back, sl 1, k 1, repeat from * across.

Row 6: With CC, * k 1, yarn in front, sl 1, yarn to back, repeat from * across.

Rows 7 and 8: With MC, knit. Repeat these 8 rows for pattern.

AFGHAN: With double strand MC, cast on 120 sts. Work in garter st (k each row) for 24 rows (12 ridges). Join single strand CC, work in pat until piece measures 56" from start, end with row 2 of pat. Break off CC. With MC, work garter st for 24 rows (12 ridges). Bind off.

Side Border: From right side, with double strand MC, pick up and k 180 sts (about 3 sts to the inch) on one long side edge of afghan. Work in garter st for 24 rows (12 ridges). Bind off. Work border on other long side in same way.

FRINGE: Wind MC around 12" cardboard; cut on one end. Hold 3 strands tog; fold in half. With crochet hook, draw folded lp through first st on side at lower edge of afghan, pull strands through lp and tighten. Knot fringe in st at other end of same row, then knot fringe in every other st between. Fringe top edge in same way. Trim evenly. Steam-press lightly.

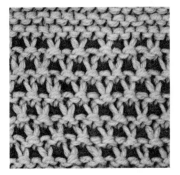

Crochet

The origins of crochet are obscure but we know that fine crochet was worked by nuns in Europe in the 16th century. In the early 1800's Ireland adopted the art and gave its name to the now universally popular Irish crochet. It spread to England as a fad, lasted for some twenty years, and kept ladies high born and low born busy turning out copies of rose point and Venetian lace. Though there is really only one stitch in crochet—interlocking loops produced with a single thread and hook—there are endless variations of the basic stitch. The most popular of these are illustrated here.

Just as some of the hooks used for crochet have changed from tortoiseshell and bone to plastic and aluminum, so the uses to which crochet has been put have kept pace with changing times. Today crochet has proved its worth for making high-style garments and everything from the lowly pot holder to tea cloths of delicacy and distinction. Boys race off to school in the morning wearing crocheted pullovers, and after dark their mothers appear at first nights carrying sequin-crocheted evening bags. You will find crochet one of the most functional of all the needle arts.

Crochet

Crochet, which originated as a method for making fine laces, has developed into a versatile technique for making many things—high-style garments and accessories, lovely table mats and cloths, bedspreads, afghans and even rugs.

Edges or trimmings of crochet combine well with fabric for a smart finishing touch. Crochet is also used for finishing knitted garments.

1. HOLD THREAD

2. HOLD HOOK

3. MAKE LOOP

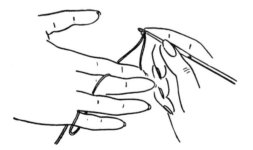

4. ADJUSTING TENSION

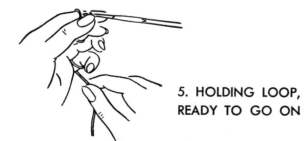

5. HOLDING LOOP, READY TO GO ON

All crochet stitches are based on a loop pulled through another loop by a hook. For a practice piece, work simple stitches until you are familiar with them, and always make a practice swatch of each new stitch before proceeding with an article.

To start, make a loop at the end of the yarn by lapping long thread over short end. Hold in place between thumb and forefinger of left hand. See Figure 1. With the right hand grasp the bar of the hook as you would a pencil (Figure 2). Insert the hook through the loop and under the long thread. Pull this thread through loop with hook. This forms a loop or first stitch (Figure 3).

Now adjust the long thread around the left hand for proper tension. Have it pass under and around the little finger and over ring finger, under middle finger and over forefinger toward the thumb (Figure 4.) Grasp the thread firmly enough to hold the tension but not so tightly as to make it difficult to pull loops through (Figure 5.)

CROCHET ABBREVIATIONS

ch—chain stitch
st—stitch
sts—stitches
lp—loop
inc—increase
dec—decrease
rnd—round
beg—beginning
sk—skip
p—picot
tog—together

sc—single crochet
sl st—slip stitch
dc—double crochet
hdc—half double crochet
tr—treble or triple crochet
dtr—double treble crochet
tr tr—treble treble crochet
bl—block
sp—space
cl—cluster
pat—pattern
yo—yarn over hook

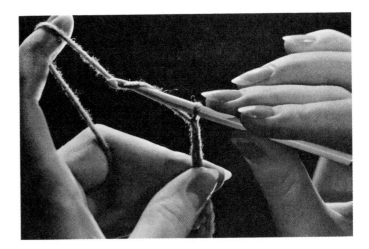

CHAIN STITCH (CH)

Chain stitch is the foundation of all crochet. The photograph and detail diagrams show how each loop is drawn through the preceding loop. Pass hook through loop under yarn to catch yarn with hook. Draw yarn through first loop to make 1 chain (ch 1). Repeat to make the required number of chains according to the directions. By holding thumb and forefinger near the stitch in work you can control the tension. Keep 1 loop always on hook until end of chain (Figures 1, 2, 3). When you begin a piece of crochet, work your starting row of chain stitches more loosely than the following rows.

SLIP STITCH (SL ST)

After forming chain of desired sts, turn, (1), insert hook in second ch from hook, (2), put yarn over hook, (3), and pull through stitch and loop.

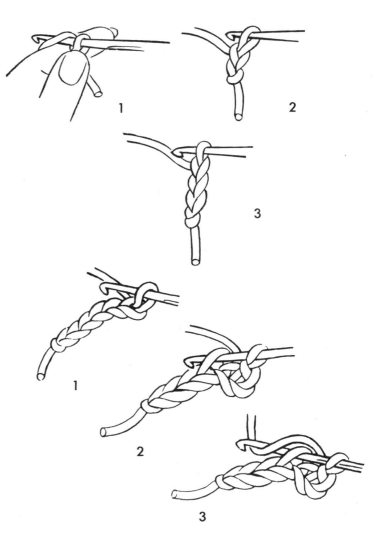

249

SINGLE CROCHET (SC)

This uses the chain as a foundation. Ch 20 sts for practice. Insert hook in top 2 threads of 2nd ch from hook (Figure 1). Draw yarn through loop making 2 loops on hook (Figures 2 and 3). Yarn over and draw through 2 loops leaving 1 loop on hook (Figures 4 and 5). This completes 1 sc. For the next sc insert hook under top 2 strands of next ch and repeat. See Figure 6.

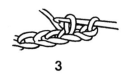

1

2

3

4

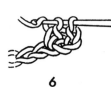

5

6

DOUBLE CROCHET (DC)

After making the starting chain (20 ch for practice swatch) pass yarn over hook, insert hook from front under top 2 strands of 4th ch from hook (Figure 1). Yarn over, draw through stitch (Figure 2). There are now 3 loops on hook (Figure 3). Yarn over (Figure 4) and draw through 2 loops, with 2 loops left on hook (Figure 5). Yarn over again (Figure 6) and draw through remaining 2 loops with 1 loop remaining on hook (Figure 7). 1 dc is now completed. For next dc, yarn over, insert hook from front under top 2 threads of next chain (Figure 8). Repeat these steps until there is a dc in each ch. At the end of the row ch 3, turn and repeat. This turning ch 3 is always counted as the first dc of next row. Therefore first dc of each row is always skipped.

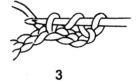

1

2

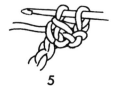

3

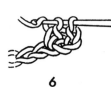

4

5

6

7

8

HALF DOUBLE CROCHET (HDC)

With 1 loop on hook put yarn over hook, insert hook in stitch, put yarn over hook, draw through st, yarn over hook and draw through all 3 loops. See photograph.

HALF DOUBLE CROCHET

TREBLE OR TRIPLE CROCHET (TR)

With loop on hook put yarn over hook twice, insert in 5th st from hook, pull loop through. Yarn over and draw through 2 loops at a time 3 times. Repeat. At end of row, ch 4 and turn. See photograph.

TREBLE OR TRIPLE CROCHET

TO INCREASE

When directions call for an increase make 2 sts in 1 st. This forms an extra st in the row.

TO DECREASE SINGLE CROCHET

Complete 1 sc to point where 2 loops are on hook. Then begin another sc until 3 loops are on hook (Figure 1). Bring yarn through 3 loops at once to work 2 sc together and form the decrease (Figure 2).

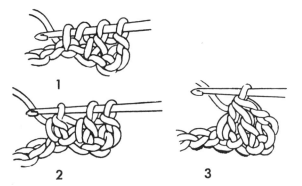

TO DECREASE DOUBLE CROCHET

Complete 1 dc to point where 2 loops are on hook. Begin another dc until 4 loops are on hook (Figure 1). Yarn over, draw through 2 loops (Figure 2), yarn over again, draw through 3 loops. 1 loop remains on needle ready to resume work (Figure 3).

TURNING SINGLE CROCHET

HOW TO TURN YOUR WORK

In crochet a certain number of ch sts are needed at the end of each row to bring work into position for the next row. Then work is turned so reverse side is facing the crocheter. Follow the stitch table below for the number of ch sts required to make a turn.

Single crochet (sc)	Ch 1 to turn
Half double crochet (half dc or hdc)	Ch 2 to turn
Double crochet (dc)	Ch 3 to turn
Treble crochet (tr)	Ch 4 to turn
Double treble crochet (dtr)	Ch 5 to turn
Treble treble crochet (tr tr)	Ch 6 to turn

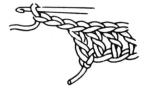

TURNING DOUBLE CROCHET

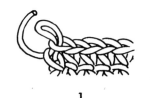

1

2

HOW TO END WORK

Do not make a turning chain at end of last row. Cut working strand about 3 inches from work (Figure 1). Bring loose end through the final loop remaining on hook and pull through. This fastens the end of the work. (Figure 2). Do not cut this strand but pass end through eye of yarn needle or darning needle and weave back into body of work so it is hidden.

HOW TO FOLLOW CROCHET DIRECTIONS

An asterisk (*) is often used in crochet directions to indicate repetition. For example, when directions read "* 2 dc in next st, 1 dc in next st, repeat from * 4 times" this means to work directions after first * until second * is reached, then go back to first * 4 times more. Work 5 times in all.

When () (parentheses) are used to show repetition, work directions within parentheses as many times as specified. For example, "(dc, ch 1) 3 times" means to do what is within () 3 times altogether.

"Work even" in directions means to work in same stitch without increasing or decreasing.

SLIP STITCH FOR JOINING

When directions say **join** always use a sl st. Insert hook from front under 2 top threads of stitch. Yarn over and with one motion draw thread through stitch and loop on hook. One loop still remains on hook for continuing work.

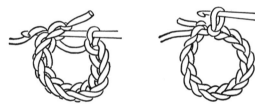

JOINING WITH SLIP STITCH

PICOT (P)

With loop on hook, turn and ch 7, slip st in 4th ch from hook to form a picot, ch 3, skip 3 sts of foundation crochet, sc in next st and repeat across. See photograph. There are variations in size for the picot. These are given with the crochet directions.

The importance of gauge in crochet

Before crocheting a garment, make a swatch to check your gauge using the yarn and hook called for in the directions.

Start with a chain about four inches long and work the swatch in the pattern stitch of the garment until piece is about three inches deep. Block swatch by smoothing it out, pinning it down along edges and steam-pressing it. Measure across two inches, counting the number of stitches to the inch. If you have *more* stitches to the inch than directions call for, you are working too tightly; try a new swatch with a larger hook or work more loosely. If you have *fewer* stitches to the inch, you are working too loosely; try a smaller hook or work more tightly.

If you wish to substitute one yarn for another, be sure the substitute yarn produces the proper gauge. By crocheting a swatch you will be able to check your gauge and determine the texture of the substitute yarn in the pattern stitch.

In crocheting household designs, you may wish to alter the appearance of the design by choosing a different thread from the one recommended. In this case be sure to work a small sample first, then check the appearance and gauge to be sure you will obtain the result you wish.

The three examples illustrated here show a single motif worked in six cord mercerized crochet thread of three different sizes: the smallest motif in size 80, the middle motif in size 60, largest motif in size 30.

Crochet Hooks — Their Sizes and Uses

Crochet hooks come in a large range of sizes, from the very fine No. 14 steel hook for fine crochet cotton to larger hooks of aluminum or plastic for coarser cotton, wool or other yarns.

STEEL CROCHET HOOKS

These are 5″ long and come in sizes 00 (large) to 14 (very fine). Steel hooks are generally used for cotton threads, but the larger sizes are often used for other yarns.

PLASTIC, BONE AND ALUMINUM HOOKS

Plastic crochet hooks are 5½″ long and come in sizes D to J. These hooks often carry a number, too. The numbers, however, are not standardized.

Bone crochet hooks are 5″ long and come in sizes 1 to 6, roughly the equivalent of B to G shown in illustration.

Aluminum crochet hooks are 6″ long and come in sizes B to K.

Afghan hooks of aluminum and plastic are 9″ to 14″ long and have a straight, even shaft. They range from sizes 1 to 10 and F to J. When afghan hooks are sized by number, the shaft of each hook is roughly equal to the same size in knitting needles. When they are sized by letter, they are equivalent to crochet hooks sized in the same way.

WOODEN CROCHET HOOKS

These are 9″ or 10″ long and are used for jiffy work.

Useful Crochet Pattern Stitches

FILET MESH

Make a ch of desired length. **Row 1:** Dc in 8th ch from hook (1 sp), * ch 2, sk 2 ch, dc in next ch, repeat from * across ch. Ch 5, turn.

Row 2: Dc in next dc, * ch 2, dc in next dc, repeat from * across to last dc, ch 2, sk 2 ch of turning-ch, dc in next ch. Ch 5, turn.

Repeat row 2 for pattern.

CLUSTER STITCH

A cluster stitch is a group of 3 or more stitches gathered together at the top to form one pattern stitch. For a practice piece, make a ch of 20 sts.

Row 1: Yarn over hook 3 times (for 1 dtr), insert hook in 6th ch from hook and draw loop through (5 loops on hook); yarn over and draw through 2 loops at a time 3 times (2 loops remain on hook); work another dtr in next ch until 3 loops remain on hook; work another dtr in next ch until 4 loops remain on hook; yarn over and through all 4 loops on hook— 1 cluster made. * Ch 4, work dtr cluster in next 4 ch, repeat from * across.

PUFF STITCH PATTERN

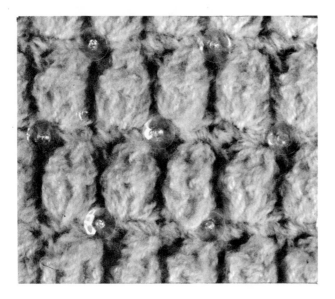

This pattern uses the cluster stitch. Make a ch of desired length.

Row 1 (wrong side): Holding back on hook last loop of each dc, work 4 dc in 4th ch from hook, yarn over and through 5 loops on hook, ch 1 loosely (puff st made), * sk next ch, puff st of 4 dc in next ch (include the ch 1), repeat from * across row. Ch 1, turn.

Row 2 (right side): Sc in top 2 loops of first puff st, * sc in each of ch-1 sp and top 2 loops of next puff st, repeat from * across row. Ch 1, turn.

Row 3: Pull up loop on hook to height of puff st, puff st in next sc, * sk 1 sc (this is over sp between 2 puff sts), puff st in next sc, repeat from * across row. Ch 1 more, turn. Repeat rows 2 and 3 for pattern. In illustration, pattern is decorated with sewn-on sequins and seed beads.

FAN SHELL STITCH

Multiple of 6 ch.

Row 1: Work 2 dc in 3rd ch from hook, ch 1, 3 dc in same ch, sk 2 ch, 1 sc in next ch, * sk 2 ch, 3 dc in next ch, ch 1, 3 dc in same ch, sk 2 ch, 1 sc in next ch, repeat from * across row, ch 3, turn.

Row 2: 2 dc in first sc, * sk 3 dc, 1 sc in ch-1 sp, sk 3 dc, 3 dc in sc between 2 shells, ch 1, 3 dc in same st, repeat from * across row, end sk 3 dc, 1 sc in ch-1 sp, sk 2 dc, 3 dc in last st, ch 1, turn.

Row 3: * 3 dc in next sc (between shells), ch 1, 3 dc in same st, sk 3 dc, sc in next ch-1 sp, sk 3 dc, repeat from * across row, end with shell in last sc, sk 2 dc, 1 sc in last st (top of turning-ch), ch 3, turn.

Repeat rows 2 and 3 for pattern.

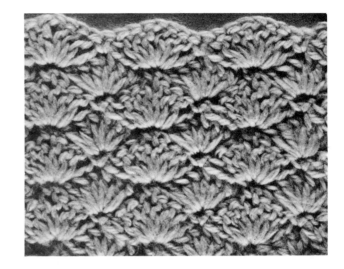

BOX STITCH

Multiple of 6 ch.

Row 1: Dc in 3rd ch from hook, dc in each of next 2 ch, sk 2 ch, sl st in next ch, * ch 2, dc in each of next 3 ch, sk 2 ch, sl st in next ch; repeat from * across, ending last shell with dc in last 4 ch. Turn.

Row 2: Sl st across top of 4 dc, sl st under ch-2 loop of shell, * ch 2, 3 dc under same ch-2 loop, sl st under ch-2 loop of next shell; repeat from * across to last shell, make shell in ch-2 loop of last shell. Turn.

Repeat row 2 for pattern, having same number of shells in each row.

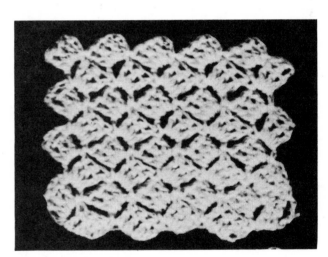

KNOT STITCH

Multiple of 6 ch. Make ch desired length.

Row 1: * Pull up loop on hook to ½″ length, draw yarn through this loop and hold single strand at back of loop between thumb and middle finger; insert hook under this single strand and work sc; repeat from * once (double knot st made); sk 3 ch, 1 sc in each of next 3 ch, repeat from first * across, end 1 sc in each of last 3 ch.

Row 2: Work double knot st to turn. * Work 1 sc in loop on one side of knot st of previous row, work 1 sc in loop on other side of same knot st; work double knot st, repeat from * across row.

Repeat row 2 for pattern.

Crocheted pullovers

Easy to make pullovers for the men in the family feature pattern stripes worked in long single crochet. The yarn is knitting worsted; the main color here is gray, the bands navy and red. Shawl collars are crocheted in one with the fronts. Directions are given for boys' sizes 6-10, men's sizes 38-44.

SIZES: Directions for boys' size 6. Changes for boys' sizes 8, 10 and men's sizes 38, 40, 42 and 44 in parentheses.

Body Chest Size: 24″ (26″-28″-38″-40″-42″-44″).

Blocked Chest Size: 27″ (29″-31″-41″-43″-45″-47″).

MATERIALS: Knitting Worsted, 12 (14-16-24-26-28-30) ozs. oxford, main color (MC); 1 (1-1-2-2-2-2) ozs. navy (N) and 1 oz. scarlet (S). Aluminum or plastic crochet hooks, sizes H and J.

GAUGE: 3 sc=1″; 4 sc rows=1″ (size J hook).

Note: Before making garment, circle sts and measurements in size you plan to make. This will facilitate reading directions.

To Bind Off: At beg of row, sl st loosely across specified sc, ch 1, work sc across; **at end of row,** leave specified sc unworked. Ch 1, turn.

To Dec 1 Sc: Pull up a lp in each of 2 sc, yo and through 3 lps on hook.

To Inc 1 Sc: Work 2 sc in same sc.

PULLOVERS: BACK: Beg at lower edge, with MC and size J hook, ch loosely 41 (45-47-63-65-69-71). Sc in 2nd ch from hook and in each ch across— 40 (44-46-62-64-68-70) sc. Ch 1, turn.

Pattern Stripe: Row 1 (wrong side): With MC, sc in both lps of each of first 1 (1-2-2-1-1-2) sc, * sc in front lp of each of next 2 sc, sc in both lps of each of next 2 sc, repeat from * across, end last repeat sc in both lps of last 1 (1-2-2-1-1-2) sc. Drop MC. Tie in N yarn, ch 1, turn.

Note: Conceal yarn ends by working over them on the following rows.

Row 2 (right side): With N, sc in back lp of first 1 (1-2-2-1-1-2) sc, * insert hook in back lp of next sc as before on 2nd row below and pull up a long lp to reach top of last row, yo and through 2 lps on hook (long sc made), make a 2nd long sc in back lp of next sc as before on 2nd row below, sc in back lp of each of next 2 sc on last row, repeat from * across, end last repeat sc in back lp of last 1 (1-2-2-1-1-2) sc. Ch 1, turn.

Row 3: With N, sc in both lps of each of first 3 (3-4-4-3-3-4) sc, * sc in front lp of each of next 2 sc, sc in both lps of each of next 2 sc, repeat from * across, end last repeat sc in both lps of each of last 3 (3-4-4-3-3-4) sc. Cut N. With MC, ch 1, turn.

Row 4: With MC, sc in back lp of each of first 3 (3-4-4-3-3-4) sc, * long sc in back lp of each of next 2 sc as before on 2nd row below, sc in back lp of each of next 2 sc on last row, repeat from * across, end last repeat sc in back lp of each of last 3 (3-4-4-3-3-4) sc. Ch 1, turn.

Row 5: With MC, repeat row 1. Drop MC. Tie in S, ch 1, turn.

Rows 6 and 7: With S, repeat rows 2 and 3. Cut S. With MC, ch 1, turn.

Rows 8 and 9: With MC, repeat rows 4 and 1. Drop MC. Tie in N, ch 1, turn.

Rows 10 and 11: With N, repeat rows 2 and 3. Cut N. With MC, ch 1, turn.

Row 12: With MC, repeat row 4. Pattern stripe completed. With MC, ch 1, turn.

Working in both lps of each sc, work MC sc until piece measures 7" (7½"-8"-12"-12"-13"-13") from start or 2¾" less than desired length to underarm, end on right side. Ch 1, turn. Check gauge; piece should be 13½" (14½"-15½"-20½"-21½"-22½"-23½") wide. Work the 12 rows of pattern stripe as before. With MC, ch 1, turn. Work even in MC sc until piece measures 10½" (11"-11½"-15½"-15½"-16½"-16½") from start, end on wrong side. Ch 1, turn.

Shape Armholes: Bind off (see To Bind Off) 2 (3-3-4-4-4-4) sc each side of next row. Dec 1 sc each side every other row 2 (2-2-3-3-5-5) times—32 (34-36-48-50-50-52) sc. Work even in sc until armholes

measure 6" (6½"-7"-9½"-9½"-10"-10") above first bound-off sts.

Shape Shoulders: Bind off 4 sc each side of next 2 (2-2-3-3-3-3) rows, then 2 (2-3-4-4-4-4) sc each side of next row. End off. 12 (14-14-16-18-18-20) sc remain for back of neck.

FRONT: Work as for back until armhole decs are completed, end on wrong side. Ch 1, turn.

Front Opening and Shawl Collar: Left Half: Sc in each of first 16 (17-18-24-25-25-26) sc. Ch 1, turn. Working on left half only, work even in sc for 1", end at center edge. Ch 1, turn. Continue in sc, inc 1 sc (see To Inc) in 2nd sc from center edge on next row, then every 1" 3 (3-3-5-5-5-5) times—20 (21-22-30-31-31-32) sc. Work even until armhole measures same as back, end at arm side.

Shape Shoulder: Bind off 4 sc at arm side of next 2 (2-2-3-3-3-3) rows, then 2 (2-3-4-4-4-4) sc at arm side of next row—10 (11-11-14-15-15-16) sc remain. Work even on remaining sc for 2" (2¼"-2¼"-2½"-3"-3"-3¼"). End off.

Right Half: From right side, join MC at neck edge, work as for left half.

SLEEVES: Beg at lower edge, with MC and size H hook, ch loosely 25 (25-27-35-37-37-39). Sc in 2nd ch from hook and in each ch across—24 (24-26-34-36-36-38) sc. Ch 1, turn. Work the 12 rows of pattern stripe as for back. With MC, ch 1, turn. Change to size J hook. Work in MC sc, inc 1 sc each side of next row, then every 1½" (1"-1"-2"-2"-2"-2") 4 (6-6-6-6-6-6) times—34 (38-40-48-50-50-52) sc. Check gauge; piece above last inc row should be 11½" (12½"-13½"-16"-16½"-16½"-17½") wide. Work even in sc until piece measures 11½" (13"-14½"-18½"-18½"-19"-19") from start or desired length to underarm. Ch 1, turn.

Shape Cap: Bind off 2 (3-3-4-4-4-4) sc each side of next row. Dec 1 sc each side every other row 5 (6-7-11-11-12-12) times. Bind off 2 sc each side of next 3 (3-3-2-2-2-2) rows. End off.

FINISHING: Run in all yarn ends on wrong side. Block pieces to measurements. Sew seams with MC, overcasting seams tog on wrong side as follows: Sew shoulder seams. Sew in sleeves. Matching pattern stripes, sew side and sleeves seams. Steam-press seams flat on wrong side. Turn pullover to right side. Turn collar down to right side. From right side, weave short ends of collar tog. Sew neck edge of collar to neck with seam at center back of neck. Beg at center back of collar, from right side, with MC and size H hook, work 1 row sc evenly around entire outer edge of collar. Join in first sc. Ch 1, turn. Sl st loosely in each sc around edge of collar. End off.

Crocheted bonnet and sacque, edged with loop stitch

The delicate loop-stitch edging adds appeal to these cuddly garments for your favorite baby. Use white baby wool or nylon yarn for the sacque and bonnet. Use the same yarn in traditional baby pink or blue for the loop-stitch trimming.

SIZE: Infants' size.

MATERIALS: Baby wool or nylon, 3-ply, 3 1-oz. balls white (W), 1 ball blue (B). Plastic crochet hook size F or 4. Two yards blue satin ribbon.

GAUGE: 3 pats=1"; 5 pat rows=1".

PATTERN STITCH: Row 1: Sc in 2nd ch from hook, draw up a lp in same ch (2 lps on hook), * sk 1 ch, draw up a lp in next ch (3 lps on hook), yo and through 3 lps on hook, ch 1 (1 pat made); draw up a lp in same ch as last st, repeat from * across, end ch 1, sc in last ch (with last st of last pat). Ch 1, turn.

Row 2: Sc in first sc, draw up a lp between first sc and first pat of last row (2 lps on hook), * draw up a lp between next 2 pats (3 lps on hook), yo and through all 3 lps on hook, ch 1, draw up a lp in same sp as last st, repeat from * across to last pat, work pat over last pat, ch 1, sc in sc of previous row. Ch 1, turn. Repeat row 2 for pattern st.

LOOP-STITCH TRIMMING: Row 1 (right side): With B, sc across work. Ch 1, turn.

Row 2 (wrong side): With yarn over left index finger, insert hook in first sc, * draw 2 strands (strand on top of index finger and strand under index finger) through st forming 1" loop on index finger; remove finger from loop, hold loop in back, yo and through 3 lps on hook (1 loop st made on right side of work). Insert hook in next sc, repeat from * in each sc. Ch 1, turn. **Row 3:** Sc in each loop st. Ch 1, turn.

Row 4: Repeat row 2. End off.

JACKET: BACK: Beg at lower edge, with W, ch 56. Work in pat (27 pats) until piece measures 5½". Make sc at end of row, ch 33 for sleeve. Drop lp off hook. With another strand of W, make lp on hook, sl st in sc at opposite end of last row, ch 31 for sleeve. End off. Pick up dropped lp, turn.

Work row 1 of pat st on ch 33 until there are 15 pats, draw up a lp in same ch as last st, sk last ch and sc, draw up a lp between sc and first pat, yo and through 3 lps on hook, ch 1, work in pat across back, draw up a lp in same sp as last st, sk sc, draw up a lp in first ch of ch 31, yo and through all 3 lps on hook, ch 1, work 15 pats across ch; end ch 1, sc in last ch (with last st of last pat)—59 pats. Ch 1, turn. Work even in pat until sleeves measure 3½" straight up from sleeve ch. Ch 1, turn.

Right Shoulder and Front: Work 24 pats, sc in same sp as last st. Ch 1, turn. Work 2 more rows of 24 pats for shoulder. Ch 9 for front, turn. Work 4 pats on ch 9, 1 pat over sc at neck edge, continue across in pat—29 pats. Work even on 29 pats until sleeve is 3½" from top of shoulder, end center front edge. Ch 1, turn. Work across 14 pats for front, sc in same sp as last st. Ch 1, turn. Work even on 14 pats until front measures same as back to sleeve. End off.

Left Shoulder and Front: Sk 11 pats for back of neck on last row of 59 pats. With lp on hook, join W with sl st in sp before next pat, sc in sp. Work in pat on next 24 pats to end of row. Work 2 more rows of 24 pats, end at sleeve edge. Drop lp off hook. Attach a separate strand of W at neck edge (beg of last row), ch 8. Break off. Pick up lp at sleeve edge, ch 1, turn.

Work across 24 pats, work 1 pat over sc at neck edge, work 4 pats on ch 8—29 pats. Complete left front as for right front. Sew side and sleeve seams.

Trimming: Row 1: With B, from right side of work, beg at left front neck edge, work 1 row of sc along front and bottom edges, making 1 sc in end of each row on front edges, 2 sc in each pat on bottom edge and 3 sc in each corner; end at right front neck edge. Ch 1, turn. Work rows 2-4 of Loop-Stitch Trimming.

From right side, join B to right front neck edge in end st of trimming. Ch 1, work sc around neck edge, skipping every 5th st to hold in neck edge slightly. Ch 1, turn. Work row 2 of Loop-Stitch Trimming around neck edge. End off.

From right side, join B to cuff edge of sleeve at underarm seam, work 30 sc around cuff edge. Sl st in first sc. Ch 1, turn. Work rows 2-4 of Loop-Stitch Trimming, joining each rnd with sl st before turning.

Steam-press jacket. Cut two 12" lengths of ribbon. Sew at neck edge for ties.

BONNET: Crown: With W, ch 4, sl st in first ch to form ring. **Rnd 1:** 6 sc in ring. Do not join rnds; mark ends of rnds. **Rnd 2:** 2 sc in each sc—12 sc.

Rnd 3: * Sc in next sc, 2 sc in next sc, repeat from * around—18 sc.

Rnd 4: * Sc in each of next 2 sc, 2 sc in next sc, repeat from * around—24 sc. Continue to inc 6 sc each rnd, having 1 more sc between incs each rnd, until there are 11 sc between incs—78 sc. Work even in sc for 3 rnds. Ch 1, turn.

Front: Row 1: Sc in first sc, draw up a lp in same st, * sk 1 sc, draw up a lp in next st, yo and through 3 lps on hook, ch 1 (1 pat made); draw up a lp in same sc as last st, repeat from * until there are 32 pats, end ch 1, sc in next sc. Ch 1, turn. Work in pat for 11 more rows—12 rows of 32 pats. Do not ch 1 at end of last row; end off W; turn.

Cuff: Join B in first st, sc in first st, * 2 sc in each of 3 pats, 1 sc in next pat, repeat from * across—58 sc. Ch 1, turn. Work rows 2-4 of Loop-Stitch Trimming. End off. Turn back cuff to right side.

Neck Edge: From right side, attach W to left front cuff edge. Working along side edge of front, catching in side edge of cuff, make 11 sc along side edge; continue across back edge of crown, making 10 sc on back edge; make 11 sc along other side edge, catching in side edge of cuff—32 sc. Ch 1, turn. Work 2 more rows of sc. End off. Cut 24" lengths of ribbon for ties. Fold one end of each piece into 3 graduated loops; sew looped end to side of bonnet.

Girls' Afghan-square sweater

SIZES: Directions for size 2. Changes for sizes 4, 6, 8, 10 are in parentheses.

Body Chest Size: 21″ (23″-24″-26″-28″).

Blocked Chest Size: 24″ (26″-28″-30″-32″).

MATERIALS: Knitted Worsted, 4 ply, 8 (9-10-12-13) 1-oz. skeins blue (B); 4 (4-5-5-6) skeins white (W). Plastic crochet hook size G. Large-eyed sewing needle. Snap fastener. Small button for sizes 6, 8 and 10.

GAUGE: Small motif=2″. Medium motif=2⅛″. Large motif=2¼″. 7 sc=2″ (waistband, cuffs, collar).

SMALL MOTIF (see gauge): Beg at center with W, ch 4. Join with sl st to form ring. **Rnd 1** (right side): With W, in ring make (sc, ch 2, dc, ch 2) 4 times. Join with tight sl st in ring. End off.

Rnd 2: From right side, join B in back lp of any sc, ch 3, in same st as ch-3 make dc and hdc; working in back lp of each st, sc in next dc, * in next sc make hdc, 3 dc and hdc, sc in next dc, repeat from * around, end hdc and dc in same sc worked in at beg of rnd—24 sts. Join in back lp at top of ch-3. End off. Weave all ends in on wrong side.

MEDIUM MOTIF (see gauge): Beg and work rnds 1 and 2 as for small motif. Do not end off.

Rnd 3: Working in back lp of each st, from right side, * sl st loosely in each of 5 sts, sl st twice in corner st, repeat from * around—28 sts. End off.

LARGE MOTIF (see gauge): Beg and work rnds 1 and 2 as for small motif. Do not end off.

Rnd 3: Working in back lp of each st, from right side, 2 sc in same place as sl st, * sc in each of 5 sts, 3 sc in next st, repeat from * around, end last repeat with 1 sc in same st worked in at beg of rnd —32 sts. Join in first sc. End off.

HALF SMALL MOTIF: Beg at center with W, ch 4. Join with sl st to form ring.

Row 1 (right side): In ring make sc, (ch 2, dc, ch 2, sc) twice. End off.

Row 2: From right side, join B in back lp of first sc on last row, ch 3, in same st as ch-3, make dc and hdc; working in back lp of each st, sc in next dc; in next sc make hdc, 3 dc and hdc, sc in next dc; in last sc make hdc and 2 dc—13 sts. End.

HALF MEDIUM MOTIF: Beg and work rows 1 and 2 as for half small motif.

Row 3: From right side, join B in back lp at top of ch-3, sl st loosely in same st as ch-3; working in

back lps, (sl st in each of 5 sts, 2 sl sts in corner st) twice—16 sts. End off.

HALF LARGE MOTIF: Beg and work rows 1 and 2 as for half small motif.

Row 3: From right side, join B in back lp at top of ch-3, 2 sc in same st as ch-3; working in back lps, sc in each of 5 sts, 3 sc in corner st, sc in each of 5 sts, 2 sc in last st—17 sc. End off.

BLOUSE: For Size 2: Make 92 small motifs and 2 half small motifs.

For Size 4: Make 112 medium motifs and 2 half medium motifs.

For Size 6: Make 161 small motifs and 2 half small motifs.

For Size 8: Make 175 medium motifs and 2 half medium motifs.

For Size 10: Make 185 large motifs and 2 half large motifs.

JOINING: Beg at lower edge of front, following chart page 264 with B, sew motifs tog catching tog back lps st by st from one corner st to the other until 3 (4-5-6-6) motif rows are joined, omitting the half motifs at underarms shown by dotted lines. Check gauge; piece should measure 6″ (8½″-10″-12¾″-13½″) in length, 12″ (13″-14″-15″-16″) in width. Leaving an opening at front of neck, continue to join motifs as shown on chart to lower edge of back, filling in corners at front of neck with half motifs.

FINISHING: Fold work across shoulders, with lower edges of back and front meeting. Sew side and sleeve seams in same way to within 1 motif of underarm. Sew one motif to each underarm, forming gussets as shown on chart by dotted lines; one corner will meet side seam and opposite corner will meet underarm sleeve seam.

Waistband: Rnd 1: From right side, join B at lower right side seam; working in back lp of sts around lower edge, ch 1, work 42 (46-49-52-56) sc across front and 42 (45-49-52-56) sc across back—84 (91-98-104-112) sc. Join in ch-1. Do not turn.

Rnd 2: Working in back lps, * sc in each of 4 (5-5-6-6) sc, pull up a lp in each of next 2 sc, yo and through 3 lps on hook (1 dec made), repeat from * 13 (12-13-12-13) times—70 (78-84-91-98) sts. Join in ch-1. Do not turn.

Rnd 3: Ch 1, sc in back lp of each sc around. Join in ch-1. Repeat rnd 3 until waistband measures 1½″ (1½″-1½″-1″-1″). End off.

Cuffs: From right side, join B at lower side seam of sleeve; working in back lp of sts, ch 1, work 28 (30-36-36-40) sc on sleeve edge. Join in ch-1.

Rnd 2: Working in back lps, ch 1, * sc in each of 2 (3-2-2-2) sc, dec 1 sc, repeat from * 6 (5-8-8-9) times—21 (24-27-27-30) sc. Join in ch-1. Beg with rnd 3 of waistband, complete cuffs as for waistband or desired sleeve length.

Crocheted afghan squares, each with a flower center, are sewn together to make an unusual sweater of knitting worsted.

Collar: Beg at neck edge with B, ch 36 (38-41-44-49) to measure 10″ (10½″-11½″-12″-13¼″).

Row 1: Sc in 2nd ch from hook and in each ch across—35 (37-40-43-48) sc. Ch 1, turn each row.

Row 2: Sc in back lp of each sc across.

Row 3: Sc in front lp of each sc. Repeat last 2 rows 1 (2-2-3-3) times more. Repeating rows 2 and 3 alternately, dec 1 sc at each side of next 3 rows—29 (31-34-37-42) sc. End off. Work 1 row sc around outer edge of collar.

Beg at opening edge of front neck, from right side, with B, work 35 (37-40-43-48) sc evenly around neck edge. Ch 1, turn. Work 1 (1-2-2-2) rows more of sc around neck edge. End off.

On Sizes 2 and 4: Sew neck edge of collar to neck with ends at center front opening. Close at neck with snap fastener.

On Sizes 6, 8 and 10: Beg 1″ from right front neck opening, sew collar to neck edge, ending at front opening and to within 1″ of end of collar (collar overlap). Close side opening with button and button-loop. Close corner of collar overlap with snap fastener inside edge of collar of right front (bringing ends of collar to center front).

TIES: Make 2 chains desired length. Sew ties under front edges of collar. Trim ends of ties with W pompons. (See Index for directions, "How to Make a Pompon.")

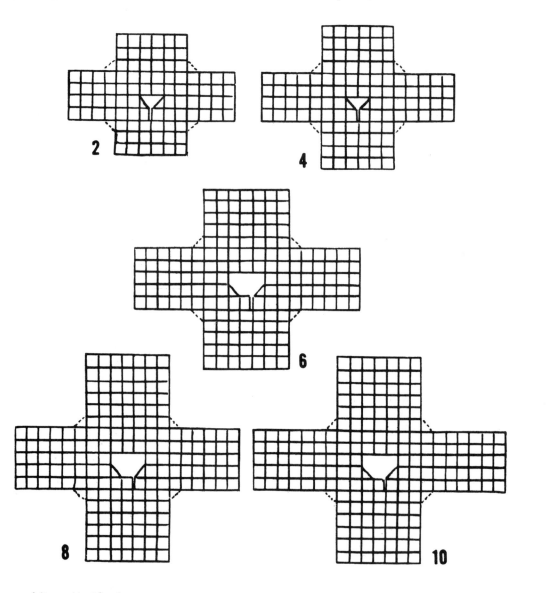

Chart for assembling Motifs for Girls' Afghan-Square Sweater

Making any or all of these 6" square picture pot holders is an easy matter with heavy cotton rug yarn. Directions for each, instructions for changing from one color to another, and how to work reverse single crochet are on pages 266-267.

Picture pot holders

GENERAL DIRECTIONS: Design Note: When a row has more than one color, start extra color or colors at beginning of row. Work over color not being used.

When changing colors, work last sc or reverse sc of one color until there are 2 lps on hook, drop strand to wrong side of work. Pick up new color and finish sc.

GAUGE: 4 sts=1"; 7 rows=2".

PATTERN: Row 1 (right side): Sc in 2nd ch from hook and in each ch across—23 sc. Ch 1, turn.

Row 2: Work in reverse sc as follows: * Holding yarn in front of work, insert hook under yarn from back to front in next sc, pull lp through and complete sc, repeat from * across. Ch 1, turn.

Row 3: Sc in each sc. Ch 1, turn. Repeat rows 2 and 3 for pat.

BORDER: Rnd 1: From right side, work sc around entire edge of pot holder, making 3 sc in each corner. Join with sl st in first sc.

Rnd 2: Working in back lp of sts, work sl st in each sc around. Join in first sl st. End off.

RING: Ch 8, join with sl st in first ch. Cut yarn, leaving an end for sewing. Sew ring to top of pot holder.

PINE TREE POT HOLDER: Materials: Heavy cotton rug yarn, 1 skein each of white, evergreen and dark green. Aluminum crochet hook size G or H. Large-eyed sewing needle.

Design Section: With white, ch 24. Following General Directions and Pine Tree Chart, work in pat for 20 rows. End.

Border and Ring (see General Directions): Work with dark green.

STAR FLOWER POT HOLDER: Materials: Heavy cotton rug yarn, 1 skein each of medium blue, white, yellow and evergreen. Alumninum crochet hook size G or H. Large-eyed sewing needle.

Design Section: With medium blue, ch 24. Following General Directions and Star Flower Chart, work design in pat for 20 rows. End off.

Border and Ring (see General Directions): Work border with white, ring with medium blue.

SAIL BOAT POT HOLDER: Materials: Heavy cotton rug yarn, 1 skein each of white, red, national blue, medium blue; small amount of black. Aluminum crochet hook size G or H. Large-eyed sewing needle.

Design Section: With national blue, ch 24. Following General Directions and Sail Boat Chart, work design in pat for 20 rows. End off.

Mast: Untwist a piece of black yarn and with 2 strands, embroider mast in outline st.

Border and Ring (see General Directions): Work border with white, ring with red.

TULIP POT HOLDER: Materials: Heavy cotton rug yarn, 1 skein each of white, dark green and cerise. Aluminum crochet hook size G or H. Large-eyed sewing needle.

Design Section: With white, ch 24. Following General Directions and Tulip Chart, work pat for 20 rows. End off.

Border and Ring (see General Directions): Work cerise border, white ring.

BUTTERFLY POT HOLDER: Materials: Heavy cotton rug yarn, 1 skein each of light yellow, yellow, turquoise and black. Aluminum crochet hook size G or H. Large-eyed sewing needle.

Design Section: With light yellow, ch 24. Following General Directions and Butterfly Chart, work design in pat for 20 rows. End off.

Antennae: Untwist a piece of black yarn and with 2 strands, embroider antennae in outline st.

Border and Ring (see General Directions): Work border with yellow, ring with turquoise.

COUNTRY COTTAGE POT HOLDER: Materials: Heavy cotton rug yarn, 1 skein each of white, black, dark green, medium blue and national blue; small amount of red. Aluminum crochet hook size G or H. Large-eyed sewing needle.

Design Section: With dark green, ch 24. Following General Directions and Country Cottage Chart, work design in pat for 19 rows. End off.

Tree Trunk: Untwist a piece of black yarn and with 2 strands, embroider tree trunk in outline st.

Border and Ring (see General Directions): Work border with white, ring with medium blue.

To follow any of these charts: Begin at lower right-hand corner of chart and work back and forth until chart is completed.

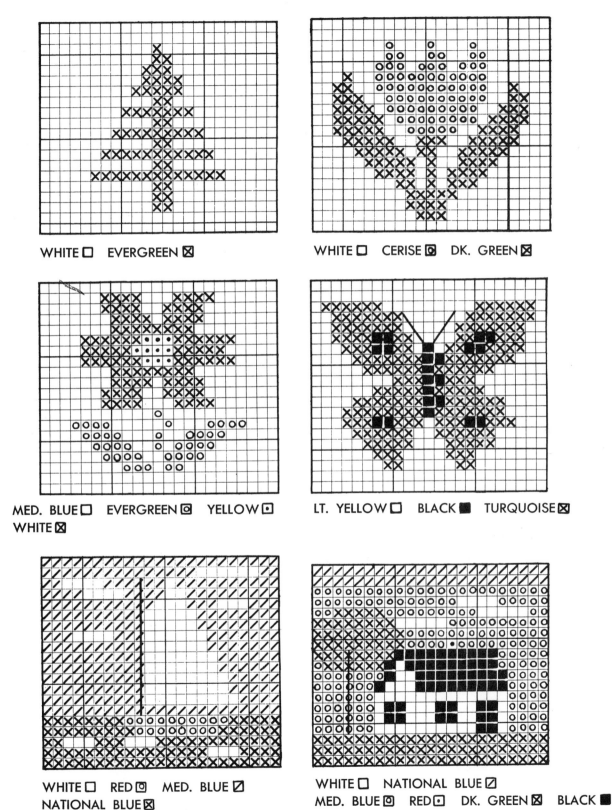

WHITE □   EVERGREEN ☒

WHITE □   CERISE ◉   DK. GREEN ☒

MED. BLUE □   EVERGREEN ◉   YELLOW ⊡
WHITE ☒

LT. YELLOW □   BLACK ■   TURQUOISE ☒

WHITE □   RED ◉   MED. BLUE ⧄
NATIONAL BLUE ☒

WHITE □   NATIONAL BLUE ⧄
MED. BLUE ◉   RED ⊡   DK. GREEN ☒   BLACK ■

Crocheting with Beads or Sequins

Many attractive accessories can be made of bead or sequin crochet. It is possible, too, to work a design of beads or sequins into a crocheted garment. Or separate collars and cuffs can be crocheted to decorate a knitted garment.

The yarns used for crocheting with beads or sequins should be smooth, and fine enough to fit through the holes of the beads or sequins. For seed beads, use fine crochet cotton or metallic

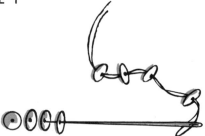

FIGURE 1

FIGURE 2.   STRINGING SEQUINS ON THREAD

FIGURE 3.   TYING THREAD AROUND YARN

FIGURE 4.   SLIDING SEQUINS ONTO YARN

thread. Medium-size beads or pearls can be strung onto heavier crochet cottons, wool yarns such as 3-ply fingering yarn, metallic yarns and fine mohair. Wooden beads with large holes can be used with bulky yarns.

Sequins can be strung onto knitting and crochet cotton, fingering yarn, and fine smooth dress yarns. Large bangles can be threaded onto any yarn, including bulky yarns.

STRINGING BEADS

If the beads are not already strung on a fine thread, thread a needle, fine enough to go through beads, with nylon thread. Knot end securely and string 12" to 18" of beads on thread. Remove needle. Tie end of thread around yarn to be used in crocheting. Slide beads gently over knot onto crochet yarn (Figure 1), taking care not to break the finer thread on which beads are strung. Remove bead thread. Thread as many beads onto yarn as you expect to use in crocheting that amount of yarn.

STRINGING SEQUINS

If sequins are not already strung, thread them on doubled sewing thread, using needle small enough to pass through center hole of sequin. Be sure right sides of sequins are facing needle (Figure 2). Inside of cup is right side of cup sequins. About 10" of threaded sequins pushed tightly together is equivalent to one strand (about 120 flat sequins or 105 cup sequins per inch).

If crochet cotton is to be used for working sequin crochet, sequins may be strung directly onto the yarn. Thread end of crochet cotton into an embroidery needle the right size to accommodate both the sequin and the yarn. Have needle 12" to 15" from end of yarn.

Pick up sequins with needle with right side of sequins facing you as they are picked up. Use a flat tray or dish to hold sequins while threading them. Do not push sequins past the double thread until they have been measured.

THREADING SEQUINS ON YARN

Holding strand of sequins with right side of sequins facing yarn, tie end of thread around yarn (Figure 3). Do not tie yarn around thread.

Slide all sequins carefully over knot onto yarn. (Short yarn end doubles back as sequins are slipped on; Figure 4.) Thread one strand of sequins onto one skein of yarn. Cut off empty thread.

When last sequin on yarn has been worked and additional sequins are needed, cut yarn 3" from last stitch made, repeat threading procedure.

BEAD CROCHET

Beads are crocheted into the work from the wrong side. String required number of beads onto yarn and push beads down on the yarn, out of the way, until ready for use. Work background of sc with yarn, ending on right side of work.

Bead Row (wrong side): Sc in each sc to place where bead pattern should begin, * pull up a loop in next sc, slip a bead up close to last loop made, hold bead in back of work, yarn over hook and through 2 loops on hook (beaded sc made), sc in next sc, repeat from * for bead pattern.

Work all right side rows in plain sc.

1. Position of sequin when hook picks up thread. Push sequin firmly against hook. With taut thread pass thread and sequin over hook for a dc.

SEQUIN DOUBLE CROCHET STITCH

In this stitch, the sequins are crocheted onto the right side of the work. Each sequin requires 3 sts (1 sequin st and 2 plain sts). Thus, for a row of 30 sequins, you will need 90 sts, plus 1 for the end st. Two rows complete the pattern, the dc row with sequins and a plain sc row.

Thread required number of sequins onto yarn with right side of sequins going on first. Slide sequins out of the way on yarn and make a ch the required length.

Row 1: 1 sc in 3rd ch from hook, 1 sc in each remaining ch. Ch 3, turn.

Row 2: Push a sequin firmly against hook, throw thread and sequin over hook, as for a dc, insert hook in top of 2nd sc (making certain sequin is toward you and right side up); take lps off hook 2 at a time *behind* the sequin, thus completing a sequin dc; 1 dc (without sequin) in each of next 2 sc. * Push a sequin firmly against hook and make a sequin dc, 1 dc (without sequin) in each of next 2 sc; repeat from * across row, ending with 2 dc (without sequins). Ch 1, turn.

Row 3: Sc in top of 2nd dc of sequin row, 1 sc in each of remaining dc of row, ending with sc in turning ch-3 of sequin row. Ch 3, turn. Repeat rows 2 and 3 alternately for pattern.

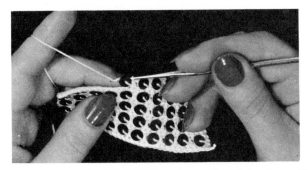

2. Start of dc with sequin position. Insert hook in top of sc below. For flat work hold sequin toward you right side up.

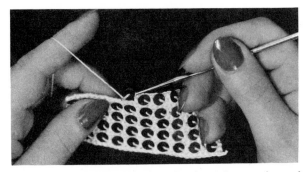

3. Completed dc position of sequin. Take lps off hook, 2 at once, behind sequin to complete dc. Make 1 dc without sequin in each of next 2 scs.

Sequin crochet with chain loops

This method for working sequin crochet is the one used most often for jackets, blouses and dresses. The sequin row is worked from the wrong side, using a simple chain loop and single crochet. If sequins are small, a ch-1 lp (chain one loop) is used for a closely-worked surface of sequins. The evening bag and eyeglass case shown on opposite page are made with ch-1 lps. Larger sequins can be worked with ch-2 or ch-3 lps.

Thread sequins on yarn as directed, page 268.

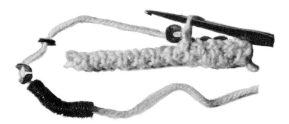

ILLUSTRATION 1:
BACK OF SEQUIN AGAINST STITCH

ILLUSTRATION 2:
SEQUINS RAISED TOWARD TOP

ILLUSTRATION 3:
SEQUINS RAISED TOWARD BOTTOM

SEQUIN CROCHET WITH CH-1 LPS

To work sequin row, slide one sequin close to st on hook. Back of sequin will be against hook; Illustration 1. Holding sequin firmly at back of work and with yarn taut so that sequin will lie flat, make 1 sc in ch-1 lp of row below. * Ch 1, slide one sequin close to ch 1 on hook, sc in next ch-1 sp, repeat from * across row.

Sequins placed after the ch 1 and before the sc as in directions above, will be raised toward top of work; Illustration 2. When article is worked from top down, this method is generally preferred.

Sequins placed after the sc and before the ch 1 will be raised toward bottom of work; Illustration 3. When article is worked from bottom up, this method is generally preferred.

Big enough to hold everything you need and decorative at the same time is this sequin-crochet evening bag made with chain-one loops. It measures 10½" x 7". Directions for making both bag and eyeglass case are on P. 272.

Sequin-crochet bag

SIZE: 10½″ wide x 7″ deep.

MATERIALS: Velveen or fingering yarn, 3 1-oz. skeins. Four strands No. 6 cup sequins. Steel crochet hook No. 5. 8″ metal sew-on bag frame. ½ yard satin for lining. Piece of Pellon, 14″ x 18″. Cardboard, 2½″ x 10″. Sewing thread. Buttonhole twist.

GAUGE: 5 sequins=1″; 4 sequin rows (8 rows) =1″.

Note: Follow directions for threading sequins onto yarn, page 268.

BAG (make 2 pieces): Starting at top of bag, with sequin-threaded yarn, ch 113.

Row 1 (right side): Sc in 3rd ch from hook, * ch 1, sk 1 ch, sc in next ch; repeat from * across— 56 sps. Ch 2, turn.

Row 2 (sequin row): * Slide sequin close to hook, sc in ch-1 sp, ch 1, repeat from * across, making last sc in turning-ch-sp—56 sequins. Ch 2, turn.

Row 3: Sc in first ch-1 sp, * ch 1, sc in next ch-1 sp, repeat from * across—52 sps. Ch 2, turn. Repeat rows 2 and 3 until piece measures 6¾″ from start, end row 3—27 sequin rows. Ch 2, turn.

Base: Next Row (sequin row): Sc in first sp, (ch 1, sc in next sp) 4 times, ch 1, work in sequin crochet until there are 46 sequins, (ch 1, sc in next sp) 5 times. Ch 1, turn.

Next Row: Sl st in each sp and sc to sp before first sequin; ch 2, sc in next ch-1 sp, * ch 1, sc in next ch-1 sp, repeat from * across to sp in back of last sequin—46 sps. Ch 2, turn. Work in sequin-crochet until there are 5 rows of 46 sequins. Work 1 row of ch-1 sps. End off.

FINISHING: Cut two pieces of Pellon same size and shape as crocheted pieces. Whip Pellon pieces together along side edges down to indentations at base of bag. Whip bottom edges together. Close openings formed by indentations each side.

Place cardboard piece inside Pellon interlining to fit snugly at base.

From wrong side, with yarn, sew crocheted pieces together.

Cut lining satin 13½″ wide x 18″ long. If pocket for mirror is desired, cut piece 5½″ x 8″; fold in half crosswise, wrong side out; stitch side seams taking ½″ seams. Turn to right side; press. Insert piece of Pellon, 4½″ x 3½″, inside pocket; close bottom edges. Stitch pocket to lining. Fold lining in half crosswise, wrong side out; stitch side seams. Place lining inside interlining. Fold excess at bottom corners of lining neatly under cardboard; tack. Tack lining to interlining at seams. Place lining inside bag; turn under raw edges around top and hem to bag. Sew bag to bag frame along top edges of frame only with buttonhole twist.

Sequin eyeglass case

SIZE: 6″ x 3¼″.

MATERIALS: Velveen or fingering yarn, 1 1-oz. skein. One strand No. 6 cup sequins. Steel crochet hook No. 5. ¼ yard satin for lining. Cardboard, two pieces 3″ x 6″.

GAUGE: 5 sequins=1″; 4 sequin rows (8 rows) =1″.

Note: Follow directions for threading sequins onto yarn, page 268.

EYEGLASS CASE (make 2 pieces): Starting at closed end of case, with sequin-threaded yarn, ch 31.

Row 1 (right side): Sc in 3rd ch from hook, * ch 1, sk 1 ch, sc in next ch, repeat from * across—15 sps. Ch 2, turn.

Row 2 (sequin row): Sc in first sp, * slide sequin close to hook, ch 1, sc in next sp, repeat from * across—14 sequins. Ch 2, turn.

Row 3: Sc in first sp (behind sequin), * ch 1, sc in next sp, repeat from * across—15 sps. Ch 2, turn. Repeat rows 2 and 3 until there are 23 rows of sequins, end row 3. End off.

FINISHING: Cover both sides of two pieces of cardboard, 3″ x 6″, with satin. Sew one to wrong side of each crocheted piece. From right side, whip crocheted pieces together, leaving one end open and 1″ each side of end. Make twisted cord from 3 strands of yarn, cut 2½ yards long. Twist strands together very tightly until cord buckles. Place finger at center, double strands and allow to twist together. Knot ends. Sew cord around one open edge of case, continue around case and around other open edge.

Afghan Crochet Stitches

Afghan crochet is worked on a long hook, called an afghan hook, which can hold a number of stitches at one time. Illustration shows finished piece of plain afghan stitch. Directions for working the basic stitches are given below.

PLAIN AFGHAN STITCH: Work with afghan hook. Make a ch desired length.

Row 1: Keeping all lps on hook, sk first ch from hook (lp on hook is first st), pull up a lp in each ch across; Figure 1.

To Work Lps Off: Yo hook, pull through first lp, * yo hook, pull through next 2 lps, repeat from * across until 1 lp remains; Figure 2. Lp that remains on hook always counts as first st of next row.

Row 2: Keeping all lps on hook, sk first vertical bar (lp on hook is first st), pull up a lp under next vertical bar and under each vertical bar across; Figure 3. Work lps off as before. Repeat row 2 for plain afghan stitch.

EDGE STITCH: Made at end of rows only to make a firm edge. Work as follows: Insert hook under last vertical bar and in lp at back of bar, pull up 1 lp; Figure 4.

TO INC 1 AFGHAN ST: Pull up 1 lp under ch between 2 vertical bars; Figure 5.

TO DEC 1 AFGHAN ST: At beg of a pat row, keep to pat, insert hook under 2nd and 3rd vertical bars and pull up 1 plain lp for plain or cross st, or pull up 1 purl lp for purl st; keep lp on hook; Figure 6. **At end of a pat row,** insert hook under 3rd and 2nd vertical bars from end and dec as for beg row, then make edge stitch, as described above.

PURL STITCH: Holding yarn with thumb in front and below hook, pull up a lp under vertical bar; keep lp on hook; Figure 7.

CROSS STITCH: Sk next vertical bar; yarn in back, pull up a lp under next vertical bar, yarn in back, pull up a lp under skipped bar. Keep lps on hook.

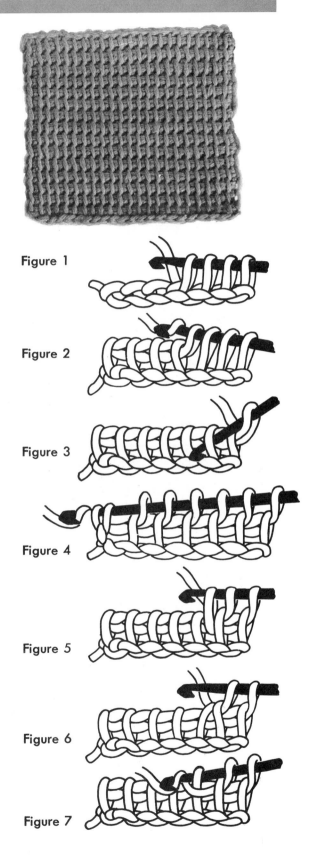

Figure 1

Figure 2

Figure 3

Figure 4

Figure 5

Figure 6

Figure 7

Afghan stitch makes the center of this bronco buster afghan for cowboy fans. The striped corral "fence" is crocheted in colors to match horse and rider. Directions are on P. 276.

274

Pretty protection against winter winds with this pullover and cap crocheted in diagonal afghan stitch. Directions for sizes 8-14 are on P. 278.

Bronco Bustin' Afghan

DETAIL OF CROSS-STITCH EMBROIDERY ON AFGHAN STITCH

Shown on Page 274
SIZE: About 44″ x 50″.

MATERIALS: Knitting Worsted, 3 4-oz. skeins Yellow, main color (MC); 1 skein each Blue (A), Brown (B), Black (C), White (D) and Red (E). Afghan hook size J. Crochet hook size G. Tapestry needle.

GAUGE: 7 sts=2″; 3 rows=1″ (afghan st). 3 dc=1″; 3 dc rows=2″.

AFGHAN ST: Work with afghan hook.

Row 1: Keeping all lps on hook, with MC, pull up a lp in 2nd ch from hook and in each ch across.

To Work Lps Off: Yo hook, pull through first lp, * yo hook, pull through next 2 lps, repeat from * across until 1 lp remains. Lp that remains on hook always counts as first st of next row.

Row 2: Keeping all lps on hook, pull up lp under 2nd vertical bar and under each vertical bar across. Work lps off as before. Repeat row 2 for afghan st.

STRIPED PATTERN: Work 1 dc rnd each of A, MC, B, C, D and E. Repeat these 6 rnds.

AFGHAN: CENTER SECTION (20″ x 26″): With MC and afghan hook, ch 70 to measure 20″. Work in afghan st for 78 rows. **Next Row:** Work sl st loosely under 2nd vertical bar and in each bar across.

BORDER: From right side, work around entire center section as follows:

Rnd 1: With A and crochet hook, make lp on hook; beg in a corner st, make 5 dc in each corner, 70 dc across top and bottom edges, 78 dc at each side edge. Join rnd with sl st in first dc. End off. Continue in striped pat for 14 rnds more, beg and ending as for first rnd, making 5 dc in each corner dc. Continue for 3 rnds more, making 7 dc in each corner dc. End off.

EMBROIDERY: Following chart, work cross-stitch cowboy on center. Each square on chart represents 1 afghan st. Work cross-stitch over vertical bar of st. See detail photograph.

CHART FOR CROSS-STITCH COWBOY

WHITE ⊡
RED ⬓
BLUE ⬕
BROWN ⊠
BLACK ■

Afghan crochet pattern stitches

FEATHER STITCH PATTERN (multiple of 4 sts plus 2): **Note:** Work with afghan hook. See Afghan Stitches, page 273.

Row 1: Work same as for row 1 of Plain Afghan Stitch. Work lps off in same way.

Row 2: Keeping all lps on hook, sk first vertical bar (lp on hook is first st), * make cross st, 2 purl sts, repeat from * across to last bar, yarn in back, make edge st. Work lps off as before.

Row 3: Keeping all lps on hook, sk first vertical bar (lp on hook is first st), * make purl st, cross st, plain st, repeat from * across to last bar, make edge st. Work lps off as before. Repeat rows 2 and 3 for feather st pat.

FEATHER STITCH

TWILL ST PATTERN (multiple of 4 sts plus 2): **Note:** Work with afghan hook. See Afghan Stitches, page 273. **Row 1:** Work same as for row 1 of plain afghan st. Work lps off in same way.

Row 2: Keeping all lps on hook, sk first vertical bar (lp on hook is first st), * make cross st, 2 purl sts, repeat from * across to last vertical bar, make edge st. Work lps off as before.

Row 3: Keeping all lps on hook, sk first vertical bar (lp on hook is first st), * make 2 purl sts, make cross st (this moves cross st 1 st to the right of cross st on row below), repeat from * across to last vertical bar, make edge st. Work lps off as before. Repeat rows 2 and 3 for twill st pat, always having 2 purl sts between cross sts and moving across sts 1 st to the right of cross sts on row below.

TWILL STITCH

BLOCK PATTERN

AFGHAN ST BLOCK PATTERN (multiple of 8 sts plus 7): **Note:** Work with afghan hook. See Afghan Stitches, page 273. **Row 1:** Work same as row 1 of plain afghan st. Work lps off same way.

Rows 2, 3, 4, 5: Keeping all lps on hook, sk first vertical bar (lp on hook is first st), make purl st, cross st, * make (purl st, cross st) twice, make purl st, plain st, repeat from * across to last 11 bars, make (purl st, cross st) 3 times, make purl st, edge st. Work lps off as before.

Row 6: Keeping all lps on hook, sk first vertical bar (lp on hook is first st), make 10 purl sts, 1 plain st over plain st of previous rows (block completed), * make 7 purl sts, 1 plain st over plain st of previous rows (block completed), repeat from * across to last 11 bars, make 10 purl sts, edge st. Work lps off as before. Repeat rows 2-6 for block pat.

TO BIND OFF PATTERN STS (work loosely): **At beg of a pat row,** start with 2nd vertical bar; if cross st is next st of pat, work first part of st, pull lp through lp on hook thus making a sl st (1 st bound off), work 2nd part of same st, pull lp through lp on hook thus making a sl st (1 st bound off); if purl or plain st is next st of pat, make a purl or plain st, pull lp through lp on hook thus making a sl st (1 st bound off). Continue in this way for specified number of sts. **At end of a pat row,** leave specified number of sts unworked. Work lps off as before. **Note:** As each section of garment is completed, with afghan hook, work sl st across unworked bound-off sts, keeping to pattern as established.

Afghan stitch set

Shown on Page 275

SIZES: Directions for size 8. Changes for sizes 10, 12, 14 are in parentheses.
Body Chest Size: 26″ (28″-30″-32″).
Blocked Chest Size: 30″ (32″-34″-36″).

MATERIALS: Knitting worsted, 4 (5-5-6) 4-oz. skeins. Afghan hooks Nos. 5/G and 6/H; steel crochet hook No. 00. Five ⅜″ pearl buttons.

GAUGE: 9 sts=2″; 3 rows=1″ (diagonal afghan st pat, No. 6/H hook). 9 sts=2″ (fringe trim, No. 00 hook).

DIAGONAL AFGHAN ST PATTERN (multiple of 3 sts plus 2): Work with afghan hook. **Row 1:** Keeping all lps on hook, sk first ch from hook, pull up a lp in each ch across.

To Work Lps Off: Yo hook, pull through first lp, * yo hook, pull through next 2 lps, repeat from * across until 1 lp remains. Lp that remains on hook always counts as first st of next row.

Row 2: Keeping all lps on hook, sk first vertical bar (counts as first st), * sk next vertical bar, yarn in back, pull up a lp under next vertical bar, yarn in back, pull up a lp under skipped vertical bar (diagonal st made), holding yarn with thumb in front and below hook, pull up a lp under next vertical bar (purl st made), repeat from * across to last bar, yarn in back, insert hook under last bar and in st at back of bar, pull up 1 lp (edge st made). This makes a firm edge. Work lps off as before.

Row 3: Keeping all lps on hook, sk first vertical bar (counts as first st), * purl 1 st, make diagonal st over next 2 bars, repeat from * across to last bar, make edge st. Work lps off as before.

Row 4: Keeping all lps on hook, sk first vertical bar, purl 2 sts, * make diagonal st, purl 1 st, repeat from * across to last 3 bars, end purl 2 sts, make edge st. Work lps off as before. Repeat rows 2, 3 and 4 for diagonal afghan st pat, keeping to gauge.

To Bind Off (work loosely): **At beg of a row,** start with 2nd vertical bar; if diagonal st is next st of pat, work first part of st, pull lp through lp on hook thus making a sl st (1 st bound off), work 2nd part of diagonal pat, pull lp through lp on hook thus making a sl st (1 st bound off); if purl st is next st of pat, make a purl st, pull lp through lp on hook thus making a sl st (1 st bound off). Continue in this way for specified sts. **At end of a row,** leave specified sts unworked.

To Dec 1 Afghan St: At beg of a row, insert hook under 2nd and 3rd vertical bars and pull up one lp; **at end of a row,** insert hook under 3rd and 2nd vertical bars from end and pull up one lp, make edge st.

To Inc 1 Afghan St: Pull up 1 lp in ch between 2 vertical bars.

PULLOVER: BACK: With No. 5/G afghan hook, ch loosely 68 (71-77-83). Work in diagonal afghan st pat for 1½″. Change to No. 6/H afghan hook. Continue in pat until piece measures 12½″ (13″-13½″-13½″) from start or 1″ less than desired length to underarm. Check gauge; piece should measure 15″ (16″-17″-18″) in width.

Shape Armholes (see to Bind Off and Dec): Keeping to pat, bind off 4 (4-5-5) sts each side of next row, then dec 1 st each side every row 3 (3-4-5) times—54 (57-59-63) sts. Work even for 1 row.

Back Opening: Right Half: Work in pat on first 27 (28-29-31) sts for 6½″ (6¾″-7¼″-7½″) above first bound-off sts.

Shape Shoulders: Bind off 9 sts at arm side once, then 9 (10-10-11) sts once. Bind off remaining 9 (9-10-11) sts for back of neck. End off.

Left Half: Beg at start of back opening, sk 0 (1-1-1) st, join yarn and work on last 27 (28-29-31) sts as for right half.

FRONT: Work as for back until armhole shaping is completed—54 (57-59-63) sts. Work even until armholes measure 4½″ (4¾″-5″-5¼″) above bound-off sts.

Shape Neck: Left Half: Work in pat on first 18 (19-19-20) sts until armhole measures same as back.

Shape Shoulder: Bind off 9 sts at arm side once, then 9 (10-10-11) sts once. End off left half.

Right Half: Join yarn in next st at start of neck shaping, bind off center 18 (19-21-23) sts, work in pat to end of row. Work as for left half.

SLEEVES: With 5/G afghan hook, ch loosely 41 (44-47-50). Work in diagonal afghan st pat for 1½″. Change to 6/H afghan hook. Continue in pat, inc 1 st each side every 5th row 5 (6-6-6) times—51 (56-59-62) sts. Check gauge; piece should be 11½″ (12½″-13″-13½″) wide. Work even until piece measures 12″ (12½″-13″-13½″) from start or 1″ less than desired length to underarm.

Shape Cap: Bind off 4 (4-5-5) sts each side of next row, then dec 1 st each side every row until 19 (20-21-20) sts remain. Bind off remaining sts. End off.

Keeping to pat, work sl st across unworked sts (see To Bind Off at beg of a row) at left underarm and left shoulder of back; on right underarm and right shoulder on front; on unworked sts at end of rows on cap of sleeves.

COLLAR: Beg at neck edge with 6/H hook, ch loosely 72 (72-80-80). Work row 1 of diagonal afghan st pat.

Inc Row: Sk first vertical bar, * (make diagonal st over next 2 sts, purl 1 st) twice, sk next vertical bar, inc by pulling up a lp in ch before next bar, pull up a lp in skipped bar (diagonal st made), purl

1 st, repeat from * 7 (7-8-8) times, (make diagonal st, purl 1 st) twice, make edge st—80 (80-89-89) sts. Beg with row 3 of pat, work in pat until piece measures 2½″ from start. Bind off sts.

FINISHING: Steam-press pieces. Sew shoulder seams. Sew in sleeves. Sew side and sleeve seams. With ends of collar at back opening sew neck edge of collar to neck, easing in edge of collar to fit neck. From right side, with No. 00 crochet hook, work 1 row sc around back opening, making 5 buttonloops of ch 3, sk ⅛″ of edge, evenly spaced on left back opening. With No. 00 hook, work 1 row sc on sides of collar. Sew buttons on right back opening.

FRINGE TRIM: Loop Stitch: Row 1: Beg at side seam, from right side, with No. 00 crochet hook, work sc in each ch of starting-row around lower edge of back and front—136 (142-154-166) sc. Do not join row. Ch 1, turn.

Rows 2 and 4: * Insert hook in next sc, wrap yarn over first finger of left hand to form 1″ lp, pull yarn under finger through sc, remove finger, hold lp in back, then yo and through 2 lps on hook (loop st made), repeat from * around. Ch 1, turn.

Rows 3 and 5: Sc in each st. Ch 1, turn. End off. Sew seam of trim. Cut loops to make fringe. Work fringe trim on each sleeve edge, having 41 (44-47-50) sts.

CAP: First Half: Beg at lower edge with 6/H afghan hook, ch loosely 50. Work in diagonal afghan stitch pat for 3½″. Piece should measure 11″ in width. Dec 1 st each side every row until 22 sts remain. Bind off sts. Piece should measure 8″ in length.

Second Half: Work as for first half. Sew halves tog. From right side, with No. 00 crochet hook, work 1 row sc around lower edge of cap, dec to desired fit. Steam-press seams.

FRINGE: Wind yarn around a 1″ cardboard; cut at one end. Fold strand in half. With crochet hook, draw folded lp through st, pull strands through lp. Knot 1 strand in this way in each diagonal st of every other diagonal st stripe around cap. Trim top of cap with pompon.

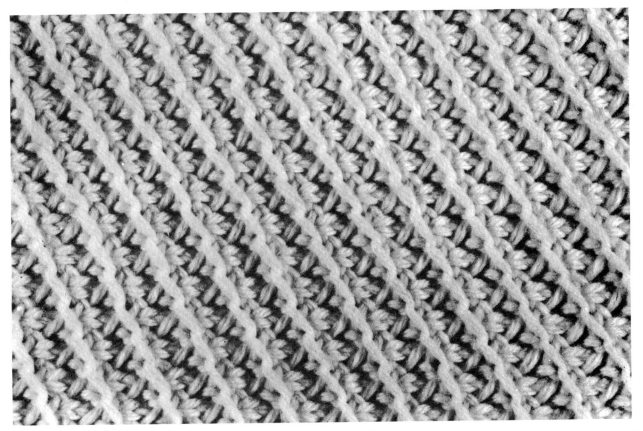

DIAGONAL STITCH

Afghan stitch pot holder

GENERAL DIRECTIONS: AFGHAN STITCH:
With afghan hook, make a chain desired length.

Row 1: Keeping all lps on hook, sk first ch from hook (lp on hook is first st), pull up a lp in each ch across.

To Work Lps Off: Yo hook, pull through first lp, * yo hook, pull through next 2 lps, repeat from * across until 1 lp remains. Lp that remains on hook always counts as first st of next row.

Row 2: Keeping all lps on hook, sk first vertical bar (lp on hook is first st), pull up a lp under next vertical bar and under each vertical bar across. Work lps off as before. Repeat row 2 for afghan stitch.

To Change Colors: Drop color just used to back of work. Pull up a lp of new color in next vertical bar. Carry unused color loosely across back of work. When carrying unused color for more than 5 sts, twist it around new color every 3 or 4 sts. Work each lp off in same color as lp.

To Read Chart: Each square on chart is one stitch. Plain squares are background color, crossed squares are pattern color. Each row on chart is one row of afghan stitch (lps pulled up on hook and worked off). Work each row to top of chart, turn chart upside down and work back to first row, omitting center row which is not repeated.

SIZE: 6″ square.
MATERIALS: Quick knitting and crochet cotton, 1 ball each of Spice (S) and White (W). Metal afghan hook size F.
GAUGE: 6 sts=1″; 5 rows=1″.
See General Directions for Afghan Stitch.
POT HOLDER: First Side: Row 1: With S, ch 31. Pull up a lp in 2nd ch from hook and in each ch across—31 lps. Work lps off hook.

Beg with row 2 of chart, work to top of chart (center row). Turn chart upside down and, omitting center row, work back to first row.

With S, sk first vertical bar, sl st in each vertical bar across last row. End off.

Second Side: Work as for first side.
FINISHING: Pin out pieces as square as possible. Steam-press. When dry, pin pieces tog, right sides out.

Edging: Starting at one corner and working through both edges at once, attach W, sc in first st, ch 1, * sc in next st, ch 1, repeat from * around four edges, making 2 sc in each corner st; end with sl st in first st; keep lp on hook.

Loop: Ch 8, drop lp off hook; count back 3 sts on edge, insert hook in st and pull lp through. Ch 1, work 11 sc over lp. End off.

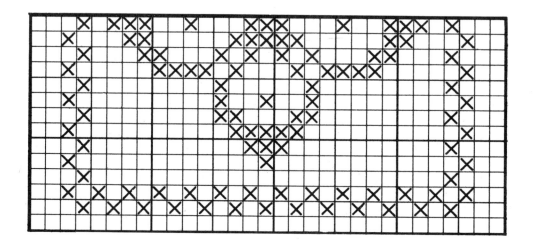

An unusual technique in afghan stitch makes this gay two-color pot holder, which is double thick for extra protection. The 6" square holder, with its stylized floral pattern, works up quickly in heavy crochet cotton. The decorative edging adds interest to the pot holder which we did in spice-brown and white. Easy-to-follow directions on opposite page.

Filet Crochet

Filet crochet is the technique of forming designs with little solid and openwork squares called blocks and spaces. Usually the background is worked in the openwork mesh with the design formed by the blocks. In this section, we show some simple variations of filet crochet.

Here, one large motif worked in blocks, forms a table-protecting place mat, 17" x 18". Mat is worked in white knitting and crochet cotton, glistening with silver. Crocheted rose leaf is appliquéd to napkin. Directions and chart for this filet rose place mat and leaf motif are on pages 284-285.

Leaf-and-scroll design of filet crochet borders a linen place mat. Flowers are worked separately and sewn to the background for a three-dimensional effect. Lacet stitch, a variation of filet crochet, adds interest to the border 4″ deep; mat measures 20″ by 15½″ overall. Chart and directions for the Embossed Daisy Mat are on pages 286-287.

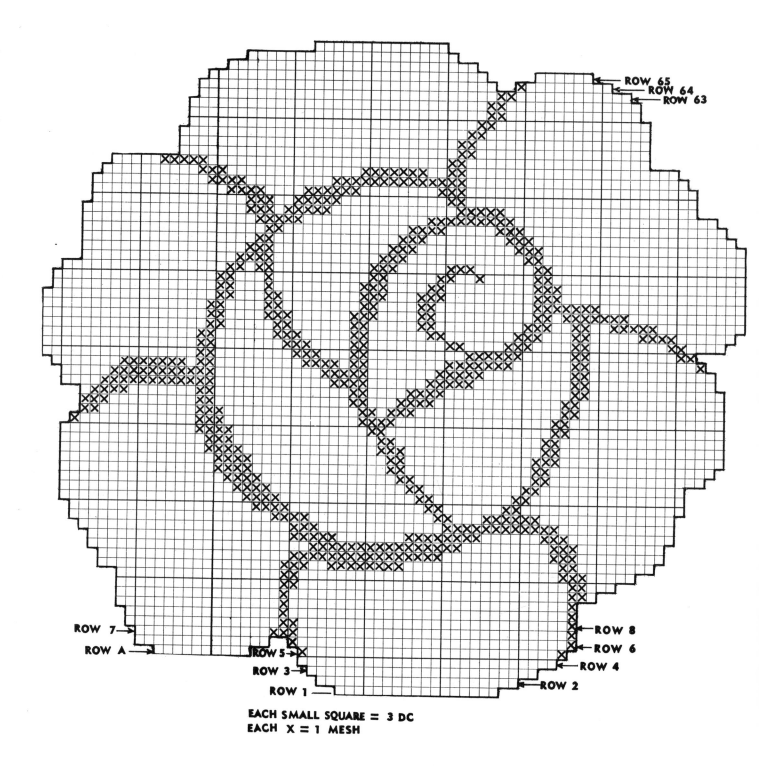

EACH SMALL SQUARE = 3 DC
EACH X = 1 MESH

CHART FOR FILET ROSE PLACE MAT

284

Filet rose place mat and leaf motif

SIZES: Mat, 17" x 18". Napkin, 16" square.

MATERIALS: Knitting and crochet cotton with metallic thread, 11 175-yd. balls, white with silver for three mats and three 3-leaf cluster motifs. Steel crochet hook No. 10. Piece of linen 17" x 17", for each napkin.

GAUGE: 12 dc=1"; 4 rows=1".

GENERAL DIRECTIONS: Each square on chart represents 3 dc; each X represents 1 mesh.

To Inc One or More Dc Squares on Chart: At beg of row, ch 6 for a dc square inc, ch 3 more for each additional square; dc in 5th ch from hook, dc in next ch (1 square), dc in each of 3 ch for each additional square. **At end of row,** yo, draw up a lp in top of turning ch last dc was worked in; holding last lp close to work, yo, draw through one lp on hook (this st is base st), yo and through 2 lps on hook twice for 1 dc, * yo, draw up a lp in base st, yo and through 1 lp on hook for next base st, yo and through 2 lps on hook twice for 1 dc, repeat from * once (a dc square inc made); work from first * to 2nd * 3 times for each additional square inc.

To Inc One Mesh: At beg of row, ch 7, dc in first dc. **At end of row,** ch 2, yo hook 3 times, draw up a lp in turning ch last dc was worked in, yo and through 2 lps 4 times (tr tr made for mesh).

To Dec One Dc Square or One Mesh: At beg of row, ch 1, sl st across 3 sts of each dc square or mesh, then sl st in next dc. Ch 5, sk next 2 dc, dc in next dc if row starts with a mesh (ch 3, dc in next dc if row starts with dc squares), finish row. **At end of row,** leave 3 sts of each dc square or mesh unworked.

MAT: Ch 54 Row 1 (wrong side): Dc in 5th ch from hook and in each ch across—51 dc, counting turning ch. Turn each row.

Rows 2-4: Work in dc, inc dc squares (see General Directions) as shown in chart—81 dc.

Row 5: Ch 5, dc in 4th dc (mesh made at beg of row), dc in each st across, inc 1 mesh at end of row.

Row 6: Inc 1 mesh at beg of row, 2 dc in next mesh, dc in each dc to last mesh, 2 dc in mesh, dc in 3rd ch of ch 5, inc 1 mesh at end of row, ch 5. End off. Put work aside.

Row A on Chart: Ch 33. Dc in 5th ch from hook and in each ch across—30 dc, counting turning ch. Turn.

Joining Row: Ch 9, drop lp off hook, insert hook in 5th ch at end of row 6 on first piece worked and draw dropped lp through; working back on 2nd piece, dc in 5th ch from hook and in each of 4 ch, dc in each st across, inc 2 dc squares at end of row —42 dc on 2nd piece. Turn, do not twist pieces.

Row 7: Ch 3, dc in 2nd dc (always beg even dc edge this way), dc in each of next 40 dc, ch 2, sk next 2 ch of first piece, dc in next ch, ch 2, sk 2 ch, dc in top of tr tr of mesh, ch 2, sk next 2 ch of same mesh, dc in next dc (3 meshes made), dc in each dc across to last mesh, ch 2, sk 2 ch of turning ch, dc in next ch (mesh made over mesh at end of row).

Row 8: Ch 5, sk 2 ch, dc in next dc (mesh made over mesh at beg of row), dc in each dc to next mesh, (ch 2, dc in next dc) twice, 2 dc in next mesh, dc in next dc (dc square worked over mesh), dc in each st across, inc 1 dc square at end of row.

Rows 9-63: Follow chart for pat and shaping.

Shape Top of Petals: First Petal: Row 64: Dec 2 dc squares, work dc to within 3 dc of next mesh, ch 2, sk 2 dc, dc in next dc. Turn.

Row 65: Dec each side as on chart—18 dc. End off.

Second Petal: Row 64: Make lp on hook, sk next 2 meshes on row 63 from first petal, dc in last dc of 2nd mesh, dc in each st across—93 dc. Work to top of chart on 2nd petal. End off.

Steam-press mat, using steam iron or dry iron and damp cloth.

THREE-LEAF CLUSTER MOTIF: Center Leaf: Ch 19, sc in 2nd ch from hook and in each of 17 ch —18 sc. Mark beg of following rnds.

Rnd 1: Ch 1; working on other side of starting ch, * sl st in each of 2 sts, sc in each of 2 sts, hdc in next st, ch 1, sk 1 st, dc in next st, ch 1, sk next st, tr in next st, ch 1, (tr, ch 1) in each of 4 sts, sk 1 st, dc in next st, ch 1, sk 1 st, hdc in next st, sc in next st *, 3 sc in turning ch at point; working on other side, work from 2nd * back to first *, sl st in first ch 1.

Rnd 2: Ch 1, * work 2 sl sts, 2 sc, 1 hdc, (dc in next sp, dc in next st) twice, 2 dc in next sp, dc in next st, 2 tr in next sp, tr in next st, 2 tr in next sp, dc in next st, 2 dc in next sp, dc in next st, dc in next sp, hdc in next st, hdc in next sp, hdc in next hdc, sc in each of next 2 sc *, 2 sc in next sc (tip), ch 4, sl st in last sc made, sc in same sc last worked in; working on other side, work from 2nd * back to first *, sl st in first ch 1.

Rnd 3: Ch 1, sl st in back lp of each st around, join. Do not end off.

Stem: Make 1¼" ch, sl st in 2nd ch from hook and in each ch, sl st at base of leaf. End off.

Outer Leaves (make 2): Work as for center leaf for 3 rnds. Do not end off, join with sl st to center of stem.

FINISHING: Holding leaves closely tog, place cluster motif at one corner of linen with tip of center leaf ½" in from corner. Sew cluster motif in place. Make ¼" hem around napkin, following outline of cluster at corner.

Actual-size detail

CHART FOR EMBOSSED DAISY MAT

⊡ BL   ▢ CH-2 SP

M LACET ST   ▭ CH-5 SP

Embossed daisy mat

Shown on Page 283

SIZE: 20″ x 15½″.

MATERIALS: Mercerized Crochet Cotton, size 30. Steel crochet hook No. 13. Piece of linen, 13″ x 8½″.

GAUGE: 6 sps=1″; 6 rows=1″.

Note: Daisies are made separately.

LACE EDGING: Rnd 1: Beg at inner edge, * (ch 8, tr in 8th ch from hook) 19 times across one end, ch 4, tr in 4th ch from hook (corner), (ch 8, tr in 8th ch from hook) 35 times, ch 4, tr in 4th ch from hook (corner), repeat from * once, join with sl st (with work untwisted) in base of first tr at A on chart. Keep lps on inner edge. Turn.

Rnd 2 (right side): Ch 3, 2 dc over tr-bar of last corner, * 7 dc through 2 threads in center of same bar, 2 dc over balance of same bar, dc between bars, make (5 dc over next tr-bar, dc between bars) across to next corner, 2 dc over bar of corner, repeat from * 3 times, end 5 dc over last tr-bar, join in top of ch 3. Sl st in next 6 dc (corner). Turn.

Rnd 3: Ch 6, sk next 2 dc, sc in next dc, ch 3, sk 2 dc, dc in next dc (lacet st), * make (ch 3, sk 2 dc, sc in next dc, ch 3, sk 2 dc, dc in dc between bars) across to center dc at corner (21 lacet sts), ch 5, dc in same corner dc, make 37 lacet sts to next corner *, ch 5, dc in same corner dc, repeat from first * to 2nd * once, ch 2, join with dc in 3rd ch of ch 6, ending at exact corner. Turn.

Rnd 4: Ch 9, sk first sp, dc in next dc, * (ch 5, dc in next dc) across to first dc at corner, ch 5, dc in corner sp, ch 5, dc in next dc, repeat from * around, end ch 5, sl st in 4th ch of ch 9. Turn.

Rnd 5: Ch 5, dc in center of first sp, ch 2, dc in next dc, * (ch 2, dc in next sp, ch 2, dc in next dc) 8 times, (ch 3, sc in next sp, ch 3, dc in next dc for lacet st) 5 times, (ch 2, dc in next sp, ch 2, dc in next dc) 9 times to corner dc, ch 5, dc in same dc, following chart across wide end, make 32 sps, 7 lacet sts, 32 sps to next corner dc *, ch 5, dc in same dc, ch 2, dc in center of next sp, ch 2, dc in next dc, repeat from first * to 2nd * once, end ch 2, dc in 3rd ch of ch 5 (exact corner). Turn.

Rnd 6: Ch 5, sk first sp, dc in next dc, * following chart from C to B, make 15 ch-2 sps, (2 dc in next sp, dc in next dc for 1 bl) 5 times, make 12 sps, 7 ch-5 sps, 12 sps, 5 bls, 16 ch-2 sps to corner sp, ch 5, 3 dc in balance of corner sp, dc in next dc, 4 bls, 14 ch-2 sps, 5 ch-5 sps, 14 ch-2 sps, 5 bls *, ch 5, dc in corner sp, ch 2, dc in next dc, repeat from first * to 2nd * once, end ch 2, dc in 3rd ch of ch 5 (corner). Turn.

Rnd 7: Ch 4, 3 dc in top of corner dc (½ corner shell), * following chart from B across narrow end, 2 dc in corner sp, dc in next dc, 4 sps, continue across, make 2 dc in next corner sp, 7 dc in 3rd ch of same sp, 4 sps, continue across wide end *, make 6 more dc in same corner ch, repeat from first * to 2nd * once, end ch 2, 3 dc in same st with first half shell, join with sl st in top of ch 4. Turn.

Rnds 8 and 10: Ch 4, 3 dc in corner dc, * following chart from C to B, work across wide end to next corner, make 6 more dc in corner dc (7 in all), continue across narrow end *, make 6 more dc in corner dc (7 in all), repeat from first * to 2nd * once, end ch 2, 3 dc in same st with first half shell, join in top of ch 4. Turn.

Rnd 9 (wrong side): Following chart from B to C, begin, work corners, and end as for rnd 8. Turn.

Rnd 11: Ch 3, dc in each of next 3 dc (1 bl), * following chart from B to C, work across narrow end to next corner (ending 2 sps), dc in each of next 3 corner dc, ch 5, dc in dc last worked in, dc in each of next 3 corner dc (1 bl), continue across wide end (ending 3 sps) *, work corner as before, repeat from first * to 2nd * once, end 1 bl, ch 2, join with dc in top of ch 3 (exact corner). Turn.

Rnd 12: Ch 5, sk first sp, dc in next dc, * following chart from C to B, work across wide end to 3rd ch of corner sp, ch 5, dc in same ch, continue across narrow end to 3rd ch of next corner sp *, ch 5, dc in same ch, repeat from first * to 2nd * once, end ch 2, join with dc in 3rd ch of ch 5 (exact corner). Turn.

Rnd 13 (wrong side): Following chart from B to C, begin, work corners, and end as for rnd 12. Turn.

Rnds 14-23: Repeat rnds 12 and 13 alternately.

Rnd 24: Ch 6, sk first sp, sc in next dc, ch 3, dc in next dc, * continue in lacet st to center ch of next corner sp, ch 3, dc in same ch, repeat from * around, end ch 3, join with sl st in 3rd ch of ch 6. Do not turn.

Rnd 25: * Ch 7, sc in next dc, repeat from * around, end ch 7, sl st in first lp. Do not turn.

Rnd 26: In each lp around, make (4 sc, ch 4, sl st in last sc for p, 4 sc); join end of rnd and end off.

DAISY (make 8): * Ch 20, sk 2 ch, sc in next 2 ch, hdc in next ch, dc in next 2 ch, (tr in next 2 ch; holding back last lp of each of the following tr, make tr in next 2 ch, yo and through 3 lps on hook) twice, dc in next 3 ch, hdc in next ch, sl st in end ch, repeat from * 5 times more—6 petals. Ch 1, make sc in base of each of 6 petals. Ch 5, turn. Holding back last lp of each tr, make tr in each of 5 sc, 2 tr in last sc, yo and through 8 lps on hook. End off.

FINISHING: Turn daisies right side up, sew in place on edging as shown on chart. Stretch and pin edging, right side down, in true shape, pinning out each lp on inner and outer edges. Steam and press dry through a damp cloth.

Place edging, right side up, over linen. Baste inner edge of edging to linen. Hem down inner edge of rnd 2 (dc row) and lps of rnd 1. Cut linen ¼″ outside stitching, turn under edge next to edging and hem.

A European import, this small doily with its smart, contemporary pattern of leaves on miniature squares can be crocheted very quickly, using the chart method detailed on the opposite page.

SMALL CONTEMPORARY DOILY

SIZE: 8½″ in diameter.

MATERIALS: Tatting-Cotton, 1 ball white. Steel crochet hook No. 13.

Ch 8, join with sl st to form ring.

Rnd 1: Ch 4 (counts as 1 tr), 3 tr in ring leaving last lp of each tr on hook, thread over and through all lps on hook, * ch 4, 4 tr cluster in ring, repeat from * 4 times, ch 4, join. Complete doily from chart, following General Directions.

GENERAL DIRECTIONS: This doily is worked from a chart of stitch symbols rather than from row by row directions. The symbols are given with the chart. Doily has six equal sections or repeats. The chart gives one complete section.

At right of chart are numbers marking beginning of each rnd. Start at number for each rnd, work sts for that rnd to the left-hand edge of chart and repeat sts 5 times. This completes rnd. Rnd 1 is shown in its entirety.

Ch 4 at beg of each rnd to count as 1 tr.

Join all rnds with sl st in top of ch 4.

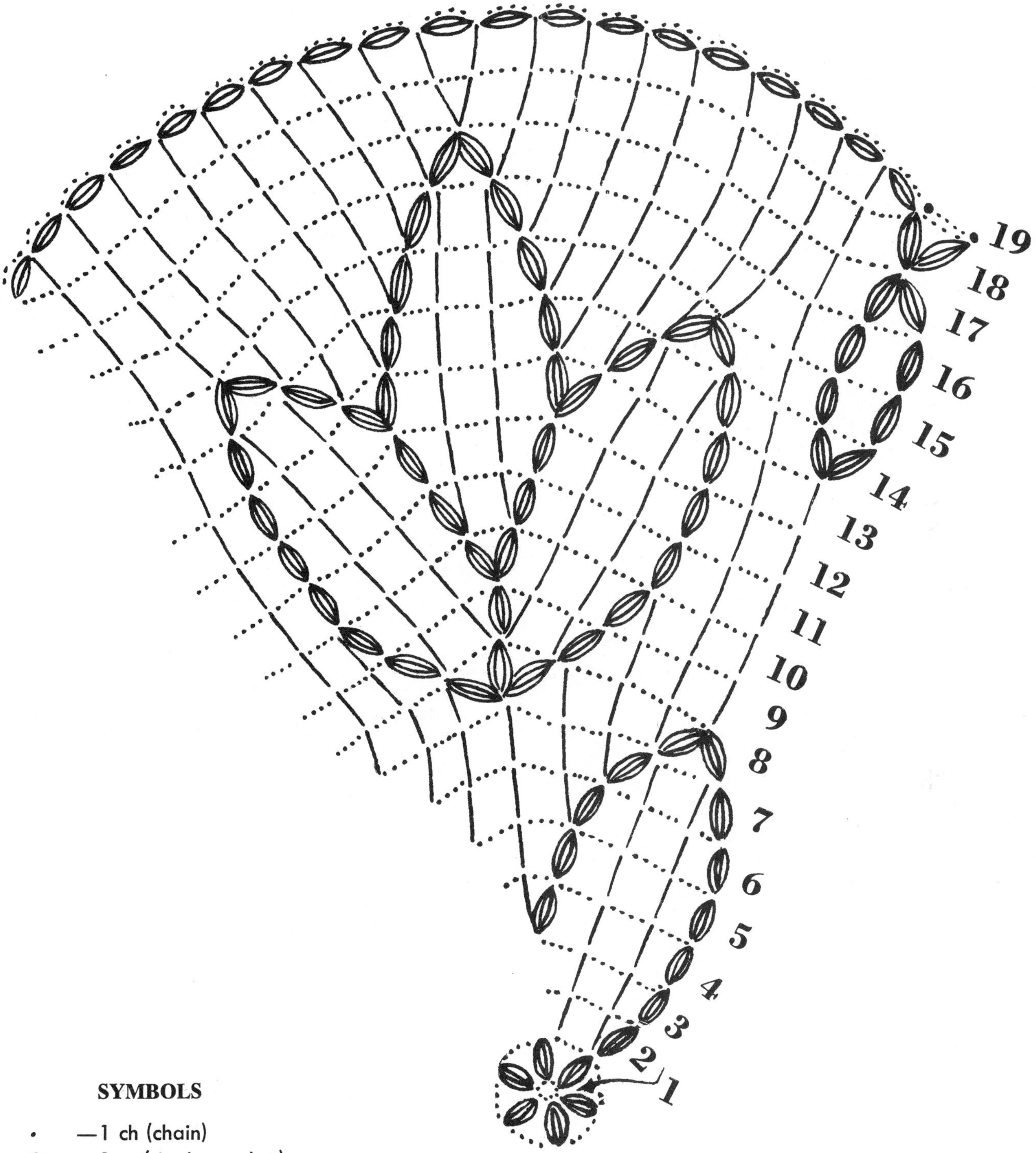

19
18
17
16
15
14
13
12
11
10
9
8
7
6
5
4
3
2
1

SYMBOLS

· —1 ch (chain)

● —1 sc (single crochet)

╱ —1 tr (treble crochet)

⬮ —4 tr cluster (4 tr in same space leaving last lp of each tr on hook, thread over and through all lps on hook)

⬯ —rice st (ch 4, 3 tr in 4th ch from hook leaving last lp of each tr on hook, thread over and through all lps on hook)

Tea cloth

SIZE: 41″ square.

MATERIALS: Mercerized crochet cotton, size 30, white. Steel crochet hook No. 13. White sewing thread. ⅞ yard colored linen.

GAUGE: Block=5½″ square.

Note: Work tightly for best results.

CENTER MOTIF: Beg at center, ch 8, join with sl st to form ring.

Rnd 1: Ch 1, 12 sc in ring. Join with sl st in first sc.

Rnd 2: Ch 8, tr in same sc as sl st, * ch 10, sk 2 sc, (tr, ch 3, tr) in next sc, repeat from * twice, ch 5, join with tr in 5th ch of ch 8—4 ch-3 sps and 4 ch-10 lps.

Rnd 3: * 3 tr in next ch-3 sp, ch 4, sl st in last tr (p made); in ch-3 sp last worked in make (4 tr, p) twice and 3 tr, sc in next ch-10 lp, repeat from * twice, join with sl st in first tr of rnd—4 petals.

Rnd 4: * Ch 7, (tr, ch 5, dtr) in 3rd tr after next p, ch 7, (dtr, ch 5, tr) in 2nd tr after next p, ch 7, sc in sc between petals, repeat from * 3 times, end rnd with sl st.

Rnd 5: Ch 3; holding back on hook last lp of each dc, make 2 dc in next sp, yo and draw tightly through 3 lps on hook (½-cl made), * 4 dc in balance of sp, dc in next tr, 5 dc in next sp, dc in next dtr, 3 dc in next sp, (2 dc, p, 2 dc) in center ch of same sp (corner), 3 dc in balance of same sp, dc in next dtr, 5 dc in next sp, dc in next tr, 4 dc in next sp; holding back on hook last lp of each dc, make tight cl of (2 dc in same sp, dc in sc between petals and 2 dc in next sp, yo and draw tightly through 6 lps on hook), repeat from * 3 times, ending last repeat with first 2 dc of cl, insert hook in first ½-cl of rnd, yo and draw tightly through cl and 3 lps on hook. End off.

BLOCK: Border: Beg with inner 4 sides of block, (ch 6, dc in 6th ch from hook) 48 times. Join with sl st in starting st of border, forming a ring with ch-lps on inside edge and straight dc-sps on outside edge of border.

First Corner Section: Ch 3, 2 dc in same place as sl st, ** (3 dc in next dc-sp, dc in st between dc-sps) 6 times, 2 dc in next dc-sp, ch 7, turn. Sk 4 dc, sl st in next dc, ch 1, turn.

9 sc in lp just made, sl st in top side of last dc, dc in balance of sp on border, dc between dc-sps, 3 dc in next dc-sp, dc between dc-sps, 2 dc in next dc-sp, ch 5, turn.

Tr in 2nd sc over lp, ch 5, sk 2 sc, (3 tr, ch 5, 3 tr) in next (center) sc, ch 5, sk 2 sc, tr in next sc, ch 5, sk 7 dc over border, sl st in next dc, ch 1, turn.

(3 sc, p, 3 sc) in first sp, sc in next tr, (3 sc, p, 3 sc) in next sp, sc in each of 3 tr, 5 sc in next sp, sc in each of 3 tr, (3 sc, p, 3 sc) in next sp, sc in next tr, (3 sc, p, 3 sc) in end sp, sl st in top side of last dc, dc in balance of dc-sp on border, dc between dc-sps, 3 dc in next dc-sp, dc between dc-sps, 2 dc in next dc-sp, ch 5, turn.

Sk 7 dc, dtr in next dc, (ch 5, tr in sc over next tr) twice, ch 5, (3 tr, ch 5, 3 tr) in center sc over next sp between 3-tr groups (center sp), ch 5, sk 4 sc, tr in next sc, ch 5, tr in sc over next tr, ch 5, dtr in same dc at base of last row, ch 5, sk 7 dc on border, sl st in next dc, ch 1, turn.

(3 sc, p, 3 sc) in each of next 4 sps, sc in each of next 3 tr, 5 sc in next sp (center sp), sc in each of next 3 tr, (3 sc, p, 3 sc) in each of last 4 sps, sl st in top side of last dc on border, dc in balance of dc-sp, dc in st between dc-sps, 3 dc in next dc-sp, 3 dc in st between dc-sps (first half-corner made), ch 5, turn.

Sk 7 dc, tr in next dc, (ch 5, dc in center sc between next 2 p) 3 times, ch 5, tr in sc over next tr, ch 5, (3 dtr, ch 7, 3 dtr) in center sc over next sp, ch 5, sk 4 sc, tr in next sc, (ch 5, dc in center sc between next 2 p) 3 times, ch 5, tr in same dc at base of last row, ch 5, sk 7 dc over border, sl st in top of ch 3, ch 1, turn.

(3 sc, p, 3 sc in next sp, sc in next st) 6 times, sc in each of 3 dtr, in next sp (center sp) make (sc, a ch-4 p, 4 sc, a ch-7 p, 4 sc, a ch-4 p, sc), sc in each of 3 dtr, (3 sc, p, 3 sc in next sp, sc in next st) 6 times, sl st in top side of last dc of corner 3-dc group made over border, make 3 more dc at base of same corner 3-dc group (2nd half-corner made) **. Make 3 more corner sections, working from first ** to 2nd **, omitting 2nd half-corner at end of last repeat, join with sl st to top of ch 3 at beg of first section. End off.

Stretch the 4 inner sides of dc border of block to form a true square. Cut a square of linen 1/16″ larger all around than outside edge of dc border that forms inner square of block. Pin or baste dc border around edge of linen. Hem down inner edge of dc border and tack down center of each ch-5 lp. Working on back of work, turn edge of linen under against back of dc border and hem down.

Stretch and pin center motif right side down on ironing board. Steam through a doubled wet cloth, then press dry through a doubled dry cloth. Pin motif in center of linen and hem down around outside edge. On back of work, cut out linen ¼″ inside stitching; turn this ¼″ edge under against dc border and hem down.

Make 49 blocks. Join blocks 7 x 7 as follows:

Joining-Edge, First Block: Join thread with sc in 3rd sc to right of a corner p on first bl (block), * (4 dc, ch 7, 4 dc) in corner p, sk 2 sc, sc in next sc, (ch 10, sc midway between next 2 p) 13 times, ch 10, sc in 2nd sc to left of next p, repeat from * around, joining final ch-10 with sl st to first sc. End off.

Joining-Edge, 2nd Block: Join thread with sc in 3rd sc to right of a corner p on 2nd bl, 4 dc in corner p, ch 3, join with sl st in 1 lp of center st of a corner ch-7 lp on first bl, ch 3, 4 dc back in same corner p on 2nd bl, sk 2 sc, sc in next sc, (ch 5, join with sl st under next ch 10 of first bl, ch 5, sc back midway between next 2 p on 2nd bl) 13 times, ch 5, sl st in next ch-10 lp on first bl, ch 5, sc back in 2nd sc to left of next p on 2nd bl, 4 dc in next corner p, ch 3, join with sl st in 1 lp of center ch of next corner lp on first bl, ch 3, 4 dc back in same p on 2nd bl, sk 2 sc, sc in next sc. Complete edge as for first bl. Forming square, join 3rd bl to 2nd bl, then join a 4th bl to first and 3rd bls in same way. **Note:** Where 4 corners meet, always join to same st where first 2 corners were joined. Continue in this way until all bls are joined.

EDGE: Rnd 1: Join thread with sc in right-hand end of ch-7 lp at one corner of cloth, ** ch 13, sc in left end of same lp, (ch 10, sc in next ch-10 lp) 14 times, * ch 10, sk 4 dc, sc in right end of next joined corner sp, ch 10, sc in left end of next joined corner sp, (ch 10, sc in next ch-10 lp) 14 times *, repeat from first * to 2nd * across side, ch 10, sc in right end of corner ch-7 lp, repeat from ** around. Omit last ch-10 lp, make ch 5 and join with tr in first sc.

Rnd 2: ** Ch 4, 3 dtr in 5th ch of corner ch-13 lp, (ch 5, sk next ch of same lp, 3 dtr in next ch) twice, ch 4, sc in next ch-10 lp, * (ch 4, 3 dtr in 5th ch of next ch-10 lp, ch 5, 3 dtr in next ch of same lp, ch 4, sc in next lp) *, repeat from first * to 2nd * across side, repeat from ** around, end with sl st instead of sc.

Rnd 3: Sl st in each of 4 sts of next ch, sl st in next 3 dtr, sl st in next sp, ch 7, (2 dtr, ch 5, 3 dtr) in same sp, ** ch 5, sk next dtr, 3 dtr in next dtr, (ch 5, 3 dtr) twice in next sp, * in center sp of next shell make (3 dtr, ch 5, 3 dtr, ch 5, 3 dtr) *, repeat from first * to 2nd * across side, sk first 3 dtr at corner, (3 dtr, ch 5, 3 dtr) in next sp, repeat from ** to end of rnd, end rnd at 2nd *, join with sl st in top of ch 7.

Rnd 4: Sc in each of next 2 dtr, 5 sc in next sp, * sc in each of next 2 dtr, make ch-4 p, sc in next dtr, 2 sc in next sp, ch 10 lp, turn, sk p, sl st in 2nd sc over next sp, ch 1, turn, (6 sc, p, 6 sc, 1 sl st) in ch-10 lp just made, ch 1, 3 sc in balance of ch-5 sp, repeat from * twice, sc in each of next 2 dtr, sk 2 dtr (1 each side of angle), ** sc in each of next 2 dtr, 5 sc in next sp, sc in each next 2 dtr, make p, sc in next dtr, 2 sc in next sp, ch 10 lp, turn, sk p, sl st in 2nd sc over next sp, ch 1, turn, (6 sc, p, 6 sc, sl st) in ch-10 lp just made, ch 1, 3 sc in balance of ch-5 sp, sc in each of next 2 dtr, sk next 2 dtr (1 each side of angle), repeat from ** across side, repeat from beg of rnd, join with sl st in first sc.

Placing a rustproof pin in each scallop, pin cloth right side down on padded board, stretching to 41″ x 41″. Steam through a wet cloth, press dry.

Crocheted lace cloth

SIZE: 34″ square.

MATERIALS: Six Cord Crochet Cotton, size 50, 14 240-yard balls. Steel crochet hook No. 14.

GAUGE: 1 motif=1¼″ square.

FIRST MOTIF: Ch 8, sl st in first ch to form ring.

Rnd 1: Ch 3, 15 dc in ring—16 dc counting ch 3 as 1 dc. Join with sl st to top of ch 3.

Rnd 2: Ch 4, dc between first and next dc, * ch 1, dc between next 2 dc, repeat from * around, ch 1, join to 3rd ch of ch 4—16 dc with ch 1 between.

Rnd 3: Ch 5, * dc in next ch-1 sp, ch 2, repeat from * around, join to 3rd ch of ch 5.

Rnd 4: Sl st in first sp, ch 4; holding back last 2 lps of each tr, make 3 tr in same sp, thread over hook and through all 4 lps on hook (4-tr cluster made); * ch 5, 4-tr cluster in next sp, ch 5, 4-tr cluster in next sp, ch 14, 4-tr cluster in next sp, turn work around, 7 sc over half of ch 14, ch 7, turn work around, 4-tr cluster in next sp, repeat from * around, end ch 7, sl st in top of first cluster. End off.

2ND MOTIF: Work as for first motif through rnd 3. **Rnd 4:** Sl st in first sp, ch 4, make tr-cluster in first sp, ch 2, sl st in corresponding (2nd) ch-5 lp on one side of first motif, ch 2, tr-cluster in next sp of 2nd motif, ch 2, sl st in next ch-5 lp (to left) of first motif, ch 2, tr-cluster in next sp of 2nd motif, ch 7, sl st in 7th ch at corner of first motif, ch 7, tr-cluster in next sp of 2nd motif, turn work around, 7 sc over ch-7 just made, ch 7, turn work around, 4-tr cluster in next sp, repeat from * of rnd 4 of first motif twice, ch 5, 4-tr cluster in next sp, ch 5, 4-tr cluster in next sp, ch 14, 4-tr cluster in last sp, turn work around, 7 sc over half of ch 14, turn work around, sl st in 7th ch at corner of first motif, ch 7, sl st in top of first cluster of 2nd motif. End off.

Join 3rd and succeeding motifs in same way, always joining motifs at ch-5 lps and at sides of corners. Make cloth 26 by 26 motifs, or desired size.

BORDER: Rnd 1: Join thread at corner of cloth, sl st to ch-7 lp, ch 6, 4-dtr cluster (ch 6 counts as 1 dtr) in ch-7 lp, † * ch 5, 4-dtr cluster in same lp, ch 5, (4-dtr cluster in next sp, ch 5) twice, 4-dtr cluster in next ch-7 lp, ch 5, 4-dtr cluster in same ch-7 lp, ch 5, 4-dtr cluster in next ch-7 lp, repeat from * across one side, ending 2 clusters with ch-5 between in end ch-7 lp, ch 7 for corner, 4-dtr cluster in next ch-7 lp on next side, repeat from † around, end ch 7 for last corner, join to top of first cluster.

Rnd 2: Sl st to first sp, work 4-dtr cluster in each ch-5 sp on side with ch 5 between clusters; work 2 clusters with ch 7 between in ch-7 lps at corners. Join to top of first cluster. **Rnd 3:** Repeat rnd 2.

Rnd 4: * 5 sc in each of next 2 sps, ch 4, sl st in 4th ch from hook for picot, repeat from * around. Join in first sc.

Pin out cloth to square shape. Steam-press.

This delicately webbed crocheted lace can be made in any size from a bridge table cover to a banquet cloth by combining 1¼″ motifs and edging them with a cluster stitch border. Make the size of your choice with crochet cotton. Directions are on page 292.

Flower and fern mat

SIZE: 16″ diameter.

MATERIALS: Mercerized crochet cotton, size 30, 2 balls. Steel crochet hook No. 12.

CLUSTERS: 3-Dc Clusters (cls): At beg of a rnd, ch 3 (counts as first dc), holding back on hook last lp of each dc, make 2 dc in same sp, yo and through 3 lps on hook; **on rnd,** holding back on hook last lp of each dc, make 3 dc in same sp, yo and through 4 lps on hook.

3-Tr Cls: At beg of a rnd, ch 4 (counts as first tr), holding back on hook last lp of each tr, make 2 tr in same sp, yo and through 3 lps on hook; **on rnd,** holding back last lp of each tr, make 3 tr in same sp, yo and through 4 lps on hook.

MAT: Beg at center, ch 9, join with sl st to form ring.

Rnd 1: In ring, make 8 3-dc cls with ch-4 sp between each cl, ch 4, join in top of first cl.

Rnd 2: Sl st in first sp, make 2 3-dc cls with ch-3 sp between in same sp, * ch 3, 2 3-dc cls with ch-3 sp between in next sp, repeat from * around, end ch 3, join in top of first cl—16 cls.

Rnd 3: 3-dc cl in first cl, * ch 3, 3-dc cl in next sp, ch 3, 3-dc cl with ch-3 sp between in each of next 2 cls, repeat from * around, end last repeat with 1 cl, ch 3, join in first cl—24 cls.

Rnd 4: 3-dc cl in first cl, * ch 3, 2 3-dc cls with ch-3 sp between in next cl, ch 3, 3-dc cl with ch-3 sp between in each of next 2 cls, repeat from * around, end last repeat with 1 cl, ch 3, join in first cl—32 cls.

Rnd 5: 3-dc cl in first cl, ch 3, 3-dc cl in next cl, * ch 3, 3-dc cl in next sp, ch 3, 3-dc cl with ch-3 sp between in each of next 4 cls, repeat from * around, end last repeat with 2 cls, ch 3, join—40 cls.

Rnd 6: * 3-dc cl with ch-3 sp between in each of 5 cls, ch 5, repeat from * around, join ch 5 in first cl—40 cls.

Rnd 7: * 3-dc cl with ch-3 sp between in each of 5 cls, ch 9, repeat from * around, join ch 9 in first cl—40 cls.

Rnd 8: 3-dc cl in first cl, * ch 3, 3-dc cl with ch-1 sp between in each of next 3 cls, ch 3, 3-dc cl in next cl, ch 6, dc in 5th ch of ch 9, ch 6, 3-dc cl in next cl, repeat from * around, omit last cl, join ch 6 in first cl—40 cls.

Rnd 9: 3-dc cl in first cl, * ch 3, 3-dc cl in next cl, ch 1, sk next cl, cl in next cl, ch 3, cl in next cl, ch 6, (dc, ch 7, dc) in next dc, ch 6, cl in next cl, repeat from * around, omit last cl, join ch 6 in first cl—32 cls.

Rnd 10: 3-dc cl in first cl, * ch 1, sk next cl, cl in next ch-1 sp, ch 1, cl in next cl, ch 7, dc in next dc, ch 7, dc in 4th ch of next ch 7, ch 7, dc in next dc, ch 7, cl in next cl, repeat from * around, omit last cl, join ch 7 in first cl—24 cls.

Clusters and chain loops arranged in a variety of leaf and petal forms give this circular mat its charm.

Rnd 11: 3-dc cl in first cl, * ch 1, sk next cl, 3-dc cl in next cl, ch 7, dc in next dc, ch 7, (dc, ch 5, dc) in next dc, ch 7, dc in next dc, ch 7, 3-dc cl in next cl, repeat from * around, omit last cl, join ch 7 in first cl—16 cls.

Rnd 12: Sl st in first ch-1 sp, 3-dc cl in first sp, * ch 12, sc in next dc, ch 12, sk next sp, sc in next ch-5 sp, ch 12, sk next dc, sc in next dc, ch 12, 3-dc cl in next ch-1 sp between cls, repeat from * around, omit last cl, join ch 12 in first cl—8 cls.

Rnd 13: Sl st to 5th ch of first ch-12 sp, 3-tr cl in next ch of same sp, * ch 11, 2 tr in 6th ch of next ch-12 sp, ch 11, 3-tr cl in 6th ch of next ch-12 sp, repeat from * around, omit last cl, join ch 11 in first cl—16 cls and 16 groups of tr.

Rnd 14: 3-tr cl in first cl, * ch 5, 5 tr in next tr, ch 2, tr in same tr, tr in next tr, ch 2, 5 tr in same tr (shell made), ch 5, 3-tr cl in next cl, repeat from * around, omit last cl, join ch 5 in first cl—16 shells, 16 cls.

Rnd 15: 3-tr cl in first cl, * ch 1, 3-tr cl in same cl, ch 4; holding back on hook last lp of each tr, make 1 tr in each of first 5 tr of shell, yo and through 6 lps on hook (5-tr cl st made); ch 5, 3 tr in next tr, 2 tr in next tr, ch 5, 5-tr cl st over last 5 tr of same shell, ch 4, 3-tr cl in next cl, repeat from * around, omit last cl, join ch 4 in first cl.

Rnd 16: 3-tr cl in first cl, * ch 4, tr in next ch-1 sp, ch 4, 3-tr cl in next cl, ch 7, sk first 5-tr cl st of shell, sc in each of next 5 tr, ch 7, sk last 5-tr cl st of same shell, 3-tr cl in next 3-tr cl, repeat from * around, omit last 3-tr cl, join ch 7 in first cl.

Rnd 17: 3-tr cl in first cl, * ch 6, tr in next tr, ch 6, 3-tr cl in next cl, ch 7, 5-tr cl st over next 5 sc, ch 7, 3-tr cl in next cl, repeat from * around, omit last 3-tr cl, join ch 7 in first cl.

Rnd 18: 3-tr cl in first cl, * ch 8, (tr, ch 3, tr) in next tr, ch 8, 3-tr cl in next cl, ch 6, sc in next 5-tr cl st, ch 6, 3-tr cl in next cl, repeat from * around, omit last cl, join ch 6 in first cl.

Rnd 19: 3-tr cl in first cl, * ch 8; 5 tr in next tr, ch 2, 2 tr in next ch-3 sp, ch 2, 5 tr in next tr (shell); ch 8, 3-tr cl in next cl, ch 6, sc in next sc, ch 6, 3-tr cl in next cl, repeat from * around, omit last cl, join ch 6 in first cl.

Rnd 20: 3-tr cl in first cl, ch 8, sl st in top of cl just made (p), * ch 8, 5-tr cl st over first 5 tr of shell, ch 5, 5 tr in next tr, ch 2, tr in same tr, tr in next tr, ch 2, 5 tr in same tr, ch 5, 5-tr cl st over last 5 tr of same shell, ch 8, 3-tr cl in next cl, ch 8, sl st in top of last cl made (p), 3-tr cl in next cl, repeat from * around, omit last ch-8 p and 3-tr cl, join in first cl.

Rnd 21: Sl st in first p, (3-tr cl, ch 7, 3-tr cl) in first p, * ch 8, sk first 5-tr cl st of shell, 5-tr cl st over next 5 tr, ch 5, 5 tr in next tr, ch 2, tr in same tr, tr in next tr, ch 2, 5 tr in same tr, ch 5, 5-tr cl st over next 5 tr, ch 8, sk last 5-tr cl st of same shell, (3 tr cl, ch 7, 3-tr cl) in next p, repeat from * around, omit last 2 cls, join ch 8 in first cl.

Rnd 22: 3-tr cl in first cl, * ch 5, 3-tr cl in next sp, ch 5, 3-tr cl in next cl, ch 7, sk first 5-tr cl st of shell, 5-tr cl st over next 5 tr, ch 7, 3 tr in next tr, 2 tr in next tr, ch 7, 5-tr cl st over next 5 tr, ch 7, sk last 5-tr cl st of same shell, 3-tr cl in next cl, repeat from * around, omit last 3-tr cl, join ch 7 in first cl.

Rnd 23: 2 3-tr cls with ch 3 between in first cl, * (ch 4, 2 3-tr cls with ch 3 between in next cl) twice, ch 10, sk first 5-tr cl st of shell, sc in each of next 5 tr, ch 10, sk last 5-tr cl st of same shell, 2 3-tr cls with ch 3 between in next cl, repeat from * around, omit last 2 cls, join ch 10 in first cl.

Rnd 24: 3-tr cl in first cl, * (ch 3, 3-tr cl in next sp, ch 3, 3-tr cl in next cl, ch 4, 3-tr cl in next cl) twice, ch 3, 3-tr cl in next sp, ch 3, 3-tr cl in next cl, ch 9, 5-tr cl over next 5 sc, ch 9, 3-tr cl in next cl, repeat from * around, omit last 3-tr cl, join ch 9 in first cl.

Rnd 25: 3-tr cl in first cl, * (ch 3, 3-tr cl in next cl) twice, (ch 4, 3-tr cl with ch 3 between in each of next 3 cls) twice, ch 8, sc in next 5-tr cl, ch 8, 3-tr cl in next cl, repeat from * around, omit last cl, join ch 8 in first cl.

Rnd 26: 3-tr cl in first cl, * (ch 2, 3-tr cl in next cl) twice, (ch 4, tr in next sp, ch 3, tr in same sp, ch 4, 3-tr cl in next cl, ch 2, 3-tr cl in next cl, ch 2, 3-tr cl in next cl) twice, ch 8, sc in next sc, ch 8, 3-tr cl in next cl, repeat from * around, omit last cl, join ch 8 in first cl.

Rnd 27: 3-tr cl in first cl, * (sk next cl, 3-tr cl in next cl, ch 4, tr in next tr, ch 4, tr in next sp, ch 4, tr in next tr, ch 4, 3-tr cl in next cl) twice, sk next cl, 3-tr cl in next cl, ch 4, tr in cl last worked in, tr in next cl, ch 4, 3-tr cl in cl last worked in, repeat from * around, ending with last tr in same place as first cl, ch 4, join in first cl.

Rnd 28: Sl st between first 2 cls, ch 11, sl st in 6th ch from hook (p), ch 7, sl st in same ch as before (2nd p), ch 6, sl st in same ch as before (3rd p), tr between first 2 cls, * (ch 6, sc in next tr, ch 6, tr in next tr; **make 3-p group:** ch 6; sl st in top of last tr worked for first p, ch 7, sl st in same place for 2nd p, ch 6, sl st in same place for 3rd p; tr in same tr as last tr was worked in, ch 6, sc in next tr, ch 6, tr between next 2 cls, make 3-p group, tr in same sp as last tr was worked in) twice, ch 6, sc between next 2 single tr, ch 6, tr between next 2 cls, make 3-p group, tr in same sp as last tr was worked in, repeat from * around, ending last repeat with ch 6, sc between next 2 single tr, ch 6, join in first tr of rnd. End off. Block mat.

Irish Crochet

Raised petals and picot loops are characteristic. In the square motif shown here, ridged leaves are crocheted separately and appliquéd to the corners. The Irish Crochet motif can be used for bed- spreads, insertions for linens, or in lightweight wool yarn, for a lacy afghan or carriage cover. On Page 242, this motif is shown as an appliquéd border for a bedspread and as a pillow top.

IRISH CROCHET MOTIF

In bedspread cotton, with steel crochet hook No. 6, motif should measure 4″ square.

In size 30 mercerized crochet cotton, with steel crochet hook No. 13, motif should measure 3″ square.

In 3-ply fingering yarn or baby yarn, with steel crochet hook No. 1, motif should measure about 6½″ square.

DIRECTIONS: Beg at center of rose, ch 7, sl st in first ch to form ring.

Rnd 1: Ch 1, 16 sc in ring. Join in first sc of rnd.

Rnd 2: * Ch 5, sk 1 sc, sl st in next sc, repeat from * around—8 lps.

Rnd 3: (1 sc, 5 dc, 1 sc) in each lp around. Sl st in joining-st of last lp.

Rnd 4: * Ch 6, sl st in back of work between next 2 petals, repeat from * around, ending with sl st between last and first petals.

Rnd 5: (1 sc, 6 dc, 1 sc) in each lp around. Sl st in joining-st of last lp.

Rnd 6: Repeat rnd 4.

Rnd 7: (1 sc, 7 dc, 1 sc) in each lp around. Sl st in joining-st of last lp.

Rnd 8: * (Ch 9, sl st in 6th ch from hook for

picot) twice, ch 3, sc in sp between next 2 petals, (ch 13, sl st in 6th ch from hook for picot) twice, ch 7, sl st in same sp between petals (corner), (ch 9, sl st in 6th ch from hook) twice, ch 3, sc in sp between next 2 petals, repeat from * 3 times, ending with sl st in joining-st of rnd 7.

Rnd 9: Sl st to center of next lp, keeping picot to front, * (ch 3, ch-6 picot) twice, ch 3 (picot-lp made), sc in next lp between picots, repeat from * around, sl st in last sl st at beg of rnd.

Rnd 10: Sl st to center of next lp keeping picot to front, * make picot-lp, sc in next sc at corner, (picot-lp, sc in next lp between picots) 3 times, repeat from * around, ending with sl st in last sl st at beg of rnd.

Rnd 11: Sl st to center of next lp keeping picot to front, * make picot-lp, sc in next lp between picots, repeat from * around, sl st in last sl st at beg of rnd. End off motif.

To Join Motifs: Mark two adjacent corners of first motif with safety pins (corners are at center of picot-lps). Join 2nd motif to first motif through 8 picots on one side as follows:

2nd Motif: Work as for first motif through rnd 10.

Rnd 11: Sl st to center of next lp, keeping picot to front, ch 3, picot, ch 6, join to corresponding picot of first motif, ch 2, sl st in 4th ch of ch-6, * ch 3, sc between picots in next lp of 2nd motif, (ch 6, join to next picot of first motif, ch 2, sl st in 4th ch of ch-6) twice, repeat from * twice, ch 3, sc between picots in next lp of 2nd motif, ch 6, join to next picot of first motif, ch 2, sl st in 4th ch of ch-6 (8 picots joined), ch 3, picot, ch 3, sc between picots in next lp, complete motif as for first motif.

Leaf (make 4 for each motif): Ch 10, sc in 2nd ch from hook and in each of next 7 ch, 3 sc in last ch; working on opposite side of ch, make sc in each of next 6 ch, * ch 3, turn; working in back lp of sts, make sc in each of next 6 sc, 3 sc in next sc, sc in each of next 6 sc, repeat from * 4 times. End off. Appliqué leaves to corners of motifs, joining tips of leaves of each motif to tips of leaves of adjacent motifs.

IRISH-CROCHET EDGING: Row 1: Ch 9, tr in 9th ch from hook, * ch 9, tr in tr, repeat from * for desired length. End off.

Row 2: With right side of ch-9 lps towards you, attach thread in center of first ch-9 lp, sc in same place, * ch 4, sl st in sc for picot, sl st in same ch-9 lp, ch 7, sl st in 4th ch from hook for picot, ch 3, sc in next ch-9 lp, repeat from * across. End off.

CROCHET-TRIMMED BEDSPREAD AND PILLOW

SHOWN ON PAGE 242

SIZE: Twin size bedspread with 9″ ruffle. 9″ square pillow with 2″ ruffle.

MATERIALS: For bedspread and pillow: 6 yards yellow fabric, 45″ wide. Seven yards yellow bias cording. Seven yards yellow bias binding. Mercerized sewing thread: yellow and white. Kapok or other stuffing for pillow. For crochet: Mercerized Bedspread Cotton, 11 250-yard balls white for bedspread used with bolster (13 balls for longer bedspread), pillow and edging. Steel crochet hook No. 6.

CUTTING AND SEWING DIRECTIONS: If bolster is to be used with bedspread, cut piece for top of bedspread, 75″ long and 42″ wide. If no bolster is to be used, cut piece for top, 96″ long and 42″ wide. Cover bolster, if any, with yellow fabric, inserting bias cording in seams at ends of bolster. Cut remaining fabric lengthwise into 11″ wide strips. From end of one strip, cut two pieces for pillow, each 10″ square. Use 3″ wide strip left over from bedspread top to make pillow ruffle.

Make 1″ hem at top of bedspread. From right side, baste and stitch bias cording to sides and bottom of bedspread top, 1″ in from edges, raw edges out. Join 11″ wide strips in one continuous strip to measure twice the distance around three sides of bedspread top. Make narrow hem at each end and along one long edge. Gather in remaining edge to fit around sides and bottom of bedspread. With right sides together and raw edges even, baste and stitch gathered edge of ruffle to bedspread top, stitching close to cording. Trim seams; cover with bias binding.

Cut 3″ wide strip, 2 yards long, for pillow ruffle. Join ends. Make a narrow hem around one edge. Gather other edge to measure one yard. Baste and stitch gathered edge around pillow top, right sides together, raw edges even, taking ½″ seam. Stitch remaining 9″ square to pillow top and ruffle, ruffle inside, raw edges even, leaving opening for turning and stuffing pillow. Turn pillow to right side, stuff, close opening.

Make two strips of Irish crochet 18 motifs long for sides of bedspread (23 motifs long for longer bedspread), one strip 8 motifs long to fit across bottom between long strips. Block strips, pinning each picot at sides and ends of strips so that each motif is 4″ square.

Sew strips to bedspread with white sewing thread, catching down each picot.

Make Irish-crochet edging for edges of bedspread. Sew to hemmed edges of ruffle with yellow thread.

Pillow: Work one motif. Work 2nd motif, joining to first motif in last rnd as for bedspread. Join 3rd motif to side of 2nd motif. Join 4th motif to first and 3rd motifs. Appliqué leaves to motifs, four leaves touching at center. Sew piece to pillow top with white thread, catching down each picot around edge.

Make Irish-crochet edging for edge of pillow ruffle. Sew to hemmed edge with yellow thread.

Crocheted Upholstery Fabrics

Colorful crocheted fabrics for upholstery are functional as well as beautiful, thanks to closely-worked, firm textures which are easy to achieve. An additional advantage of such fabrics is that you can crochet them to the exact size you need for a specific use. The crochet cotton needed for these is available in vibrant, decorator colors, some with metallic glints for extra interest. Directions for crocheting six of these fabrics are given on Pages 300 and 301.

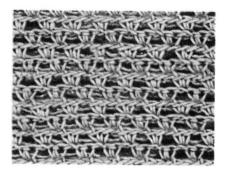

A Ridged pattern of ecru worked over gold-decorated pink, spice, brown

B Silvershot spice and ecru, accents of bittersweet, brown

C Bold stripes of brown and spice, pencil-striped with aqua, ecru

D Easy-crochet fabric of ecru, robin's-egg blue

E Diagonals of orange, brown nubs on metallic ecru ground

F Stripes, brown and orange chains on a spice fabric

A McCALL'S NEEDLEWORK & CRAFTS MAGAZINE FEATURE

Jewel-hued afghan is crocheted of knitting worsted in easy-to-handle 7" x 9" oblongs. Its fringes are a uniform 1¼" long. Directions for making it are on P. 301.

Crocheted fabrics

FABRIC A

MATERIALS: Knitting and crochet cotton, ecru, brown, spice. Metallic knitting and crochet cotton, rose. Steel crochet hook No. 6 or 7.

GAUGE: 10 sts=1"; 6 rows=1".

With ecru, make a ch slightly longer than desired width of fabric.

Row 1: Place ends of spice, brown and rose tog and, working over them with ecru, sc in 2nd ch from hook, sc in next ch, ch 1, * sk 2 ch, 2 sc in next ch, ch 1, repeat from * across, end with 2 sc, sk 2 ch, 1 sc in last ch. Ch 1, turn.

Row 2: Working over 3 strands as before and picking up front lp only, make 2 sc in first sc, ch 1, * 2 sc in next ch, ch 1, repeat from * across, end with 2 sc in ch, 1 sc in last sc. Ch 1, turn.

Row 3: Working over 3 strands as before and picking up back lp only, repeat row 2. Repeat rows 2 and 3 alternately for pat. Work in pat until piece is desired length. Break off. Block.

FABRIC B

MATERIALS: Knitting and crochet cotton, brown. Metallic knitting and crochet cotton, spice, ecru. 3-ply nylon and wool yarn, coral. Steel crochet hook No. 6 or 7.

GAUGE: 7 sc=1"; 7 rows=1".

With spice, make a ch several inches longer than desired width of fabric.

Row 1: Sc in 2nd ch from hook and in each ch across until row measures 2" longer than desired width. Cut off remaining ch. Ch 1, turn each row.

Row 2: Sc in each sc across. Drop spice, attach ecru.

Row 3: Working over 1 strand each of coral and brown, sc in first sc, * ch 1, sk next sc, sc in next sc, repeat from * across. Drop coral and brown.

Row 4: Working in front lp only, sc in each st across; drop ecru, pick up spice.

Row 5: Sc in each sc across.

Row 6: Working over strands of coral and brown, sc in each sc across. Drop spice, attach ecru. Repeat rows 3-6 for desired length. Block to measurements.

FABRIC C

MATERIALS: Knitting and crochet cotton, brown, ecru, aqua. Metallic knitting and crochet cotton, spice. Steel crochet hook, No. 6 or 7.

GAUGE: 7 sc=1"; 1 stripe pat=1¼".

With brown, make a ch slightly longer than desired width of fabric.

Row 1: DC in 4th ch from hook, * yo hook, insert hook in front lp of lower half of dc and pull lp through, insert hook in next ch and pull lp through, yo and draw through 2 lps on hook, yo and draw through last 3 lps on hook (connected dc made), repeat from * across until row is desired width of fabric and has an even number of dc. Ch 1, turn.

Row 2: Sc in each st across. Drop brown, attach ecru. Ch 1, turn.

Row 3: Sc in each sc across. Ch 1, turn.

Row 4: Sc in each sc across. Drop ecru, attach spice. Ch 3, turn.

Row 5: Insert hook in 2nd ch from hook and draw lp through, insert hook in 3rd ch from hook and draw lp through, insert hook in each of next 2 sc and draw lp through, yo and draw through all lps on hook, ch 1 to fasten. * Insert hook in ch 1 and draw lp through, insert hook in back of last lp made and draw lp through, insert hook in each of next 2 sc and draw lp through, yo and draw through all lps on hook, ch 1 to fasten, repeat from * across. Ch 1, turn.

Row 6: Picking up back lps only, sc in first ch 1, * ch 1, sc in next ch 1, repeat from * across, end with sc in last ch 1, sc in turning ch. Drop spice, pick up ecru. Ch 1, turn.

Row 7: Picking up back lp only, sc in each st across. Ch 1, turn.

Row 8: Sc in each sc. Drop ecru, attach aqua.

Row 9: Sc in each sc across. Break off.

Row 10: Pick up brown, ch 3, * make a connected dc in next sc, repeat from * across. Repeat rows 2-10 for desired length of fabric. Break off. Block.

FABRIC D

MATERIALS: Knitting and crochet cotton, ecru, aqua. Steel crochet hook No. 6 or 7.

GAUGE: 9 sc=1"; 11 rows=1".

With ecru, make a ch longer than desired width.

Row 1: Sc in 2nd ch from hook, sc in each ch across until row is desired width and number of sc is a multiple of 4 sts plus 3. Ch 1, turn each row.

Row 2: Sc in each sc. Drop ecru, attach aqua.

Row 3: Sc in first 3 sc, * sc in next sc on row below (long sc made), sc in next 3 sc, repeat from * across, end with sc in last 3 sc.

Row 4: Sc in each sc across. Drop aqua, pick up ecru.

Row 5: Picking up back lp only, sc in each sc across.

Row 6: Repeat row 2.

Row 7: Sc in first sc, * long sc in next sc on row below, sc in next 3 sc, repeat from * across, end with long sc, sc in last sc.

Row 8: Repeat row 4.

Row 9: Repeat row 5. Repeat rows 2-9 or desired length of fabric. Break off. Block to measurements.

FABRIC E

MATERIALS: Metallic knitting and crochet cotton, ecru. Knitting and crochet cotton, brown, orange. Steel crochet hook No. 6 or 7.

GAUGE: 8 sc=1"; 6 rows=1".

With ecru, make a ch 2" longer than desired width of fabric.

Row 1: Sc in 2nd ch from hook and in each ch across. Ch 1, turn each row. With ecru, work over 1 strand each of brown and orange throughout.

Row 2 and All Even Rows: Sc in each sc across.

Row 3: Sc in each of next 3 sc, * (insert hook in sc on previous row below last sc made; with orange and ecru draw lp through to height of last sc made, yo hook) twice, draw through all lps on hook, drop orange (long group st made), sk 1 sc, sc in each of next 6 sc, repeat from * across.

Row 5: * Sc in each of next 6 sc; with brown and ecru, make a long group st as before, sk 1 sc, repeat from * across.

Row 7: Sc in each of next 2 sc, * long group st with orange and ecru, sk 1 sc, sc in each of next 6 sc, repeat from * across.

Row 9: Sc in each of next 5 sc, * long group st with brown and ecru, sk 1 sc, sc in each of next 6 sc, repeat from * across.

Row 11: Sc in first sc, * long group st with orange and ecru, sk 1 sc, sc in next 6 sc, repeat from * across.

Row 13: Sc in each of next 4 sc, * long group st with brown and ecru, sk 1 sc, sc in each of next 6 sc. Repeat from * across.

Row 15: Sc in each of next 7 sc, * long group st with orange and ecru, sk 1 sc, sc in each of next 6 sc, repeat from * across.

Rows 16-29: Repeat rows 2-15 reversing colors of group sts. Repeat rows 2-29 for desired length.

FABRIC F

MATERIALS: Metallic knitting and crochet cotton, spice. Knitting and crochet cotton, brown, orange. Steel crochet hook No. 6 or 7.

GAUGE: 9 sts=1"; 7 rows=1".

With spice, make a ch 2" longer than desired width of fabric.

Row 1: Dc in 4th ch from hook and in each ch across. Ch 1, turn.

Row 2 (wrong side): Picking up front lp only, sc in each dc across. Ch 3, turn.

Row 3 (right side): Picking up back lp only, dc in each sc across. Ch 1, turn. Repeat rows 2 and 3 alternately for desired length. Break off.

With double strand of orange, make lp on hook. With right side facing and thread underneath, start at one side edge, insert hook down between 2nd and 3rd dc of first dc row, pull up lp through lp on hook. Work a row of sl sts in this way over first dc row, making each sl st over 2 dc. Ch 2. * Working in opposite direction, sl st over next dc row in same way. Ch 2. Repeat from * to last dc row.

With wrong side of work facing and double strand of brown, work sl sts across each dc row below and above orange sts—2 rows of brown sl sts to each dc row. Break off. Block to measurements.

Jewel afghan

Shown on Page 299

SIZE: About 54" x 63".

MATERIALS: Knitting Worsted, 64 ozs. National Blue (NB), 6 ozs. each Golf Green (GG) and Peacock (P), 5 ozs. Sea Green (SG). Plastic crochet hooks, sizes I and F. Tapestry needle.

GAUGE: 10 sc=3"; 7 rows=2" (sc ridge rows, size I hook).

Note: Motifs, 7" x 9", are crocheted and fringed separately, then sewed tog. For afghan, approximately 54" x 63", make 54 motifs.

MOTIF: With NB and size I hook, ch 30 loosely, to measure about 9". **Row 1:** Sc in 2nd ch from hook and in each remaining ch—29 sc. Ch 1, turn.

Row 2: Sc in each sc across. Ch 1, turn.

Row 3 (ridge row): Working through back lp of sts only, sc in each st across. Ch 1, turn.

Row 4: Working through both lps of sts, sc in each st. Ch 1, turn.

Rows 5-24: Repeat rows 3 and 4 alternately 10 times—11 ridge rows. Cut yarn leaving a 15" end for sewing.

FRINGE: Wind all four colors of yarn separately or together over a 1¾" cardboard. Cut through yarn at one edge to make strands for fringe.

To Knot Fringe: Insert size F hook from bottom up through 1 free lp on ridge row, fold one strand of yarn cut for fringe in half over hook, pull folded end through st to form a loop on hook, pull 2 ends of strand down through loop; pull ends to tighten knot.

Fringe Pattern: Row 1: Beg at lower right corner of motif and knotting fringe in each of 29 sts of first ridge row, knot 2 GG, 2 NB, 1 SG, 1 P, 1 SG, 2 GG, (2 NB, 1 P) 3 times, 2 NB, 2 GG, 1 SG, 1 P, 1 SG, 2 NB, 2 SG.

Row 2: Skip next ridge row. In next ridge row above, beg from right edge, knot 2 SG, 2 NB, 1 SG, 1 P, 1 SG, 2 GG, 2 NB, 1 P, 2 GG, 1 P, 2 SG, 1 P, 2 NB, 2 GG, 1 SG, 1 P, 1 SG, 2 NB, 2 P.

Row 3: Skip next ridge row. In next ridge row above, beg from right edge, knot 2 P, 2 NB, 1 SG, 1 P, 1 SG, 2 GG, 2 NB, 1 P, 2 SG, 1 P, 2 GG, 1 P, 2 NB, 2 GG, 1 SG, 1 P, 1 SG, 2 NB, 2 GG.

Skipping 1 ridge row between fringe rows, repeat rows 1, 2 and 3 once more.

FINISHING: Sew 9 motifs along 9" width, one above the other, with fringe going in one direction, using ends left for sewing. Make 5 more strips of 9 motifs in same way. Sew strips together side by side. With NB, work 1 row of sc around afghan, working 1 sc in each st at top and bottom of afghan, 1 sc in end of each row at sides, 3 sc in each corner. Join with sl st to first sc; end off. Trim fringe evenly.

Crocheted and woven mats

Place mats which simulate weaving so closely that even experts are deceived can be made easily by threading colored and metallic yarns through filet mesh. Crochet your mesh first, then "weave," using a tapestry needle. The sturdy yarns woven through give sufficient body to the mats to keep warm plates from marring the finish of a table, and yarn ends make the fringes pictured here.

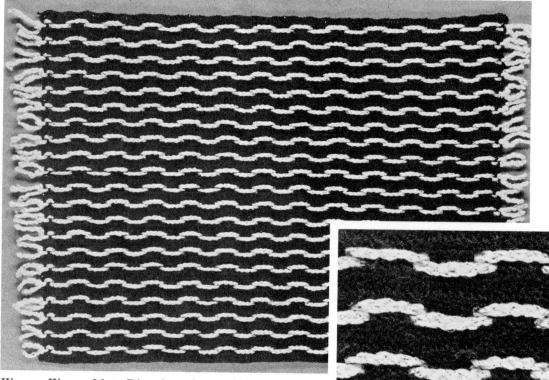

Woven Waves Mat. Directions for making this handsome mat, with white and silver crocheted chains interwoven through the black ground, are given below.

SIZE: About 18″ x 12″ (without fringe).

MATERIALS: Knitting and crochet cotton, 3 balls Black (B) for background. Metallic knitting and crochet cotton, 2 balls white and silver (W) for weaving. Steel crochet hook No. 7. Tapestry needle.

GAUGE: 8 dc=1″; 7 rows=2″.

PLACE MAT: BACKGROUND: Beg at wide side, with B, ch 152.

Row 1: Dc in 4th ch from hook and in each ch across—150 dc, counting turning ch. Turn each row.

Row 2: Ch 3 (counts as 1 dc), dc in 2nd dc, * ch 2, sk 2 dc (sp), dc in each of 4 dc (bl), repeat from * across, end ch 2, sk 2 dc, dc in each of 2 dc—25 sps.

Row 3: Ch 3, dc in 2nd dc, * 2 dc in next sp, dc in each of 4 dc, repeat from * across, end last repeat with 2 dc—150 dc. Repeat rows 2 and 3 for pat until piece measures 12″ from start, end row 2 of pat. End off.

WEAVING: Work from right to left edge each time.

Woven Stripe: Step 1: With W, make a 21″ ch. Conceal loose ends of ch by drawing them back through ch. With ch and tapestry needle, weave under first st of first sp row, over next dc, * under next bl, over next bl, repeat from * across, end under 2nd dc from end, over last dc. Pull row out flat, leaving 1¼″ fringe each side.

Step 2: With W, make a 21″ ch. Making fringe as before, weave ch over first st of same sp row, under next dc, * over next bl, under next bl, repeat from * across, end over 2nd dc from end, under last dc. Pull row out flat. Tie ends of fringe tog in a single knot. Stitch knot securely on each edge. Work woven stripe in each sp row to top edge.

Steam-press to measurements, using steam iron or dry iron and damp cloth.

Diagonal Stripes Mat. Directions below will tell you how to make this mat with its diagonal aqua stripes and a lacing of gold thread crossing a fudge-brown background.

SIZE: About 18″ x 12″ (without fringe).

MATERIALS: Knitting and crochet cotton (A), 3 balls brown for background. Cotton rug yarn (B), 2 skeins aqua, and metallic knitting and crochet cotton (C), 1 ball aqua for weaving. Steel crochet hook No. 7. Tapestry needle No. 20.

GAUGE: 2 bls and 1 sp=1″; 7 rows=2″.

PLACE MAT: BACKGROUND: Beg at wide side, with A, ch 170.

Row 1: Dc in 4th ch from hook and in each of 3 ch, * ch 2, sk 2 ch (sp), dc in each of 4 ch (bl), repeat from * across, end last repeat dc in each of 5 ch—28 dc bls, 27 sps. Turn each row.

Row 2: Ch 3 (counts as 1 dc), dc in 2nd dc, * ch 2, sk 2 dc, dc in next dc, 2 dc in next sp, dc in next dc, repeat from * across, end dc in top of turning ch—27 bls, 28 sps.

Row 3: Ch 3, dc in 2nd dc, * 2 dc in next sp, dc in next dc, ch 2, sk 2 dc, dc in next dc, repeat from * across, end dc in top of ch 3. Repeat rows 2 and 3 for pat until piece measures 12″ from start.

WEAVING: Work from right to left edge each time.

First Woven Stripe: Step 1: Cut B strand 44″ long. Using strand doubled in tapestry needle, weave under first st of first row, * over next bl, under next bl, repeat from * across, end under last 4 dc, over last dc. Pull row out flat, cut B, leaving 1″ fringe each side.

Step 2: With 44″ C strand doubled and working across same row, weave between the 2 B strands, weaving over the sts worked under and under the sts worked over previously.

Second Woven Stripe: Step 1: With 44″ B strand doubled, weave over first st of next row, under next dc, * over next bl, under next bl, repeat from * across, end under 2nd dc from end, over last dc.

Step 2: Work as for step 2 of first woven stripe.

Third Woven Stripe: Step 1: With 44″ B strand doubled, weave over first st of next row, * under next bl, over next bl, repeat from * across, end over last 4 dc, under last dc.

Step 2: Work as for step 2 of first woven stripe.

Fourth Woven Stripe: Step 1: With 44″ B strand doubled, weave under first st of next row, over next dc, * under next bl, over next bl, repeat from * across, end over 2nd dc from end, under last dc.

Step 2: Work as for step 2 of first woven stripe. Repeat these 4 stripes alternately, forming diagonal stripes, to top edge.

FINISHING: Sew fringe securely to mat. Trim fringe evenly. Steam-press to measurements.

303

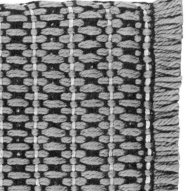

Cross-Woven Mat. Directions for making this striking mat with black ground, a rich autumn brown pattern, and spice-and-silver vertical stripes are given below.

SIZE: About 18″ x 12″ (without fringe).

MATERIALS: Knitting and crochet cotton (A), 3 balls black for background. Cotton rug yarn (B), 2 skeins brown, and metallic knitting and crochet cotton (C), 1 ball spice for weaving. Steel crochet hook No. 7. Tapestry needle No. 20.

GAUGE: 2 bls and 1 sp=1″; 4 rows=1″.

PLACE MAT: BACKGROUND: Beg at wide side, with A, ch 174.

Row 1: Dc in 4th ch from hook and in each of 2 ch, * ch 2, sk 2 ch (sp), dc in each of 4 ch (bl), repeat from * across—29 bls, 28 sps. Turn each row.

Row 2: Ch 3 (counts as 1 dc), sk 1 dc, dc in each of 3 dc, 2 dc in sp, * dc in next dc, ch 2, sk 2 dc, dc in next dc, 2 dc in next sp, repeat from * across, end dc in each of last 3 dc, dc in top of turning ch.

Row 3: Ch 3, sk 1 dc, dc in each of 3 dc, * ch 2, sk 2 dc, dc in next dc, 2 dc in next sp, dc in next dc, repeat from * across, end ch 2, sk 2 dc, dc in each of 4 dc. Repeat rows 2 and 3 for pat until 49 rows are completed. End off.

WEAVING: Work from right to left edge.

First Woven Stripe (right side): Cut B strand 44″ long; use strand doubled in tapestry needle. Working across first row, weave under first st, over 2 dc, under 1 dc, * over 4 dc, under 1 dc, over 2 dc, under 1 dc, repeat from * across row—15 short B sps, 14 long B sps. Pull row out flat, cut B, leaving 1″ fringe each side.

Second Woven Stripe (right side): With 44″ B strand doubled and working across next row, weave (under 1 dc, over 2 dc) twice, (under 2 dc, over 6 dc) 13 times, under 2 dc, (over 2 dc, under 1 dc) twice—13 long B sps; make fringe as before. Repeat these 2 stripes alternately to top edge. Sew fringe securely to mat. Trim fringe evenly.

First Vertical Stripe (edge): With 4 C strands about 3½ yards long, start on right side of mat at lower right-hand corner. Leaving 1″ end (weave this end in on wrong side later), work as follows: Weave under first 2 B strands of first short B sp, * over next 2 B strands above, under next 2 B strands above, repeat from * to top edge. Pull row out flat. Pass C through center of next bl to the left, thus bringing C to wrong side.

Second Vertical Stripe: From wrong side, weave under next line of long B strands to lower edge. Pull row out flat. Turn to right side. This stripe is visible through the background sps.

Third Vertical Stripe: From right side with C, * weave under short B sp, over next long B sp above, repeat from * to top edge. Pull row out flat. Pass C through center of next bl to the left, thus bringing C to wrong side. Repeat last 2 vertical stripes alternately across mat, ending with 2nd vertical stripe. Turn to right side, work edge as for first stripe. Cut C, leaving 1″ end. Weave in ends on wrong side.

Steam-press to measurements, using steam iron or dry iron and damp cloth.

How to Make Hairpin Lace

Use a crochet hook and a hairpin lace loom. Width of hairpin lace depends on the size of hairpin loom used. This loom is sometimes called a fork or staple.

With crochet hook, make a loose chain stitch. Take hook out of stitch and insert left-hand prong of loom through chain stitch. Draw out ch (loop) until knot is halfway between prongs. Then bring thread to front and around right-hand prong to back (Fig. 1). Insert crochet hook up through loop on left-hand prong, draw thread through and make a chain (Figs. 2 and 3). * To get crochet hook in position for next step, without drawing out loop on hook, turn handle of crochet hook upward parallel with prongs, then pass it through the prongs to back of loom (Fig. 4). Now turn loom toward you from right to left once (a loop over right prong). With a loop on hook, insert crochet hook up through loop on left-hand prong, in back of front thread, draw thread through (Fig. 5) and complete single crochet. Repeat from *

Note: Some prefer to withdraw crochet hook from loop, turn loom over as directed and reinsert hook, instead of method illustrated in Fig. 4.

When loom gets crowded, remove base, slide most of loops off, leaving last few on and replace base.

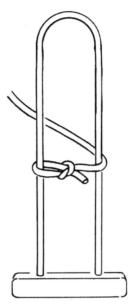

FIGURE 1

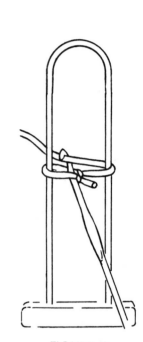

FIGURE 2

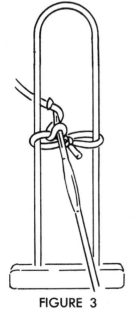

FIGURE 3

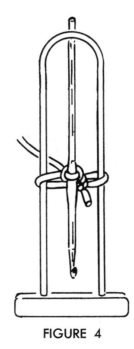

FIGURE 4

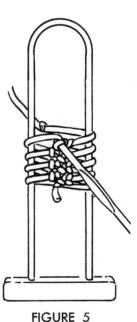

FIGURE 5

Ribbon-woven carriage cover

SIZE: Approximately 30″ x 36″ (finished).

MATERIALS: Baby yarn, 3 ply, 9 1-oz. balls. 3/16″ acetate taffeta knitting ribbon, 2 50-yd spools. Steel crochet hook No. 4. One 1½″ hairpin lace loom. One bodkin or safety pin for weaving. Sewing thread.

GAUGE: 4 mesh=1″; 3 mesh rows=1″. 6 sc=1″.

MESH PATTERN: Row 1: Dc in 6th ch from hook, * ch 1, sk 1 ch, dc in next ch, repeat from * across, turn.

Row 2: Ch 5, dc in 2nd dc, * ch 1, dc in next dc, repeat from * across, end ch 1, dc in 4th ch of turning ch, turn. Repeat row 2 for mesh pat.

BLANKET: Ch 244 loosely. Work in mesh pat (120 mesh) for 116 rows, turn.

Edge: Ch 1, work 1 row sc around edge of shawl, making 1 sc in each ch 1 and dc across top and bottom, 3 sc in each corner, 2 sc in end st of each row on sides. Steam-press blanket, using a damp cloth.

TO WEAVE RIBBON: Use ribbon directly from spool. **Row 1:** With bodkin or small safety pin, weave ribbon loosely through mesh on first row of blanket. Smooth out ribbon so that work does not pull. Cut ribbon, leaving ½″ at each end. Turn under ends of ribbon; with sewing thread, sew to sc row.

Row 2: Work as for row 1, weaving under the mesh previously worked over. Continue in this manner to last row of blanket. Pin to a flat surface and press, using a dry cloth.

LACE EDGING (make 2 strips): Following directions that come with loom, make hairpin lace strip with yarn double, until there are 552 double lps each side. End off. Pin one strip, along sc at center, over edge where ribbon ends were sewed, placing 148 lps on each side edge, 128 across each end. Half of lace's width extends beyond edge. With yarn, sew strip in place. Sew 2nd strip, in same way, on other side of blanket to make it reversible.

This light weight, reversible carriage blanket is crocheted of baby yarn in a mesh pattern, then woven with taffeta knitting ribbon and trimmed with hairpin lace. A generous 30″ x 36″ size.

Wool cover of hairpin lace

SIZE: Approximately 44″ x 66″.

MATERIALS: Sport yarn, 17 ozs. main color (MC) and 11 ozs. contrasting color (CC). Hairpin looms 3″ and 1½″ size. Crochet hooks No. H/8 and B/1.

WIDE STRIP (make 15): Use MC, 3″ loom and No. 1 hook. Following directions that come with loom, make strip until there are 459 lps on each side. Finish off.

NARROW STRIP (make 16): Using CC, 1½″ loom and No. 1 hook, work same as wide strips.

JOINING STRIPS: Use No. 8 hook. Insert hook through first 3 lps on narrow strip, pick up first 3 lps on wide strip and pull them through lps on hook, * pick up next 3 lps on narrow strip and pull them through, pick up next 3 lps on wide strip and pull them through. Repeat from * to top. Place safety pin through last 3 lps to hold. Always starting at same end with first 3 lps of narrow strips, join another narrow strip to other side of wide strip and continue joining wide and narrow strips alternately.

FINISHING: Finish side edges by drawing 2 lps through 2 lps. Using a double strand of MC and No. 8 hook, attach yarn at top right corner. Working across top of afghan, ch 3 loosely, sc in joining between strips (through 3 lps held by pin), * ch 3, sc in center of MC strip, ch 3, sc in next joining, ch 3, sc in next joining. Repeat from * across. Repeat edging at bottom.

FRINGE: Cut 4 strands CC 10″ long. Always working from same side of afghan, insert hook through first ch-3 lp, catch center of these strands and pull them part way through, forming a lp, then draw cut ends through lp and pull tight. Make 2 pieces of fringe in each ch-3 lp in this manner, using colors to correspond with colors of strips.

Striped wool coverlet of hairpin lace alternates wide and narrow strips of lace in contrasting colors. Make it of sport yarn in afghan size, 44″ x 66″, add two-color fringe at top and bottom.

PLACE MAT MOTIF

SIZE: Each motif, 2″ in diameter.

MATERIALS: Mercerized crochet cotton, No. 20, white. One ¾″ wide hairpin lace loom. Crochet hook size 12.

MOTIF: Make 28 lps of hairpin lace on each prong. Remove from loom, and join last sc made to first sc neatly to form a circle. Cut thread and fasten off.

To Make Center: Join thread in one lp at center (keeping the lps straight). Sc in two lps at center, sc in next 2 lps, repeat around. Tie threads and cut.

Outer Edge: Fasten thread in one lp. * Ch 7, sc in next lp, repeat from * around. Fasten off.

2ND AND OTHER MOTIFS: Join with 4 side lps, (ch 3, sl st in ch-7 of corresponding motif, ch 3) 4 times.

FILL-IN MOTIF: Ch 7, sl st in a free lp between group of 4 motifs, ch 7, sl st in first ch made, * ch 7, sl st in next loop, ch 7, sl st in center, repeat from * around. End with a sl st in first ch made (12 lps in all). Tie ends and fasten off.

Wheels of hairpin lace are edged with crochet and joined together with fill-in motifs to make a square or rectangular tablecloth or place mat. Actual-size detail of hairpin lace and fill-in motifs, worked of crochet cotton No. 20, shown above; directions right.

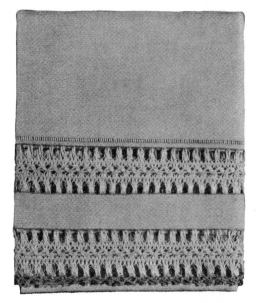

Hairpin lace turns a plain towel into a pretty guest towel. Edging and insertion are done in two colors, can match your own color scheme. Made of No. 30 crochet cotton. Towel insertion and edging directions are given here.

TOWEL INSERTION AND EDGING

MATERIALS: White crochet cotton No. 30; contrasting color (CC) cotton No. 70. One ¾″ hairpin lace loom. Steel crochet hooks Nos. 8 and 14.

INSERTION: With white cotton and No. 8 crochet hook, make 2 strips of hairpin lace in length desired (for a 17″ wide towel, 168 lps). Fasten off. Insert hook in 3 lps of first strip, * pick up 3 lps of 2nd strip, draw through lps of first strip, draw through lps on hook; repeat from * to end. With CC and hook No. 14, insert hook in first 3 outside lps of strip, make 1 sc, * 5, 1 sc through next 3 lps; repeat from * across. Ch 8, make half turn; working along end, * 1 sc in sc, ch 8, repeat from * twice more, work along opposite side to correspond. Fasten off.

EDGING: Work hairpin lace as for insertion. With CC finish one side as for insertion. On opposite side, work edging as follows:

Row 1: * 1 sc in next 3 lps, ch 6, repeat from * across.

Row 2: Ch 6, turn, * 1 sc in next lp, ch 6, 1 sc in 3rd ch from hook (picot), ch 3; repeat from * across. Fasten off.

Hairpin lace trimmings

Hairpin lace can be used for smart and decorative trimmings on suits, coats and dresses. Many yarns are suitable for making the braids and edgings: wool yarns from fingering weight to bulky types; novelty yarns, such as knitting ribbon in taffeta or silk organdy, metallic yarns, and cordé.

Ribbon hairpin lace, ½″ or ¾″ wide, makes a trimming braid which can be formed into scallops, loops, frogs, initials or other designs. If design curves a great deal, as in forming loops or initials, do not edge the hairpin lace with crochet; Figure 1. Unedged hairpin lace is elastic and can be easily curved and stretched.

For crisper, sharper trimming, edge the lace with single crochet; Figure 2. Edged hairpin lace can be curved somewhat as in the intertwined design of two braids illustrated. The two braids may be made in two different colors for variety, or the hairpin lace may be worked in one color and the crocheted edges in another. For a scalloped edge, fold braid over at each inner point, as illustrated.

Before sewing ribbon braid to garment, steam-press, then pin in place in desired design. Sew it in place from wrong side of garment along center of trimming.

Fringed hairpin lace trimming has one edge finished in crochet, the other edge left in free-hanging loops. If a wool yarn is used, loops can be cut to form fringe. To make fringed hairpin lace trimming, Figure 3, use a 2″ hairpin loom and make lace in usual way with a multiple of 5 loops. On one edge, place 5 twisted loops together, one over the other and work 5 single crochet in each cluster of loops across. Be sure all loops twist in same direction.

A smart scalloped braid can be made by working scallops of crochet on both edges of the hairpin lace. Make 1½″ lace a little longer than desired length having multiple of 4 loops each side. With matching or contrasting yarn, crochet groups of loops together on both sides of lace as follows:

Make lp on hook; place first 4 loops tog, sl st these loops tog, make 5 sc in same place as sl st (spread loops apart as you work; scallop should measure ½″), * sl st next 4 loops tog, make 5 sc in same place as sl st, repeat from * across. Repeat scallops on other edge of hairpin lace directly opposite scallops of first side, or alternate scallops by working first 2 loops together, then repeating from * across and working last 2 loops together.

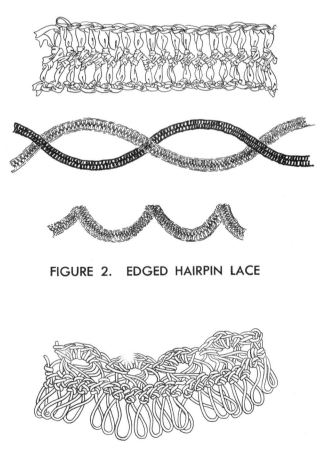

FIGURE 1.   UNEDGED HAIRPIN LACE

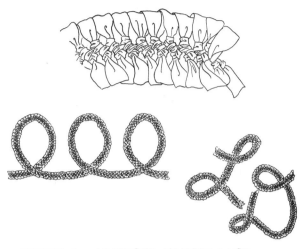

FIGURE 2.   EDGED HAIRPIN LACE

FIGURE 3.   FRINGED TRIMMING

Crocheted trimmings

CROCHETED TUBULAR CORD

May be used for a tie belt or, pressed flat, for a trimming braid. Use yarn single or double and suitable steel crochet hook.

Rnd 1: Ch 2, 6 sc in 2nd ch from hook. Do not join rnds.

Rnd 2: Sc in front lp of each sc around. Repeat rnd 2 for desired length. Sc in every other sc around. Cut yarn leaving 8″ end. Thread end in yarn needle, draw end through remaining sts, fasten off securely.

CROCHETED SOUTACHE

Makes a beautiful braid for a suit or dress. Make a chain with soutache a little longer than you need for edge to be trimmed. Single crochet in each chain for desired length. Use wrong side of crochet for right side of braid.

CROCHET-COVERED BUTTONS

Rnd 1: Ch 2, 12 sc in 2nd ch from hook. Do not join rnds.

Rnd 2: * Sc in next sc, 2 sc in next sc, repeat from * around. Continue around is sc, inc as necessary to keep work flat, until piece is same size as button mold.

Next Rnd: * Pull up a lp in each of next 2 sts, yo and through 3 lps on hook (dec made), sc in next sc, repeat from * around. Insert button mold. Continue to dec as necessary to cover back of button mold.

CROCHETED BUTTONS

Buttons can be made without molds, following directions above and stuffing with cotton.

RING BUTTONS

Lightweight buttons can be made by using plastic rings as a base. With same yarn used in garment, work sc closely around ring. Join with a sl st in first sc. Turn crochet to inside of ring to fill center and sew center stitches together, leaving end for sewing to garment. For larger rings, 2 or 3 rnds of sc may be required to fill center with decreases on each rnd. A small shank type button, beads or rhinestones may be sewn to center of ring button for decoration. Rings may be covered with soutache, too.

CROCHET-COVERED BUCKLES

A self-belt made for a knitted or crocheted dress should always have a buckle to give the belt a professional look. Buy a buckle in proper size for belt, sc closely over buckle with same yarn as belt, keeping top of stitches at outer edge of buckle.

RING BUCKLE

One, two, three or more plastic rings can be used to make a buckle. With same yarn used in belt, work sc closely around ring. Join with sl st in first sc. Sew rings together as shown. Lap one end of belt through ring at one side; sew end to wrong side. Lap other end of belt through ring at other side; finish with snap fastener.

RING BUTTONS

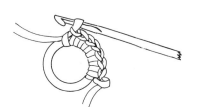

Single Crochet Around Ring

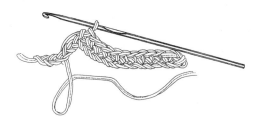

CROCHETED SOUTACHE

Turn Crochet To Inside

COVERED RINGS USED AS BUCKLE

Tatting

Stitches and picots which produce rings and half-rings are the essentials of tatting. Varying arrangements of these produce different designs. The French call tatting "frivolité," the Italians call it "occhi," which means "eyes," and in the Orient the work is referred to as "makouk" which describes the shuttles on which tatting is done, rather than the needlecraft itself.

Tatting, which is simply another method of lace-making, looks very delicate, but is actually quite strong because every stitch is a unit all by itself which does not lean on its neighbors for strength. The two stitches which are the basis of the craft are reversals of each other, and once learned, can be done easily and in large part without even watching the work in progress.

Edgings are perhaps the most popular use for tatting today, with round or square table mats close seconds.

The technique is somewhat difficult to describe. If you do not know how to tat and would like to learn, try to augment the information in this chapter with a lesson or two from a friend who knows the art.

How to Tat

Tatting is the technique for forming lace designs of loops, rings and picots by means of a shuttle and thread. The tool used is called a tatting shuttle and may be of steel, plastic, bone or tortoise shell. Some are made with a hook at one end but these are harder for the beginner to use. For practice work, use mercerized crochet cotton size 20 or 30 in the shuttle.

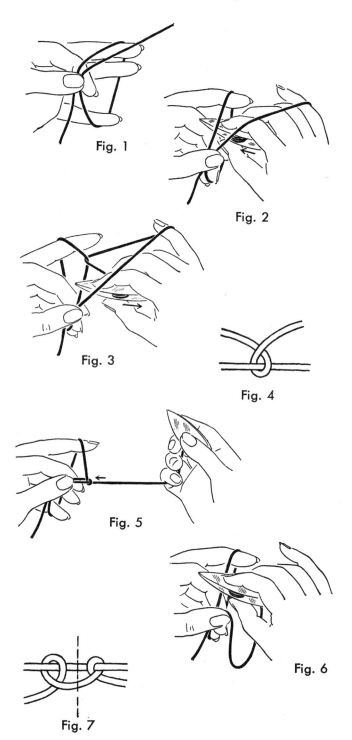

Fig. 1

Fig. 2

Fig. 3

Fig. 4

Fig. 5

Fig. 6

Fig. 7

TO WIND THE SHUTTLE BOBBIN: If there is a hole in the bobbin center, insert thread through hole, tie a knot and wind bobbin. If bobbin is removable, wind it and replace it in shuttle. Only wind enough thread to fill shuttle without projecting at the sides.

TO HOLD THREAD AND SHUTTLE: Hold end of thread between thumb and forefinger of left hand. Bring thread around back of left hand, spreading fingers, and grasp thread again between thumb and forefinger for a ring of thread; Fig. 1. Unwind shuttle so thread is about 12″ long. Hold shuttle between thumb and forefinger of right hand with pointed end facing left hand and thread coming from back of bobbin.

TO MAKE DOUBLE STITCH: First Half: With shuttle in right hand, pass shuttle thread under fingers of right hand, then over back of hand; Fig. 2. Bring shuttle forward and slide flat top of shuttle *under* ring thread on left hand; Fig. 2. (Do not let go of shuttle; the ring thread will pass between shuttle and fingers.) Then slide shuttle back over ring thread; Fig. 3. Pull shuttle thread taut and *at the same time,* drop middle finger of left hand so that ring of thread lies loose. This will cause loop to turn over; Fig. 4. Keep shuttle thread taut (this is very important) while you raise middle finger of left hand again. Loop will pull close to left thumb as you pull ring thread taut; Fig. 5. Hold loop firmly between thumb and forefinger.

Second Half: The second half of double stitch is made in reverse. Allow shuttle thread to fall slack without putting it over right hand. Slide shuttle *over* ring thread, Fig. 6, back under ring thread and over shuttle thread. Pull shuttle thread taut and *hold it taut* as you slacken ring thread and tighten it again. Second half of stitch slips into place beside first half; Fig. 7.

By pulling the shuttle thread, stitch should slip back and forth. If it does not, the stitch has been locked by a wrong motion and must be made over again. Practice double stitch, the basic stitch of tatting, until you can make it without looking at instructions. When loop around hand becomes too small to work in, pull shuttle thread at left of stitches to enlarge loop.

TO MAKE RINGS AND PICOTS: Rings and picots are characteristic of all tatting. To make first ring, work 4 double stitches (4 d), then make first half of another double stitch; slide it on thread, stopping about ¼″ from last stitch. Complete double stitch and draw entire stitch in position next to 4 d, forming picot (p); Fig. 8. Work 3 more d, work another picot, 3 more d, work another picot and 3 more d. Hold stitches firmly in left hand, draw shuttle thread until first and last stitches meet, forming a ring.

TO JOIN RINGS: Wind thread around left hand as for first ring and work first double stitch of next ring about ¼″ from ring just made. Work 3 more d. If you are using a shuttle with one pointed end, or a hook at one end, insert this end through the last picot of previous ring (or use a crochet hook) and pull ring thread through. Pull up a loop large enough to insert shuttle. Draw shuttle through this loop, Fig. 9, and draw shuttle thread tight. This joins the rings and counts as the first half of a double stitch. Complete double stitch, work 3 more d, a picot, 4 d, a picot, 4 d, close ring same as first ring.

TO REVERSE WORK: Turn work so that base of ring just made is at the top and work next ring as usual.

TO JOIN THREADS: Use a square knot to fasten a new thread close to the end of last ring or chain. Continue work and cut off ends later. Never attach a new thread in ring as the knots will not pass through the double stitch.

TO WORK WITH TWO THREADS: By using two threads, a wider range of patterns can be made. One method of working with two threads is to use the ball of thread for making chains and the shuttle thread for making rings. Tie ball and shuttle threads together. Use shuttle thread to form a ring. When ring is completed turn it so base is held between thumb and forefinger. Stretch thread from ball over back of fingers and loop it twice around little finger; Fig. 10. Work over ball thread with the shuttle in the usual way to form a chain, pull stitches together when chain is finished and resume work with the shuttle thread only for next ring.

When two colors are used in making rings, two shuttles must be used. These colors may be alternated, or the second color may be worked over the first as described in making a chain with a shuttle and a ball.

TO MAKE A JOSEPHINE KNOT: Work a small ring consisting of only the first half of double stitches.

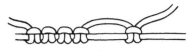
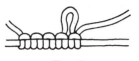

Fig. 8

Fig. 9

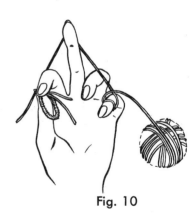

Fig. 10

TATTING ABBREVIATIONS

r—ring	d—double stitch
ch—chain	rw—reverse work
rnd—round	sep—separated by
j—join	lr—large ring
p—picot	sm—small
cl—close	sp—space
	beg—beginning

Tatted edgings

WILD ROSE EDGING

MATERIALS: Tatting cotton. Tatting shuttle. Steel crochet hook No. 14. Handkerchief.

Use ball and shuttle.

Rnd 1: J thread in edge of handkerchief ⅛″ before one corner. * Ch (4 d, p) 3 times, 4 d, j in edge of handkerchief on other side of same corner ⅛″ past corner. ** Ch (4 d, p) 3 times, 4 d, j in edge of handkerchief ¼″ from last joining. Repeat from ** across to within ⅛″ of next corner. Repeat from * around. Tie and cut.

Rnd 2: J in center p of corner ch. * Ch (4 d, p) 3 times, 4 d, j in center p of next ch. Repeat from * around. Tie and cut.

Rnd 3: R 3 d, j in first p of first ch after corner ch, 3 d, cl r. * Leave ¼″ thread, r 3 d, j in next p of same ch, 3 d, cl r. Leave ¼″ thread, r 3 d, j in same p, 3 d, cl r. Leave ¼″ thread, r 3 d, j in last p of same ch, 3 d, cl r. Leave ¼″ thread, j in center p of next ch. Leave ¼″ thread, r 3 d, j in first p of next ch, 3 d, cl r. Repeat from * around. Tie and cut.

STAR FLOWER EDGING

MATERIALS: Tatting cotton. Tatting shuttle. Steel crochet hook No. 14. Handkerchief, with rolled, hemstitched edge.

Use ball and shuttle.

Rnd 1: J thread in edge of handkerchief at one corner. * Ch 6 d, p, 6 d, rw. R 3 d, p, (4 d, p) twice, 3 d, cl r, rw. Ch 6 d, p, 6 d, j in edge of handkerchief ⅜″ from last joining †. Ch 4 d, j in edge ⅛″ from last joining, repeat from * across to next corner ending at †. Repeat from * around edge of handkerchief. Tie and cut.

Rnd 2: J thread in edge at same corner between first and last motif. * Ch (3 d, p) 3 times, 3 d, j in first p of r, ch 3 d, p, (4 d, p) twice, 3 d, j in same p. Ch 3 d, j in next p of same r, ch 3 d, p, (4 d, p) twice, 3 d, j in same p. Ch 3 d, j in last p of r, ch 3 d, p, (4 d, p) twice, 3 d, j in same p. Ch (3 d, p) 3 times, 3 d, j over ch in edge between motifs. Repeat from * around, joining center p of first round ch to center p of last round ch of last motif. Tie and cut.

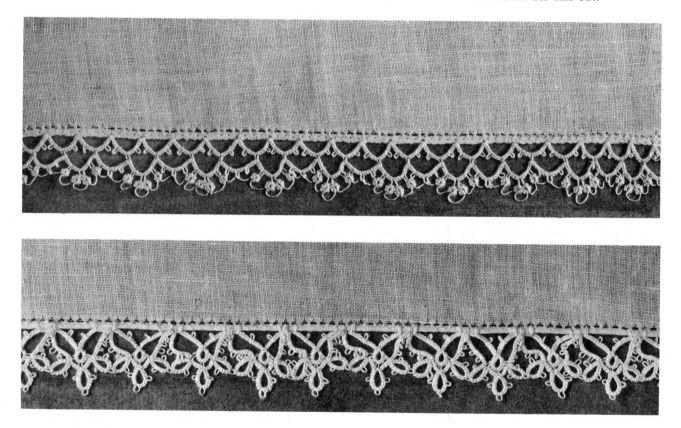

Tatting makes a rich and delicate lace for edging handkerchiefs. Wild Rose and Star Flower Edgings, ⅝″ and ¾″ wide, are joined to the hemstitched handkerchiefs during the first round of tatting.

Tatted doily

SIZE: 10″ in diameter.

MATERIALS: Six Cord Crochet Cotton, size 10. Tatting Shuttle. Steel crochet hook No. 8.

Center Motif: Rnd 1: Make r of (3 d, p) 11 times, cl r, rw.

Rnd 2: Draw thread in last p, (ch 3 d, j in next p, make sm p) 11 times.

Rnd 3: J in p, * ch 6 d, p (9 d, p) twice, 6 d, j in same p (ch-lp made), ch 2 d, j in next p last rnd, repeat from * around, joining first p of new ch-lp to last p of last ch-lp. At the end of rnd, j last p of ch-lp to first p of first ch-lp. Tie and cut. There are 11 ch-lps with ch 2 d between. Center motif completed.

Rnd 4: * Make r of 4 d, j in p at point of ch-lp, 4 d, cl r, rw. Ch 5 d, p, (10 d, p) twice, 5 d, rw. Repeat from * around, j in first r. Tie and cut.

Rnd 5: * Make r of 5 d, j in p at point of ch, 5 d, cl r, rw. (Ch 5 d, p) 7 times, 5 d, rw. Repeat from * around, j in first r. Tie and cut.

Rnd 6: First Motif: Work rnds 1 and 2 as for center motif. **Next Rnd:** J in p, (4 d, j in next p) twice, work from first * to 2nd * of rnd 3 until there are 7 ch-lps, (4 d, j in next p) twice, tie to center p of ch on rnd 5, cut thread. Make 10 more motifs in same way, joining center p of first ch-lp new motif to center p of last ch-lp last motif. At end of rnd, j center p of last ch-lp to center p of first ch-lp first motif.

Rnd 7: * Make r of 4 d, j in center p of 2nd ch-lp on a motif, 4 d, cl r, rw. (Ch 5 d, p, 10 d, p, 10 d, p, 5 d, rw. R 4 d, j in center p of next ch-lp same motif, 4 d, cl r, rw) 4 times. Repeat from * around, j in first r. Tie and cut.

Rnd 8: * Make r of 4 d, j in center p of ch to right of double r last rnd, 4 d, cl r, rw. (Ch 5 d, 7 p sep by 5 d, 5 d, j in center p of next ch) twice, ch 5 d, 7 p sep by 5 d, 5 d, rw. R of 4 d, j in center p of next ch, 4 d, cl r, rw. Repeat from * around, j in first r. Tie and cut.

Tatted doily design suggests a medieval rose window framed in smaller flowers and petals. In size 10 cotton, an easy size for the beginner to work with, doily is 10″ in diameter.

Tatted squares

MATERIALS: Mercerized crochet cotton, size 30. Tatting shuttle.

FOUR-LOOP SQUARE: R 5 d, 7 p sep by 2 d, 5 d, cl r.

* R 5 d, j in last p of last r, 2 d, 6 p sep by 2 d, 5 d, cl r*. Repeat from * to * twice more joining last p of 4th r to first p of first r.

Second Four-Loop Square: Work as for first square, joining to first square by 5th p of first r and 3rd p of 2nd r. Make 9 squares in all, joining to form a cross 5 squares high by 5 squares wide.

CORNER MOTIF: R 2 d, 3 p sep by 2 d, 2 d, j in 4th free p of r at end of cross, 2 d, 3 p sep by 2 d, 2 d, cl r.

* Rw, ch 2 d, 5 p sep by 1 d, 2 d. Rw, ** r 2 d, p, 2 d, j in next to last p of last r, 2 d, p, 2 d, j in middle p of next r of square, 2 d, 3 p sep by 2 d, 2 d, cl r *.

Repeat from * to *, ch 3 d, p, 3 d.

Rw, r 2 d, p, 2 d, j in next to last p of last r, 2 d, p, 2 d, j in middle p of next r of square, 2 d, p, 2 d, j in middle p of next r of square, 2 d, 3 p sep by 2 d, 2 d, cl r.

Rw, ch 3 d, j in p of last ch, 3 d. Repeat from ** to *. Repeat from * to * twice, ch 7 d, p, 7 d, p, 5 d.

Rw, r 3 d, p, 3 d, j in middle p of 2nd from last ch, 3 d, p, 3 d, cl r.

Rw, ch 3 d, r 3 d, 11 p sep by 2 d, 3 d, cl r. Ch 3 d, rw, r 3 d, j in last p of last r, 3 d, j in middle p of next ch, 3 d, p, 3 d, cl r.

Rw, ch 5 d, p, 7 d, p, 7 d. Cut and tie in first r. Fill in other 3 corners in same way.

Join medallions by middle picots of adjacent rings and chains. Where four corner motifs meet, join 3 large rings in middle picot of large ring of first medallion.

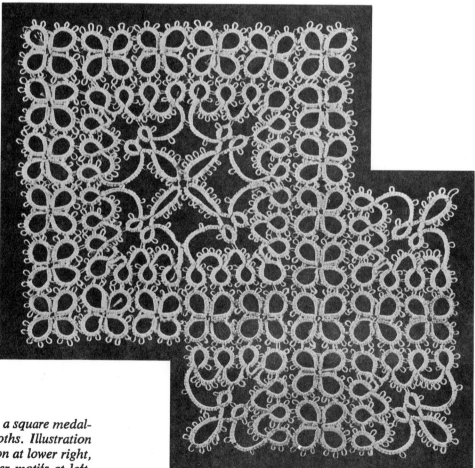

Two motifs combine to form a square medallion for place mats, tablecloths. Illustration shows one complete medallion at lower right, method of joining four corner motifs at left.

Tatted daisy doily

MATERIALS: Mercerized crochet cotton, size 30, 1 ball white, 1 ball yellow; 2 shuttles.

CENTER MEDALLION: Row 1: With yellow, r 1 d, 10 p sep 1 d, cl.

Row 2: * Ch 2 d, small p, j to next p. Repeat from * making 10 p.

Row 3: * Ch 3 d, small p, j p. Repeat from * around.

Row 4: * Ch 2 d, small p, 2 d, small p, j p. Repeat from * around. Tie and cut.

With white, tie to a p, ch 10 d, p, 8 d, p, 2 d, p, 8 d, p, 10 d, j next yellow p, 10 d, j last p previous. **Ch** 8 d, p, 2 d, p, 8 d, p, 10 d, j next yellow p. Repeat around. (10 petals made.) Tie and cut.

Tie thread at j of petals. Ch 10 d, p, 10 d, j next petal j. Continue around. Tie and cut. Ch as previous round, making 11 d.

SIDE MEDALLIONS: With yellow, 2 rows same as center medallion.

Row 3: Ch 2 d, p, 2 d, j p, 2 d, p, 2 d, j p. Continue around 10 times. Tie and cut.

Make 7 white petals same as center medallion. For second rnd, j p center medallion at same time to end p of new medallion. Ch 10 d, j at joining, 10 d, p, 10 d, etc., j next free p center medallion. Tie and cut. Make 5 side medallions joining last one to first one.

EDGE: Row 1: With yellow, r 3 d, p, 6 d, j to p of sixth petal, 6 d, p, 3 d, cl. R 3 d, j last p last r, 6 d, 2 p sep 6 d, 3 d, cl. R 3 d, j p last r, 6 d, j second petal next medallion, 6 d, p, 3 d, cl, rw. With white ch 9 d, 3 p sep 9 d, rw. With yellow * r 9 d, j next petal, 9 d, cl, rw. With white ch 9 d, 3 p sep 9 d, 9 d, rw. Yellow r 9 d, j same petal, 9 d, cl, rw. White ch 9 d, p, 9 d, rw. Repeat from * twice, then ch 9 d, 3 p sep 9 d, 9 d, rw. Repeat from beginning with 3 r group. Join to correspond. Tie and cut.

Row 2: White thread, j to p of long ch, ch 9 d, 3 p sep 9 d, 9 d, rw. Yellow r 3 d, p, 6 d, j end p same loop, 6 d, p, 3 d, cl. R 3 d, j p last r, 6 d, j next ch, 6 d, p, 3 d, cl. R 3 d, j p last r, 6 d, j next long ch, 6 d, p, 3 d, cl, rw. White ch 9 d, 3 p sep 9 d, 9 d, j next p same loop. Repeat once from beginning of row, ch 9 d, 3 p sep 9 d, 9 d, rw. Yellow r 9 d, j second p next loop, 9 d, cl. R 9 d, j first p next loop, 9 d, cl, rw. White ch 9 d, 3 p sep 9 d, 9 d. Repeat around. Tie and cut.

Row 3: With white, r 3 d, p, 3 d, cl, rw. Ch 13 d, j center p on ch previous row, 13 d, rw. R 3 d, p, 3 d, cl. Repeat around. Tie and cut.

Row 4: With white, r 3 d, j r previous row, 3 d, cl, rw. Ch 13 d, p, 13 d, rw. R 3 d, j p next r, 3 d, cl, rw. Ch 13 d, p, 13 d, rw. R 3 d, j same p, 3 d, cl. Continue around.

Outside medallions are made same as side ones, except that they are completed with 10 petals, joining to previous row with a petal to long loop, next two to next ch's, and fourth to next long loop.

Tat a field of daisies for your table. Tatted doily, 11¾" across, makes a pretty place mat in yellow and white. Motif of daisy is shown actual size. In two-color tatting, two shuttles are used.

Padded tatting motif

MATERIALS: Six Cord Crochet, size 10. Tatting shuttle.

Note: In padded tatting, all joinings are made with ball thread, as it would be difficult to draw 4 strands through a picot.

FLORAL MOTIF: Center (make 2): Make r of (l d, p) 6 times; cl r, j in last p. **Rnd 1:** Ch (2 d, j in next p, make smp) 6 times.

Rnd 2: Ch (3 d, j in smp, make smp) 6 times.

Rnd 3: Ch (4 d, j in smp, make smp) 6 times.

Rnd 4: Ch (5 d, j in smp, make smp) 6 times.

Rnd 5: Ch (6 d, j in smp, make smp) 6 times. Tie and cut thread.

Petals: For padding, measure about 6 yards of crochet cotton size 10, fold into 4 equal lengths; tie the 4 strands to shuttle and wind on. Tie the 4 strands to ball thread. Draw through picot of one flower center and ch (3 d, p, 20 d, p, 3 d, j in next p) 6 times, joining first p of every ch to last p of previous ch; do not join last petal to first petal. Rw and ch back, 3 d, j in last p, ch (22 d, j where chains are joined) 6 times, joining last ch in first p of first petal.

Stem and Leaves: Rw, ch 60 d for stem, p, ch 25 d, p, ch 25 d, j in p of stem, 30 d, j in p at point of leaf. Tie and cut. Join in smp of 2nd flower center, ch 30 d, j in bottom p of stem, ch 30 d, j in same p of tatted center. Tie and cut.

Floral motifs in padded tatting ring a circular cloth of pastel linen. Flower petals shown in detail, stems and leaves, are formed over "padding" of four strands of cotton.

Hand Loom Weaving

The looms discussed in this section have little in common with the large 2- and 4-harness looms used by professional weavers which often require considerable space. Weave-It Looms, Loomettes, Multi-Shape Looms, Looper Looms, Crazy Daisy Winders, and Knit-Wits are small, easily portable, and simple to use. Most depend on needles or hooks for interweaving yarns to make a variety of items. They produce relatively small rosettes, squares or rectangles which you must join together to turn out larger articles. Almost all are readily available in art needlework departments, yarn shops, and variety stores.

These looms are mere babies in needlecraft terms: the Looper Loom, for instance, was first manufactured in the mid-1920's as a result of a waste product in the hosiery industry (a loop from the toe of a sock or stocking). The loop stretches to about 7", and the loom was made to accommodate it. The rosettes which the Knit-Wit turns out are an even more recent invention, though rosette *shapes* were in use for such open-work articles as bedspreads four or five hundred years ago in Europe. Early rosettes were made by several different methods, one of which used a board with nails as the basic implement.

These small looms are an answer not only for needleworkers who want to adopt a quick and easy portable craft but for such diverse groups as Scouts and occupational therapists.

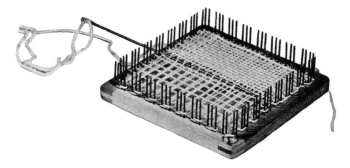

CLOWN

SIZE: 17″ tall.

MATERIALS: Knitting worsted, 2 oz. red; 1 oz. each of white and yellow; ⅓ oz. each of green and orange; small amount of black. 4″ Weave-It loom. Steel crochet hook No. 1. Scraps of black, white and red felt. Matching sewing thread. Cotton for stuffing.

CLOWN: Following directions that come with loom, weave twelve red squares for suit and hat, two white squares for head.

Head: Fold under four corners of both white squares (measure 1″ from corner on each edge); whip squares together, leaving opening for neck. Sew on small black felt circles for eyes, a red circle for nose. Cut out red felt mouth and sew to face with matching sewing thread. With black yarn, embroider around eyes and make straight stitches at outer edges as shown. Embroider a black lazy daisy stitch (see Index) with a yellow stitch in the center above and below each eye. Make a white stitch in center of eye. Cut out white felt ears and sew to head. Stuff head.

Hair: Make three orange tassels as follows: Wind yarn around a 1½″ piece of cardboard 20 times. Tie at one edge; cut at the other. Sew one tassel to each side of head, third one to center back of head.

Hat: Baste from center of one side of a red square to corners of opposite side, forming a triangle; repeat on another red square. Sew sides together on basted lines; turn. Sew hat to head, spreading tassels to look like hair as you work.

Crocheted Brim: With green, ch 53. Dc in 4th ch from hook, * 2 dc in next ch, 1 dc in next ch, repeat from * across. End off. Sew to hat.

Upper Body: Fold two top corners of two red squares same as for head and sew together on folds (shoulders). Sew center opening to head.

Sleeves (make 2): Fold red square in triangle. Fold under each corner at apex (measure 1¼″ from corner on each edge); sew folded edges together, having points of apex inside sleeve. Sew with running stitch along seam and pull to make a slight curve (inside of arm). Stuff sleeve. Sew with running stitch around top of sleeve and round it for armhole; sew between front and back of body and finish sewing side seams of body. Stuff body. Close bottom of sleeve, inserting white felt hand as you sew.

Lower Body: Sew a red square to each of front and back upper body. Sew side seams and stuff. Close center of bottom with three or four stitches, leaving an opening each side for leg.

Legs: For each leg, fold a red square in half and sew side seam. With seam at inside of leg, sew to leg openings of body; stuff and gather at bottom to close.

Foot (make 2): With green, ch 4.

Row 1: Sc in 2nd ch from hook, sc in next 2 ch.

Row 2: Ch 1, turn; 2 sc in first sc, one sc in next sc, 2 sc in last sc—5 sc.

Row 3: Ch 1, turn; 2 sc in first sc, sc in each of next 3 sc, 2 sc in last sc—7 sc. Continue to sc in 7 sc until piece measures 2″. Dec 1 sc at beg of each row until 3 sc remain. End off. Make another piece in same way. Sew together, stuffing as you go. Sew foot to bottom of leg.

Side Pockets (make 2): Fold red square in a triangle; pin. Sew fold to leg about ½″ from waist seam. Sew lower seam of triangle; leave top open.

Dolls (make 2): Wind white yarn around a 3″ piece of cardboard twenty-one times. Tie at one edge of cardboard and cut at other edge as for tassel. Arrange tied end of yarn over a tiny cotton ball and tie about 1″ below top for neck. Cut ten 2½″ strands and tie together ¼″ from each end (arms). Slip arms through center of yarn and tie again (waist). Leave yarn free at bottom for skirt and tie a bow to top of head for girl doll. For boy doll, divide yarn at bottom in two equal parts and tie ¼″ from ends for pants. With black yarn, embroider doll's face. Place a doll in each pocket.

FINISHING: Make six small yellow pompons. Sew three to hat and three to suit as shown.

Wrist Ruffles (make 2): With yellow, ch 23. **Row 1:** Sc in 5th ch from hook, * ch 3, sk 1 ch, sc in next ch, repeat from * across row.

Row 2: Ch 5, turn; sc in first lp, * ch 5, sc in next lp, repeat from * across. End with sl st, leaving a long end. Gather ch to fit around wrist and sew in place.

Ankle Ruffles (make 2): With yellow, ch 33. Work rows 1 and 2 as for Wrist Ruffle.

Row 3: Ch 6, turn; sc in first lp, * ch 6, sc in next lp, repeat from * across row. End with a sl st, leaving a long end for sewing. Gather row of ch to fit around ankle and sew in position.

The clown is made on the 4" Weave-It Loom. The Weave-It squares are sewn together, trimmed with embroidery, stuffed and decorated with pompons.

Weave-it afghan

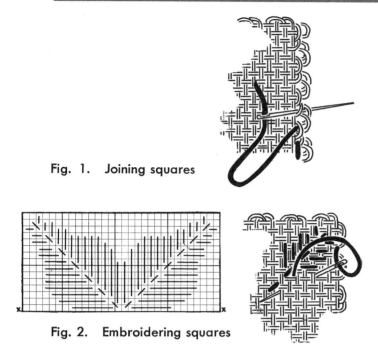

Fig. 1. Joining squares

Fig. 2. Embroidering squares

JOINING WEAVE-IT SQUARES

For a neat joining, it is necessary to know the right side of the squares. To determine right side, hold square so that starting end is in lower left-hand corner, finishing end in upper right. The side facing you is right side.

Place two squares together, right sides facing. Line up edges so that double loops of back square appear between loops of front square, Fig. 1.

Thread long finishing end in needle, insert needle through first loop of front square to back; then through first loop of back square and second loop of front square to front. Continue working in running stitch through first loop of next group on front square and last loop of group on back square; then to front through first loop of next group on back to second loop of group on front.

Draw yarn up snug but not tight. Fasten at end with a slip knot.

AUTUMN LEAVES AFGHAN

SIZE: 34″ x 57″.

MATERIALS: Knitting worsted: 24 ozs. white; 1 oz. each orange, tangerine, and brown. 4″ Weave-It loom. Large-eyed, blunt needle.

DIRECTIONS: Weave 135 white squares for afghan; embroider squares **before** removing from loom to keep tension even. Following chart, embroider over square in straight stitches, working each stitch over front and back so afghan will be reversible (Fig. 2). Each line of chart represents a strand of the woven square. Embroider eight squares with orange flowers, following chart and starting at top of square; X's on chart will be at center; repeat chart in reverse to complete flower. Embroider seven squares with tangerine flowers in same manner. Embroider sixty squares with brown leaves, following chart with row X at one edge of square. Do not embroider remaining squares.

Join squares as directed; sew plain and embroidered squares together to form block design of nine squares. Join blocks, alternating orange and tangerine flowers, to form afghan.

Autumn Leaves Afghan

Adjustable Looms

The multi-shape looms are designed for winding various patterns which are held in place by tying at intersections of yarn. Looms have deep prongs to accommodate several strands of yarn, so that patterns of desired thickness and density can be wound. Below is a sturdy doormat made on rectangular loom of oblong winding held in place with two-way knots.

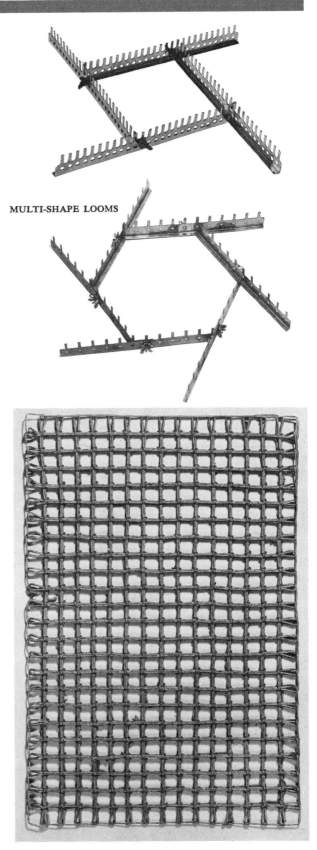

MULTI-SHAPE LOOMS

JUTE DOORMAT

MATERIALS: Jute wrapping cord, seven 50-foot balls. Dritz Multi-Shape Loom. Small flat paint brush. Half pint flat varnish. Turpentine. Two wood strips ¼″ thick and 1″ wide, 12″ and 18″ long.

Put loom together following directions that accompany it, for a 12″ x 18″ mat. Place the two ¼″ strips of wood inside frame, centered one on top of other, to support ends and sides of loom. Wind six layers of cord, according to directions for oblong winding that come with loom. Wind bobbin and tie each intersection with two-way knots (directions with loom).

Leave mat on the loom, dampen well with water. Let dry several days. When dry, remove from frame carefully.

Mix equal parts varnish and turpentine. Paint both sides, saturating mat. Let dry outdoors for a week.

The jute doormat pictured at right is an ideal project for scout troops.

Looper Looms

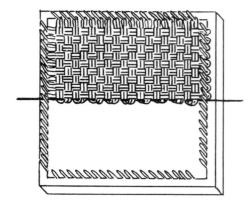

Fig. 1. HALF-SQUARE ON LOOM

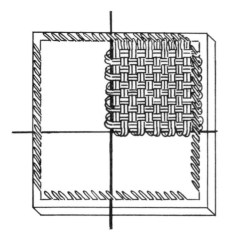

Fig. 2. QUARTER-SQUARE ON LOOM

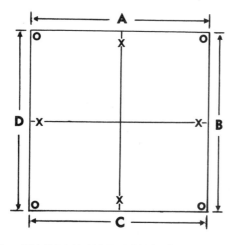

Fig. 3. DIAGRAM FOR JOINING

An unusual use for Looper Loom squares! Now you can make amusing stuffed animals as well as the popular pot holders! Full, half, and quarter squares make Mama Horse and her Baby.

MAMA HORSE AND BABY

EQUIPMENT: Looper loom about 7¼″ square with manufacturer's directions for weaving squares and joining. Two double-pointed knitting needles. Large-eyed needle. Large crochet hook. Scissors. Safety pins.

MATERIALS: Jersey loopers in various colors. Heavy duty thread. Cotton for stuffing. Buttons and beads for eyes.

GENERAL DIRECTIONS: Weave full squares following manufacturer's directions. To weave half-square, see Fig. 1. Place a knitting needle across loom between center prongs; hold in place by hooking the ends of a looper across the back of loom and over ends of knitting needle. Stretch loopers across loom in same direction as knitting needle, filling half of loom. Cross-weave one looper over and under stretched loopers from edge of loom at corner, to knitting needle; bring looper around knitting needle and weave back to next prong on same edge. Repeat with more loopers to fill prongs on one side of loom.

For a quarter-square, see Fig. 2. Place a knitting needle across center of loom as for half-square; place another knitting needle across center of loom in opposite direction and anchor with a looper stretched across back. Stretch a looper from one corner to knitting needle, bring looper around needle and back to next prong on same edge as start. Continue stretching loopers in this manner to fill prongs up to knitting needle placed in opposite direction. Cross-weave by starting a looper on adjacent side of same corner as start, weave over and under loopers to knitting needle, around needle and back to same edge. Continue weaving loopers to fill prongs up to knitting needle.

Before removing squares from loom, run a stay string of heavy thread over and under strands of loopers around edge of weaving just inside loom. It is not necessary to use a stay string on sides that have knitting needles; unhook looper at back that holds needle and leave needle through loopers.

To join squares and lace edges, follow instructions that come with loom, using crochet-hook method.

Make Mama Horse's body by joining four full-size squares together; Baby Horse's body is one square. To form bodies, join sides (Fig. 3) A and B, from O to X's; slip safety pin through last loop. Join sides B and C from O to X's; join sides C and D from O to X's; join sides D and A from O to X's, holding last loops with safety pins. Stuff with cotton. Slip a string through last loops and tie together; remove pins.

For heads, use one square for Mama Horse, a quarter-square for Baby. Following Fig. 3, join sides A and B from O to X's. Repeat for sides B and C, holding last loops with safety pins. On side D, fold corners O to center X, join loops across this end from corners to center. Join edges C and A halfway to first joining; lace loops around remaining opening, tack last loops.

For neck, weave a half-square for Mama Horse and a quarter-square for Baby. Fold half-square in half crosswise; fold quarter square in half. Join ends and tack last loop. Stuff with cotton. Sew one open end to front of body with neck joining up. Sew opposite open end of neck to opening of head. Knot contrast-ing color loopers through neck seam from back, over top of head for mane. Use full loopers for Mama Horse; cut 4″ long strands of loopers for Baby Horse.

Sew on white button eyes with black bead pupils. Sew red or pink felt tongues to bottom of heads. For tails, cut nine loopers in half for Mama; use three 4″ strands for Baby. Run tail loopers through back, making ends even; tie together with short piece of looper, close to body.

For Mama Horse's saddle, weave a half-square in two colors. Insert ends of two loopers through center of narrow end of saddle and pull long ends of loopers through short ends to secure. Braid loopers and tack ends. Repeat at other side of saddle. Place saddle on back and sew ends of braids together under body. For Baby Horse's saddle, wrap two loopers around body and sew ends together at underside. Sew two small looper circles at sides of saddle for stirrups.

For Mama Horse's reins, make two looper braids by joining four loopers at center front of saddle and dividing them in half to make a braid on each side of neck. Join braids at front and tack under body.

Daisy Winder

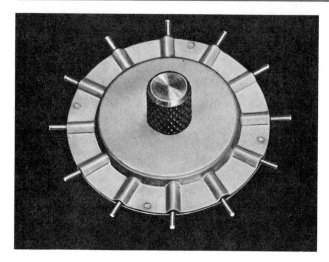

DAISY AFGHAN

SIZE: 48" x 70".

MATERIALS: 34 ozs. Shetland and wool yarn. Daisy Winder. Steel crochet hook No. 2. Tapestry needle.

GAUGE: 1 daisy=2" (with edge).

Follow directions given with Daisy Winder. Make 782 daisies with 12 double petals. Afghan has 34 rows of 23 daisies.

AFGHAN: Note: Join daisies on right side, working in double lps of each of 12 petals. **Row 1:** With yarn, make lp on crochet hook, sc in lps at end of a daisy petal, do not twist petals, * (ch 2, sc) in each of next 3 petals; **for free picot,** ch 5, sl st in front and side lp of last sc, repeat from * once, (ch 2, sc) in 8th and 9th petals; sc in petal of a new daisy, ch 2, sc in next petal of new daisy; **for sl-st joining,** drop lp off hook, insert hook in sc of 8th petal of last daisy and pull dropped lp through, ** ch 2, sc in 3rd petal of new daisy; **for picot-joining,** ch 2, drop lp off hook, insert hook in center ch of p (picot) of last daisy and pull dropped lp through, ch 2, sl st in front and side lp of last sc of new daisy to complete picot-joining; (ch 2, sc) in each of next 3 petals of new daisy, make free p, (ch 2, sc) in each of 7th and 8th petals of new daisy †; sc in petal of a new daisy, ch 2, sc in next petal of new daisy, make sl-st joining as before in 7th petal of last daisy (first and 2nd petals of new daisy joined to 8th and 7th petals of last daisy) **. Repeat from ** to 2nd ** until 23 daisies are joined, end at †. Do not end off. Work as follows:

Complete Edge on Free Petals: Ch 2, sc in 9th petal, make free p as before, * (ch 2, sc) in each of next 3 free petals, make free p, ch 2, make sl-st joining in top of joining-st between last and next daisy, ch 2, sc in next free petal, make picot-joining in cen-

ter ch of last p of last daisy, repeat from * across, ending in 10th petal of 23rd daisy; (ch 2, sc) in each of 11th and 12th petals, ch 2, sl st in sc of first petal, make free p. End off. Mark last p starting point for following daisy rows.

Row 2: Make lp on hook, sc in petal end of a new daisy, (ch 2, sc) in each of next 3 petals; working from right to left across last worked edge of last row, make picot-joining in center ch of marked p, * (ch 2, sc in next petal of new daisy, make sl-st joining in sc of next petal of daisy on last row) twice, ch 2, sc in new petal of new daisy †, make picot-joining in center of the 2 joined p on last row, (ch 2, sc) in each of next 2 petals of new daisy; sc in petal of a new daisy, ch 2, sc in 2nd petal of new daisy, make sl-st joining in sc of 2nd from last joined petal of last daisy of new row, ch 2, sc in 3rd petal of new daisy, make picot-joining in center of the 3 joined p, repeat from * until 23 daisies are joined, end at †, make picot-joining in center ch of free p on last row, (ch 2, sc) in each of 7th and 8th petals of new daisy. Do not end off. Complete edge of free petals as for row 1. Repeat row 2 until 34 rows of 23 daisies are joined.

BORDER: Make lp on hook, from right side, † work sc in 2nd ch-2 sp to left of free corner p, * make p of ch 3 in sc last worked, ch 2, sc in next ch-2 sp, ch 2, sc and p of ch 3 in joining-st between next 2 p, (ch 2, sc) in each of next 2 ch-2 sps of next daisy, repeat from * to within 1 ch-2 sp of next corner; make p of ch 3 in sc last worked, ch 2, sc in next ch-2 sp, ch 2, sc and p of ch 3 in center ch of corner p, ch 2, sc in next ch-2 sp, ch 2, repeat from † 3 times. Join with sl st in first sc. End off. Run in ends on wrong side.

Steam-press afghan lightly, stretching slightly to 48" x 70".

The directions which come with the winder will show you how to make the daisies; the instructions here tell you how to put the daisies together to make the finished afghan opposite.

Daisies done on a Crazy Daisy Winder are joined to make this pretty white afghan.

A McCALL'S NEEDLEWORK & CRAFTS MAGAZINE FEATURE

The Knit-Wit

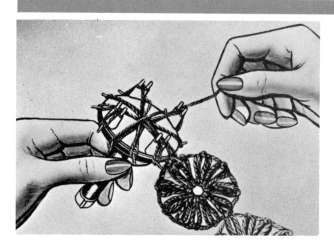

Versatile Knit-Wit can be used to turn out both rosettes and pompons. Two different kinds of articles which can be made with it are pictured on these pages—a baby's set and a panda.

INFANT'S ROSETTE SET

SIZE: Infants'.

MATERIALS: 3 ozs. pompadour yarn. Knit-Wit. Two yards satin ribbon, ½″ wide. Matching sewing thread.

GENERAL DIRECTIONS: Following directions that come with Knit-Wit, make square rosettes with open centers, winding yarn twice around prongs. If fine pompadour is used, wind yarn 3 or 4 times around prongs.

JACKET: BACK: Make 16 rosettes; join in a square, 4 x 4.

FRONTS: Make 16 rosettes; join in 2 separate pieces, 2 x 4.

SLEEVES: Make 18 rosettes; join in 2 separate pieces, 3 x 3. Join opposite sides of one piece to form a tube 3 squares long. Repeat with other piece.

COLLAR: Make 4 rosettes; join in a strip.

FINISHING: Place fronts over back. Join fronts to back at sides for 2½ squares from bottom edge, leaving 1½ squares free at sides for sleeves. Beg at sleeve edge, join 1 square at top of each front to 1 square at each side of back for shoulders, leaving 2 center squares of back and 1 square of each front free for neck edge. Join sleeves to fronts and back at sleeve openings. Join collar to neck edge. For ties, cut 1 yard of ribbon in half. At one end of each piece, form bow by pleating ribbon: first pleat 1½″ deep, 2nd one 1″ deep, 3rd one ½″ deep. Tack bow with matching sewing thread; sew to either front at neck edge under collar.

BONNET: Make 22 rosettes. Join in 3 pieces as follows:

BACK: Join 4 rosettes in a square, 2 x 2.

SIDES AND TOP: Join 12 rosettes in a rectangle, 2 x 6.

CUFF: Join 6 rosettes in a strip.

FINISHING: Place one long edge of piece for sides and top around 3 sides of square for back. Join. Sew cuff to front of cap. Make ribbon ties as for jacket; tack to either side of bonnet over cuff, sewing through cuff and sides of bonnet.

Clip Knit-Wit rosettes to make this appealing stuffed Panda's fur coat.

PANDA

EQUIPMENT: Knit-Wit. Large-eyed needle. Regular sewing needle. Scissors. Ruler. Pencil. Paper.

MATERIALS: Black and white knitting worsted, 1-oz. each. White felt 8″ x 10″. Black felt 6″ x 8″. Black and white thread. India ink. Cotton for stuffing. Round black elastic.

DIRECTIONS: Using patterns on Page 330, cut from white felt two body pieces and a 1¾″ diameter circle for seat. From black felt, cut two arms, two legs, two ears and two eye patches.

Sew body pieces together around head and sides. Stuff firmly with cotton. Sew edge of seat around bottom of body. Cut two ¼″ circles of white felt for eyes and two black felt dots for pupils. Sew pupils to eyes and eyes to eye patches; sew eye patches to either side of head as indicated by dash line on pattern. Draw nose and mouth on head with India ink as shown. Make approximately 46 white yarn Knit-Wit rosettes and 28 black yarn rosettes. Cut all loops on rosettes and trim ends. Sew the white rosettes to body as indicated by X's, on both sides of body (if there appear to be any gaps between rosettes, add more as needed). Sew black rosettes on arm and leg pieces at X's; at double X's sew a rosette on opposite side of felt piece.

Sew arms and legs to body with black elastic, matching dots on limbs and body patterns. Make two tucks on each straight edge of ears. Separate strands of yarn on head at place indicated by dash lines on pattern; sew ears to head.

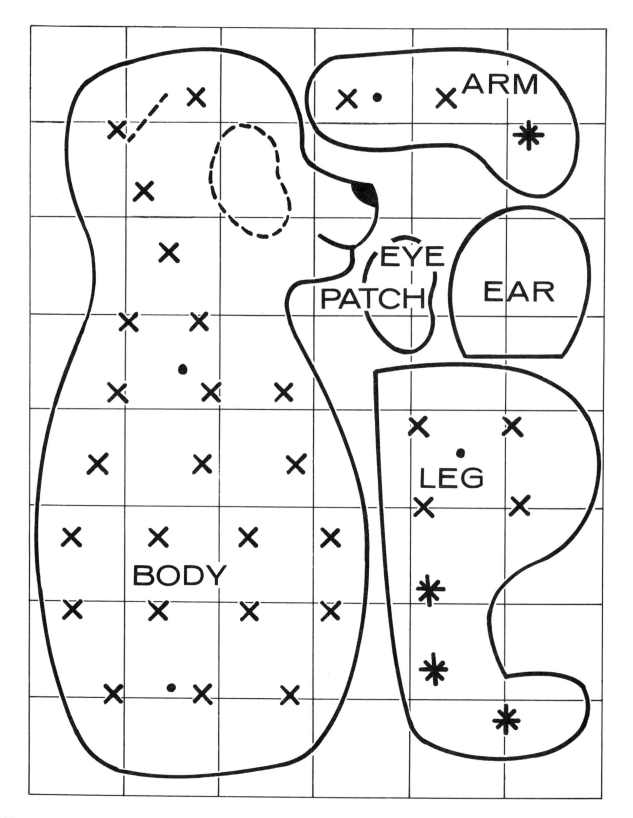

Netting
Laces
Braids

Netting is probably as old as the first primitive peoples who caught fish in nets and small game in snares, but the earliest pictorial evidence we have of it is in Egyptian tombs where figures are shown wearing tunics of netting. Netting, an art all by itself, is the foundation for filet lace when embroidery is worked over the finished netting. Embroidery worked over net meshes ranges from the ancient Persian art of gold and silver threads on silk net, through the modern method of working simple stitches in varying kinds and thicknesses of threads to produce transparent effects.

Bobbin lace (sometimes called pillow lace) gets its name from the bobbins around which the threads to make it are wound. Pins are placed in a predetermined pattern on a bolster pillow; then threads are woven in and out with the various bobbins. Bobbin lace was introduced, apparently, in Genoa in the sixteenth century and its popularity spread rapidly.

Netting

Netting is one of the ancient crafts, and you may want to try your hand at making something in netting—such as a glamorous carry-all bag for evening. Netting ranges from fine to coarse, depending on the thread you use and the size of the mesh sticks which are the basic tools of the craft. The netting lesson given on this and the following two pages will help you learn to net.

DEFINITIONS AND STITCHES

Net Plain: Over needle or mesh stick, net 1 knot (or stitch) in each loop all around.

Net Together: Over knitting needle or mesh stick, draw a given number of loops together with netting needle, and net.

Twin Loops: Two loops coming from one loop in preceding rnd.

Fullness: To prevent circular netting from becoming too tight it is necessary to add fullness to make it lie flat. This is done by netting 2 knots or more in each loop over the mesh stick according to the size required. In a large piece it is necessary to add fullness several times.

Asterisks: An asterisk (*) followed by the word "repeat" means that directions in asterisks should be repeated throughout rnd.

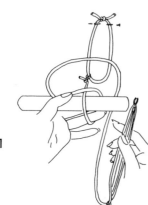

Fig. 1

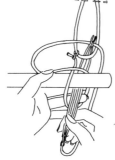

Fig. 2

GENERAL DIRECTIONS

Start counting stitches in foundation loop with the first netted knot. Do not count the tie-in knot.

Mesh sticks are sometimes measured by their circumference, sometimes by width. Follow directions carefully. These sticks are used to obtain wide loops, while knitting needles are used for finer netting. Thread used may be crochet cotton, tatting cotton, or sewing thread for very fine work; knitting worsted, twine and novelty yarns produce a bold effect. To practice, use a coarse crochet cotton.

To thread netting needle, the thread is put through the small hole and firmly knotted with a small knot just large enough to prevent its being pulled back through the hole. The thread is then wound around the ends of the needle through each eye. It is important not to wind too much thread on the needle at one time, since it will not pass through the smaller loops. Cut thread.

To begin netting, first make the foundation loop. This is a piece of thread 9 to 12 inches long securely knotted into a loop and pinned to a firm pillow. Tie end of thread from the netting needle securely onto the foundation loop, using a square knot, or other non-slipping knot, leaving approximately ¼" end. Grip mesh stick between thumb and forefinger of left hand as pictured in Fig. 1.

To tie knot:

Step 1: Take threaded netting needle in right hand and pass the thread over in front of mesh stick, around the two middle fingers, then in back of the mesh stick and up. Grip thread between forefinger and thumb and loop it up and around in a figure-eight fashion (Fig. 1).

Step 2: Pass netting needle over little finger, under the mesh stick, through loop around middle fingers, up through the foundation loop, and over the top of figure-eight loop as in Fig. 2.

Step 3: Draw needle through, pulling it away from you and hooking the trailing looped thread on little finger.

Step 4: Continue pulling thread away from you and release thread held by thumb. Then release loop around the two middle fingers pulling thread away from you until all slack is drawn tight around the mesh stick. Still holding loop with little finger, place knot on top of mesh stick (Fig. 3).

Step 5: Release loop around little finger and pull thread toward you and down over the mesh stick (Fig. 3), holding a taut line from pillow with left hand. Draw thread and knot tight. **Be sure not to release loop around little finger until the knot is on top of mesh stick.**

Make succeeding knots to right of first knot, repeating steps 1 through 5 until desired number of stitches have been taken in the foundation loop. Practice simple knot until you are proficient in tying the knots and making all loops the same length.

Practice: Proceed as in steps 1 to 5 above, netting 10 stitches in the foundation loop over the mesh stick. When the end of the row is reached, remove mesh stick, turn your work over, and start another row beginning with step 1, and net once in each loop (Figs. 1A, 2A and 3). To widen work, net twice in each inside loop. Continue practice until loops are uniform and knots tight.

When tying on a newly threaded needle, leave at least a two-inch thread on your work. Tie the joining knot as close to the netted knot as possible. You cannot pull a knot through netting.

Correcting Mistakes: Netting knots may be untied quite easily by using a sewing needle. If round is too tight it may be necessary to cut off entire round. This may be done by cutting as close to the knots as possible until you get near the starting point. Then untie knots with a needle to clear about a 2-inch thread. Tie new thread onto this thread end and continue. Go back around work and untie all the other knots with needle to get out the small pieces of thread.

Note: If wider mesh sticks are used than specified in directions, also use a size larger knitting needle than size specified.

When directions state that thread is to be put twice around needle, remember that you have the thread over the needle to start, so once more around will make the loop twice as long, giving the desired stitch.

If your round comes out short a loop, net 2 in last loop to add. If you have too many loops net 2 together to subtract.

"Net three in each, or more" means net three knots.

Always have thread over mesh stick or knitting needle to start netting. All other threads go back of mesh stick.

Circular Netting: Prepare the foundation loop and net the desired number of stitches into it over a mesh stick. Remove foundation loop from pillow and, with thumb and forefinger, force all netting onto one end of foundation loop, being careful not to entangle the netting. Holding netting with one hand, tie a square

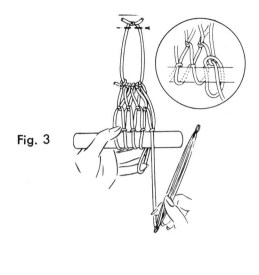

Fig. 3

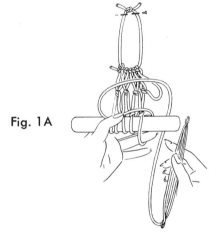

Fig. 1A

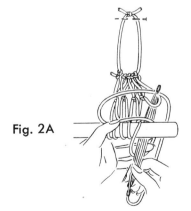

Fig. 2A

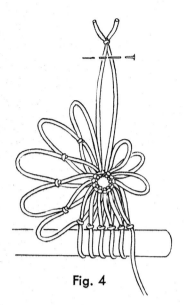

Fig. 4

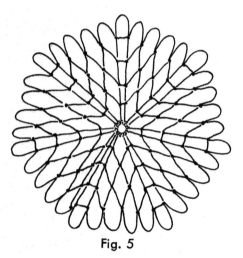

Fig. 5

knot with both threads of the foundation loop. Force this knot down against netting to form a small circle in the center of work. This knot must be secure or the center of your work will pull loose. After the center is tied, pin the foundation loop back onto a pillow and spread netting out in a circle as in Fig. 4. Now begin netting the 2nd round. (Remove the mesh stick at end of each round and begin as in step 1.) Mark beginning of round so you will know when a round is completed. Net 3rd round, 4th round, etc. When the article is finished, thread a sewing needle with both threads of the foundation loop and weave around the center of work over and under loops of first round. This will reinforce the center thread. It is well to leave a ¼″ thread end when tying knots or ending in order to prevent pulling out or raveling of ends of thread.

Circular Netting with Increasing: Net 7 loops into the foundation loop and tie up ring together. Net two stitches in each loop on the 2nd round. For the 3rd round, net 2 stitches in first loop, 1 plain and repeat. In succeeding rounds, net 2 stitches in first loop and add an additional plain stitch to the number netted between the increases in the preceding round (Fig. 5).

Gold mesh carry-all

EQUIPMENT: Extra-large netting needle. ¾″ mesh stick. Large-eyed needle. Firm pillow; pin. Scissors. Colorless nail polish. Crochet hook size 00.

MATERIALS: Narrow gold soutache braid, about 30 yards. Chiffon scarf and one yard of matching velvet ribbon, if desired.

DIRECTIONS: Cut the braid into three-yard pieces for working ease; dab colorless nail polish on each cut end to prevent fraying. Prepare a foundation loop (see General Directions) and net 15 stitches into it. Proceed as for Circular Netting. To make bag size shown, net 20 rounds; net fewer rounds if smaller bag is desired. Tie on new threads at the point a netting knot would be made. When bag is completed, trim all ends and dab again with nail polish.

For handle, crochet two soutache chains, each about 18″ long. Weave each chain in and out of last round of netting from opposite directions. Tie together ends of each chain; weave ends back into chain, using large-eyed needle. (Or make handle of velvet ribbons.)

Note: This bag may be made of nylon knitting worsted if a more utilitarian carry-all is desired.

*A practical carry-all bag to make in gold sou-
tache braid for dress occasions, or in strong
yarn for everyday use.*

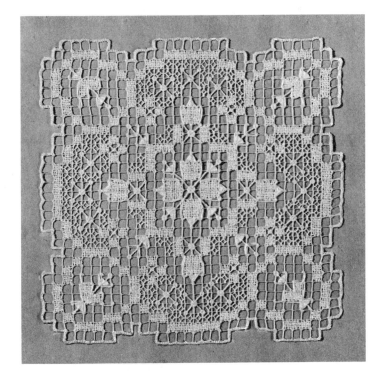

*The foundation of filet lace is netting. Net
meshes are ornamented with variations of
simple weaving, buttonholing, and darning
—and a lace is born! To make the Flower
Centered Doily above, net is sewn in a frame;
when embroidery is complete, outline of
doily is buttonholed and net beyond is cut
away. Both ground and embroidery are in
No. 50 linen thread. This 7¼" square is
worked over 32 meshes.*

Filet lace

The novice lace maker should begin by working a lace sampler like the one on this page, using the motif instructions on the next page. Netting is the foundation for the embroidery which consists basically of darning, weaving and buttonholing stitches. Endlessly varied combinations of these make up the exquisite finished designs so much admired in handmade lace.

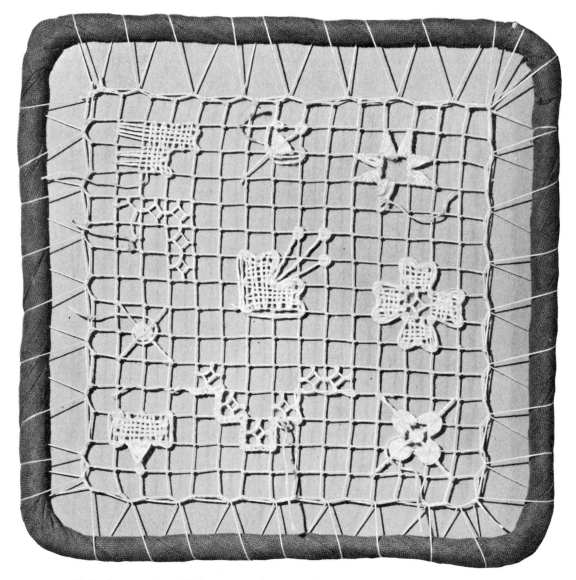

Netted square is pulled taut on a home-made frame for practicing filet lace making.

MATERIALS: Netting needle. Mesh stick ½″ in circumference. Tapestry needle for embroidery. Linen or cotton thread—for netting, No. 50 to 100; for embroidery, No. 30 to No. 50. For frame—stiff steel wire, strips of outing flannel, bias binding tape.

To practice the netting and embroidery, use a coarse cotton.

To Net Filet Square: Tie thread to foundation loop and follow instruction for Lesson in Netting, netting 2 stitches in the foundation loop to start. Turn work over and make next row as follows: Net once in first loop, twice in last loop. Work succeeding rows by netting once in each loop except last; net twice in last loop. Continue in this manner until there is one more loop in row than number of meshes required for embroidery design. Work one row of knots without increasing, then on next row decrease one knot by putting netting needle through last two loops in row at one time, netting them as one knot. The buttonholing worked around design area will be easier to do if two extra rows of mesh are netted. Netting is used as foundation for the embroidery.

To make frame for embroidering: Bend wire to the shape required, making it bigger than netted piece. Fasten ends and wrap strips of flannel around wire. Then wrap with tape, sew end down. Secure netted piece inside frame by taking long stitches through net and over frame, stretching net evenly all around.

Edges of doilies are finished with buttonholing done over mesh threads. Netting outside buttonholing is then cut away close to knots.

Filet lace motifs

Note: Motifs are in three columns; start at top left of Sampler on Page 336.

No. 1: Cloth stitch is plain darning stitch. The number of threads darned in each netted mesh depends on size of mesh. Four rows of threads were used in each mesh in sampler and in doily. Darn under and over in one direction to cover foundation netting. Then darn under and over threads and netting in opposite direction.

No. 2: Loop stitch is done in buttonhole-stitch fashion, from left to right. Take stitches from one horizontal bar of mesh to another, leaving loops between stitches. On return row, turn work around and work stitches over next row of horizontal bars and catch loops to vertical bars by passing needle over loop, under bar, over loop.

No. 3: To make a rosette, fasten thread in center of four meshes, make four diagonal spokes from center to corner and back, twisting threads as you go, then to opposite corner and back and to remaining corners in same way. At center, weave over and under spokes and mesh.

No. 4: Make cloth stitch (No. 1) first over two squares. Then work weaving stitches around end and half of side by weaving over and under meshes. To make point, do a series of buttonhole stitches in pyramid shape on vertical bar at center by weaving around horizontal bar at one side, then buttonholing on vertical bar and weaving around horizontal bar at other side, etc., until point is formed. Continue weaving stitches along other half of side and end.

No. 5: Make a single spoke from one corner of a mesh, diagonally across two meshes to opposite corner, with a small rosette at end. Bring thread halfway back, twisting around first thread. Weave triangular section over and under side threads of mesh and spoke. Carry thread back to point of triangle and make weaving stitches from point, along sides, to corners and back.

No. 6: Work cloth stitch (No. 1) over three meshes in an L shape. Bring thread to center of L and make the three spokes with rosettes, as shown. Then work weaving stitches all around cloth stitch.

No. 7: For edging, work loop stitch (No. 2) to form desired shape; at same time, do two rows of long padding stitches on outer edge. Work buttonhole stitch over padding; cut away meshes outside.

No. 8: Star flower is made by first taking two buttonhole stitches on the long side of the petal. Then take weaving stitches from end of buttonhole stitches to center, crossing threads, with the last thread at pointed end of petal, over netted knot. There are two petals on each side. Finish with loop stitch in the center mesh if desired.

No. 9: The four-petal flower is composed of cloth stitch (No. 1) squares around a center of loop stitch (No. 2). Outline the petals with weaving stitches.

No. 10: Tie thread at corner of mesh for center, make a diagonal spoke to opposite corner above and back. Continue spoke diagonally over two meshes and back to center, then make two more spokes in opposite direction and back to center. Weave around center a few times. Work petals separately in outer meshes by weaving over and under one spoke and two mesh threads on each side eight times.

The elaborate-appearing results of filet lace are achieved by combining the basic stitches above, which are forms of weaving, buttonholing and darning.

Edges of doily are finished with buttonholing done over mesh threads in desired shape. Netting outside buttonholing is then cut away close to knots.

Follow illustration for placing and combining Filet Lace Motifs to make doily shown on page 335.

Bobbin Lace

Bobbin lace is made by winding thread on bobbins, which are crossed and twisted over a paper pattern held in place by pins on a bolster. (To construct bolster, see Index: Lace Loom.) The threads must be tied snugly around the pins to keep the mesh even and show no unsightly loops or irregularities. The paper pricking over which lace is made determines width and mesh of lace although details of design may vary. If pricking is cared for by inserting pins carefully and at right angles to bolster, the lace will evolve with mathematical accuracy and pattern will last a long time. A plastic spray will lengthen the life of a pricking.

Before starting to weave a piece of lace, notice, especially, that the larger the space between points to be spanned, the more twists are needed in the threads to keep the lace firm and clean-cut.

TO MAKE PRICKINGS

Place piece of 3″ x 16″ tough wrapping paper under pricking patterns. Bottom edge of paper should be flush with bottom of patterns. Hold wrapping paper in place firmly with pieces of Scotch tape. Prick all dots of patterns through. Remove wrapping paper and repeat to complete 12 inch long pattern pricking. (Cut through Scotch tape to remove; pulling away may tear paper.) Draw in lines showing repeats of pattern. Copy large and small numbers to pattern at least 3 repeats. Cut patterns apart.

Note: Attach bobbins at points directly below large numbers on patterns. Number indicates number of bobbins to attach. Small numbers indicate order in which pins are placed as work proceeds. (Unless otherwise indicated, pin is always placed between the 2 pair of threads forming last stitch.)

Apron with lace insets

This crisp, cool apron, made of sheer lawn, features two lace designs sewn together. Complete instructions for making the apron and lace insets are on the following pages.

How to make bobbin lace

THREE STEPS IN MAKING BASIC "WHOLE STITCH"

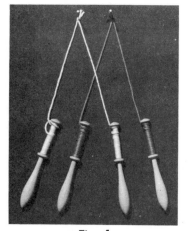

Fig. 1

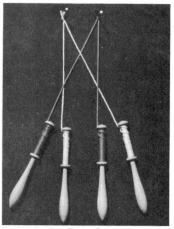

Fig. 2

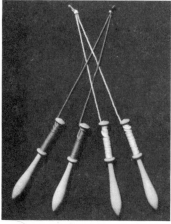

Fig. 3

TO START WORK

Remove bolster from box (see Index: Lace Loom) and pin pricking pattern around bolster with bottom of strip lapping *over* top end and two repeat lines coinciding. Place bolster back in box so numbers may be read from working position and fasten to tape at back of box.

As a rule, two pairs of bobbins are handled at a time, one pair being controlled by left hand, one pair by right. Notice in Fig. 3, how these two pairs are crossed and twisted to form the fundamental Whole Stitch. Study and practice Figs. 1, 2, and 3 before starting to make lace. Half Stitch is merely the last two movements of the Whole Stitch, or Twist and Cross, Fig. 4.

A continual repetition of half stitches makes what is called a Braid. Tie threads of 4 bobbins together, attach to pillow and practice making a braid.

HINTS WHILE WORKING

When about 2 inches of lace have been made, start taking pins from rear of bolster to use in front as you need them.

When lace starts to ride up on pins, instead of lying flat against pattern, free bolster tape; turn bolster back a bit, and re-fasten tape with pin.

When thread on bobbin is all used, rewind bobbin and tie new thread end to old with weaver's or square knot. Clip close.

Fig. 1. Cross: Wind 4 bobbins, as illustrated, making loop around head as shown on first bobbin, left. Tie thread ends in pairs and attach pairs to bolster, 1″ apart, with pins. A Cross is always made by placing left center bobbin over the right center bobbin.

Fig. 2. Twist: When making Cross, two bobbins change positions; nevertheless, the first two bobbins left are *always* pair No. 1, the third and fourth bobbins are *always* pair No. 2. A Twist is made by placing right bobbin of each pair over left bobbin.

Fig. 3. Whole Stitch is made in three movements, 1) Cross, 2) Twist, 3) Cross again. Cross and Twist are made. Make another Cross and complete the Whole Stitch. Put a pin between pairs 1 and 2 and repeat whole stitch until it becomes familiar.

Two lace designs

ABBREVIATIONS

P—Point
C—Cross
Pr—Pair
T—Twist
Bobs—Bobbins
H St—Half Stitch
TC—Twist and Cross
Wh St—Whole Stitch

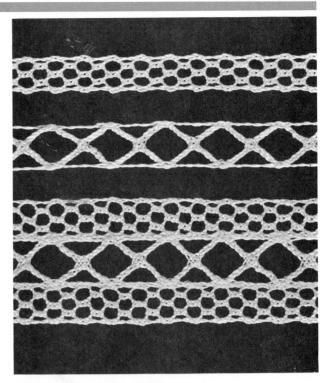

PEEP-HOLE INSET A

MATERIALS: Wind 12 bobbins with No. 50 linen thread.

Step 1: With Prs 1 and 2, T C twice, insert pin at P 1, T C twice.

Step 2: With Prs 2 and 3, T C twice, insert pin at P 2, T C twice. Continue making 2 T C's before and after inserting pins at consecutive points, each time using a new pair of bobbins. When P 5 has been tied, start with Prs 1 and 2 again, tying point at extreme left, moving to right.

TOP: PEEP-HOLE INSET "A".
CENTER: CRISSCROSS INSET "B".
BOTTOM: COMBINES "A" AND "B".

CRISSCROSS INSET B

MATERIALS: 12 bobbins wound with No. 50 linen thread.

The length of braid in lace calls for 4 half-stitches. Braid to P 1 means T C 4 times in the direction of P 1. Attach 6 bobs at each of points in pattern B.

Step 1: With Prs 4 and 5, braid to P 1.

Step 2: With Prs 2 and 3, braid to P 1.

Step 3: With Prs 3 and 4, Wh St; with Prs 4 and 5, Wh St; with Prs 2 and 3, Wh St.

Step 4: Insert pin at point 1 (between Prs 3 and 4). Pull all threads snugly around pin. Repeat Step 3 and pull threads again snugly around pin.

Step 5: With Prs 4 and 5 braid to P 2; with Pr 6, T 5 times; with Prs 5 and 6, Wh St; with Prs 4 and 5, Wh St; insert pin at P 2.

Step 6: With Prs 4 and 5, Wh St; with Prs 5 and 6, Wh St.

Step 7: With Prs 2 and 3, braid to P 3; with Pr 1, T 5 times; with Prs 1 and 2, Wh St; with Prs 2 and 3, Wh St; insert pin at P 3.

Step 8: With Prs 2 and 3, Wh St; with Prs 1 and 2, Wh St. Repeat from Step 1.

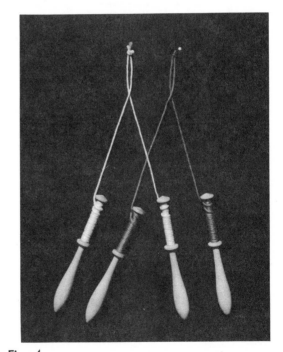

Fig. 4
"HALF STITCH" USED FOR CRISSCROSS AND PEEP-HOLE LACES.

Apron with lace insets

MATERIALS: 1 yd. sheer lawn; 69″ of Peep-Hole Inset A, 34½″ of Crisscross Inset B; No. 100 sewing thread.

To Make Inset (A & B): Cut Peep-Hole Inset in half and overcast one piece to either side of Crisscross Inset. Cut inset A and B into 2 pieces, one piece 7½″ and 1 piece 27″ long.

Cutting: Mark out and cut all apron pieces on thread lines from chart measurements. Note dotted lines on chart, one 10″ and one 11½″ from bottom of pattern. These indicate threads pulled to within 1″ of apron side edges.

Apron Skirt (A): Cut selvages from lawn. Baste and then sew each edge of 27″ inset A & B along one of the lines made by pulling threads, beginning ½″ from end of inset (right side up) and 1″ from edge of cloth. Sew to within 1″ from other side, and clip lace ½″ from end of sewing. Starting at center, cut away material from back of inset ¼″ from sewing, being careful not to cut lace. Cut to within 1¼″ of edges of cloth. Cut 4 diagonals from these points to ends of sewing. Fold back raw edges of material

all around lace. Push lace ends through to wrong side of apron and baste to folds. Turn in side hems of apron to meet folds and cover lace ends. Baste and hem. Turn up apron hem to edge of inset. Baste and hem. Trim material at other edge of inset to about ⅛″ and whip (Fig. 4). Make double gather at top of apron ¼″ from edge, and pull in to 17″. Do not fasten off threads until waistband is in place.

Pocket (B & C): Turn in long edges of B, bring folds together, raw edges inside. Baste. Overcast one edge of 7½″ piece of inset to double fold. Whip other long edge of C. Fold back 3 raw edges of pocket ¼″ and baste pocket to apron as shown on chart. Slipstitch neatly in place.

Waistband (D) and Ties (E 1 & 2): Make ⅛″ hem on one end of each tie. Pleat other end to make it 1″ wide. Fold waistband in middle, lengthwise. Backstitch pleated ends of ties to band, one at each end and on same side of fold. Backstitch side of band with ties attached to apron top. Fold in other 3 edges of band ¼″. Hem long edge to gather line of apron. Hem band ends to ties.

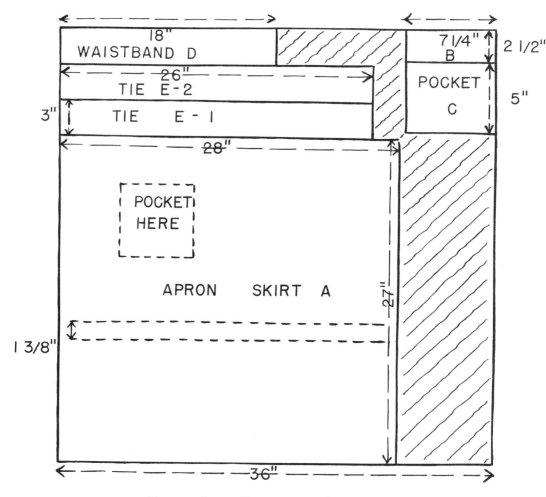

Diagram for making apron with lace inset.

Finishing and joining laces

Finishing Raw Ends of Lace: When desired length of lace is made, allow plenty for joining or turning back the ends. Cut off bobbins close to pins. Remove all pins carefully. Seal ends with any transparent cement to prevent raveling. Inset pieces, such as are used in the apron, opposite, should be measured, motifs matched and cut accurately, ends cemented and turned back so that folded part is entirely hidden by the pattern of the lace. With No. 80 thread, sew end firmly in this position for ½" from fold, using same method as for mitering corners (Fig. 2). Cut close to sewing. Use No. 100 thread for sewing finer laces.

Making Turned Corners: Most laces made to encircle an entire article must be mitered at four corners (Figs. 1 & 2) before sewing to cloth or other lace pieces. Note how corner is brought to a right angle at the most convenient point for sewing. When lace has been sewn to preserve this perfect angle, cut on fold, separate ends and couch them down to flatten and hide them.

Attaching Lace to Material: There are two distinctly different methods used in attaching handmade lace to material. **1. Overcasting** is the most popular and is used to join two pieces of lace or to join lace to a hemmed edge of material after laces have been basted together. **2. Whipping** (Fig. 4) makes a beautiful finish for fine linens and should be used whenever practical. A thread should be pulled out 3/16" from edge of material. The lace, right side up, should then be basted and overcast along this line (Fig. 3) with small invisible stitches, the article turned over, edge of material folded back at edge of lace, turned under and whipped, with needle piercing fold and edge of lace.

All straight edges of cloth used for making beautiful finished pieces should be cut on a thread. Articles should be pressed on wrong side under a damp cloth and over a Turkish towel or padded board.

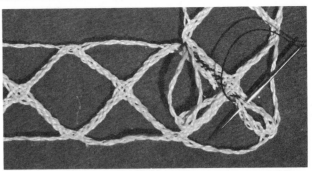

Fig. 1.   To miter lace, form right angle, sew before cutting fold.

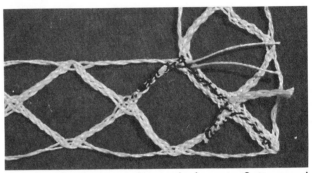

Fig. 2.   Separate ends, couch down to flatten and hide ends neatly.

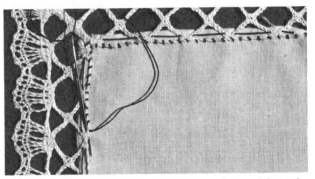

Fig. 3.   Baste lace to pulled thread on right side of linen, and overcast invisibly.

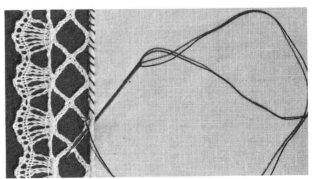

Fig. 4.   Edge of linen is rolled, hemmed on wrong side, lace flush with finished edge.

Braiding and Knotting

Create bands of trimmings with bobbins and yarns. Designed with a flexible "on-the-bias" character to fit smoothly around curved edges, they are a stunning finish for knit or crocheted garments. The width of the braid is controlled by the number of strands and weight of the yarn. A lacelike openwork effect is obtained by knotting at regular intervals.

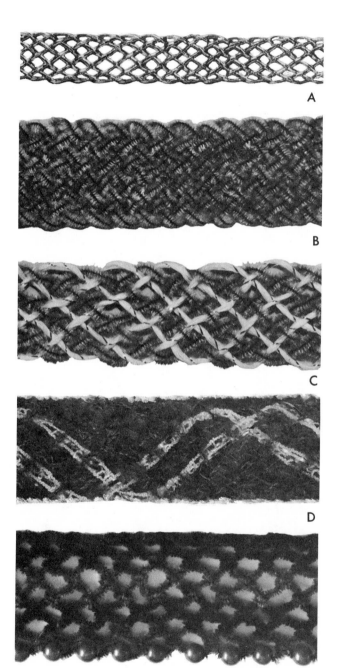

BRAIDED AND KNOTTED TRIMS

EQUIPMENT: Working surface: All trims shown must be made on a foundation into which pins may be pushed and held in an upright position. This foundation may be a piece of Celotex or other soft wallboard, a "pillow" such as used in making bobbin lace (see Index: Lace Loom). Trims made on a revolving loom work up more quickly than those made on a flat surface because work does not have to be removed from pattern until finished. Use a 17″ square of wallboard for a good flat surface; pad it with a piece of blanket or other thick material; cover padding with soft, dark cloth.

Bobbins: Use a special bobbin made for this work or a knitting bobbin, hand weaving shuttle bobbin or handmade paper bobbin will do.

Pins: You will need about 60 pins. If a "pillow" or revolving bolster is used, ordinary dressmaker pins will do. If a wallboard surface is used, glass-headed pins are better—small heads of ordinary pins are hard on fingers.

Patterns: Two are given on the opposite page— No. 1 is for fine yarns or close-meshed trims; No. 2, for heavier yarns or open-meshed trims.

Make patterns from strips of pliable cardboard. Use a 10″ strip for a flat surface; for a revolving bolster, use a strip long enough to encircle bolster.

Trace pattern. Place cardboard strip under tracing. Hold cardboard firmly in place and prick through all dots with a pin. Move up cardboard, lining up bottom row of holes on cardboard with top row of dots on diagram. Continue pricking until entire length of cardboard has been marked. Now, with pencil, connect pricked points as shown on diagram, and print on letters and numerals. Fasten pattern to top center of flat surface, or around revolving bolster.

See page 347 for directions for making the four braided trims, A, B, C, and D; and page 348 for the knotted trim, E.

MATERIALS: Estimate amount of yarn needed by the following chart.

For 1 yd. of braided trim:
Over pattern No. 1—1¾ yds. per strand
Over pattern No. 2—1½ yds. per strand

For 1 yd. of knotted trim:
Over pattern No. 1—4 yds. per strand
Over pattern No. 2—3 yds. per strand

Variations in yarns and in the individual handling of them will make some difference in amount of yarn required. To gauge amount of yarn needed and help to familiarize yourself with the technique, make a trial piece of knotting or braiding with ½ yd. strands of yarn before beginning actual full-length trim.

Note: Chenille yarns are apt to twist together when being cut. A gentle shake as you pull them apart will untwist them.

GENERAL DIRECTIONS: Wind required number of bobbins with yarn, leaving an 8″ end. Knot ends of yarn together in pairs—six-ply trims will have three pairs; eight-ply trims, four pairs; etc. Pin knots to lettered points on top line of pattern and allow all strands to hang straight from pins without crossing one another. *First strand on left is always referred to as bobbin 1, second strand is bobbin 2, etc.* As braiding or knotting progresses, strands, of course, change places.

Working Procedures: While working, be sure that pins are upright at all times. Leave enough pins in place along edge of trim to hold it firmly in position. Knotted trims require fewer "holding" pins than braided trims because knots themselves tend to hold trim in shape.

When working braiding on a flat surface, complete 10″ of braiding, then remove work and move 5″ of it up beyond top of pattern. Re-pin remaining 5″ to top half of pattern and continue braiding. When working knotting on a flat surface, remove completed 10″ and move up, re-pinning at least 14 of the completed knots at top of pattern. Match knots to holes by piercing each knot and pinning in hole.

If joining is necessary, free bobbin, leaving at least 6″ of thread; wind bobbin with second length and join strands with square knot. Continue braiding. When within 2″ of knot, pierce knot with pin and insert pin 2″ above finished braid so that new strand is held taut at point of braiding. Continue braiding. When work is off pattern, knot may be cut ½″ from braid and ends sewn invisibly to wrong side of braid.

Finishing Trims: Before removing finished trim, fasten ends of yarn with a piece of Scotch tape. Then remove trim and stitch across yarns close to tape.

PATTERN NO. 1

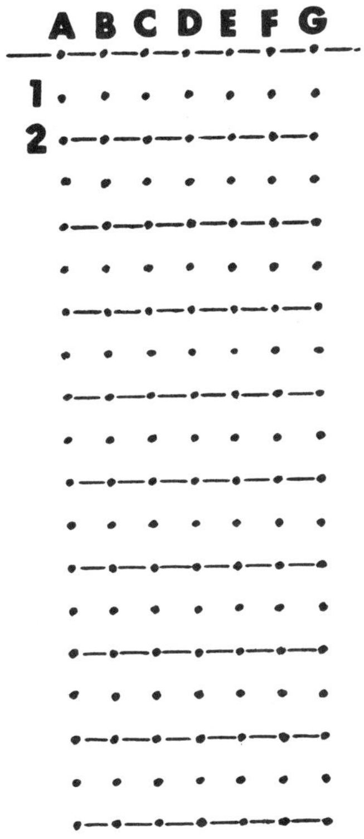

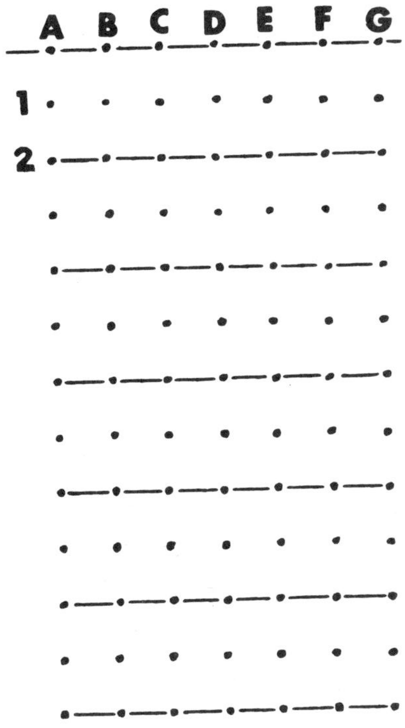

PATTERN NO. 2

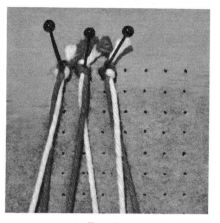

Fig. 1

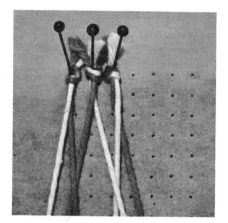

Fig. 2

BRAIDING: The preliminary steps in working a braid consist in "setting up" and "lining up" the strands. The set-up is simply the fastening of the paired strands to the top of pattern. The line-up is the arranging of strands before starting to braid.

Six-Ply Braid (Figures 1 to 4): **To set up:** Attach six bobbins, one pair at each of points A, B and C. (See P. 345. Use either Pattern 1 or Pattern 2, depending on the thickness of your yarn.) **To line up:** Place bobbin 2 over bobbin 1, 4 over 3, 6 over 5 (Fig. 1). Place 2 over 3, 4 over 5 (Fig. 2). Place 4 over 3 (Fig. 3).

To braid: Step 1—Place a pin at point A1, between bobbins 1 and 2. Place another pin at point C1, between bobbins 5 and 6. Step 2—With bobbin 1, weave under 2, over 3. With bobbin 6, weave over 5, under 4, over 3.

Continue, repeating steps 1 and 2, placing two pins directly below two preceding pins. (Fig. 4).

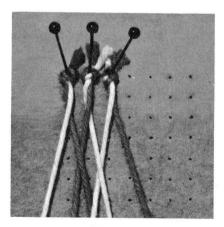

Fig. 3

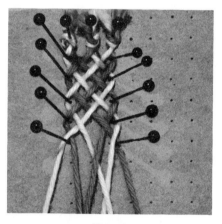

Fig. 4

Eight-Ply Braid (Fig. 5): **To set up:** Attach eight bobbins, one pair at each of points A, B, C and D. (See Patterns 1 and 2 on page 345.) **To line up:** Place bobbin 2 over bobbin 1, 4 over 3, 6 over 5, 8 over 7. Place 2 over 3, 4 over 5, 6 over 7. Place 4 over 3, 6 over 5. Place 4 over 5.

To braid: Step 1—Place a pin at point A1, between bobbins 1 and 2. Place a pin at point D1, between bobbins 7 and 8. Step 2—With bobbin 1, weave under 2, over 3, under 4. With bobbin 8, weave over 7, under 6, over 5.

Repeat steps 1 and 2, placing two pins directly below two preceding pins.

Ten-Ply Braid (Fig. 6): **To set up:** Attach ten bobbins, one pair at each of points A, B, C, D and E. (See page 345.) **To line up:** Place bobbin 2 over bobbin 1, 4 over 3, 6 over 5, 8 over 7, 10 over 9. Place 2 over 3, 4 over 5, 6 over 7, 8 over 9. Place 4 over 3, 6 over 5, 8 over 7. Place 4 over 5, 6 over 7. Place 6 over 5.

To braid: Step 1—Place a pin at point A1, between bobbins 1 and 2. Place a pin at point E1, between bobbins 9 and 10. Step 2—With bobbin 1, weave under 2, over 3, under 4, over 5. With bobbin 10, weave over 9, under 8, over 7, under 6, over 5.

Continue, repeating steps 1 and 2, and placing two pins at points directly below two preceding pins.

Figs. 5 and 6 show eight- and ten-ply braid lined up.

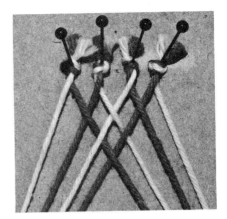

Fig. 5

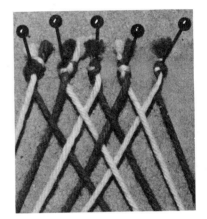

Fig. 6

DIRECTIONS FOR BRAIDED TRIMS
Shown on Page 344

BRAID "A": Eight-ply braid of gold cordé is made on pattern No. 1 (page 345).

BRAID "B": Ten-ply braid of chenille is made on pattern No. 2 (page 345).

BRAID "C": Ten-ply braid of chenille and a contrasting yarn is made on pattern No. 2 (page 345). Bobbins 1, 4, 5, 8, and 9 are chenille; bobbins 2, 3, 6, 7, and 10 are contrasting yarn.

BRAID "D": Ten-ply braid of chenille and a contrasting yarn is made on pattern No. 2 (page 345). Bobbins 1, 4, 5, 6, 7, 8, 9, and 10 are chenille; bobbins 2 and 3 are contrasting yarn.

Note: Braids may be individualized to your own needs by using other yarns.

Detail A: If you need to join yarns to make a finished braid, see instructions on P. 345.

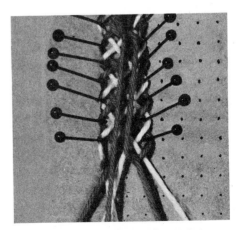

DETAIL A: JOINING YARN

HOW TO KNOT

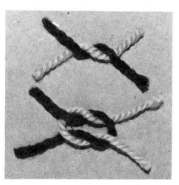

Fig. 1

Fig. 2

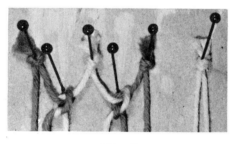

Fig. 3

KNOTTING: Knotted trims can be close and thick or open and lacy, depending upon the pattern used. A thin yarn, knotted over pattern 2, (See Page 345) will be open and lacy; a heavy yarn, knotted over pattern 1, (Page 345) will be close and thick.

Directions given here are for an eight-ply knotted trim. Six-, ten- and twelve-ply trims are tied in same way except, of course, that fewer or more strands are attached to pattern. Granny's Knot is shown in Fig. 1, Square Knot is shown in Fig. 2.

Eight-Ply Knotting (Fig. 3): **To set up:** Attach eight bobbins, one pair at each of points A, C, E and G. **To tie:** Step 1—Place pins at points B1, D1, and F1, between the pairs of strands. Step 2—Tie Granny's Knots around these three pins, using one strand from each of the two pairs nearest each pin. Step 3—Place pins at A2, C2, E2 and G2, dividing strands into three pairs with a single strand at each edge. Step 4—Tie Granny's Knots around these four pins as in Step 2. Repeat these four steps, placing pins in holes directly below preceding pins.

KNOTTED AND BEADED TRIM "E"
Shown on Page 344, Worked on Pattern No. 2

MATERIALS: Equal amounts of navy and bright red chenille (allow 1 yd. per strand for each 10″ of finished fringe); red beads ¼″ in diameter (24 for 10″ of fringe); eight bobbins.

To set up: Wind four bobbins with blue chenille, four bobbins with red. Thread one red strand with 24 beads. Attach one pair blue chenille at each of points A and E, one pair red at each of points C and G. Allow beaded strand to hang in position of bobbin 8.

To tie: Step 1—Place pins at points B1, D1 and F1 between the pairs of strands.

Step 2—Tie square knots (Fig. 2) around these three pins, using one strand from each of the two pairs nearest each pin.

Step 3—Place pins at A2, C2, E2 and G2, dividing strands into three pairs with a single strand at each edge. Push one bead up close to pin directly above.

Step 4—Tie square knots around these four pins, as in step 2. Knot at G2 should close bead into space above. Repeat steps 1 to 4.

Technical Aids

The current professional approach to designing, making, and finishing handwork has taken needlework of all kinds away from the homemade look and out of the amateur field. Today's needlework has been developed to a very high degree of perfection and the handmade item is the prestige item. This doubtless is one of the reasons why hand-knitted and crocheted garments have become high fashion, and unusual handmade accessories for the home are sought by leading decorators. In this section we give you much of the technical know-how for obtaining these professional results.

The choice of equipment is of utmost importance The good workman also knows and understands the materials with which he is creating an object, so he chooses the material which is best suited to the purpose.

While this is a learn-and-make book, it is our hope that readers will not only learn the basic techniques of needlework but will develop to the point where they can create their own designs. In this section we have given you many helpful aids for designing, working and finishing needlework. Here is one more important suggestion. Be sure that you know how to do the stitch or stitches with which you plan to execute the designs, and have tried out the stitches with the type of yarns you plan to use on a sample of the background material. Then design within the limitations of your materials and take full advantage of them.

Embroidery Equipment

Once you decide to make an embroidered piece, it is important to collect the proper equipment. Not many items are needed, so choose the best you can afford. Good tools produce good work. Learn to use your embroidery accessories properly and you will find your work to be neater.

Different embroidery techniques require different needles. For embroidery on fabric, be sure your needles are smooth and sharp. Embroidery needles are rather short and have a long, slender eye. They are made in sizes 1 to 12; the higher numbers are the finest. Blunt needles are used for needlepoint, huck weaving and embroidery on net. Keep a good selection of needles on hand and protect them by storing them in a needle case. It is also advisable to run your needles through an emery strawberry occasionally to clean and sharpen them. To thread yarn or stranded floss through the needle eye, double it over the end of the needle and slip it off, holding it tightly as close as possible to the fold. Push the flattened, folded end through the needle eye and pull yarn through.

You will need proper scissors. Embroidery scissors should be small, with narrow, pointed blades and must be sharp. Protect the blade points by keeping them in a sheath.

You may or may not find it convenient to embroider with a thimble. But you will find that in some instances a thimble is necessary. Generally, metal thimbles are better than plastic or bone.

Be sure that the closed end and sides are deeply indented to prevent the needle end from slipping off when in use. Thimbles come in different sizes. Try on a few for correct fit before you buy one.

Embroidery is usually worked in a frame. With the material held tautly and evenly, your stitches are more likely to be neat and accurate than if the fabric were held in the hand while working. Many embroidery hoops and frames are equipped with stands or clamps to hold the embroidery piece and leave both your hands free.

There are two main types of frames, round and rectangular. The round frame or hoop consists of two pieces, a smaller hoop which fits into the larger one. There is usually a spring or screw adjustment to keep them fitting snugly. The fabric for embroidery is placed over the smaller hoop and the larger hoop is pressed over the fabric onto the smaller hoop. These frames may be of either wood or metal. When embroidering on very delicate fabric, it is advisable to place tissue paper over the inner hoop first, or wrap the inner hoop with a thin material to prevent marking the fabric.

The rectangular frame consists of four pieces: two roller pieces at top and bottom and either two screw-type ends for tightening, or flat ends with holes for adjusting. The embroidery piece or tapestry is tacked onto the strips of fabric on the roller pieces and laced onto the ends to hold it taut. Specific instructions for mounting the embroidery fabric will come with each frame.

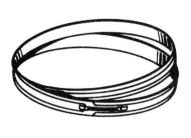

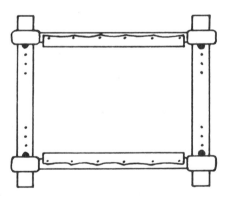

Threads For Embroidery

The appearance of your work is greatly influenced by the material that you choose. You can make a delicate piece of work with fragile fabric and a fine thread, or translate the identical design onto coarser fabric, using a heavier thread. In needlepoint, for instance, the yarn required for each canvas is chosen for its covering quality. Crewel wool used single would not cover the mesh of gros point canvas; a heavier yarn is required, or two or more strands of fine wool. The needle to use with each yarn or floss should have an eye large enough to accommodate the yarn, but not larger than needed. Some types of embroidery traditionally use a certain yarn or floss, while others technically require a specific kind. Chart relates threads and needles to type of work.

Materials or Type of Work	Thread	Needle*
Fine Fabrics or thin material	Six-strand Embroidery Thread (Split for very fine work) Twisted cotton or fine Mercerized Thread Rayon floss or cord	Embroidery or crewel needle No. 1 to 10
Medium Textures such as linen, pique (or other cottons); or light-weight sweaters of wool, nylon, or angora	Pearl cotton No. 3 or 5 Six-strand Embroidery Thread combining number of strands Rayon embroidery floss Fine wool yarns	Crewel No. 1 to 12 Tapestry No. 20 or 22 Darning No. 14 to 18
Heavyweight or coarse fabrics such as Monk's cloth, burlap, felt, wool suitings, or heavy sweaters	Double strand Pearl Cotton Metallic Cord Tapestry Yarn or Crewel Yarn Sock and Sweater Yarn, Nylon Angora, Chenille, Germantown	Crewel No. 1 to 12 Tapestry No. 18 to 22 Chenille No. 16 to 22 Darning No. 14 to 18
Cutwork	Mercerized Pearl Twist Pearl Cotton No. 8	Embroidery or crewel No. 1 to 10
Huck Weaving	Pearl Cotton No. 5 Six-strand Embroidery Thread Fine wool yarn	Tapestry No. 20 or 22
Quilting or *Appliqué*	50-60 to 100 Mercerized Thread Quilting Thread (one size)	Quilting No. 7 to 8
Beading, Sewing on Sequins, or *Stringing Beads*	Buttonhole Twist Mercerized Sewing Thread	Beading No. 16
Machine Embroidery See specific instructions		
Candlewick Embroidery or for heavy yarns worked through sweaters or fabrics	Candlewick Yarn Rug yarn of cotton, wool, or rayon luster	Candlewick needle
Petit Point *Needlepoint* *Gros Point* *Quick Point*	Crewel Wool Tapestry Wool Tapestry Wool (2 strands) Rug Yarn	Tapestry No. 20 to 23 Tapestry No. 18-19 Tapestry No. 17 Large-eyed rug needles

*In embroidery and sewing needles the largest number is the finest needle.

How to Transfer Designs

If you are spending your own precious time to create an heirloom for tomorrow you will want to be sure the design is as attractive as possible.

If you have a fine museum in your neighborhood study the lovely embroidery designs they show. Sometimes you can choose an embroidery motif from a bed hanging and apply it around the border of a luncheon cloth. Sometimes you may choose to translate a painting into needlepoint.

If you have a research library with fine books on art or design, on rare old china, or beautiful linens, then you can use these sources.

If you plan to copy a museum design, or a print from some other source, place tracing paper over the photograph of the design and carefully copy the complete design; to protect the print, place a piece of glassine between the design and the tracing paper. Mark the correct colors and shades, using colored crayons or pencils. The design, if it is to be used in the same size, is now ready to be used on your fabric; there are a number of ways of transferring a design.

CARBON PAPER: Typewriter carbon may be used between your fabric and the tracing. However, this is apt to be smudgy and can soil the fabric. Dressmakers' carbon is better to use for this purpose and comes in light and dark colors. Anchor the fabric to a smooth surface with masking tape; place carbon face down on fabric with tracing on top in correct position; tape in place. With an instrument such as a dry ball point pen, carefully mark all lines of design, using enough pressure to transfer clearly.

BACK TRACING: A design may also be transferred to a smooth fabric by going over all lines on back of tracing with a soft pencil. Then tape tracing onto your fabric, right side up, and trace all lines again, using a hard pencil.

DIRECT TRACING: If the fabric and tracing are not too large and unwieldy, the design can be transferred by means of a light box, or ordinary glass window. With this method, the fabric must be of a light color and not very heavy. Place tracing (which must be marked with heavy, dark lines) right side up on a light box, or tape to window in bright daylight. Tape fabric on top of tracing. With the light coming from the back, the traced design will show clearly through the fabric and can be traced directly on the fabric, using a sharp pencil.

PERFORATED PATTERN: There is another method, which makes a good permanent pattern, called perforating. In many large cities it is possible to have a perforated pattern made professionally from your tracing. Look for such a company under Perforated Patterns in the classified directory. To make your own perforated pattern, mark design accurately on heavy quality tracing paper. Then the traced design is perforated on all outlines. With tracing on a lightly padded surface, use a pin or unthreaded sewing machine to make the holes in the tracing paper, about 1/16″ apart. Hold the pin straight up and push through paper enough to make clear holes. When the perforating is finished, place it over your fabric, smooth side up and weight it down around edges to hold it in place while transferring. The design may be transferred by means of a perforating powder called pounce, and a pouncer. To make a pouncer, roll up a strip of flannel or felt tightly, sewing it so it remains rolled. Dip the end of the pouncer in powder, tap off excess; then dab and rub it over the perforated outlines. Carefully lift up corner of perforated pattern to see if design has been transferred clearly. If not, go over it again with pounce. When the transferring is completed, carefully lift off pattern. Perforating paste may be used instead of powder. Directions for its use will come with the paste.

TRANSFER PATTERN: If you do not wish to create your own design, you can use one of the lovely designs already prepared for you, ready to be transferred to your fabric by means of a hot iron. The McCall's Transfer Patterns which are printed in blue will transfer on both light and dark fabrics. These transfers are available at pattern departments.

To use the transfer pattern always cut away the pattern name or number or any other parts that you do not wish to use. Shake the paper to remove any loose particles. Lay the fabric on an ironing board or lightly padded surface and pin in position so it will not slide. Pin transfer design in place, design side down on fabric.

Experiment first with a small piece of transfer on a sample of material. Before stamping test heat of the iron with the number or trial sample on a sample of the material, *selecting a low heat or rayon heat for all materials.* Transfer design with a downward stamp of the iron (never press slowly and heavily as in ironing). If your test sample is not clear, the heat of iron is not correct.

When the iron is the correct temperature, stamp the design. Before removing the transfer lift a corner to see if the design has been transferred satisfactorily. When completely stamped, remove the transfer by running the warm iron lightly over it. This prevents the transfer ink from sticking to the paper as it is pulled away from the material.

How to Enlarge or Reduce Designs

There are various ways of enlarging or reducing a design so that all parts of the design will be enlarged or reduced in proportion. Two methods are given here. The most commonly used is the "square" method, No. 1. Another simple procedure is the "diagonal" method, No. 2.

If you wish to keep the original design unmarked, trace outlines of design onto tracing paper, as explained on opposite page, "How to Transfer Designs."

Method No. 1: Mark off squares over the design to be enlarged if they are not already there. Use ⅛" squares for small designs and ¼", ½" or 1" squares for proportionately larger designs. Make the same number of squares, similarly placed, in the space to be occupied by the enlarged design. Copy outline of design from smaller squares to corresponding larger squares. Reverse procedure for reducing designs.

A "trick of the trade" is to place a fine wire screen over the original design for "squaring off." Another short cut is to transfer original design to graph paper.

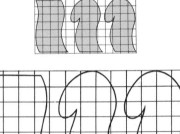

Method No. 1. Small "m" enlarged by squares to place-mat size.

Method No. 2: Make a rectangle to fit around design to be enlarged. Draw a diagonal line from corner to corner and extend line far enough to form diagonal of a rectangle to fit desired size.

Subdivide large and small rectangles by first making opposite diagonals to find center. Then draw lines to quarter the space. Make diagonal of quarter sections to find centers. Draw lines to quarter the space. Copy outlines of design from smaller areas to larger areas or vice versa. An easy way to divide the rectangles into spaces described above is to fold the paper into halves, quarters and eighths, then draw diagonal lines into folds.

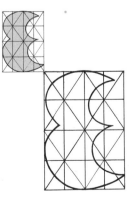

Method No. 2. By drawing diagonals, small "e" becomes place-mat size.

Aids in Designing

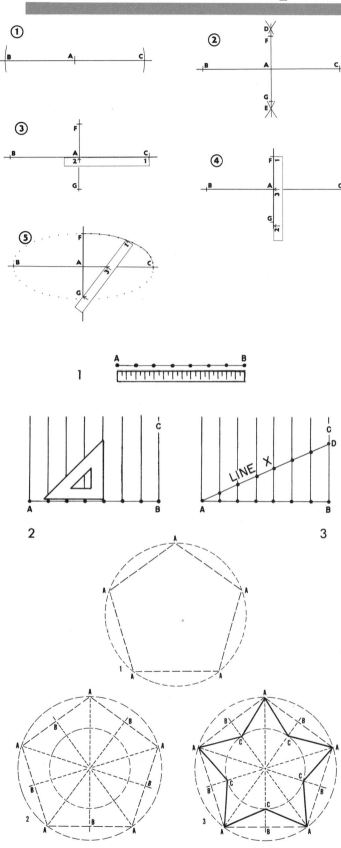

HOW TO DRAW AN OVAL

Here is the simple geometrical method of making ovals large or small to fit any desired space.

Fig. 1: Draw a straight line length of, or longer than, desired length of oval. At center of line establish point A. With compass (or pencil tied to string) swing arcs to establish B and C, the length of oval.

Fig. 2: From B and C swing arcs above and below line BC. Connect their intersections with line DE, On this line mark points F and G equal distances from A, to establish width of oval.

Fig. 3: Mark points 1 and 2 to match A and C on a straight, firm strip of paper.

Fig. 4: Turn this measuring paper vertically along line FG so that point 1 is at F. Mark point 3 at A.

Fig. 5: Rotate the measuring paper clockwise, moving point 3 along line AC and point 2 along AG. Make dots opposite point 1. Connect these dots with a line which completes the first quarter of the oval. Repeat this procedure in the other three parts or make a tracing and transfer curve to complete oval.

HOW TO DIVIDE ANY LINE INTO EQUAL PARTS

Fig. 1: The line to be divided will be called line X. Rule off line AB shorter than line X by marking off AB into the desired number of equal parts, using simple divisions on ruler such as ½″, ¼″, etc.

Fig. 2: With a draftsman's triangle, or holding an ordinary ruler at right angles to line AB, raise perpendicular lines at each division.

Fig. 3: Measure line X and mark off length on ruler. Place ruler so that line X extends from A to line BC; where it touches is point D. Line X is now divided into equal parts.

HOW TO MAKE A STAR

1. Draw a circle desired size of star. With compass or dividers, find five equidistant points A on circumference of circle. Draw lines to connect points to form a pentagon.

2. Using same center of circle, draw another circle inside larger circle as illustrated (distance of inner circle from outer circle controls depth of star points). Find centers of five sides of pentagon (points B). From these centers, draw lines through center of circle to opposite points A.

3. Draw lines from points A of pentagon to where dividing lines intersect inner circle (points C).

How to Design a Crest

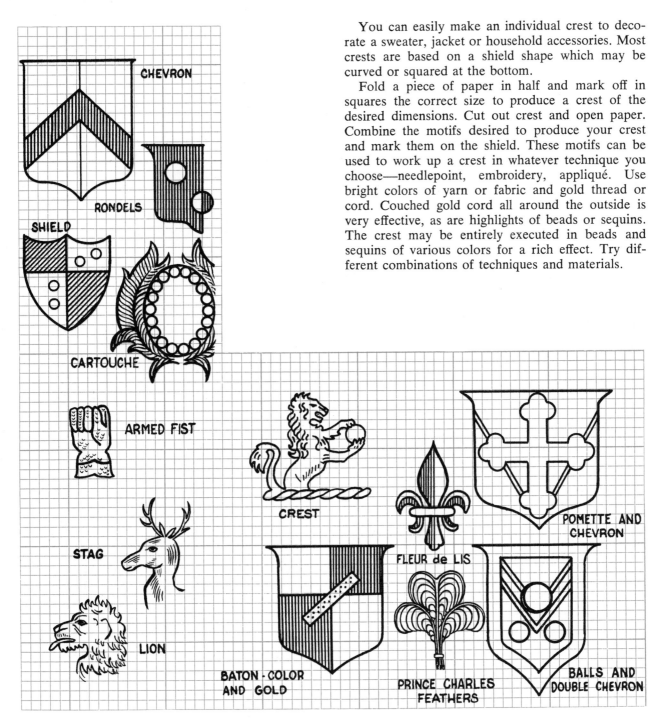

You can easily make an individual crest to decorate a sweater, jacket or household accessories. Most crests are based on a shield shape which may be curved or squared at the bottom.

Fold a piece of paper in half and mark off in squares the correct size to produce a crest of the desired dimensions. Cut out crest and open paper. Combine the motifs desired to produce your crest and mark them on the shield. These motifs can be used to work up a crest in whatever technique you choose—needlepoint, embroidery, appliqué. Use bright colors of yarn or fabric and gold thread or cord. Couched gold cord all around the outside is very effective, as are highlights of beads or sequins. The crest may be entirely executed in beads and sequins of various colors for a rich effect. Try different combinations of techniques and materials.

CHEVRON

RONDELS

SHIELD

CARTOUCHE

ARMED FIST

STAG

LION

CREST

FLEUR de LIS

PRINCE CHARLES FEATHERS

BATON - COLOR AND GOLD

POMETTE AND CHEVRON

BALLS AND DOUBLE CHEVRON

Care of Embroidery

When your needlework is completed, it often needs to be pressed or blocked into shape. Sometimes it is soiled from working and must be laundered. This should always be done with care to preserve as much of the freshness of the fabric and thread as possible. Treat embroidery gently.

To help keep your work neat and clean, keep it in a plastic bag when not embroidering. When your embroidered piece is completed, finish off the back neatly by running ends into the back of the work and clipping off any excess strands. If wool embroidery or needlepoint is not really soiled but needs just a little freshening, simply brushing over the surface with a clean cloth dipped in carbon tetrachloride or other good cleaning fluid may be satisfactory. This will brighten and return colors to their original look.

FABRIC EMBROIDERY: Better results will be obtained by blocking (directions below) rather than pressing an embroidered piece for a picture or hanging. However, articles that are hemmed, such as tablecloths or runners, should be pressed as blocking would damage the edge of the fabric. To press your embroidered piece, use a well-padded surface and steam iron, or regular iron and damp cloth. Embroideries that have been worked in a frame will need very little pressing. If the embroidery was done in the hand it will no doubt be quite wrinkled and may need dampening. Sprinkle it to dampen and roll loosely in a clean towel. Embroidery should always be pressed lightly so that the stitching will not be flattened into the fabric. Place the embroidered piece face down on the padded surface and press from the center outward. For embroidery that is raised from the surface of the background, use extra thick, soft padding, such as a thick blanket.

If beads or sequins are added to embroidery, take care not to use too hot an iron, as some of these may melt. These should also be pressed wrong side down. The padding below protects them from breaking.

Embroideries made of colorfast threads and washable fabrics can be laundered without fear of harming them. Wash with mild soap or detergent and warm water, swishing it through the water gently—do not rub. Rinse in clear water without wringing or squeezing. When completely rinsed, lift from the water and lay on a clean towel; lay another towel on top and roll up loosely. When the embroidery is sufficiently dry, press as described above.

After blocking or pressing, an embroidered picture should be mounted right away to prevent creasing. To store other embroidery, place blue tissue paper on front and roll smoothly, face in, onto a cardboard tube. Then wrap outside in tissue.

TO REMOVE STAMPING FROM THE MATERIAL: It is almost impossible to remove transfers from light colored fabrics that cannot be washed. Try soaking in cleaning fluid for about ten minutes. Rub carefully and rinse in clean fluid, until material is clean; let dry, and press. For woolens, place material right side up with a blotter under the fabric. Rub gently with a clean cloth saturated in cleaning fluid. As the cloth absorbs the color use a fresh cloth.

Washable fabrics may have the blue transfer pattern removed by washing them with a good laundry soap and warm water, rubbing by hand until the marks disappear. For wash silks or rayons, soak the fabric in cleaning fluid for about five minutes, rubbing lightly. This will loosen and spread the transfer. Then wash in lukewarm water with a mild soap rubbing carefully until the marks disappear. After rinsing thoroughly, place fabric wrong side up. Cover with a damp cloth and press with medium hot iron.

TO BLOCK NEEDLEPOINT: If a small piece of needlepoint is pulled slightly askew through working, sponge the surface on the wrong side. Lay it face down on a damp towel, pull into shape and pin all around the edges. Cover with another damp towel and steam press with a regular iron.

For larger pieces that become badly out of shape, the needlepoint should be blocked as follows: Cover a soft-wood surface with brown paper. Mark the canvas size on this, being sure corners are square. Place needlepoint right side down over guide and fasten with thumbtacks about ½" apart all along edges of canvas. Wet with cold water thoroughly and let dry. Repeat as many times as necessary.

TO BLOCK EMBROIDERED PICTURE: With needle and colorfast thread, following the thread of the linen and taking ¼" stitches, mark guide lines around the entire picture to designate the exact area where the picture will fit into the rabbet of the frame. The border of plain linen extending beyond the embroidery in a framed picture is approximately 1¼" at sides and top and 1½" at bottom. In order to have sufficient linen around the embroidered design for blocking and mounting, 3" or 4" of linen should be left around the embroidered section. Now, matching corners, obtain the exact centers of the four sides and mark these centers with a few stitches.

If the picture is soiled, it should be washed, but it should be blocked immediately after washing. In preparation, cover a drawing board or soft-wood bread board with a piece of brown paper held in place with thumbtacks, and draw the exact original size of the linen on the brown paper. Be sure linen is not pulled beyond its original size when the measurements are taken. (Embroidery sometimes pulls linen slightly out of shape.) Check drawn rectangle to make sure corners are square.

Wash embroidery in mild soap with plenty of suds; squeeze suds through material; do not rub embroidery. Rinse thoroughly, but do not wring or squeeze. Let drip for a few moments. Place embroidery right side up on the brown paper inside the guide lines and tack down the four corners. Tack centers of four sides. Continue to stretch the linen to its original size by tacking all around the sides, dividing and sub-dividing the spaces between the tacks already placed. This procedure is followed until there is a solid border of thumbtacks around the entire edge. In cross-stitch pictures, if stitches were not stamped exactly even on the thread of the linen, it may be necessary to remove some of the tacks and pull part of embroidery into a straight line. Use a ruler as a guide for straightening the lines of stitches. Hammer in the tacks or they will pop out as the linen dries. Allow embroidery to dry thoroughly.

TO MOUNT EMBROIDERED PICTURE: Cut a piece of heavy white cardboard about ⅛" smaller all around than the rabbet size of the frame to be used. Stretch the embroidery over the cardboard using the same general procedure as for blocking the piece. Following the thread guide lines, use pins to attach the four corners of the embroidery to the mounting board. Pins are placed at the centers of sides, and embroidery is then gradually stretched into position until there is a border of pins completely around picture, about ¼" apart. When satisfied that the design is even, drive pins into the cardboard edge with a hammer. If a pin does not go in straight, it should be removed and reinserted. The edges of the linen may be pasted down on the wrong side of the cardboard or the edges may be caught with long zigzag stitches. Embroidered pictures can be framed with glass over them, if desired.

TO MOUNT NEEDLEPOINT PICTURE: After canvas has been blocked, stretch it over heavy cardboard or plywood cut same size as worked portion of canvas. Use heavy cardboard for small pictures (12" or less); for larger pictures and panels, use ¼" plywood. If cardboard is used, hold canvas in place with pins pushed through canvas into edge of cardboard. If canvas is mounted on plywood, use carpet tacks. Push pins or tacks only part way into edge; check needlepoint to make sure rows of stitches are straight. Carefully hammer in pins or tacks the rest of the way. Using a large-eyed needle and heavy thread, lace loose edges of canvas over back of cardboard or plywood to hold taut; lace across width then length of picture.

Frame mounted picture as desired, without glass.

TO REFINISH OLD FRAMES: Here are a few

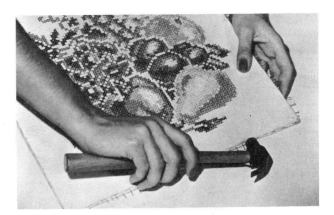

Illustration shows how basting was used to outline the exact area of linen where it fits frame. Pins show how needlework has been stretched over cardboard following basting thread.

hints for redoing frames, which you may find useful.

There are a number of easy ways to modernize or change the color of frames. In oversize gold frames you will find that most of the very wide and elaborate ones are actually two or three frames, one inside the other. Place frame face down on a rug and remove the outer frame by pulling out with pliers the few small nails that hold it.

To glaze gold frames: You have seen gold frames coated with an off-white, cream or other soft tint. The gold shows through only at the high spots, giving a very modern and pleasing effect. It is the simplest thing in the world to give your own gold frames this "new look." Materials needed are: Small can of flat white paint. One or two tiny tubes of artists' oil colors. A small inexpensive varnish brush. A half pint of turpentine or paint thinner. A soft rag.

To tint with oil colors: Raw sienna will make a cream color; raw umber makes a nice off-white; burnt sienna gives a dull pinkish cast. To paint, pour a little turpentine into a dish. Dip the varnish brush in the turpentine and brush lightly on a sheet of clean paper to remove dust and grease. Wipe lightly with a soft cloth. Stir flat white paint well and pour into dish. In a separate cup squeeze a small amount of oil color and add a few drops of turpentine. Stir the color with a knife until there are no lumps. Now add some color to the white and stir it. Add the color a little at a time until you get the depth of tint desired. With varnish brush apply a coat quickly to entire frame. Immediately start wiping the color off the high spots with a cloth until the right amount of gold shows through. Do not rub hard. If color does not come off easily, moisten the cloth with turpentine. If you wipe off too much on any spot, apply more paint with brush and wipe again. On flat surfaces wipe with long even strokes. Allow to dry overnight.

How to Design Needlepoint

Today, more and more women are interested in finding a medium of self-expression. Needlepoint is one way to fill this need. Once the basic stitches are mastered, the competent needlewoman is ready to take the further step of creating her own designs. Therefore, we offer some how-to suggestions on creating individual needlepoint designs. It is really quite a simple matter to design a piece of needlepoint to fit your personal requirements and taste. The satisfaction of "making your own" rather than executing a ready-made design is well worth the effort and time required.

WHERE TO FIND A DESIGN

Those who are talented in drawing will have no trouble creating an entirely original needlepoint design. Others may wish to obtain the aid of an artist friend, or the art teacher in a local school. However, even those who have no creative talent and wish to "do it themselves" may still obtain distinctive results by using the following suggestions.

1. Take your inspiration from something purely personal—a favorite picture in your home, your pet, a pictorial representation of your hobby, a sampler of daily activities, your coat of arms.

2. Work out a design inspired by your decor—repeat a motif taken from your wallpaper, or drapery fabric. Change the size or proportion to suit your needs and to fit the item you plan to make. You can enlarge a small design for a bold, contemporary effect, reduce a large one to repeat for allover pattern. Use the colors of your decor.

3. Research designs—look up and copy old designs from books on needlepoint in your library, or study actual pieces in museums. Use them as shown, or vary designs to suit your own taste. Usually illustrations have been reduced from the size of the original; perhaps your library or museum has a photostating service, so that you can get the design you wish to use blown up to full size. If not, for "How to Enlarge by Squares," see Index. Trace the design carefully and do the enlarging at home. (Note: When making a copy, remember not to use someone else's design for an item to be sold unless the design is in public domain.)

4. Adapt designs from other needlework. Cross-stitch designs are worked on squares, for example, and can be adapted easily to needlepoint.

CHOOSING YOUR MATERIALS

For delicate, traditional designs, small stitches are most suitable; simple, bold, contemporary designs should be worked in large stitches.

Petit point employs the smallest stitches, and is suited to small designs, detailed traditional designs and delicate effects, such as are used on evening bags and French boudoir chairs. Choose a fine canvas and fine yarn such as crewel wool.

Needlepoint is suited to upholstery, pictures, etc.

Use a medium single or double thread canvas, and two strands of crewel wool, or one of tapestry yarn.

Gros point is suited to upholstery, as well as to pictures, pillows and rugs. Use medium large double thread canvas, one or two strands of tapestry yarn.

Quick point is especially suited to bold designs and for making rugs. Use a large mesh canvas and rug wool, or two or more strands of tapestry yarn. In using this for upholstery, care should be taken that when mounted on a chair or stool seat, it is not too bulky for inserting into the frame.

Note: Knitting worsted is not considered desirable for needlepoint, as it does not have enough twist, and may wear thin in working. However, it may be used in pictures, where there will be no wear.

PUTTING A DESIGN ON CANVAS

There are three ways of getting your design on the canvas. One is to make the design into a chart or graph, each square of which represents one stitch, with symbols to indicate the colors; you follow this chart in working the canvas. Another way is to work from a design with outlines filled in with color. You draw the design outlines on your canvas and fill in the colors with embroidery. The easiest method for the needleworker to follow is to have the design painted on canvas, with various areas colored to correspond exactly to the wools to be used.

1. How to Make a Chart or Graph

Draw the design on a piece of graph paper with the count the same as your canvas (i.e., 10-squares-to-the-inch paper represents 10-mesh-to-the-inch canvas); each square represents a stitch. On most graph papers you can fill in color areas with water colors. If paper buckles, use colored pencils.

Another method is to rule lines representing canvas threads over the design, scaled to exact size of finished piece. If necessary, enlarge or reduce design before ruling lines.

2. How to Mark Outline on Canvas

Place design, heavily outlined, under canvas; trace lines that show through; complete outline with India ink and a very fine brush, or with a felt-tipped marker. In using this method (particularly good for coarse canvas), paint curved lines as curves; do not attempt to indicate where individual stitches fall. Planning placement of stitches while working is interesting.

Outlines of design may also be perforated (see Index) at close intervals, placed over your canvas and stamped with a felt pad and stamping paste.

With small meshed canvas, you can transfer your design directly to the canvas. Thumbtack canvas to a flat surface; establish a vertical and a horizontal center as placement guides. Cover canvas with carbon paper; center pattern over carbon, and trace around outline of design with a blunt point such as tip of a knitting needle. After transferring is completed, paper towels should be placed over outline and pressed with a hot iron to remove any excess carbon that might discolor yarn. Go over outlines with India ink.

HOW TO PAINT IN THE DESIGN

1. For a simple design with few colors, color areas can be filled in with wax crayons. Fix colors by pressing canvas under paper towels with warm iron.

2. For complex designs, painting design on canvas with oil paints is not difficult. Use decorator oils (they are less expensive). Buy the following colors: white, lemon yellow, cadmium light, yellow ochre, vermilion, alizarin crimson, ultramarine blue, cobalt blue, cerulean blue, emerald green, veridian, Vandyke brown, burnt sienna, black. With these colors, desired shade can be mixed to match yarns.

Canvas to be painted is stretched tightly on a board over a piece of brown paper to absorb oil. Colors are mixed and then thinned to consistency of light cream with cleaning fluid (naphtha). This cuts oil and keeps colors from spreading; it makes paint dry quickly. Skill is required to learn how to mix exact consistency of paint so that it is not so thin it changes color when applied and not so thick it clogs canvas.

Some colors, black, for instance, have a tendency to take a long time to dry. In this case, add a tiny bit of Japan drier to naphtha. Usually, oil paint thinned with naphtha alone will dry overnight.

Use soft, pointed brushes for painting. Japanese water-color brushes are very good for this purpose; they hold quite a bit of paint, and have a good point. You need turpentine for washing brushes frequently.

CHOICE OF STITCHES

The stitch used has a great deal to do with the wearing quality of the embroidery. There are three familiar methods of working needlepoint: half cross-stitch, continental stitch and the diagonal method.

1. Half cross-stitch, practical for pictures or areas that receive little wear, works up quickly and saves yarn. This method barely covers canvas, and must be done carefully for good coverage on front; there is practically no yarn on back.

2. Continental stitch uses more yarn, covers canvas front and back. The work is more attractive, wearing quality is increased by slight padding on back.

3. The diagonal method is best for needlepoint that will receive the most wear, particularly chair seats or rugs. It uses the same amount of yarn as the continental stitch, covers the front of the canvas well, and also forms a durable web which reinforces the back of the canvas.

PROFESSIONAL TIPS

For a professionally finished piece, plan to leave a margin of bare canvas around work; embroidering more needlepoint than will show on the surface of the finished piece is a waste of yarn and time. The bare edge of the canvas is turned back on a sampler, turned under in upholstery, or covered with a frame for a picture. In deciding what size of canvas to buy, allow at least 1½″ margin to leave bare for blocking finished piece.

Wetting needlepoint for blocking softens glue sizing of the canvas. When piece dries, canvas resets and holds its shape unless it is unmounted, as in rugs, or subject to handling, as with handbags. For such pieces, it is advisable to stiffen the back of the work with glue while it is wet and fastened face down. Dry glue can be obtained at a hardware store. Mix one-half cup of dry glue with one-half cup of boiling water, then thin with three cups of cold water; mixture should be brushed on back of embroidery.

In making a bag or other item made of more than one piece, do not sew pieces together on a sewing machine. Trim unworked canvas margin to ½″ or 1″; turn margin to back and whip to embroidery; finish each piece as a separate section. Join pieces at the edges with a connecting row of needlepoint; or sew together by hand with a slipstitch and cover the joining with a twisted cord. When joining two pieces, match design stitch by stitch.

FINAL FINISH FOR WOOL EMBROIDERY

Pieces embroidered in wool yarns and needlepoint pieces often become quite fuzzy from working and handling. It is advisable to remove this fuzz to bring design outlines back into clear focus and give a clean, professional look to the embroidery. For this process, a long thin wax lighting taper (waxed wick) is used. Light the taper, and holding it just above the surface of the embroidery, move it rapidly back and forth, singeing the fuzz off the embroidery. Blow away the singed fuzz, or brush it lightly with a soft brush. This process may be repeated if necessary.

Aids to Upholstering with Needlepoint

Designs become bolder and simpler with large stitches and finer and more detailed with small stitches. The character of the design is thus in keeping with the stitch count of the needlepoint which in turn should harmonize with the character of the furniture it is to cover.

Petit point is ideal for very delicate furniture such as French chairs. Needlepoint and gros point are well suited to average weight chairs such as Chippendale and Queen Anne. Quick point goes well with bulky, unembellished contemporary furniture and some Provincial styles.

Technically, almost any chair can be upholstered with petit point and gros point. However, the bulkiness of quick point limits its uses slightly. It should not be recommended for upholstering chair seats or stool tops which fit down into a frame unless the stool or chair has been specially built to allow for the extra bulk. If a piece of needlepoint too bulky for such a chair is forced into its frame, the frame may split when sat upon. Examples of such chairs and stools are given below, and comments as to which weight of needlepoint should be used.

French period chair, ideally upholstered with petit point.

Medium-weight chair, suitable for gros point.

Contemporary chair, loose cushions, best for quick point.

Contemporary chair, with a removable seat, boxing, suitable for quick point.

Stool top fits into framework, not recommended for quick point.

HOW TO MAKE A PATTERN OF AREA TO BE EMBROIDERED

The second bit of advice is to work only that area of the canvas which will show after the piece has been upholstered. It is a mistake to fill in the background to the edge of the canvas.

Important are the money and time saved by working only the necessary area; important to the upholsterer is ease in upholstering without extra bulk of worked canvas at miterings and tucking-in places.

One must also remember when choosing a suitably-sized piece of needlepoint canvas that at least a 1½″ margin for blocking and upholstering must extend around the embroidery.

You must be able to place the center of the embroidered design motif ½″ in front of center line of seat pattern to adjust visual balance of background area in perspective on chair.

In order to determine the exact area to be embroidered, a muslin pattern is made as follows:

On a square piece of muslin, a little larger than enough to cover the seat, mark a vertical and horizontal line at the center with a soft pencil, using the thread of the muslin as a guide.

On the seat of the chair or stool, draw corresponding center lines. Place muslin on chair seat along these lines. Beginning at center of the seat and working towards edges on all four sides, place pins 3″ apart (Fig. 1). Continue pinning muslin at either side of pins at edges of seat, alternating from side to side to keep muslin from pulling out of shape. Slash muslin to fit around back legs and tuck it down in. Pin the corners to make miters wherever necessary.

Using a soft pencil, mark all around the lower edge of the chair seat; mark around the legs, reaching down into tucked-in area; mark on both sides of all mitered corners; make a line to indicate top area of chair seat to be used later in placing design correctly on chair seat pattern.

With a tape measure, verify the muslin pattern against the length and width of the chair seat. The measurements of center lines on the chair and the muslin should correspond exactly. Pin muslin down on a board, threads straight. You will find that despite great care, the shape of the muslin is slightly irregular. Being sure that all distances are the same, make a perfectly symmetrical version of pattern on brown paper, with horizontal and vertical lines corresponding to those on the muslin. Cut out on edge (Fig. 2).

Place paper pattern on the canvas on which a horizontal and vertical line has also been established through center of needlepoint design. Horizontal line on paper should be placed ½″ *behind* horizontal line on canvas for proper placing of chair design as described above. Leave a 1½″ margin all around for blocking (Fig. 3).

Pin the brown paper pattern to the canvas and mark the outline on the canvas with India ink or indelible marking pen. This will slightly enlarge the chair pattern and allow for possible work shrinkage. Save the brown paper pattern and use it later as a guide when blocking the embroidered needlepoint.

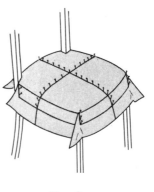

Fig. 1

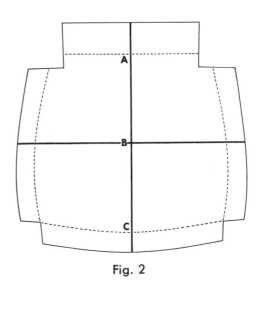

Fig. 2

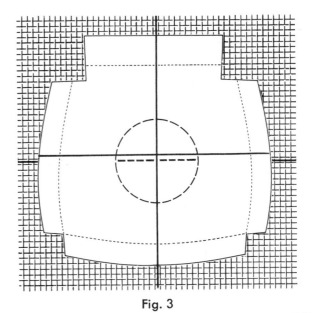

Fig. 3

361

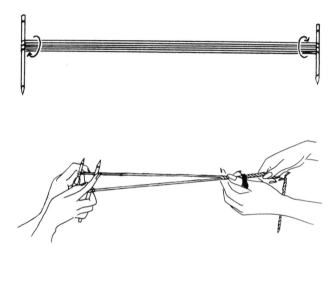

TWISTED CORD

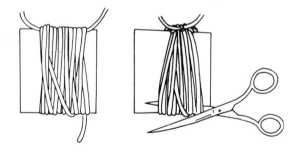

TASSEL Directions for this are on opposite page.

HOW TO MAKE A NEEDLEPOINT PILLOW

If a foam rubber form is used, the finished needle-point should be exactly the size of the foam rubber. If a pillow form is used which is filled with kapok, feathers or similar material, the finished needlepoint should be about ¼″ smaller all around so that the pillow form will fit well into corners.

To make pillow with boxing strips, cut off canvas after blocking to within ¾″ of embroidery. Turn canvas back on edge of embroidery on pillow top and boxing strips and whip-stitch to hold in place. Join boxing pieces to top by whipping them to top at right angles; whip corners together with matching wool. Prepare material for back of pillow in the same way as for top and whip to edge of three boxing strips. Insert pillow form. Whip fourth boxing strip to back of pillow. Cover joining at top and back with twisted cord. (To make, see below.)

TO UPHOLSTER CUSHIONS FOR CHAIRS AND STOOLS

If unattached, use same method as for pillow.

TO UPHOLSTER CHAIRS WITH REMOVABLE SEATS

Remove seats. Using vertical and horizontal lines marked on canvas of embroidered needlepoint piece, place needlepoint in position on chair. Use the un-worked canvas for tacking to the bottom of seat; tack center front and center back at edges, then tack centers of sides, working toward corners. Pull needle-point in position, but not too tightly.

TO UPHOLSTER A CHAIR WHEN FABRIC IS ATTACHED TO FRAMEWORK OF CHAIR SEAT

Usually, when removing the old upholstery fabric of a chair or stool, it will be seen how upholstery was handled before, and the same method can be used. Needlepoint differs from fabric in that only the un-worked canvas should be turned back in mitering corners to avoid bulkiness.

Because a piece of needlepoint is too valuable for the average amateur upholsterer to handle, have this kind of furniture upholstered by a professional.

HOW TO MAKE A TWISTED CORD

(Method requires two people). Tie one end of yarn around a pencil. Loop yarn over center of second pencil, then back to first, around first pencil and back to second, making as many strands between pencils as desired for thickness of cord. Length of yarn between pencils should be 2½ times length of cord desired. Each person holds end of yarn just below pencil with one hand and twists pencil with other hand, keeping the yarn taut. When yarn begins to kink, catch it over a doorknob; keep yarn taut. One person now holds both pencils together while other grasps center of yarn, sliding hand down yarn and releasing yarn at short intervals, letting it twist.

HOW TO MAKE TASSELS

See details on opposite page. Wind yarn around a cardboard cut to size of tassel desired, winding it 25 to 40 times around, depending on thickness of yarn and plumpness of tassel required. Tie strands tightly together around top as shown, leaving at least 3″ ends on ties; clip other end of strands. Wrap a piece of yarn tightly around strands a few times about ½″ or 1″ below top tie and knot. Trim ends.

HOW TO MAKE POMPONS

One method is to cut two cardboard disks the desired size of pompon; cut out ¼″ hole in center of both disks. Thread needle with two strands of yarn. Place disks together; cover with yarn, working through holes. Slip scissors between disks; cut all strands at outside edge. Draw a strand of yarn down between disks and wind several times very tightly around yarn; knot, leaving ends for attaching pompon. Remove disks by cutting through to center. Fluff out pompon and trim uneven ends.

HOW TO MAKE FRINGE

Cut strands of yarn double the length of fringe desired. Fold strands in half. Insert a crochet hook from front to back of edge where fringe is being made, pull through the folded end of yarn strand as shown in Fig. 1. Insert the two ends through loop as shown in Fig. 2 and pull ends to tighten fringe. Repeat across edge with each doubled strand, placing strands close together, or distance apart desired. For a fuller fringe, group a few strands together, and work as for one strand fringe.

The fringe may be knotted after all strands are in place along edge. To knot, separate the ends of two adjacent fringes (or divide grouped fringes in half); hold together the adjacent ends and knot 1″ or more below edge as shown in Fig. 3. Hold second end with one end of next fringe and knot together the same distance below edge as first knot. Continue across in this manner. A second row of knots may be made by separating the knotted ends again and knotting together ends from two adjacent fringes in same manner as for first row of knots.

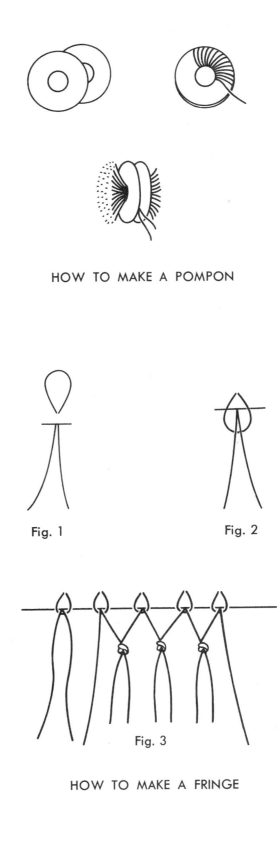

HOW TO MAKE A POMPON

Fig. 1   Fig. 2

Fig. 3

HOW TO MAKE A FRINGE

363

How to make a Bobbin Lace Loom

The loom shown here was designed so that it can be knocked down and stored easily. It consists of three parts: a box attached to a base; a bolster; a spread, or working field. This little loom was made from materials easily available in the home; it is easy to keep clean and simple to make. It was designed for use on a table. If it is to be held in the lap, place a second, and larger base under it.

Materials Required for Base: Piece of stiff corrugated board, or fibreboard, cut 12″ x 19½″. ½ yard blanketing. Bed padding or cotton wadding to pad spread. 1¼ yards of any strong cotton fabric to cover base, box side, bolster and make spread lining.

For Bolster: Strips of any kind of closely woven, heavy fabric or paper, cut 4½″ wide and 1 to 7 yards long, depending on thickness of material chosen (bed sheeting is good). One piece of ½″ diameter curtain rod 6¼″ long. One pair brass curtain rod fixtures (inside casing type), size to hold rod.

For Box and Spread: Piece of smooth wrapping paper, cut 24″ x 16″ for spread pattern. Stiff cardboard, or thin corrugated board, 22″ x 28″, or smaller odd pieces. ½ yard 36″ wide black velveteen or other soft dark fabric to cover spread and bolster. 12″ of strong, narrow ribbon or tape. Five strong tapes or cloth strips, four cut 4″ long, one cut 3½″ long.

Working Materials: Scotch tape. Glue. Awl or upholsterer's needle.

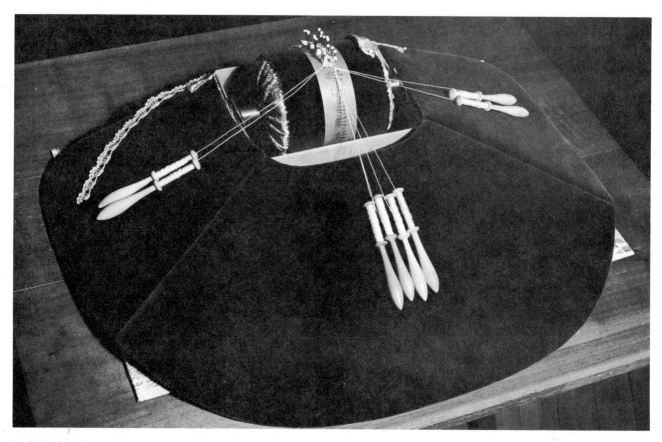

Bobbin lace loom in operation with pattern in place, showing how bobbin threads twist around pins to make lace.

STEP-BY-STEP DIRECTIONS

Box Sides: From thick cardboard or corrugated board, cut pieces for back and front of box, each 3″ x 6¾″, and two ends, each 3″ x 5″. From cotton fabric, cut coverings for box, two pieces 8″ x 7½″ and two pieces 8″ x 5¾″. Fold coverings in half crosswise with right sides facing, to make two pieces 4″ x 7½″ and two 4″ x 5¾″. Stitch each piece along two short sides ¼″ from edges. Turn right side out. Insert matching cardboards, pushing snugly to folded top edge. Turn in raw edges at bottom ¼″ and baste; run a second basting close to bottom edge of cardboards, stretching the fabric tightly to make a ¾″ flap along bottom of all four pieces.

Base: Cut base cover 21½″ x 26″. Find center of one 21½″ edge of base cover, and center of flap of back box piece. Place center to center, allowing 1″ at edge of base cover extending beyond edge of flap, for seam allowance. Stitch flap of box back to base cover all around flap (stitching should be as close as possible to bottom of box for firm structure). Stitch other three pieces to base cover to form box, with back and front flaps out, and end flaps in. Stretch base cover over top and bottom of base with box at top center rear. Turn in seam allowances of base cover and overcast top and bottom together firmly.

Finishing Box: Mark top center of both box ends with pins. With awl or upholstery needle, make holes ⅝″ on either side of pins and ⅜″ down from top. With 6″ pieces of strong ribbon, tie curtain rod fixtures to inside of box ends, through holes, allowing half of brass fixture to protrude above top edge. Sew one end of a 4″ tape to each top corner of front; sew other two 4″ tapes to top corners of back of box, leaving ends free, one end 1″ long, the other 3″ long (the 1″ ends will hold spread in place). Raise parts of box and pin long tapes together to hold box upright. Sew the 3½″ tape to top edge of box back about 2″ from one end. This is pinned to bolster when working, to keep bolster from turning.

Bolster: Attach end of cloth or paper strip to exact center of 6½″ piece of curtain rod with Scotch tape. Roll bolster on ironing board with strip running lengthwise of board and iron holding strip taut. Wind cloth firmly around rod. When bolster measures 2″ in diameter, attach woolen strip and continue rolling to a circumference of about 12″. Pin at edges.

Cut bolster cover 8″ x 14″ and stitch 8″ ends together, with right sides facing, after fitting snugly around bolster. Turn right side out. Slip cover over bolster, turn in ¼″ on one side edge with strong thread and gather; pull gathers tight around rod and fasten. Gather opposite side, turning in fabric to make a perfect fit when thread is drawn up and fastened. Wind with dark 14″ long strip of fabric matching spread, and pin in place. (When bobbin lace pattern is pinned around bolster, if added circumference is needed, build up bolster with woolen strips placed under dark finishing strip.) Place bolster in box, fitting rod ends into fixtures.

Spread: Pattern given on next page is half of the pattern. Enlarge pattern by copying it on paper ruled in 1″ squares; complete half-pattern. (See Index, How to Enlarge Designs.″) Cut off both ends of the pattern along dotted line. Use pattern pieces just as they are, to cut cardboard foundation, lining for foundation, and padding for foundation top. Cut three pieces of velveteen to cover spread pieces, allowing 1½″ extra all around each piece; cut center piece on bias of velveteen.

Glue linings to back of cardboard foundation pieces leaving about 2″ free at edges. Glue padding to top of foundation pieces in same way. Stretch velveteen over padded side of pieces, fold over edges and pin to lining. Turn in edges of velveteen pieces and sew neatly in place.

Assemble spread by overcasting side pieces to center piece (as indicated by dotted line on pattern) on bottom side. Place spread around bolster, with inside curve of spread resting on front corners of box. Pin short tape ends to spread to hold in place.

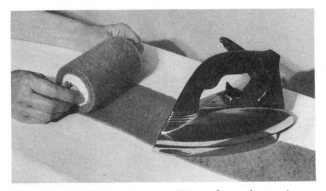

Photograph above shows rolling of woolen strip to make bolster; curtain rod is core of roll.

Back view of loom assembled, shows how bolster fits in box, and how spread fits around box.

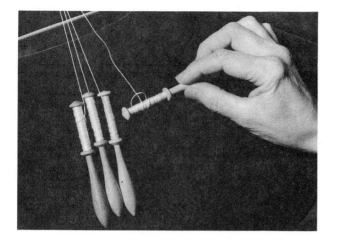

In winding the thread around bobbins, make a loop around head as shown to keep thread from unwinding while working. When thread becomes short, tip each bobbin to horizontal position and tease thread loose, unwinding as you do so.

Pattern below is for half of spread. To enlarge pattern to actual size, copy on paper ruled in 1″ squares. To complete pattern, fold paper on line indicated and cut out double. Cut pattern into three pieces, as indicated by dotted line on pattern. When cutting center section out of velveteen fabric, be sure to place straight of goods as indicated.

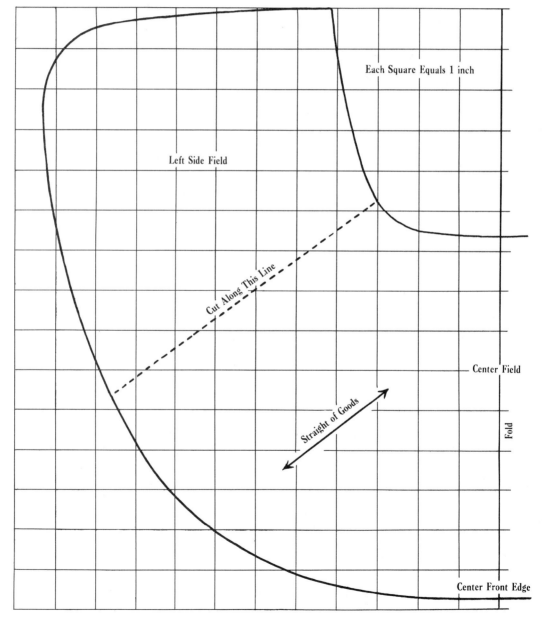

Each Square Equals 1 inch

Left Side Field

Cut Along This Line

Center Field

Straight of Goods

Fold

Center Front Edge

Yarns for Knitting and Crochet

WOOL YARNS have these advantages:

Warmth without weight. Wool fibers have the ability to trap air, thus giving an insulating effect.

Absorbency. Wool will absorb half its weight in moisture without becoming uncomfortable.

Resilience. Wool fiber can be stretched 30% beyond its length and snap back to normal.

Luxurious feel. Wool is soft to the touch. With proper care, wool keeps its "feel."

Washability. Wool can be washed successfully, provided care is used. Dry cleaning is preferred for garments with intricate construction, linings, delicate trimmings. Some yarns such as baby yarn and sock yarn are made shrink-resistant.

Color. Wool can be dyed in an infinite variety of beautiful hues and shades.

Standard or Plain. These are 2-, 3-, or 4-ply yarns in which plies of the same weight are twisted together in a uniform manner. Knitting worsted and 3-ply fingering yarn are examples.

Novelty Yarns. These use single-ply yarns of the same or different size twisted together in an irregular manner. Examples are bouclé and nubbly dress yarns.

Blends. Blended yarns are homogeneous yarns composed of two or more different fibers mixed prior to spinning into yarn. The combination of equal parts of nylon and wool is common.

Twisted Mixtures. One strand of a decorative fiber is twisted in or around the wool yarn. An example of a twisted mixture is pompadour which has a strand of rayon twisted around the wool.

Mohair. Mohair comes from the long silky hair of the Angora goat and makes a warm, lightweight, fluff-textured yarn. It is used alone or combined with wool or other fibers.

Angora. This fluffy, soft yarn is made of hairs from the Angora rabbit and is used for trimmings, accessories and sweaters.

Cashmere. Combed from the goats of Kashmir and the Himalayas, this superlatively soft and lightweight yarn is used for sweaters, scarves and accessories. Cashmere which is not as durable as most wools and is expensive is often blended with wool for extra strength and less cost.

SYNTHETIC YARNS of rayon, nylon, orlon and dacron are available in a wide variety of sizes and textures. Synthetics offer many advantages:

Luster. Rayon is especially notable for its luster. Glittering metallic yarns are available for knitting and crocheting evening wear.

Easy Care. Nylon, orlon and dacron wash easily, dry quickly.

Shape-Retention. Nylon, orlon and dacron yarns do not stretch or shrink, and require no blocking after laundering. Since synthetics do not have wool's elasticity, it is particularly important to knit to the correct stitch gauge with synthetics.

Strength. Synthetics are long-wearing.

Mothproof. All synthetics are mothproof.

Non-Allergic. Allergy-sufferers can knit and wear synthetics without difficulty.

Variety. Synthetics can be spun in many weights and types. Rayon, for instance, can appear as cordé, straw or chenille.

Blendability. Synthetics can be mixed with one another or with wool to add such qualities as strength, non-shrinkage.

COTTON YARNS offer these advantages:

Low Cost. Cotton is inexpensive.

Washability. Cotton launders without matting.

Color. Takes dye well, has true rich shades.

Ease of Handling. Does not catch or split.

Mercerized crochet cotton. Fine, strong, mercerized thread with a firm finish in 6-cord and 3-cord twists used mostly for household articles.

Bedspread Cotton. Heavier and more pliable thread used for bedspreads, home accessories.

"Quick" crochet cotton. Heavy, crisp thread for making household and fashion accessories.

Pearl cotton. Lustrous mercerized cotton with a rope twist primarily used for crocheted trimmings, edgings and fashion accessories.

Cotton rug yarn. Durable bulky yarn of all cotton or blended with rayon for rugs, casual sweaters, slippers, bags and hats.

Dress yarns. These are textured yarns of all cotton or blends of cotton and rayon or linen.

LINEN YARNS are crisp and cool and easy to care for, often blended with other fibers.

SILK YARNS are lustrous, luxurious and lightweight; are sometimes blended with other fibers.

Standard wool yarns

Most knitting is done with the basic wool yarns illustrated here. While fashion yarns for suits and dresses change considerably from year to year, these yarns remain the same. In general, when directions call for one of these yarns, any brand may be used. It is necessary, however, to check your stitch and row gauge before knitting or crocheting any article, even when you use the brand yarn specified in the directions.

There is some variation from one brand to another in the tightness of twist in each yarn. This variation does not usually affect the interchangeability of the yarn. Each yarn type is illustrated in three ways: 1. The knitted swatches show the overall appearance of the yarn knitted in stockinette stitch. 2. Each yarn is untwisted to indicate the number of plies or strands twisted together to make the yarn. (In some countries, the ply number is an indication of the thickness of the yarn: this is not so in the United States.) 3. Several brands of each yarn are photographed side by side to show variations.

KNITTED SWATCHES

YARN PLY

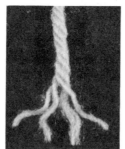

KNITTING WORSTED

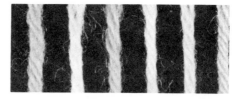

Sample strands of knitting worsted, the most widely used yarn. Heaviest of the standard yarns, it is used for outdoor sweaters, accessories, afghans.

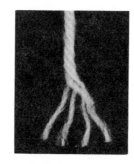

SPORT YARN, 4-PLY

Sample strands of 4-ply sport yarn, a smooth, strong knitting wool for socks, gloves, men's sweaters. Sport yarn is also available in 3-ply twist.

FINGERING YARN, 3-PLY

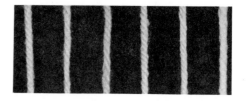

Sample strands of 3-ply fingering yarn, a soft, smooth, lightweight yarn. For men's, women's and children's lightweight sweaters, socks.

SOCK AND SWEATER, 3-PLY

Sample strands of sock and sweater yarn, 3-ply, show firm twist. Similar to sport yarn, wool is used for lightweight knitwear which requires sturdiness.

Sample strands of 4-ply sock and sweater yarn. Smooth and strong, yarn gives excellent wear in socks, gloves and medium-weight sweaters.

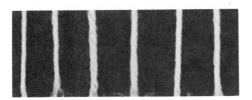

Sample strands of baby yarn, similar to fingering yarn in size but softer. Baby yarns are also made in nylon for those who prefer a quick-drying yarn.

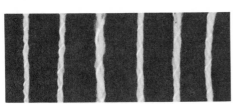

Sample strands of pompadour. Three at left are 2-ply wool, three at right are 3-ply wool, all wound with rayon thread which adds decorative touch.

YARN PLY

SOCK AND SWEATER, 3-PLY

SOCK AND SWEATER, 4-PLY

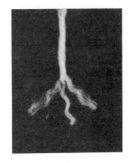

BABY YARN

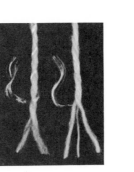

POMPADOUR, 2- AND 3-PLY

Professional Blocking and Finishing For Knitted and Crocheted Fashions

Professional blocking and finishing often make the difference between a beautiful knitted or crocheted garment and a mediocre one. A perfectly knitted item can be ruined by slipshod finishing, while even an indifferently knitted one can be made smart by careful corrective blocking and finishing. Professional techniques are given here as a guide to the shop offering finishing service and to the individual knitter who has the proper equipment and wants to do her own blocking and finishing. The most important ingredients are time and patience, a knowledge of dressmaking techniques and a feel for the fabric. Do not hurry. Allow a day to block and finish a high-style sweater or jacket, two days or more for a suit or coat or dress which requires a lining.

BLOCKING

Blocking is the method used to set a knitted or crocheted piece to desired shape, size and texture. Cables, ribs and raised patterns can be blocked by steaming to shape but should not be pressed flat. Stockinette stitch in most yarns can be pressed flat. Every piece of a garment must be blocked individually before a seam or other joining is made.

Blocking Equipment:

1. Blocking table (40" x 60" or larger).
2. Heavy rug padding nailed to table and covered tightly with muslin sheet.
3. Rust-proof T pins or large bank pins.
4. Steam iron adjusted to maximum amount of steam.
5. Transparent pressing cloth.
6. Yardsticks and tape measures.
7. Tailors' chalk (white and colored).
8. Pressing pads for bustline and darts.
9. Shaped sleeve pad.
10. Sleeve board for pressing seams and edges.
11. Heavy strings tied to large safety pins at each end to mark center of garment, and as guide to a straight line between two points.

Determining Measurements for Blocking: As many actual body measurements as possible should be taken; see Figures 1 and 2 for complete body measurements. Any adjustment for the style and fit of the design can be taken into consideration in blocking. Check with the blocking measurements recommended in the instructions and with picture of the garment.

If blocking measurements for individual pieces are not given in the instructions, figure them out, using the gauge as a guide. Note the number of stitches at bottom, hip, waist, underarm, shoulders, etc., and divide by the number of stitches per inch. Compare blocking measurements to body measurements (making same allowance for style, as shown in picture). Make notes of adjustments that should be made.

Fig. 1   Fig. 2

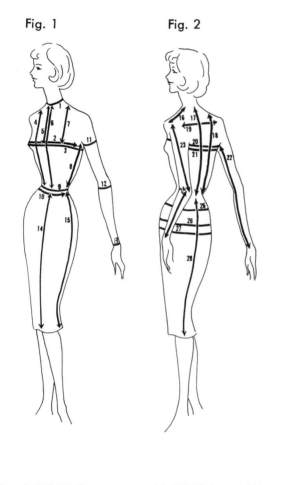

1 NECK 2 BUST FRONT	16 NECK TO END OF SHOULDER
3 BUST 4 SHOULDER TO WAIST	17 NECK TO WAIST
5 NECK TO BUSTLINE	18 SHOULDER TO WAIST
6 NECK TO WAIST	19 BACK—4" BELOW NECK
7 SHOULDER TO BUSTLINE	20 CHEST 21 BUST BACK
8 UNDERARM TO WAIST	22 UNDERARM TO WRIST
9 WAIST	23 SHOULDER TO ELBOW
10 WAIST FRONT 11 UPPER ARM	24 ELBOW TO WRIST
12 LOWER ARM 13 WRIST	25 HIPS—3" BELOW WAIST
13 WRIST 14 WAIST TO HEM—FRONT	26 HIPS—7" BELOW WAIST
15 WAIST TO HEM—SIDE	27 HIPS—9" BELOW WAIST
28 WAIST TO HEM—BACK	

Preparing Garment for Blocking: Conceal all ends of yarn by running them diagonally through several stitches on wrong side, using a tapestry needle or crochet hook. If yarn is particularly heavy, split it and run each end separately through adjoining stitches to avoid bulk.

If washing is necessary, wash pieces separately. Smooth out flat on Turkish towels, adjusting pieces so that they measure no more than finished measurements desired. Some knits stretch larger when wet so must be pushed into slight puckers (which will disappear as fabric dries). Drying process may be hastened by placing towels on window screens raised so that air can circulate underneath.

Special Considerations: Certain pattern stitches such as ribbing, cables, lacy stitches or other patterns which require stretching in width for proper effect should be blocked one to two inches wider to allow for shrinking back; if yarn contains 50% or more nylon, allow two or three inches for shrinking back.

Some yarns have considerable "hang" and measure much longer held up than lying flat on the table. The amount of "hang" should be taken into consideration and the garment should be blocked shorter and wider. This is true of extra heavy or loosely knitted garments. Mohair needs a little extra stretching in length only; otherwise it may buckle.

For the full-busted figure it is best to have an underarm bustline dart which can be sewn in when fabric is not bulky. Allowance must be made by stretching the front longer at the sides to make room for dart; Figure 3. If fabric is to be steamed, rather than pressed flat, dart allowance can be accomplished by inserting a pad from side seam toward center front, before seaming, to increase length at side.

Plan Seams: Consider what type of seam will be most suitable. In most garments a running backstitch made with #50 sewing thread or fine yarn is best and will need an allowance of only one stitch from edge. If machine zigzag stitch is to be used, allow ⅜" for seams. If fabric calls for overcast or woven seams, it is not necessary to make any allowances. Any jogs caused by increases, bind-offs, or other shaping can be evened out in blocking and taken in in seams.

Basic Pattern: It is helpful to have a McCall's Basic Try-On Pattern (McCall's Try-On Pattern 100, Misses' and Junior Sizes, and Pattern B-200, Half-Sizes, are available at pattern counters) to use as a blocking guide to proper shaping of a skirt panel, cap of set-in sleeve, shape of basic collar and neckline, etc. Be sure to consider seam allowances and darts in pattern. This pattern is also useful for linings. Darts in basic pattern may be pinned in and pads used for shaping the knitted fabric accordingly; or if more suitable for fabric to be blocked flat, leave basic pattern as is, and after blocking, shrink the extra width allowed for darts.

Pinning: After writing down all measurements to be followed in blocking, pin one section at a time on blocking table, wrong side up (except ribbons). Following measurements, place pins in edge of section as close as necessary to obtain a perfectly even edge, never more than ½" apart; place into padding in opposite direction from fabric "stretch"; Figure 4.

Fig. 3

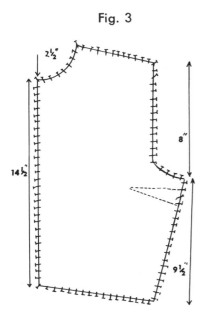

Side blocked 9½″ is 8½″ with ½″ dart sewn in.

Fig. 4

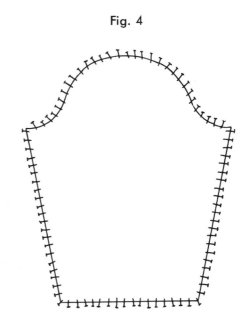

Placing of pins for blocking sleeve.

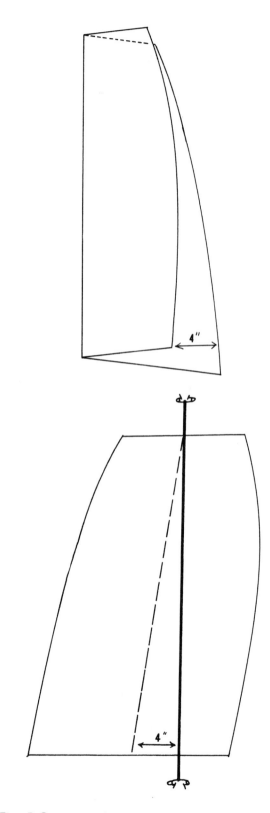

Fig. 5 Correcting bias piece.

Pressing: There are two methods of pressing knitted and crocheted pieces: flat pressing and steampressing. Consider the texture desired before touching iron to fabric. Some yarns, such as mohair, should never be pressed flat as they would lose life and texture. If a soft fluffy appearance is desirable, or if pattern stitch is any type of raised stitch, it should not be pressed flat. If in doubt, try pressing a small piece flat in an inconspicuous section; then try another section steamed without pressure and compare. Some materials, such as ribbon, can be pressed flat and afterwards steamed up slightly before unpinning to obtain an attractive texture. If there are cables separated by wide sections of plain knitting, you may wish to use a combination of two techniques, pressing only plain section flat.

For steaming technique, support weight of iron in your hand, hold as close as possible to fabric without touching it and move slowly over entire pinned piece, making certain that steam penetrates fabric. If yarn is extra heavy, it may be necessary to use a spray iron or a wet pressing cloth to provide extra steam.

To press sections flat, place organdy pressing cloth on top of pinned piece and lower iron so that weight rests on fabric. Raise and lower again over entire section; do not use a back-and-forth ironing motion. With the transparent pressing cloth it is possible to see where flat sections begin and end.

Leave pieces pinned to table until entirely dry. Drying can be hastened by the use of a small electric fan or hand dryer. If a piece has a duplicate, leave guide pins in the blocking table at intervals around the garment shape so that you have an outline for shaping the duplicate piece.

Wet Blocking: This may be desirable if the stitch used makes the finished pieces go strongly bias. Also, wet blocking may be used for articles which have been washed. Wet or wash article thoroughly, squeeze out and roll in a Turkish towel, lay the individual pieces on blocking table and pin to measurements using rustproof pins. Leave until thoroughly dry.

Bias Items: Some yarns will work up straight when knit in garter stitch or pattern stitches with no purling, but will go strongly bias when knit in stockinette stitch. This may happen with some pattern stitches and some knitters, regardless of the yarn used. Wet blocking will solve this problem, or if time and space do not permit, item can be straightened with steam blocking: First mark center stitch of item, then measure exactly how much the bias amounts to and block it the same amount in the opposite direction. Example: If the item hangs 4″ bias to the right, pin and block it 4″ to the left, and the blocked piece will hang straight; Figure 5.

Blocking Technique for Ribbon: Nearly all ribbon garments look, fit and wear best when blocked flat. Run in or sew ends on wrong side. Lay piece on blocking table right side up. Examine pieces for any imperfect stitches and straighten by placing plain end of crochet hook under the imperfect stitch to hold it straight. Apply steam to set the stitch.

Smooth piece on table right side up, pinning just enough to control curling at edges, but do not stretch material. Place pressing cloth over article and press, using steam and slight pressure on iron to flatten the stitches and set the pattern. Do not use ironing motion. Unpin pieces, consult "blocked gauge" and re-pin, stretching to desired measurements. You must consider "hang" when blocking ribbon skirts. Allow 1″ to 2″ for most ribbons and 3″ for the heavier all-rayon ribbons. Block skirt slightly wider to compensate for the "hang" which makes the skirt fit closer to the body.

Ribbon knits should be stretched after setting the stitches or the garment will gradually become longer in wearing and require alterations. If properly stretched to the blocked gauge, the garment will retain its original dimensions. Stretched and blocked ribbon pieces can be shrunk with steam, too, though in a limited range.

Ribbon knits take nicely to sewn-in darts, and an underarm bustline dart is usually desirable. Allowance should be made for this in blocking. For full-busted figures requiring a "close" fit, darts may also be taken vertically from the waist up. Allow ⅜″ to ½″ for seams in knitted ribbons. Some crocheted ribbons have zigzag edges formed by the pattern which can be meshed and sewn as an invisible seam. It is necessary to match these edges, so find the right side of each piece before blocking.

Some ribbons and some stitches look nicer if steamed slightly without cloth after pressing flat, but before removing pins. This can be determined by experimenting on a small corner of the material and is usually desirable for a "butterfly" stitch or other overlay pattern stitch.

ASSEMBLY

Many dressmaking techniques are used in assembling knitted garments and the couturier types require a good knowledge of dressmaking techniques for a successful result. In assembling knitted garments there are no helpful notches to match as in dressmaking patterns. Everything has to be measured and marked with pins or chalk to take the place of notches. Careful and precise blocking will show its value here. Some garments have definite ribs or patterns that can be matched. Plain stitches must be measured and marked at intervals and the markings matched.

It is desirable to have a form with collapsible shoulders for fitting garments. A store would need several, in different sizes.

Preliminary Try-On: Baste pieces together with contrasting thread, taking in darts and seam allowances. Try garment on form. If you find something wrong other than seam adjustments, you can shrink or stretch for desired fit. If it is necessary to stretch, the part to be stretched should be pinned to desired measurement and steam applied to just that portion. If shrinking is necessary, pin to desired measurement and form small puckers which will disappear with steam applied and a little coaxing with the fingers. The wide part of the sleeve board is useful for small adjustments which can be done without removing bastings. If garment fits form, sew the main seams. It is now ready for fitting. (If garment is to be lined, sew main seams of lining and try on at same fitting.)

Common Fitting Problems: Shoulder seams that sag can be held by a running backstitch of yarn through the seam, which is left in garment; Figure 6. Necklines can be adjusted and held by slip stitching with yarn; Figure 7.

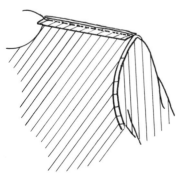

Fig. 6 Staying stitch for a shoulder seam.

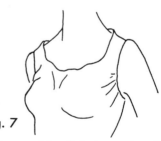

Fig. 7

Neckline is too big. Solution: Slip stitch, and shrink out the fullness.

Armhole is too small. Solution: Release crocheted edge, pin out and stretch armhole.

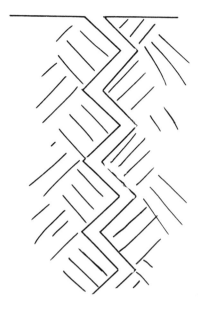

Fig. 8 Meshing crocheted box stitch patterns together: Join zigzag edges, sew back and forth holding pieces right side up.

Fig. 9 Running Backstitch.

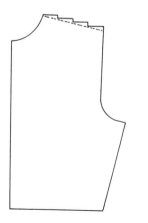

Fig. 10 Sewing shoulder seam to take in jogs of bind-offs.

If fronts of jacket or coat hang away from each other, front edge is too long and should be shortened by a staying thread as described for shoulders and shrinking; or side seam is too tight and should be stretched. If front edges hang forward and overlap more at bottom than they should, front edges are too short and are drawing (common if edges are crocheted); or side seams are too loose. Solution: Stretch front edge if it has any curve, or restitch side seams more firmly.

If wide square neckline gapes or sags in front and slides on shoulders, take more seam allowance from shoulder neck edge to nothing more at shoulder tip. Sew 1½″ wide folded piece of nylon tulle along square of neckline to hold it to desired shape. Also check bustline fit of garment, for if it is stretching through bustline, neckline will be affected.

If straight skirt ripples or flares at bottom, hips are too tight. It is best to pin zipper in place while garment is being tried on to prevent buckling of zipper. Mark positions of buttons and buttonholes, if they are to be made later. If grosgrain or nylon tulle facings are to be applied to front edges or neckline, cut and pin them in place during try-on. Mark waistline if it is fitted and pin seam binding or soft elastic in place to hold waistline.

If it is necessary to cut fabric for major adjustments, mark cutting line with chalk or basting and zigzag stitch on sewing machine ¼″ inside marked line (adjust size of zigzag stitch to fabric). Or sew by hand, being careful to catch every stitch. Then cut fabric. Raw edge can be crocheted if yarn is not too heavy, or overcast by hand. If garment is too long, excess can be removed by pulling a thread at desired length and binding off the open stitches with crochet hook in same tension as knitting.

Seams: Seams should be as nearly invisible as possible and, above all, straight and neat. They must be firm enough to hold, yet elastic enough to give with the fabric, having the same tension and resiliency as the knitting. All patterns, stripes, tops of ribbed bands, colored borders, etc., must be matched carefully. Seams may be sewn in various ways depending on type of knitted or crocheted fabric and stitch. Ribbons, unless edge patterns are to be meshed together as in Figure 8, can be sewn by machine. A zigzag stitch with #50 mercerized sewing cotton is best. Test resiliency after sewing a few stitches. A zigzag stitch will give with the fabric while a straight stitch is apt to break. Certain firm fabrics knitted of wool or other yarns also take to this machine stitching.

Hand-Sewn Seams: In every case sleeves should be set in and collars sewn on by hand. Hand sewing should be a running backstitch, Figure 9, taking in seam allowance planned, usually 1 stitch (2 stitches if finely knit). Sewing with yarn makes a bulky seam which is hard to take out, if necessary, without cutting the wrong strand. However, if yarn is desired, use very fine matching yarn or split the original yarn. Seams may also be woven or meshed when called for in a pattern. Be careful to take in bound-off stitches in seams; Figure 10.

Weaving Seams: (a) Lengthwise Woven Seam. Thread needle with matching yarn. Lay the two pieces face up on a flat surface, edges meeting. Take a vertical stitch through one edge, then a vertical stitch through the other edge. When yarn is drawn sufficiently tight it will make a running stitch seam and each stitch will meet its neighbor in the proper order; Figure 11.

(b) Crosswise Woven Seam: Thread needle with matching yarn. Lay the two edges face up on a flat surface. Starting at right-hand side, take a small stitch through both edges; then insert needle into first stitch and up through next stitch on one edge, down through second stitch and up through next stitch on other edge. Working first in one edge and then the other, insert needle into last stitch worked in and bring it up through next stitch. Continue across in this manner; Figure 12.

Setting in Sleeves and Attaching Collars: Sleeves cannot be woven into place. Because the set of a sleeve is so important, it is best to baste it in place and try on before sewing in by hand.

It is not enough to match underarm seams; you must find the center of sleeve cap and pin to shoulder seam. Then, starting at underarm, pin each side fitting sleeve carefully into armhole and ease in any slight fullness through top of sleeve cap; Figure 13. If there is too much fullness to be eased in, check cap measurements and armhole length with basic pattern and reshape if necessary. A small amount extra may be taken in when sewing sleeve in place without resorting to cutting the fabric.

Find center back of collar and neck and pin together. Pin front edges of collar in position; pin carefully and evenly between the pins placed at center and front edges; Figure 14.

If collar is double, or faced with tulle, undercollar must be smaller to allow for turndown. This also applies to lapels for proper "roll."

Join the two collars at outer edges by sewing right sides together closely along edge (if fabric is not bulky) or by single crocheting, slip stitching or overcasting along stitches at edges through both thicknesses. Sew upper collar to neck edge, taking in small seam or overcasting edge stitches together, then roll collar over your hand and pin undercollar so that it covers seam and has proper roll without bulk underneath. Sew undercollar in place.

Fig. 11   LENGTHWISE WOVEN SEAM

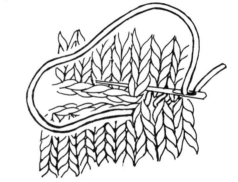

Fig. 12   CROSSWISE WOVEN SEAM

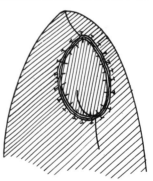

FIG. 13   SETTING IN SLEEVE

FIG. 14   PINNING ON COLLAR

Finishing

Hems: If garment is to have a hem at bottom or on sleeves, these can be picked up before or after main seams are in and facings turned. Use a size smaller needle than used in garment and work in stockinette stitch. With wrong side facing you, pick up and knit through the whole stitch at edge; pick up to within one stitch of side edges (seam allowance) and within one stitch of facing when turned.

If garment has cables starting at hemline, it is necessary to pick up hems in this way, picking up fewer stitches across cables so that hem will not buckle. This is also true of widely ribbed garments, if they need hems. If garment is finely ribbed at bottom or has a nonroll border, it does not need a hem. Another method used for hems when garment is clumsy to handle is to knit hems separately and single crochet, overcast or slip stitch to bottom edge of garment. Ribbing on bottom edges and cuffs should be flat seamed or woven together so that ribbing can be turned up without showing a "wrong side" seam.

Interfacing: Sometimes it is desirable to interface a collar with nylon tulle or bias Pellon. Cut interfacing to fit undercollar and catch stitch to entire undercollar before joining to upper collar; Figure 15. Interfacing should also be used along front edges of garments, especially tailored jackets and coats. Pin to piece to be interfaced and cut to fit.

Facings: Most facings are knitted but nylon tulle is good to use as a facing. It provides a base for sewing buttonholes, as well as a crisp front edge. Patch pockets will not sag if they are catch stitched throughout to nylon tulle. A strip of tulle will do wonders for a low neckline, the edges of slot pockets, or for cuffs. It is easy to work with, does not ravel, and is not as scratchy as coarse net.

If garment is too bulky for a knitted facing, French belting (grosgrain) can be used. This has a picot edge and can be steamed and stretched into a curve.

To face front edges of a cardigan with ribbon, wet and press ribbon before sewing to garment to preshrink it, or use nylon ribbon. Use matching grosgrain ribbon slightly narrower than front bands. If there are no front bands, use ribbon 1″ wide. Cut ribbon 1″ longer than edge to be faced. Place ribbon on wrong side of garment just inside edge; turn under top and bottom edges of ribbon; pin to neck and bottom edges of cardigan. Baste ribbon in place; whip edges of ribbon to cardigan with matching sewing thread. If cardigan does not have front band, the inner edge of ribbon can be left free. Slash rib-

bon under buttonholes. Buttonhole-stitch or overcast around slashes. Or, if desired, hem edges of slashes around the buttonholes.

Buttonholes: Although buttonholes are usually knitted in, a neater buttonhole can be made by cutting and pulling a strand out for the required number of stitches; Figure 16. Either single crochet or slip stitch with yarn through the open stitches on both sides of buttonhole. This method is especially good for bulky yarns: split the yarn to be used for crocheting the open stitches.

If garment has a facing, the buttonhole must be opened in facing as well and matched to that on outside. Except in the case of mohair or extremely bulky yarns, both buttonholes can be crocheted at the same time by inserting hook through loop of outside and inside stitches and working as one. In the above-mentioned yarns, or when facing is of a different color than garment, work each buttonhole separately and tack loosely together with thread. Make long shanks when sewing the buttons on these bulkies.

Outlined buttonholes can be made by using a contrasting yarn to single crochet or slip stitch the buttonhole. Soutache can be used for slip stitching to give a trimmed or bound effect. If it would be best to have a vertical rather than a horizontal buttonhole, mark position and baste a piece of seam binding or

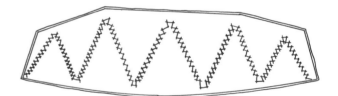

Fig. 15
Catch stitching interfacing to collar.

Fig. 16
Cutting strand for buttonhole.

narrow grosgrain ribbon slightly longer than buttonhole to wrong side of garment. Machine-stitch buttonhole using the zigzag machine. Cut with razor blade between lines of stitching and through seam binding. Work buttonhole stitch around opening with split yarn or buttonhole twist.

Buttons: Select attractive buttons that are light in weight, shank type for bulky yarns, sew-through type for fine yarns. Buttons can be made from plastic rings or button molds. Directions for these are given under Crocheted Trimmings (see Index).

Belts: A self-belt should always have a buckle to avoid a homemade look. Covered rings can be used as buckles. If rings are not used, buckles of several sizes can be purchased and crocheted over with same yarn or ribbon used in belt. If knitted belt has a neat edge, overcast grosgrain to the wrong side along edges. If belt is wide, catchstitch grosgrain back and forth, in a wide zigzag pattern, through center to hold firm and prevent rolling. Insert a strip of interfacing in extra wide belts. If edges of belt require smoothing, single crochet or slip stitch around entire belt before facing.

Skirt Tops: Tailored skirts are best fitted to waist and closed with a placket zipper. In ribbon garments, press seam allowance flat and insert zipper along seam line. In yarn garments, single crochet around zipper opening before sewing in zipper. Ease fabric into zipper and sew by hand with small running backstitch. If skirt has knitted waistband, face with grosgrain, overlap at left side and fasten with snaps. If there is no waistband, sew 1½″ wide grosgrain, cut to waist measure, on inside of skirt. If a skirt has no zipper, a crocheted elastic edge is neater than the "beading" type. Use round millinery elastic with yarn: Work one round of single crochet on top of skirt, making sure skirt will go over shoulders. On next round, hold elastic along edge of skirt and single crochet over it. Next round, single crochet without elastic, and following round single crochet over elastic. Alternate rounds in this manner, having three or four with elastic.

Finishing Edges: In finishing edges by crocheting, do not use more than one row of single crochet plus one row of slip stitch, from wrong side, if required. Some bulky yarns require only a row of slip stitch done loosely from wrong side, while some garments look best with one row of single crochet done from right side. Other patterns (usually in two colors) require one row of slip stitch from the right side, plus one row of single crochet, also from right side. It is necessary to have the proper tension in all crocheting done along edges. There should be fewer single crochet stitches to the inch than knitted stitches; do not work into every stitch or row.

To turn an outside corner, work two or three stitches into corner stitch. To turn an inside corner, decrease two stitches by pulling through loops in corner, and one stitch each side of corner, and drawing yarn through all loops on hook tightly. This decrease should also be done at the end of any opening such as a zipper placket.

Pressing Seams: Give seams final pressing, using sleeve board and point of iron, taking care not to shrink or stretch seams.

Linings: It is desirable to have a lining in most coats, and in some jackets. Mohair in particular should be lined. Lightweight taffeta lining material is easy to work with and comes in a wide range of colors. China silk or sheath lining is recommended for ribbon sheath dresses and skirts. For detailed directions on lining a coat, see next page.

In lining sheath dresses, the basic blocking pattern can be used to cut lining. Leave ample seam allowance, and slight ease at back of neck. Stitch main seams. Try dress on inside out with lining on top. Pin along main seams and around neckline, turning in edges of lining at neckline and armholes or sleeve edges. Turn edges of lining at zipper opening, and pin along zipper tape. Pin at waistline. Sew lining to dress at waistline, neck, and sleeve edges. Do not attach lining at lower seams of skirt.

Mounting on Tulle: Some ribbon dresses, especially those with full skirts, made of silk organdy ribbon in lacy patterns, are greatly enhanced by mounting entire dress on tulle, a painstaking process. Cut tulle to basic bodice pattern. Use dress as pattern for skirt panels, allowing ½″ for overlap. Do not sew seams. Try on dress inside out. Pin tulle sections to dress while on, pinning in darts. Pin tulle to dress throughout bodice in diagonal crossbar design, overlapping tulle ½″ at side seams and turning in ½″ at zipper opening. Pin sections of tulle to skirt, overlapping ½″ at waistline and wherever panels meet. Pin darts at waist for smooth fit. Turn ½″ under and pin along zipper opening. Now pin tulle to entire skirt in diagonal crossbar design. Turn small hem under and pin to bottom of skirt.

Remove dress carefully. Catch stitch tulle to dress following pin lines, conforming as closely as possible to pattern stitch. Take only tiny catch stitches in dress; run thread between dress and lining for about ½″, then catch stitch to lining with medium-size stitch. Hem around neckline, bottom edge, and zipper. Close overlapped sections of tulle with running backstitch.

Lining a handknit or crocheted coat

The technique of lining a hand knitted or crocheted coat is more involved than that of lining a cloth coat, and requires considerably more work —nearly all by hand. One should allow two to three days to finish and line the coat. However, since there is so much to be gained in appearance, fit, and wear by lining the coat, it is well worth the extra work.

Lining Materials: Choose a lining material with "body" and slight stiffness. Taffeta, satin, Milium satin, or lightweight brocade of either rayon or silk are all suitable; choice depends on style of coat. Use lightweight Pellon for interfacing, bias Pellon for collars.

Preparing Coat for Lining: The first step before blocking is to close and sew together any buttonholes; then judge the amount of "hang" of the pieces. Test for hang as follows: Lay back of coat smoothly on table and measure the length from neck to hem. Now fold in half lengthwise, armholes and shoulder seams together. Hold piece at back of neck and measure along fold while hanging in mid-air. The difference in measurement is the amount of "natural hang" before blocking. If there is a great amount of hang; the back and fronts of the coat should be blocked shorter and wider than the desired finished measurement. Width is lost to some extent, particularly at upper half of coat, as a result of hang in heavy or loosely worked pieces. One must consider also that the coat has to hang unsupported from the shoulders, unless it is to be tightly belted at the waist.

Blocking and Finishing: Block pieces following instructions on preceding pages. After the pieces have been blocked, make paper tracings of all pieces.

Sew shoulder seams, side seams, sleeve seams, and set sleeves in place. Always use matching thread and small, loose backstitches unless otherwise specified. Now hang coat on a dressmaker's form, pinning to form at neck and pinning and holding in slightly across shoulders to prevent weight of sleeves from stretching shoulder line and neck. Let hang at least overnight.

After coat has hung overnight, check length and see that the front edges hang in a straight line following pattern stitch used. Make any necessary adjustments. If length is correct and coat has a separate hem, pin hem around bottom of coat with wrong sides together, being careful not to draw in or buckle bottom of coat. It is best to do this while garment is on the form. Allow for any facings at front of coat. Overcast hem in place with matching thread; sew upper edge loosely in place.

If coat has hung to a longer length than desired, mark length with pins. If coat is knitted, pull a strand of yarn at nearest place consistent with the pattern stitch used and cut, thus removing the excess length. With crochet hook and yarn, slip-stitch through the open stitches from the wrong side, being careful not to work too tightly. Pin and overcast the separate hem in place. If coat is crocheted, turn up excess and use for hem. If coat needs to be shortened and has a knitted-on hem, open stitches at desired length and also at the "turning row" of hem to remove excess length. With wrong sides together, pin hem in place, having open stitches at bottom. With inside of coat facing, slip-stitch together with crochet hook and yarn through two open stitches (hem and coat edge), being careful to work with loose tension. Sew upper edge of hem loosely in place with matching thread.

Cutting: Cut out lining so that it will correspond to measurements of coat while it is hanging on form. Allow 1½″ extra width for a ¾″ pleat at back of neck and 1″ on each shoulder of back for ½″ darts. If garment has set-in or dolman sleeves, allow 2½″ for a 1¼″ dart on each shoulder of front; if raglan sleeves, allow 2″ for 1″ dart on each shoulder of front. Allow ½″ extra length in sleeves for "elbow room." Allow ½″ extension of lining on all edges, plus 3″ at bottom edge for hem.

Sewing: Sew darts on shoulders: taper darts on back to nothing about 4″ down; taper darts on set-in or dolman-sleeved coat fronts to nothing about 7″ down; taper darts on raglan-sleeved coat fronts to nothing about 5″ down. Sew seams of lining and press. Always press seams and joinings as in dressmaking. Press all knitted facings and hems which will not show on right side of coat as flat as possible before sewing to coat, to avoid undesirable bulk.

Interfacings: Cut neck interfacing from Pellon to conform to neck of coat. If coat is made of ribbon or ribbon and yarn, use Pellon interfacing 3″ wide at front edges as well.

Place coat on form wrong side out. Pin interfacing carefully in place and catch-stitch throughout in zigzag pattern.

Pinning Lining in Place: Remove coat and place lining on form wrong side out. Place coat right side out over lining. Pin coat to lining, starting at center back of neck and pinning toward shoulders and along shoulder seam, allowing ½″ to extend at neck edge and easing coat slightly across shoulder span for graceful drape. Pin side seam of lining to side seam of coat near underarm. Allowing ½″ of lining to extend, pin lining to coat along both front edges while it is still hanging on form.

Place a few pins along upper half of armhole and along the shoulder darts. (If coat has a raglan sleeve, pins should be placed along seam line.) Tack lightly to lining where pinned. Baste ¼" horizontal pleat in sleeve lining just below elbow (to be released later for ease). Pin lining to sleeve edge, allowing ½" to extend at bottom of sleeve.

Sew invisibly from right side along all pinned edges, ¼" from edge of coat.

Lining must extend into and turn with all edges—except for bottom hem—for a tailored and neat look. Pin and sew bottom hem of lining in place.

Make holding bars for hem by crocheting a chain 1½" long with yarn. Slip stitch to seam of coat near bottom; sew other end to inside seam of lining.

Sleeves: If sleeves have hems, trim lining just inside edge of sleeves. Sew invisibly along turn of hem. Turn and press up. Sew upper edge in place, sewing through lining to catch outside of coat sleeve lightly; then release the basted "ease pleat."

If sleeves have no hems, turn edge of lining to inside (between lining and coat) and hem in place just inside edge of sleeve; lightly sew lining to sleeve at 1" above, so that "elbow ease pleat," when released, will not cause lining to show at bottom.

Facings: If coat has separate facings, pin to front of coat, right sides together, while on form. Sew along front edges, taking in a small amount consistent with pattern stitch. Press seam open. Turn facings to inside. Press again. With inside of coat facing you, sew lightly along turned edge ¼" to ½" in from edge, taking small stitches and catching outside of coat invisibly. Take care not to draw front edge. Pin and sew inside edge of facings through lining and invisibly to front of coat.

If facings are knitted in one with front of coat, mark place where facings will turn and sew lining to coat along this line. Press lightly, trim edge of lining, and sew inside edge of facings in place in same way as separate facings. There will be a double thickness of lining inside facings.

If coat has no facings at all, trim extending edge of lining. Turn ½" on edge of coat (more, if called for by pattern) after sewing along line of prospective turn in order to hold lining inside fold for sharp edge. Pin and sew turned edge in place, catching outside of coat invisibly.

If coat is collarless, or has a set-away collar, or stand-up band set away from neck edge, finish neck by turning extending edge of lining to inside; then turn ¼" of neck edge to inside (over lining) and sew. If knitted or crocheted neck facing is provided, pin in place, then sew so that it joins turned edge of neck. Sew other edge lightly in place, catching through lining to interfacing.

Collars: If coat has a collar, face with bias Pellon, catch-stitching throughout in zigzag pattern. Cut lining, allowing ½" to turn to inside at all edges, and sew to collar on three sides leaving neck edge

open, except where knitted under-collar is provided. In this case, bias Pellon is catch-stitched to under-collar before sewing together with upper-collar. Always fold or roll collar in desired position (this applies also to lapels) before sewing under-collar or collar lining in place (under part will need to be smaller, to avoid buckling collar). Pin and sew upper part of collar to neck edge of coat, working from inside of coat. Press seam. Fold collar in position and sew under-collar or collar lining in place, covering seam. Catch-stitch invisibly through all thicknesses, 1" from outside edges of collar, using zigzag pattern.

Helpful Suggestions Regarding Collars: Stand-up band collars, although worked straight, should be blocked longer at lower edge and held in slightly at upper edge in order to stand straight up when sewn to coat. These collars are usually set farthest away at shoulder seams. Set-away collars are sewn at neck edge of front, slightly down at back of neck, and farthest away at shoulder seams. Collar is completely finished before attaching to coat. Shawl collars must be blocked considerably longer at the outside edge than at the neck edge, to prevent front of coat from pulling up. Stretch collar and under-collar at outside edge and ease at back edge. Notched collars should be woven to lapels with yarn, because edges seamed in the conventional way tend to be bulky.

Patch Pockets and Belts: If edges of pockets would not look well showing, a small amount can be turned to inside after lining. Cut Pellon to fit, and catch-stitch in place throughout. Cut lining material extending ½" at edges. Turn ½" of lining to inside and sew along edge (or turn 1 row or 1 stitch to inside for better appearance). Try on coat. Pin patch pockets in place, pinning through to lining. If coat has a back belt, interline and line it as for pockets; pin it in place at becoming position. After checking to see that lining is smooth underneath pockets, sew pockets in place through to lining from right side. This supports pockets and prevents sag. Run invisible stitches ½" from edges of belt so that lining cannot show from right side. Separate cuffs are also handled this way.

Buttonholes: If buttonholes have been knitted or crocheted in, release basting used to close buttonholes. With crochet hook and yarn, work 1 row of slip stitch around buttonhole; sew buttonhole together at ends for neat corners. Slit lining material and turn under ⅛" around buttonhole; sew in place, overcasting to buttonhole. If coat has a facing and has double buttonholes, finish each buttonhole separately with slip stitch. Slit lining and sew double buttonhole together, catching the lining material between for support. When sewing buttons in place, leave enough shank so that buttons do not dimple front of coat.

Decorative Touches for Handknits

There are many ways to decorate handknits. They can be embroidered with sequins or beads using the method described for "Beading as Trimming" in the Embroidery section (see Index). More casual knits in stockinette stitch can be embroidered with wool.

Buttonholes Formed With Knitted Bias Binding

Cable Edging

Wool Embroidery: Work embroidery after pieces have been blocked and, if possible, before they have been sewn together. Place tissue paper over the design you want to embroider and trace the outlines. Leaving a margin of paper around design, cut out motif. Baste in place.

Many yarns are suitable for embroidering sweaters: crewel wool, fingering yarn, knitting worsted, mohair, etc. Any yarn except a nubbly or bulky yarn may be used. Thread yarn in a chenille needle (sharp-pointed yarn needle). Embroider design over tissue paper, then carefully tear tissue away.

Embroidered Appliqués: If design is a large solid motif such as a flower worked entirely in satin stitch, the design can be traced or stamped on organdy and embroidered. The embroidered motif is then appliquéd to the sweater.

Duplicate Stitch: Cross-stitch or needlepoint designs which are given in chart form may be used for duplicate stitch embroidery on stockinette stitch. For the embroidery, use same weight yarn as sweater was knitted in. For Duplicate Stitch directions, see Index. In choosing the design, consider that each little square of the design will cover one stitch of the knitting. Since there are more rows to the inch than stitches to the inch in stockinette stitch, the design will appear somewhat shorter from bottom to top after it is worked on the sweater.

Bias Tubing: Satin or velvet makes attractive trimming for knitwear. It can be curved to follow the lines of the garment or formed into scrolls and other applied designs. For a flat effect, remove all or part of the stuffing in the tubing and press flat. To use tubing as a binding for necklines, collars, cuffs and pocket edges, open up seam of tubing and remove filler. With right sides together, stitch one edge of binding to edge of knitwear. Fold binding to wrong side; hem.

Knitted Bias Binding: A binding knitted in stockinette stitch of the same yarn as the garment, in matching or contrasting color, gives a couturier look to a suit or jacket. Cast on stitches required for width of binding desired taking into consideration that binding will be folded in half. Work for required length, increasing in first stitch and knitting two stitches together at end of every knit row. Sew along edge of piece to be bound with right sides together, turn and press. Sew other edge to wrong side of garment. Vertical buttonholes can be made automatically by leaving spaces when sewing on binding.

Knitted Cable Edging: A knitted cable can be made to edge coats, suits and dresses. Sport yarn weight is excellent for most purposes but knitting worsted can be used for bulkier cable trims. To make cable trim, cast on 10 stitches. Work a 6-stitch cable at center with 2 stitches each side in reverse stockinette stitch to be turned under. One edge of trimming, when turned under, forms a deeper scalloped edge than the other. Use this deeper edge for outer edge. Stitch outer edge of trimming to wrong side of garment taking in two stitches of trimming. Turn trimming to right side; turn under two stitches on opposite edge and hem in place.

Rolled Edges: A corded finishing on knitwear can be made by rolling crocheted edges over cable cord. Cable cords can be bought in several thicknesses. Work a row of single crochet from wrong side along edge to be trimmed. Work back and forth in single crochet until edging is deep enough to roll forward to right side over cable cord. A ready-made braided piping can be inserted along the edge of the roll and stitched in at the same time as the rolled edge is sewed down to the right side.

Folded Grosgrain Ribbon Trim: This makes a pointed decorative border for jackets and cardigans. Use 1″ wide grosgrain ribbon in matching or contrasting color. Fold ribbon on the bias for all folds and press each fold flat as you work. In making the folds, never bring two edges of the ribbon together.

Fold right end of ribbon to back diagonally; Fig. 1.

Working from right to left, fold ribbon to front diagonally forming a point; Fig. 2.

Continue to fold diagonally to front forming points at top and bottom for desired length of trimming; Fig. 3. Trimming can be used in this form if a saw-tooth edge is desired. Or, fold trimming through center and press; Fig. 4.

Knitted Fringe Trimming: A fringe can be knitted and sewed to the lower edges of casual sweaters, stoles and ponchos. Use knitting worsted and a pair of knitting needles No. 5. Cut a piece of cardboard as wide as you want the fringe and about 3″ long.

Cast on 8 to 10 stitches. The number of stitches you cast on will determine the depth of the knitted border above the fringe.

Row 1: Insert needle in first stitch in the usual way, place the cardboard behind your needles and in front of the yarn close up to first stitch. Hold cardboard between thumb and forefinger of left hand. Pass yarn along back of cardboard, up front and around point of right needle. Knit off the stitch. Knit to end of row.

Row 2: Slip first stitch, knit to end of row. Repeat these two rows alternately for desired length of fringe trimming. Bind off. When cardboard is full of loops, slip some loops off end and slide remainder of loops towards end of cardboard to make room for more loops. Fringe may be kept in loops or cut.

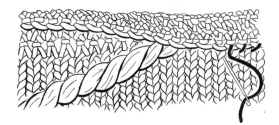

Crocheted edge rolled over cable cord

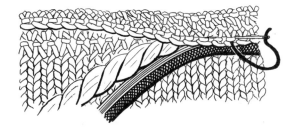

Piping inserted for extra trimming touch

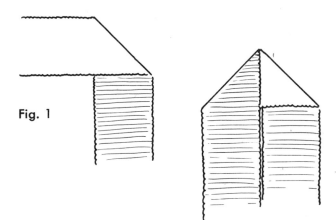

Fig. 1

Fig. 2

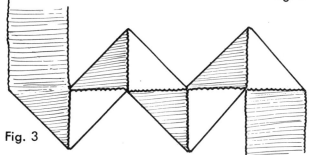

Fig. 3

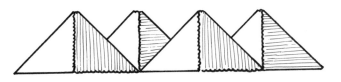

Fig. 4

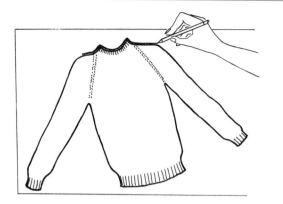

HOW TO LAUNDER SWEATERS

To maintain the proper shape, before washing a sweater, trace the outline on clean brown wrapping paper. Spread the paper out on a clean, flat surface. Put several layers of newspaper or bath towels under it to prevent damage to the surface caused by moisture. (For Orlon Sayelle, see special insructions below.)

Wools, including Angora, should be washed in lukewarm water (comfortable wrist temperature) and soap or light-duty detergent suds. Squeeze garment gently through suds and constantly support it with your hands both in sudsing and rinsing to prevent stretching. Do not twist or wring. Rinse thoroughly in water of the same temperature until all soap or detergent is removed. Do not lift out of the water as the weight of the wet garment will stretch it. In last rinsing, use a softening and fluffing agent. Squeeze water out gently, as much as possible without wringing or twisting. Place turkish towels under and over garment, roll and squeeze to remove water. Carefully place garment on brown paper, shaping to outline; pin with rust-proof pins if necessary.

If sweater is made of Angora, shake it gently to fluff up surface hairs before garment is completely dry; return to drying process. Refluff when dry.

If sweater is very fragile, with open pattern, baste it to a piece of white sheet before laundering it to help it retain its shape.

Another good way to reshape a knitted sweater is to use a cardboard form, cut to the size and shape

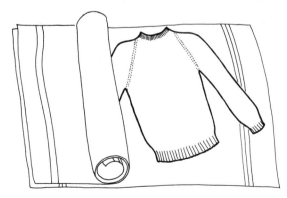

of body and sleeves before washing. Cut away cardboard sleeve shapes from rest of form so that they can be inserted separately. Place washed garment on a paper-covered surface, insert cardboard forms, pat knitted fabric to fit form. Let dry flat. During drying, garment will adjust itself to the form, which can be saved and used again.

Usually a knitted sweater needs no pressing after laundering, but a light steaming may be desirable. Use a steam iron or a regular iron with a damp cloth. Hold iron just above knitwear, so steam penetrates without applying any actual pressure.

Nylon, orlon and other synthetics should be laundered in same way as wool, but warmer water may be used. Use fluffing and softening agent in last rinse water. Dry in same manner as wool.

Garments made of Orlon Sayelle can be machine washed. Place inside out in lingerie bag or pillowcase. Set washer for five-minute cycle or the delicate fabric setting, high-water level. Use detergent. After washing, machine dry in tumble dryer.

To hand-wash Orlon Sayelle, use warm water and any detergent. Rinse well in cold water. Squeeze out excess water, roll in towels, squeeze again. Spread out on a smooth surface (not terry towels), bunch loosely into shape, allow to dry thoroughly. Do not stretch garment; do not hang to dry. Orlon Sayelle stretches when wet, returns to original shape when completely dry. Because of amount of moisture absorbed by fibers, allow two to three days to dry.

HOW TO LAUNDER CROCHETED LACE

Make a lather of soap or detergent and hot water, taking care to have all particles well dissolved. Dip lace in suds and squeeze gently until clean. Rinse in several changes of lukewarm water, once in cold water. Wrap in towel to press out excess moisture and dry immediately, starching and blocking if desired.

Starching: Use elastic starch and cold water, 2 level tablespoons of starch to each cup of water. Dissolve starch completely, dip lace in solution until saturated, roll in turkish towel, then block immediately.

Blocking: For a square or any rectangular piece, draw desired outline on padded board with pencil, taking care to make corners square. Pin lace, right side down, to outline, using only rust-proof pins. For round doily, pin center securely; for an oval doily, pin the center section in a straight line. Smooth out edges from center and pin, checking distance from center with a ruler and keeping patterns evenly spaced around. Press thoroughly through a dry cloth until all moisture has been absorbed.

Addenda: Glossary

Throughout this book, many stitches are taught and many needlework terms are explained in the section where they occur. In order to round out our information, we are adding seventeen stitches and giving a glossary of needlework terms, techniques, and materials which have not been fully explained elsewhere. If you are looking for any information not given here, consult the index.

afghan A knitted or crocheted coverlet.

afghan crochet A form of crochet made with a special afghan hook which has a long shaft of uniform thickness. A full row of stitches is worked onto the hook, then the stitches are worked off.

appliqué A form of embroidery. Material of one kind or color is sewn to a background; stitching is usually of secondary importance. Sewn-on design can consist of cutout design motifs, colored shapes to form a new design, crocheted or tatted motifs, etc.

Aran The group of three islands at entrance to Ireland's Galway Bay have given their name to the knitting done by the inhabitants. Usually worked in unbleached wool, the knitting is characterized by raised pattern stitches.

argyle A knitting in a colorful diamond and plaid pattern worked with bobbins, commonly used in socks and sweaters; named for a branch of the Scottish Campbell clan, from whose tartan the design was originally adapted.

Assisi A form of old Italian embroidery; solid cross-stitch background emphasizing unworked design areas; traditionally scarlet or blue on creamy linen, sometimes black with black outline.

bangles Ornamental flat metallic shapes (round, oval, diamond, oblong, etc.) which have a hole near one edge for stitching to garment so that bangles hang loosely.

Bargello A form of embroidery; thread worked in upright stitches on canvas to form peaked, shaded, distinctive patterns; known also as "flame work," "Hungarian point," and "Florentine stitch."

beading needle A long, very thin needle with slender, long eye, fits through tiny hole of beads; used for bead embroidery and stringing.

bead work (a) American Indians decorated skins and later clothes with tiny beads strung on short threads, massed in short rows or as outlines. Designs were accented with shells, animal teeth, and silk ribbon appliqué. (b) Victorian needlewomen worked their popular "Berlin work" patterns in beads.

Berlin work A form of needlepoint very popular during Victorian era. Brilliantly colored wools were worked in patterns on canvas; the best quality of both wool and canvas came from Berlin.

black work A form of embroidery in which designs (usually scrolls, grapes, leaves) were worked with fine black silk on white linen. First appeared in England at the time of Henry VIII. Known also as "Spanish work," it was probably introduced by Catherine of Aragon.

bobbin A core upon which yarn or thread is wound for pattern knitting, braiding, tatting, or lace-making; may be round, cylindrical or spindle-shaped depending upon its use.

bobbin lace A type of lace made by twisting and braiding threads (on bobbins) around pins arranged in a pre-determined pattern. Known also as bolster lace, or pillow lace.

bodkin A flat, blunt, large-eyed needle used to draw ribbon or tape through casings, or to turn cording right side out.

bolster The rotating cushion or pillow to which pricked patterns for bobbin lace are attached and on which the lace is made.

Bosnian An embroidery stitch used for filling; composed of straight (either vertical or horizontal) stitches and connecting diagonal stitches.

braid work The decorative application of braid, stitched in elaborate patterns to garments, pictures, or almost any article. Silk, cotton, linen, worsted, and mohair braids are used.

broderie Anglaise A simple type of cutwork embroidery consisting mostly of small oval and round eyelets; sometimes all are cut, sometimes some are worked solidly in satin stitch. Also called "Madeira."

bugle beads Small cylindrical glass or plastic beads used in decorative trimming.

bullion A cord formed by gold, silver, or metallic threads wound around wire or cotton; used generally for braids or fringes. Also, bullion stitch (see Index).

butt To join end-to-end without overlapping; used by rug braiders to form a perfect circle, oval, or square.

candlewicking (a) A form of embroidery especially popular in early American days. (b) A special heavy, soft thread used to make designs in running stitch, usually clipped to form tufts.

chain stitch embroidery One of the most ancient forms of embroidery. When worked with a hook and not with a needle, it became known as tambour work.

chenille A form of embroidery, fashionable in France during the 18th century, worked with "chenille"—the French word for caterpillar, which the thread resembles! There are two kinds: soft, unwired "chenille à broder" which can be worked to look like painting on velvet, and coarse "chenille ordinaire" used for couching or in satin stitch over large open-meshed canvas.

crêpe work The forming of imitation flowers or leaves of crêpe and sewing them to silk or satin backgrounds, or making them up on wire foundations as detached sprays.

crewel stitch One of the old embroidery stitches, the most important in crewel work, now known as stem stitch.

crewel wool A fine, loosely-twisted 2-ply wool yarn used in crewel embroidery.

crewelwork Embroidery worked in a variety of stitches with crewel wools on linen which was first in vogue during the reign of James I of England (1603-1625); also known as Jacobean work. Traditionally, designs consisted of a large stylized tree with numerous exotic fruits and flowers, sometimes with various animals and insects. From the main trunk grew curving, leafy branches to fill the required area.

cross-stitch A form of embroidery employing one simple stitch throughout; may be worked on fabric stamped with a transfer design or by counting threads. Commonly used for samplers, pictures, borders, and repeat patterns.

cut canvas work A kind of embroidery worked on coarse canvas with 4-thread soft wool, cut and combed to look like pile. (Tufts are tied and fastened to the canvas with fine thread.) Known also as "British raised work."

cutwork A form of embroidery which is worked by cutting out areas of the fabric. See also broderie Anglaise, hardanger, hedebo, reticella, Renaissance, Richelieu, Venetian, white work for specific types of cutwork.

darning on net Embroidering designs on a net background with darning stitches. See net embroidery.

double knitting A knitting stitch which results in a double thick, tubular material; English 4-ply wool similar to knitting worsted.

drawn work A form of embroidery in which threads are drawn from the fabric and the open area is decoratively stitched. See also hardanger, hemstitching, and white work.

emboss A term employed in embroidery to signify the execution of a design in relief, either by stuffing with layers of thread or a succession of stitches underneath the embroidery, or else by working over a pad made with thick materials.

embroidery floss A soft, loosely-twisted, six-strand thread of mercerized cotton.

fagoting An insertion stitch used to join two pieces of material.

Fair Isle A form of knitting originated in one of the Shetland islands, which features horizontal pattern stripes worked in stockinette stitch with two or more colors which are carried across back of work.

filet crochet A type of crochet featuring designs formed by solid "blocks" surrounded by openwork "spaces" which make up the background; originated to resemble filet lace.

filet lace An embroidery on netting background using variations of darning, buttonhole, backstitch, and filling stitches.

fish scale embroidery A kind of embroidery worked on silk, satin, or velvet foundations from flower patterns. Principal parts of the design, such as flower, leaves, butterflies, are covered over with brightly tinted fish scales sewn to the foundation with colored silks. Stems, vines, etc., are worked in satin stitch; centers, with French knots, beads, pearls, or spangles.

fishskin appliqué A form of embroidery practiced by the Aleuts and other Eskimos. Translucent strips of dried seal intestine (or, away from the coastal areas, bear or deer intestine) were painted and appliquéd to garments. Beads, fringe, and fur tufts added further decoration.

foundation fabric The background material for embroidery, hooking, or knotting. For rug making, it is the material through which strips of yarn or fabric are worked. Depending upon the hooking technique employed, it may be burlap, rug canvas, warp cloth, monk's cloth, etc.

gauge In knitting and crochet, the number of stitches and rows per inch on which each set of directions is planned.

graph paper Paper marked into squares commonly ranging from 10-to-the-inch to 4-to-the-inch; usually the inch lines are accented. Available at art supply and some stationery stores.

gros point A form of needlepoint worked in tapestry yarn on 8- to 12-to-the-inch mesh canvas.

hairpin lace A form of crochet worked on a hairpin loom, known also as a fork or a staple, to produce an exceptionally lacy crochet.

half-pattern A pattern for one half of a symmetrical design; when "flopped" it forms a complete pattern.

hardanger A form of embroidery in which threads are drawn, satin stitch squares are embroidered, and threads are cut. See also cutwork and drawn work.

hatchment An embroidered panel of a coat-of-arms worked on a black background, usually square and hung cornerwise. Upon the death of the person so memorialized, the panel was hung upon the door to give notice to the public, as a wreath is now used.

hedebo A form of embroidery in which openwork parts are cut away and filled in with a variety of lace stitches, solid areas are worked with satin stitch, and edgings are buttonholed. See also cutwork.

hemstitching A decorative needlework for making hems and borders for which threads are drawn; the exposed threads are stitched together in groups forming various patterns. See also drawn work.

hooking A rug-making technique; strips of fabric or yarn are pulled with a hook through a foundation fabric at close intervals to solidly cover surface. A large crochet-type hook is used for the traditional hand-hooked type. See also punch needle and latch hook.

huck embroidery Darning stitches worked in formalized designs on linen or cotton toweling called huck which has pairs of raised threads on the wrong side. Also known as huck-a-back darning. Not to be confused with Swedish weaving.

interfacing A material set between surface fabric and facing to provide body and shape.

interlining A material set between surface fabric and lining to provide warmth and shaping.

Irish crochet A form of crochet consisting of a background of picot loops and raised motifs of flowers or fruit and leaves.

Jacobean Characteristic of the time of James I of England, who reigned from 1603 to 1625; often refers to crewelwork.

knitting The creation of fabric for garments, accessories, afghans, etc., by interlacing yarn or thread in series of connected loops using pointed needles.

lacer A blunt, needle-like device sometimes used for lacing braid to braid with carpet thread when making braided rugs.

laid work A form of embroidery in which large, bold designs are filled with threads laid across the surface and secured with surface stitches. Simply, quickly, and inexpensively worked, it is common to almost every needleworking locality, and is often known by different names.

latch hook or latchet hook A rug-hooking device used to knot short pieces of yarn onto canvas mesh; hook has a movable latch to facilitate the work.

loopers Jersey loops used for weaving on small hand looms.

macrame A form of needlework originally Arabic; threads are knotted, braided, and fringed to produce ornamental trims and fabrics. When made in fine thread, it is referred to as macrame lace.

Madeira A form of embroidery consisting of eyelet holes, the edges caught by simple overcast stitches; sometimes called "broderie Anglaise."

mesh Openings between threads; often used as size designation for the number of openings to the inch.

mesh sticks Flat sticks with rounded ends used in netting; available in widths from ¼″ to ¾″.

miter A diagonal joining of material at a corner without overlapping.

Moravian work A name given to the gloomy memorial pictures so popular with American needleworkers in the 18th century. The fad for making them is supposed to have originated with people of the Moravian sect, immigrants from Moravia.

motif A design element used singly or repeated.

Mountmellick work A form of bold, padded white work embroidery with no drawn or open spaces; stitches lie on the surface with little thread on the wrong side; derives its name from the Irish town where it originated.

multiple The number of stitches required to work one pattern.

nap Short fibers on fabric surface which have been brushed in one direction.

needle lace A lace made using only a needle and

worked in buttonhole bars, picots, and knot stitches with a single thread.

needle gauge A piece of heavy cardboard or plastic with holes punched and numbered according to corresponding knitting needle sizes.

needlepoint An embroidery on canvas, worked to cover the area completely with even stitches to resemble tapestry. Known through the ages, it has been called in successive periods "opus pulvinarium," "cushion style," "canvas work," and "Berlin work." As a general term, it includes petit point, needlepoint, gros point, and quick point, all of which are worked in the same manner, on canvas of various sizes of mesh. Today needlepoint, specifically, is done with tapestry yarn or crewel wool on 14- to 18-to-the-inch mesh canvas. See tent stitch (Index).

needleweaving A form of drawn work in which threads are woven back and forth over the exposed area; known also as woven hemstitching or Swedish weaving.

net embroidery An embroidered pattern in a variety of stitches worked on net, usually by counting holes (or the design may be on a piece of fabric basted under the net). See also darning on net.

netting The process of making a knotted, open-meshed fabric which may be as simple as fishnet or as intricate as lace.

netting needle A special pliable "needle," split at both ends, around which netting thread is wound, and which is used in the actual netting process.

ombré A color term referring to yarn or fabric which is shaded from light to dark tones of one color.

openwork A form of embroidery in which the design is outlined and then the background is "punched" with holes by pulling and stitching the threads apart.

paillettes A general term for shiny objects (spangles, sequins, beads, etc.) with a hole for sewing on; used as decorative trim.

patchwork The sewing together of small pieces of fabric, usually to form either an allover pattern or a pattern of blocks. Also known as "pieced work."

Penelope canvas A fine, double-thread canvas sometimes used for needlepoint; and, when basted to linen, as a guide for working cross-stitch (canvas threads are removed when embroidery is complete).

petit point A needlepoint worked in fine wool yarn, silk, or cotton on single-thread canvas, 20-to-the-inch mesh or smaller.

pile Raised loops or tufts which cover the surface of a fabric.

plush stitch One of the stitches on canvas; made with loops which are cut to form a plush-like surface, or left whole to form a border or fringe; also called raised stitch.

pompon A rounded tuft or ball made by tying together strands of yarn or thread.

pounce (a) To transfer a perforated design by forcing fine powder or paste through tiny holes. (b) The powder or paste so used.

pouncer The tool used for pouncing.

pricking (a) A pattern used in making pillow lace, formed by pin-puncturing heavy paper. (b) A pattern made by hand-pricking, transferred with pouncer.

punch needle (a) A mechanically adjustable automatic needle for hooking rugs, used only with yarn. (b) A smaller version of rug punch needle used for embroidery. (c) A needle used for the traditional embroidered punch work which is fairly thick, round on top, and three-sided from the middle to the point.

punch work (a) Traditionally, a form of embroidery which is used chiefly for fillings and backgrounds. See openwork. (b) An embroidery worked with an automatic punch needle, which forms looped designs.

quick point Needlepoint worked in doubled tapestry wool or rug yarn on 5 to 7 mesh-per-inch canvas.

quill embroidery A form of embroidery worked by American Indians. Dyed porcupine quills were sewn on leather with a thin strip of sinew, or inserted through holes made in birchbark, or woven and wrapped.

quilting A decorative stitching together of two or more layers of fabric; extra padding or cording may be used for a more pronounced raised or puffed effect.

rabbet The inner edge of a picture frame into which the picture fits.

raised canvas work A form of embroidery executed from designs upon canvas with plush stitch; when completed, it is raised above the foundation and has the appearance of pile.

reticella work Another name for elaborate cut-work; also known as Renaissance work, having been extremely popular in that period.

ribbon knitting   The process of knitting with a crisp flat ribbon from ³⁄₁₆″ to ¼″ wide, woven especially for the purpose. Ribbon is usually rayon or silk or blends of the two.

ribbon work   A form of embroidery in which narrow ribbon is stitched and gathered into shape on satin foundations for ornamentation.

Richelieu   A form of cutwork embroidery which is predominated by picots and connecting buttonholed bars.

rocailles   Transparent glass seed beads.

sampler   Originally, samples of fundamental embroidery stitches worked in a rather scattered pattern arrangement, which became more formalized by the end of the 17th century. Now cross-stitch is generally used for the pictorial samplers which typically include alphabet, numbers, names, and dates, etc.

sculpturing   The scissors-trimming of pile to emphasize design areas.

seed beads   Tiny round beads.

sequins   Small metallic shapes with center holes for thread; sewn, knitted, or crocheted on as decoration.

shuttle   A thread-wound device used in tatting, lace-making, weaving, etc.

smocking   A decorative gathering of fabric worked in a number of stitches to form banded designs, usually worked in a combination of colored threads.

soutache   A narrow braid woven in a herringbone pattern.

spangle   A flat metallic sequin-type paillette, often in a novelty shape.

splicing   A method of joining strips used in rug braiding.

stab stitch   A stitch made holding the needle at a right angle to the cloth; commonly used in quilting.

stump work   An elaborate form of embroidery which flourished in the 17th century. Parts of the design were raised in high relief from the background by outlining and padding up with horsehair, wool, or pieces of wood. This was covered with thick silk or satin upon which embroidery stitches were worked.

tambour   A form of embroidery worked with a special needle resembling a crochet hook with which thread is drawn in and out of the material in a chain-like stitch. Floral designs so stitched on fine net achieve the effect of lace.

taper   (a) To become gradually narrower. (b) A long, waxed wick customarily used to light candles, sometimes used by embroiderers to singe wool fuzz from work.

tapestry wool   A tightly twisted yarn used for working needlepoint.

Teneriffe embroidery   Similar to needleweaving, but worked over embroidered bar stitches instead of through fabric as in drawn work or needleweaving.

ticking   A strong, firm cotton fabric, usually striped, used for pillows, mattresses, etc.

tracing wheel   A spiked rotating wheel on a handle; used with carbon to transfer dressmaker markings.

trame   Long laid threads indicating design and color on needlepoint canvas; stitches are worked over these threads and the canvas beneath them.

transfer   (a) To copy from one surface to another. (b) A commercial design printed in a special preparation which can be imprinted on fabric using a hot iron.

tricot crochet   English term for afghan crochet.

tubular knitting   Knitting usually worked on four needles or a circular needle to produce tube-shaped material.

tuft   A knotted cluster of short, soft threads.

Turkey work   A form of needlework copying texture and designs of early Turkish rugs, made by knotting yarn on canvas or coarse cloth.

Venetian embroidery   A kind of embroidery similar in appearance to Venetian lace, but worked with buttonhole stitch outlines in high relief; backgrounds are filled with a variety of stitches and cutouts.

warp cloth   A sturdy foundation fabric used for punch needle rugs.

warp thread   Lengthwise threads in a woven fabric.

weft thread   Crosswise (selvage-to-selvage) threads in a woven fabric.

welting   A cord covered with bias fabric strips used as seam or edge trim.

white work   Any embroidery worked in white on white. Most commonly, it refers to the especially delicate form of white work, in which drawn threads and cutwork are combined with a variety of stitches to add to the lacy effect.

Additional embroidery stitches

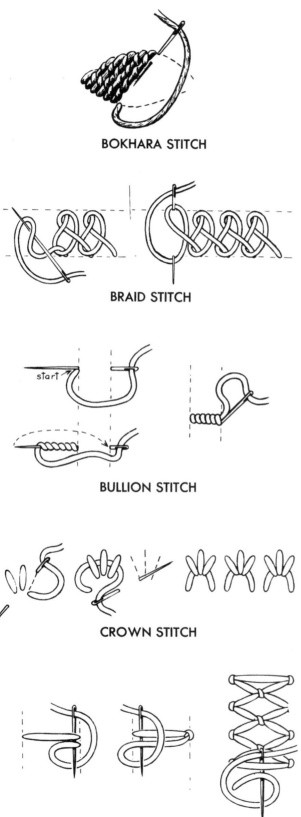

BOKHARA STITCH

BRAID STITCH

BULLION STITCH

start

CROWN STITCH

DIAMOND STITCH

BOKHARA STITCH. One thread is laid across the area at a time, and couched in place as shown with small stitches, using the same thread. Good for filling large spaces.

BRAID STITCH. This stitch should be worked closely and kept rather small. Wrap thread around needle once as shown to make an inverted loop; insert needle in fabric from top to bottom, thus twisting thread. Bring thread under needle tip. Pull needle through and tighten stitch carefully. Do not pull too tightly, or braid effect will be lost.

BULLION STITCH. Insert point of needle in and out of fabric for length of stitch desired, do not pull needle through. Wrap thread around needle a number of times as shown, enough to fill space of stitch. Hold wrapped needle and fabric firmly with thumb and finger of left hand and pull needle through, drawing the thread up; this will reverse direction of the stitch, so that it lies in the space of first stitch. Insert needle in fabric at end of stitch.

CROWN STITCH. Make center straight stitch with two slightly shorter stitches at either side as shown; bring needle to front of fabric above and to left of three stitches. Then pass needle under the three stitches, but not through fabric. Insert needle in fabric again above and to right.

DIAMOND STITCH. A good border decoration. Take a horizontal stitch from left to right and bring needle out just below as shown; pass needle under the stitch, under and over the thread and pull to make knot. Bring thread across and knot on opposite end of first stitch. Insert needle through fabric under knot and bring out a short distance below. Knot again at center of last stitch as shown; insert needle at opposite side and bring out just below.

INTERLACING STITCH Make two rows of back stitch the distance apart desired, with stitches alternately spaced as shown. With a different color thread, loop stitches under back stitches and over thread as shown, alternating on top and bottom rows.

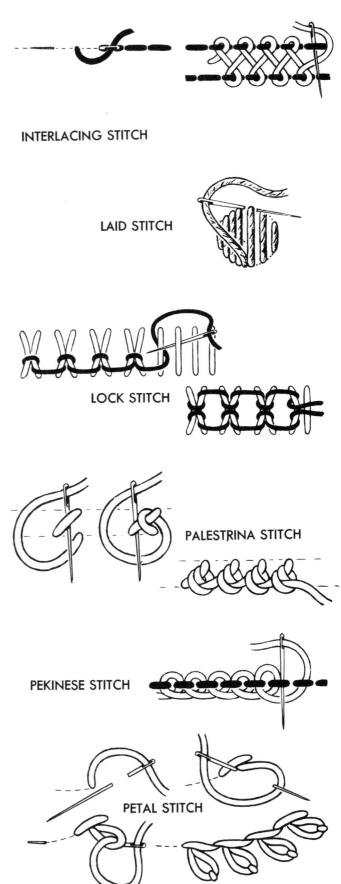

INTERLACING STITCH

LAID STITCH Take stitches across the area to be filled, allowing a space between each, the size of another stitch. Fill these spaces with another series of stitches. This method conserves yarn and produces smooth, flat stitches, which may also be couched at intervals.

LAID STITCH

LOCK STITCH This stitch may be worked in one or two colors and is a good banding design. Take a number of vertical stitches spaced as desired, either close or wide apart. With another thread, work from left to right as shown, along bottom section of stitches. Repeat across top in same manner.

LOCK STITCH

PALESTRINA STITCH To start, take a short diagonal stitch, bringing needle out below. Draw needle under stitch from top down and over thread as shown; pull up thread gently and repeat. For next stitch, insert needle to right from top to bottom, making a diagonal stitch and repeat. Keep stitches short and close together.

PALESTRINA STITCH

PEKINESE STITCH This is most effective when two colors or two different kinds of thread are used. First make a line of fairly large backstitches. Then make looped stitches through the backstitches.

PEKINESE STITCH

PETAL STITCH This is actually a combination of outline stitch and lazy daisy stitch, worked simultaneously. Take one stitch of outline, bringing needle back to middle of stitch; make lazy daisy to one side, then continue with another stitch of outline.

PETAL STITCH

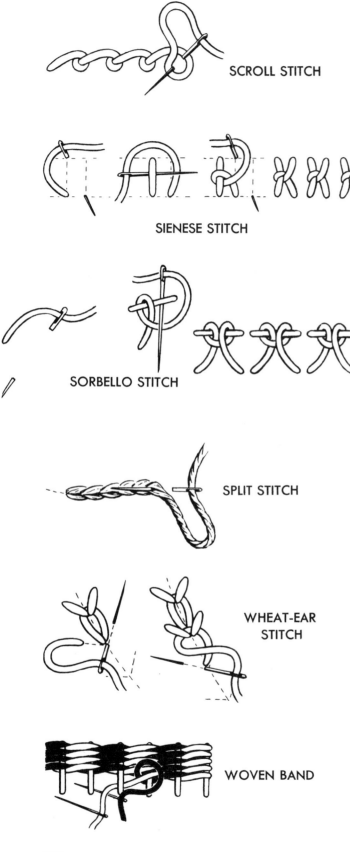

SCROLL STITCH. Working from left to right, loop thread around as shown; take a tiny stitch to the right with needle over both top and bottom of loop. Pull up thread to make knot. Space the tiny stitches far enough apart so scroll effect is clearly defined.

SCROLL STITCH

SIENESE STITCH. When worked closely, this stitch makes a good border. Make first vertical stitch, bring needle out at bottom and to right. Loop thread around vertical stitch as shown; insert needle at top to the right and bring out at bottom, ready for next vertical stitch.

SIENESE STITCH

SORBELLO STITCH. First take a horizontal stitch and bring needle out below and left. Loop thread around horizontal stitch twice as shown; insert needle below and right; bring out to right even with horizontal stitch for beginning of another stitch.

SORBELLO STITCH

SPLIT STITCH. When a fine line is desired, this stitch may be used. Work as for outline stitch, bring needle out through thread as shown, thus splitting it in half.

SPLIT STITCH

WHEAT-EAR STITCH. First make two straight stitches forming a V; bring needle out below at center. Pass needle under the two stitches and insert needle in fabric again at center below, making a chain loop.

WHEAT-EAR STITCH

WOVEN BAND. Make row of vertical foundation stitches evenly spaced. Use two needles and contrasting color yarn. Work from top down, alternating threads. Each thread is brought over one foundation stitch and under next; threads twist over each other for each stitch as shown.

WOVEN BAND

Index